William A. Miles, Charles P. Miles

The Correspondence of William Augustus Miles on the French

Revolution - 1789-1817

Vol. I

William A. Miles, Charles P. Miles

The Correspondence of William Augustus Miles on the French Revolution - 1789-1817
Vol. I

ISBN/EAN: 9783337230739

Printed in Europe, USA, Canada, Australia, Japan

Cover: Foto ©ninafisch / pixelio.de

More available books at **www.hansebooks.com**

THE CORRESPONDENCE

OF

WILLIAM AUGUSTUS MILES

ON THE

FRENCH REVOLUTION

1789–1817

EDITED BY THE

REV. CHARLES POPHAM MILES, M.A., F.L.S.

HONORARY CANON OF DURHAM
MEMBRE DE LA SOCIÉTÉ D'HISTOIRE DIPLOMATIQUE

IN TWO VOLUMES — VOL. I.

LONDON
LONGMANS, GREEN, AND CO.
AND NEW YORK: 15 EAST 16th STREET
1890

THESE VOLUMES

ARE DEDICATED TO THE

CHILDREN OF MADAME RICHARD WADDINGTON

BY THEIR

AFFECTIONATE GRANDFATHER

IN THE FERVENT HOPE THAT THEY, AS CITIZENS OF FRANCE,
WILL EVER REMEMBER THAT THE PROSPERITY AND
STABILITY OF A NATION CAN BE SECURED ONLY
BY ITS PEOPLE LIVING IN THE FEAR OF GOD

'Le premier arbre de la liberté a été planté, il y a dix-huit cents ans, par Dieu même sur le Golgotha. Le premier arbre de la liberté, c'est cette croix sur laquelle Jésus Christ s'offert, en sacrifice pour la liberté, l'égalité, et la fraternité du genre humain'—VICTOR HUGO

'If the Son therefore shall make you free, ye shall be free indeed'—*John* viii. 36

PREFACE

The circumstances which led Mr. Miles to retain copies of his political correspondence are mentioned in the Introduction to these volumes. It may be further explained that he was wont to compose a rough draft of each letter, which, after having been re-written, was copied into a book specially prepared for the purpose. Each volume, bound in leather and dated, embraced about six months. The letters selected for the present publication are in the handwriting of my mother, and were copied between the years 1803 and 1816, at which later date Mr. Miles went to Paris, where, in the following year, he died. On the return of the family to England, soon after my father's death, these MS. volumes, together with original letters and newspaper cuttings, were consigned in the first instance to Sir Charles Flint, at the Irish Office, London, and were soon afterwards transferred to the custody of my dear mother, with whom they remained until her decease at Monkwearmouth Vicarage in 1872. The letters that passed between Mr. Miles and his friends on the Continent are written in French. I am responsible for the translation. Lafayette, however, wrote to him in English. No portion of this voluminous correspondence was written for publication. The letters convey the frank expression of an intelligent, well-informed, and unbiassed mind, and were addressed on the spur of the moment to statesmen and private friends in the interests of peace. 'So anxious was I to avert the terrible calamities of war,' he wrote to one of these friends, 'that I really did not know what sleep was from October 1792 to January 1793, when the madness of the Brissotine faction in France precipitated the catastrophe which it was my study to have prevented, and by a wanton and premature declaration of war destroyed my hopes for ever.'

Probably it seldom happens that any person is able, as in the present instance, to speak of his father as having been 112 years ago in communication with literary and political men—Mr. Miles having corresponded with David Garrick, among others, so far back as the year 1778; and it may be mentioned that my half-sister, Theodosia, whose letters written in the midst of the exciting scenes of the French Revolution appear in this volume, was at school in the Abbaye Royale (le Couvent de Port-Royal de Paris) in the year 1786, or three years anterior to the fall of the Bastille.

At the age of eighty years, and after having passed more than half a century in the active service of the Church, the preparation of these volumes has not been accomplished without fatigue; but the labour has been alleviated by the conviction that the letters, which discuss important events in our national history, are instructive in their moral teaching. They deprecate in unmeasured terms the perils that have resulted, and may yet result, no less from political party-spirit and intrigue than from the spirit of anarchy fomented by less responsible people—calamities which, if not restrained by higher principles, may become as rife and dangerous as were the political convulsions at the close of the last century.

It remains to acknowledge the assistance afforded by M. Florent, who, in response to my applications, transcribed at the Foreign Office, Paris, the several despatches and other documents from which my quotations have been obtained. The Rev. H. J. Carter, Rector of Duxford, Cambridgeshire, kindly obtained for me, through the University Library or other source, any special information desired. I am indebted to the Hon. F. V. Inglott, C.M.G., late member of the Executive and Legislative Councils of the Government of Malta, for the names of the gentlemen who arrived in London, in 1802, as a deputation from Malta and Gozo. Nor can I omit to record that nearly the whole of the correspondence now published was copied by my dear wife in readiness for the press. The quotation from Victor Hugo is borrowed from Mr. Lilly's work, 'A Century of Revolutions.'

CHARLES POPHAM MILES
(*Late Vicar of Monkwearmouth*).

St. Julian, Hatherley Road, Kew Gardens:
October 1, 1890.

CONTENTS

OF

THE FIRST VOLUME

PAGE

Mr. Miles to the Duke of Leeds. Frankfort, July 12, 1789.
Illness of the Emperor and Fermentation in France the only disquietudes—Count Romanzow proceeds to London—Intended visit to the Elector of Mayence—General de Wimpffen—His vicissitudes 121

Mr. Miles to the Duke of Leeds. Frankfort, July 30.
Necker on his way to Paris—Marshal de Broglio reported at Hesse-Darmstadt—Count d'Artois expected at Frankfort—M. de Francks driven from Strasburg—France convulsed will convulse Europe 122

Mr. Miles to the Duke of Leeds. Frankfort, August 1.
Fugitives from Paris—Tumult at Wurtzburg—Troops ordered to the Austrian Netherlands 123

Mr. Miles to the Duke of Leeds. Frankfort, August 6.
Disturbances at Bâle—Prince George of Hesse-Darmstadt and the Prince of Würtemberg escape from Paris—Count d'Artois supplied with money—Frankfort unsafe for the refugees—Marshal de Broglio reported at Verdun 124

Mr. Miles to the Duke of Leeds. Frankfort, August 11.
French refugees driven back from Spires—Disturbances at Montbéliard—Revolt at Strasburg 125

Mr. Miles to the Duke of Leeds. Frankfort, August 17.
  Apprehensions of a general revolt—Discontent at Hesse—The Hereditary Prince of Orange—Elector of Mayence . . 125

Mr. T. Somers Cocks to Mr. Miles. Charing Cross, Aug. 25.
  Tranquillity in England—Health of the King—French crossing over to England—Louis XVI. and America . . . 127

Mr. Miles to the Duke of Leeds. Frankfort, September 1.
  Visit to the Elector of Mayence—Déjenner champêtre—Madame de Condenhoff—Clergy permitted to marry . . 128

Mr. Miles to Mr. Somers Cocks. Frankfort, September 1.
  Aschaffenburg a paradise—The Landgrave of Hesse-Cassel—Duke of Saxe-Meiningen—Revolution in Liège . . . 130

M. Fabry to Mr. Miles. Liège, August 26.
  Revolution—The cockade—The patriot chiefs—Fabry and Chestret Burgomasters—The Prince Bishop signs . . 132

Mr. Miles to the Duke of Leeds. Aschaffenburg, September 25.
  Circle of the Upper Rhine assemble—Alsace and the French emigrants—M. de Breteuil at Frankfort—Anecdote—Prince de Salm—Present to George III. 133

Mr. Miles to the Duke of Leeds. Frankfort, November 9.
  The Corvée—Suspicions against the British Court—French interests at Mayence—The Duke of Sussex departs . . 135

Admiral Sir Thomas Rich to Mr. Miles. London, Nov. 13.
  Quiet life—Swords into ploughshares 136

Mr. Somers Cocks to Mr. Miles. London, November 24.
  Mr. Ryder and Mr. Bland Burgess—The French and civil war—Prosperity of England—George III. at the theatre—Mr. Pitt 138

Mr. Miles to the Duke of Leeds. Frankfort, December 5.
  The Brabançons—The Electorate of Trèves—Mr. Walpole—The Prince de Conti and the Princess de Holstein Beck at Frankfort—' Cursory Reflections on Public Men and Public Measures' 140

Mr. Miles to the Duke of Leeds. Frankfort, December 30.
Insurrection among the Brabançons—The Elector of Mayence and the Courts of Berlin and London on the revolt in the Pays-Bas—Alsace—The Prince de Conti alarmed—The Chasse and the Corvée—The coronation expected—Probability of war—General D'Alton—Count Trauttmansdorff—Cardinal Rohan—Soldiers refuse to fire 141

M. Le Brun to Mr. Miles. Liège, January 13, 1790.
Publication of 'Cursory Reflections on Public Men, &c.' . 144

M. Le Brun to Mr. Miles. Liège, January 15.
Brittany and Normandy separate provinces—Requests pecuniary loan 144
Minute by Mr. Miles on M. Le Brun 145

Mr. Miles to Lord Rodney. Liège, January 28.
Hauteur of the English—Lord Torrington—Dissensions at Brussels—Liège—Disputes—Mansion in flames—Alliance with France 146

General Wimpffen to Mr. Miles. Paris, February 3.
Mirabeau again in France, *où il joue le premier rôle*—Sets up a journal—Anecdote respecting him—The Court at Versailles dependent on him 149

Mr. Miles to the Marquis of Buckingham. London, July 15.
Arrangements made for Mr. Miles to proceed to Paris on a confidential mission 150

Mr. Miles to Lord Buckingham. Paris, August 16.
Events in Paris—Lafayette and the National Guards—The Duke of Orleans faction—The Lameths—Cabal . . 150

Mr. Miles to M. Talleyrand. Paris, August 20.
Announcement of his arrival in Paris 152

M. Talleyrand to Mr. Miles. Paris, August 23.
Acknowledgment of the above letter 153

Mr. Miles to Lord Rodney. Paris, August 23.
Excitement in Paris—Execution of a priest at Liège—'Breaking on the wheel'—Palais Royal, Tuileries—The laws in England 153

Mr. Miles to Lord Buckingham. Paris, September 6.

Anarchy an argument in favour of despotism—Dangers from the populace—Dismissal of the War Minister—Threats against Marquis de Bouillé—Necker—Jealousy of the French—Libels in the Press—Hostility to Pitt—Dupont and the Family Compact—Alsace—Palais Royal infamous—Maréchale de Richelieu—Duc d'Aremberg—Jacobin Club 160

The Family Compact—'Réflexions sur le Projet de Décret proposé le 25 de ce mois, Août, 1790, par M. de Mirabeau l'aîné' 164
The Family Compact—Extracts from the speech of Mirabeau in the National Assembly 167

M. Mirabeau to Mr. Miles. Paris, September 17.

Dinner engagement postponed . . . 169

M. Pétion to Mr. Miles. Paris, September 17.

Election of Mr. Miles as a member of the Jacobin Club . 169

M. Crelet to Mr. Miles. Paris, September 24.

Election of Mr. Miles as a member of the Society of 1789 . 170

Mr. Miles to Mr. Rose. Paris, October 11.

Excitement against England—England and Spain—The mission of Mr. Miles to Paris full of promise . . . 170

Mr. Miles to Sir Edward Newenham. Paris, November 27.

Anarchy inconsistent with liberty—Confusion in Paris—Character of Mirabeau—Lafayette—Brutality of the mob—Profligacy of the higher orders—Revolt at Brest influenced Spain towards England—Condition of the royal family of France—Proposal by Mr. Miles to rescue Marie Antoinette—The clergy and nobility 171

Mr. Miles to Mr. Rose. Paris, November 30.

The Family Compact may be dissolved on condition of England's friendship—Pitt could ensure it . . . 176

Mr. Miles to Lord Buckingham. Paris, December 13.

The Family Compact—No response from England—Desire in Paris for an alliance—Negotiations between France and Prussia—The Emperor and the Netherlands—Danger from civil war—The Jacobin Club—Pitt pacific—Suspicion excited against foreign powers—England could restore calm . . . 178

Mr. Miles to Sir Edward Newenham.   Paris, December 13.

Police without authority—Nothing yet accomplished worthy of imitation in Ireland—Capacity without principle—Profligacy in the National Assembly—As much corruption as formerly . 182

Mr. Miles to the Duc d'Aremberg.   Paris, December 24.

Criticism on the writings of Burke—The Revolution good in itself, but endangered by anarchy 184

Mr. Miles to the Rev. H. H. Edwards.   Paris, December 24.

Rapid succession of events—Transition from despotism to anarchy—Dominion of one man preferable to the fury of millions—France stained by atrocities—Jacobin Club—Alarms of counter-revolution—Perilous state of the royal family—Position of Lafayette—Orleans party—Violence of the Press—Extracts—Mirabeau 185

Mr. Miles to Mr. H. J. Pye.   Paris, January 5, 1791.

Poet Laureat and politics—The National Assembly—Bastille—Despotism of the Court at Versailles succeeded by the tyranny of the mob—Incapacity of Louis XVI.—The royal family—The people absolute—Decrees against the clergy—Burke deceived—Poets and historians—Ancient *noblesse* of France—Absence of religious comfort—Mirabeau—Power of the Jacobins—Oath imposed on the clergy—Fonthill Beckford . . . 194

Mr. Huskisson to Mr. Miles.   Paris, January 28.

Desires an interview with Mr. Miles . 202

Mr. Miles to Mr. Pye.   Paris, January 30.

Society disorganised—Mr. Miles speaks at the Jacobin Club—Freedom of discussion beneficial—Assignats—Prince Charles de Hesse—German nobility—Sanguinary principles of the Jacobins—Orleans party—The Queen, Lafayette, the Mayor of Paris, hated—The Club, 'Les Amis de la Constitution monarchique'—Riots, the military, the Government—No prospect of returning order 202

Mr. Miles to Lord Buckingham.   Paris, February 3.

Intrigues at Vienna—Cabals—Alsace and Lorraine . . 208

Mr. Miles to Sir Edward Newenham.   Paris, February 16.

Anarchy, despotism—France not to be imitated—Paris without government—Lafayette—Soldiers powerless—The King's aunts

—Jacobin Club—Warning to Ireland—Baron de Robeck—
Legislation retarded 209

Mr. Miles to Lord Buckingham. Paris, February 18.
Political writers in a tempest—England—Happier times
remote—Pamphlets collected for his Lordship . . . 213

Mr. Miles to Mr. Somers Cocks. Paris, February 23.
The Lameths, Barnave—Counter-revolution—The Jacobins
and the provinces—Frenzy of the people—Families leave Paris
—The King's aunts—The municipality—The *poissardes*—Louis
XVI. and Monsieur denounced—The Luxembourg and the mob—
Lafayette firm—Brittany—Revolt in the South—Lands of the
clergy—Flight of the King's aunts arrested—Lafayette at the
Tuileries—Club for women—The Bishop of Liège returns—The
French clergy 214

Minute by Mr. Miles on the Prince Bishop of Liège . . 222

M. de Chartres to Mr. Miles. Paris, February 25 . . 222

Minute by Mr. Miles on M. de Chartres 223

Mr. Miles to Mr. Somers Cocks. Paris, February 25.
Arrest of the King's aunts—Appeal to the National Assembly
—Conduct of the mob—The Mayor, Lafayette, Montmorin—
Firmness of the Queen—The Palais Royal—Danger of the
aristocrats 223

Mr. Miles to Mr. Somers Cocks. Paris, February 28.
The military are passive—M. Bailly and the King—The Queen
—Morals of the people—Languedoc, Metz, Brussels—Necker . 231

Minute by Mr. Miles on Affairs in Paris 235

Mr. Miles to Lord Rodney. Paris, March 1.
Military sent to Vincennes—Latude—Firmness of Lafayette—
The people driving to anarchy—Madame de Lafayette—Anecdote
of Mirabeau—Santerre—Lafayette loses popularity . . 236

Mr. Miles to Mr. Pye. Paris, March 1.
Paris overcast with gloom—Smelfungus—National Assembly
—Royalty threatened—the Club monarchique—The King's aunts
—Barnave—The *poissardes*—Monsieur and the mob—The
Royalists in Languedoc—Brittany—Chaos everywhere—Credulity of the King—Robespierre the man of the future—Mirabeau
and the Bishop of Autun—The red-hot Royalists . . 238

CONTENTS OF THE FIRST VOLUME. xvii

Mr. Miles to Mr. Somers Cocks. Paris, March 1.

State of Paris—Faubourg St. Antoine in motion—Vincennes and the mob—Lafayette—Alarm at the Tuileries—The palace invaded, men armed with stilettoes seized—A secret project—Activity of the Jacobins throughout France—Mirabeau denounced—Appears at the Jacobin Club—Court of Louis XV. . . 246

Madame de Lafayette to Mr. Miles. Paris, March 10.

Hopes to obtain for Miss Miles admission to the National Assembly at an early date 252

Mr. Miles to Lord Rodney. Paris, March 12.

State of Paris—Bedlam broken loose—Intrigues by monarchists—Prussia intrigues, Austria, Sardinia—Cardinal de Rohan—Louis XVI. and the Queen under an illusion—Mirabeau votes on the Spanish question on receipt of a bribe—Talon distributes money—Tumult and suspicion—King of Prussia—Liège betrayed—Firmness of Marie Antoinette 253

Mr. Miles to M. Latude. Paris, March 13.

Duty of the Legislature towards Latude—Mr. Miles assists him 256

Minute by Mr. Miles on Latude or La Fleur . . 257

Mr. Miles to Sir Edward Newenham. Paris, March 18.

Liberty, not licentiousness—Vergennes, Brienne, Calonne, Broglio—The Revolution of 1688—The Bastille fell without a struggle—De Launay—The assignats—Church lands—Lafayette and the Lameths—Immorality of the ancient French Court—Recent incident at the Tuileries—The Prince de Condé—French emissaries in Ireland 258

Observations on Burke's Reflections on the Revolution . . 265

Mr. Miles to Lord Rodney. Paris, April 1.

Death of Mirabeau—His character and influence—Dreaded and yet influential—His courage at Versailles in 1789—The Lameths—The Marquis de St. Huruge—Mirabeau denounced at the Jacobins—Austrians on the march to Fribourg—War imminent 270

Mr. Miles to Mr. Somers Cocks. Paris, April 4.

Mirabeau is no more—Mourning for eight days—The autopsy—Lameths suspected—Mirabeau the pride and the infamy of his country—Cardinal de Rohan—Prince de Condé—Alsace opposes the Revolution—Assignats—France intrigues—Vienna and Berlin—Religious excitement in the South—Lafayette—Santerre—Wimpffen—Le Brun elected at the Jacobins . . . 272

Miss Miles to her Father. Paris, April 15.

Return of Mr. Miles to England—Nuns taking the oath at their convent—Danger of being whipped—Praises of Mirabeau—The *mandement* of Gobel 277

Mr. Miles to Sir Edward Newenham. London, April 16.

Lafayette suspects England—Russia must be controlled—Catherine II.—Her ambition—Joseph II.—France and Russia—Mr. Fox—His error—Lafayette offers to resign—The duplicity of the Court of Versailles is disseminated—No prospect of order—Lafayette in danger from the rabble 280

Miss Miles to her Father. Paris, April 22.

The King prevented from going to St. Cloud—The *poissardes*—Cardinal de Rochefoucaud in peril—Cardinal de Montmorenci—The Bishop of Senlis—Louis XVI. and the National Assembly—Mob disturbance—A counter-revolution feared . . . 284

Lord Fortescue to Mr. Miles. April 26.

Courage at an early date might have saved Louis XVI. . 287

Miss Miles to her Father. Paris, April 29.

Visit to Madame Mourgue—Opinion of a *democrat* on dogs and beggars—Attempt to stab Lafayette—Insubordination—Drums beating and troops marching—Assignats at 7 per cent. . 288

Miss Miles to her Father. Paris, May 6.

The Pope burnt in effigy—Narrow escape of Clermont-Tonnerre—The boasted liberty of France—The Pope and Avignon—Procession in honour of Mirabeau—Riot and insolence in the streets—An insolent beggar—M. Bonne-Carrère and his appointment to Liège 289

Mr. Miles to Sir Edward Newenham. London, May 11.

Honesty in politics—Pitt and Fox—The example of France a warning—The French unequal to complete their task—Lafayette suspects England—Ireland warned by example of France . 292

Miss Miles to her Father. Paris, May 20.

Resignation of Lafayette—Money at 15 per cent.—Navarre refuses taxes—Strasbourg—Alsace—Emigrations from Paris

Alarm felt by Miss Miles—Counter-revolution—The French without religion—The National Guard 295

Mr. Miles to Mr. Pitt. May 31.
General Wimpffen might be employed in the interests of England—The Rhine as the boundary of France . 298

General Wimpffen to Mr. Miles. Paris, June 17.
Uneasiness on the frontier—Mutiny in the French artillery—The Jacobins and Santerre—A general war anticipated—Madame de Staël and Narbonne 299

Miss Miles to her Father. Paris, June 26.
Letters cannot leave Paris—Return of Louis XVI. and the royal family from Varennes—Excitement in Paris . . 301

Miss Miles to her Father. Paris, June 27.
Rumours respecting the King—A Republic desired—Removal of the Queen—Her sufferings 303

A Member of the National Assembly to Mr. Miles. June 30.
The flight of the King—The Dauphin—M. de La Colombe, Lafayette, Santerre—Duc d'Aiguillon—Duchesse de Richelieu—Latude—Count de Mauldo 305

Minute by Mr. Miles on the Flight of Louis XVI. . . 306

Mr. Miles to Mr. Pitt. July 1.
Apprehensions of Lafayette respecting the British armaments—Efforts are made to remove the suspicion . . 308

Lord Fortescue to Mr. Miles. July 5.
France cannot live in perpetual anarchy—The position of the royal family 309

Mr. Miles to Mr. Joseph Smith. July 6.
Desires instructions from Mr. Pitt—Awkward position of his family in Paris 310

Lord Gower to Mr. Miles. Paris, July 8.
Acknowledges a pamphlet from Mr. Miles—Expresses hopes for its success 310

Lord Rodney to Mr. Miles. July 14.
Commends the publications of Mr. Miles—The Assembly at Paris, Paine, and the English Constitution . . 311

Mr. Miles to Sir Edward Newenham. July 14.

 Russia and the National Assembly—Passport obtained for the flight of the royal family—Certainty of an explosion—Resolve of Bouillé's officers—Confusion augments—Mrs. and Miss Miles leave Paris 311

Mr. Miles to Sir Edward Newenham. Dover, July 16.

 Waiting to receive his family—Arrival of a merchant from Bordeaux and Paris—Alarm at Bordeaux, French ships mistaken for a British squadron—Conduct of the municipality at Bordeaux—The Tuileries closed—Position of the royal family . . 312

Mr. Huskisson to Mr. Miles. Paris, August 12.

 Commissions of Mr. Miles executed—Brutus's Letters—Sheridan and Burke—Alarming state of France—The want of discipline in the army—Position of Louis XVI. . . . 313

Mr. Huskisson to Mr. Miles. Paris, September 15.

 The 'Gazette Universelle' esteemed—The 'Gazette de la Cour' stupid—General Wimpffen 314

A Member of the National Assembly to Mr. Miles. Paris, October 4.

 Intrigues of the King of Prussia—Court of Berlin aims at detaching France from Austria—Montmorin and Lessart—The Queen intermeddles—Danger of a crisis 315

Lord Fortescue to Mr. Miles. October 5.

 Unable to foresee a *dénouement* to the anarchy in France—The King's acceptance of the constitution—Mankind are not to be congratulated on the labours of the revolutionists . . 315

Mr. Miles to Lord Fortescue. December 28.

 Assignats have fallen to 40 per cent.—Temporary bankruptcy cannot be deferred, yet France will recover from her delirium and threaten the liberties of Europe—Mischief brewing in Ireland 316

Mr. Miles to Lord Buckingham. December 28.

 Ireland—Coercion necessary 317

Despatch of Lückner to the War Minister. June 1792 . 317

Mr. Aust to Mr. Miles. July 4.

 Peace in India—Prosperity of England . . . 320

M. Mourgue to Mr. Miles. Paris, July 6.

Female education—Critical position of France Scipion Mourgue attached to the Legation in London—The French not ripe for revolution—The Jacobins—The National Assembly—Champ de Mars on July 17, 1791—Bailly and Lafayette—The Legislative Assembly 321

M. Mourgue to Mr. Miles. Paris, July 13.

Hostile armies on the frontier—Position of the French—Pétion suspected—Louis XVI.—The Ministry resigns—English newspapers—The 'Moniteur'—German confederacy . . . 325

M. Scipion Mourgue to Mr. Miles. London, August 7.

Déchéance of the King demanded—General alarm—Bonne-Carrère appointed to Philadelphia 328

M. Scipion Mourgue to Mr. Miles. August 17.

Assault on the Tuileries—Clermont-Tonnerre—Le Brun, Roland, Clavière, Servan 328

Mr. Aust to Mr. Miles. August 18.

Acknowledges receipt of a memoir of Le Brun supplied to the Foreign Office 329

Mr. Huskisson to Mr. Miles. Paris, August 18.

Assault on the Tuileries—The Swiss Guard—The royal family—National Convention—Massacre 329

M. Mourgue to Mr. Miles. Paris, August 30.

Horrors of August 10—France misled—The royal family—Affairs without a parallel—Spain, England, and France—Liberty in England—No desire to re-enter the Administration . . 330

Mr. Aust to Mr. Miles. August 30.

Recall of Lord Gower from Paris 332

Mr. Lodge to Mr. Miles. Hastings, September 19.

Landing of emigrants—Subscriptions for the clergy—The Bishop of Avranches 332

Mr. Miles to Mr. Long. September 24.

M. Chauvelin and the London newspapers . . . 333

Lord Fortescue to Mr. Miles. September 26.

Tom Paine—Convention of cannibals—The émigrés . . 334

Mr. Aust to Mr. Miles. October.

    Dumouriez surrounded—Duke of Brunswick . . . 335

Minute by Mr. Miles on Lord Elgin's Despatches . 335

Sir Edward Newenham to Mr. Miles. Dublin, October 13.

    Retreat of the Prussians—Austria and Russia—Spain—The Duke of Brunswick—The Royalists—Danger in Ireland . . 335

Mr. Miles to Sir Edward Newenham. October 19.

    Prussia artful—England should avoid hostilities . . 337

M. —— to Mr. Miles. Paris, October 20.

    Perilous position of Marie Antoinette—Lusignan—Robespierre—August 10 and September 2—Paris a den of tigers . . 337

Mr. Miles to Mr. Somers Cocks. October 29.

    Conduct of Prussia—Fraudulent courts—State of Ireland—Mistake of the Duke of Brunswick—Dumouriez and Louis XVI.—Anxiety in Paris to save the King and Queen—Danger to France from internal discord—Other revolutions may follow . 338

Minute by Mr. Miles on the Retreat of Dumouriez . . 340

Mr. Miles to Mr. Somers Cocks. November 5.

    Retreat of the Prussians—Conjectures—Temerity of the French—The Landgrave of Hesse—French freebooters—King of Sardinia—Geneva, Brabant, Liège—Dumouriez—Wimpffen defends Thionville—Liberty endangered—Sedition in Ireland . 341

Mr. Miles to Mr. Long. November 12.

    Vandernoot in London—Van Eupen—Vonck—Brabant—Governments palsied—Bishop of Liège a fugitive—Civil war in Ireland Danger to England from France—Custine and Dumouriez—The Jacobins—Alliance with France—Union of parties in England 344

Mr. Miles to Lord Fortescue. November 12.

    The political atmosphere—England feels the storm—Minds of men revolutionised—Sceptres of Kings on the Continent . 346

Minute by Mr. Miles. November 13.

    M. Scipion Mourgue desires on the part of France an interview with Mr. Pitt—Le Brun—The Abbé Noël . . . 347

CONTENTS OF THE FIRST VOLUME

PAGE

Mr. Miles to Mr. Aust. November 15.
    The French Republic—Mistaken foreign policy of England—
No good to be expected from confederacy 850

Mr. Aust to Mr. Miles. November 16.
    Inquiries about M. Scipion Mourgue 350

Mr. Miles to Mr. Aust. November 16.
    Lord Grenville may be informed about M. Mourgue . . 351

Mr. Miles to Mr. Aust. November 17.
    Necessity for political union 351

Mr. Aust to Mr. Miles. November 17.
    Lord Grenville declines to receive communications from the French Executive Council 352

Minute of Conversation with Mr. Long. November 18 . 352

Mr. Miles to Mr. Long. November 19.
    Spain veers round to France—The Family Compact—England should acknowledge the Republic 354

Mr. Miles to Mr. Pitt. November 26.
    France and Spain—Count d'Aranda and the French Minister—
An alliance with England preferred by France . . . 354

Mr. Miles to Mr. Aust. November 26.
    Decree of November 19—War against all the world—The Convention surprised into the measure—France and Holland—M. Sémonville—French Admiral and Russia—Count d'Aranda—Gibraltar and Spain—Mr. Miles offers to go to Paris . . 355

Mr. Miles to M. Scipion Mourgue. November 28.
    An explanation demanded—Has M. Mourgue authority to treat with the Court of London? 356

Minute of Interview with Mr. Long on M. Mourgue's Mission. 357

Mr. Miles to Mr. Long. November 29.
    A general pacification practicable—The French impressed by the loyalty of the English 358

Mr. Miles to Mr. Pitt. November 29.

The mission of M. Mourgue—Decree of November 19—Dumouriez instructed to delay—The Scheldt 359

Mr. Miles to Mr. Pitt. November 30.

Possibility of peace—Mr. Miles offers to see M. Le Brun—Acknowledgment of the Republic desired—The emigrants—The Alien Bill 360

Mr. Miles to Mr. Long. November 30.

M. Mourgue will meet Mr. Long 361

Minute on Interview of M. Mourgue with Mr. Long . . 362

Mr. Long to Mr. Miles. December 1.

The 'Sun' newspaper—'Protest' against Paine . . 364

Minute on Interview of M. Maret with Mr. Pitt. December 2 364

Mr. Miles to M. Le Brun. December 2.

Mission of M. Scipion Mourgue—Alliance with France—Allusion to Liège 366

Mr. Miles to M. Maret. December 3.

Alliance with France—The Executive Power must abstain from interfering with the internal affairs of England . . . 366

Minute of Interview between M. Maret and Mr. Miles . . 368

Mr. Miles to Lord Buckingham. December 4.

A mission to Paris desirable—M. Le Brun might be influenced in favour of peace—War hazardous 370

Minute of Interview between M. Maret and Mr. Miles . 371

Mr. Aust to Mr. Miles. December 6.

State of Ireland—Lord Grenville declines the offer of Mr. Miles to proceed to Paris 372

Mr. Miles to M. Scipion Mourgue. December 6.

The mission of M. Mourgue—England desires peace—The Dutch must be protected—England not ripe for revolt . 372

Minute of Interview between M. Maret and Mr. Miles. . 373

Lord Buckingham to Mr. Miles. December 7.
    On the question of Mr. Miles going to Paris . . . 374

Mr. Miles to Lord Buckingham. December 8.
    War hazardous—Intentions of the Executive Council known to Mr. Miles—Proposal to the Duke of Leeds in 1790—Tyranny of the House of Austria—The Netherlands . . . 375

Mr. Long to Mr. Miles. December 9.
    Publications of Condorcet—The coalition—Mission to Paris improbable—Defence of Louis XVI. 376

Mr. Miles to Mr. Long. December 9.
    Measures taken to arrest the writings of Condorcet Defence of Louis XVI.—The ruling party in France desire to save the royal family. 377

Mr. Miles to M. Fabry. December 9.
    Opening of the Scheldt would necessitate war—Le Brun dazzled—English Cabinet pacific—The Abbé Sieyès favours war—False reports by the emigrants—Prussian emissaries in Paris—The Austrian Netherlands 378

Mr. Miles to Mr. Pitt. December 12.
    Arrival of Noël—Dumouriez and the Scheldt—Dumouriez, Noël, and Maret in favour of peace—Warning against privateers. 381

Mr. Miles to Mr. Long. December 13.
    Dumouriez and Holland—The Liégeois—The Duke of Leeds in 1790—Mr. Pitt and Lord Hawkesbury—The Scheldt—Mr. Fox desires that an agent should be sent to Paris . . 382

A Member of the Convention to Mr. Miles. Paris, Dec. 9.
    Recall of Maret—Garat, Chauvelin—Expectation in Paris of a change in the English Cabinet—The French fleet—Sémonville—War inevitable—Armed vagabonds must be employed—France not afraid—Clavière, Madame Roland 385

M. Scipion Mourgue to Mr. Miles. Paris, December 9.
    England must abandon the Scheldt—The situation critical—Peril of Louis XVI. 387

Minute of Interview between M. Maret and Mr. Miles . . 388

Mr. Miles to Mr. Pitt. December 14.
    Offers to see Le Brun, accompanied by Maret . . . 389

Mr. Miles to M. Le Brun. December 14.
    Painful state of affairs—An acceptable agent from Paris is desirable 389

Minute of Interview with Lord Buckingham . . . 390

Mr. Miles to M. Noël. December 16.
    Acknowledges the 'Journal of Brissot'—Finds hope in the return of Maret to Paris 391

Mr. Miles to Mr. Pitt. December 16.
    The States of Brabant and the Scheldt—Dumouriez—The French misled with respect to England—Lord Lansdowne—Mr. Fox—The 'Journal of Brissot' 392

Mr. Miles to M. Le Brun. December 18.
    Intrigues in Paris adverse to peace—Ill-founded suspicions in France respecting England—The aristocrats—The armaments against Spain—Mr. Pitt and the internal affairs of France—War dangerous for France—Interview of Maret with Pitt on December 2—Loyalty of the English—Le Brun and Chauvelin . 393

Minute by Mr. Miles. December 18.
    Bill for disarming foreigners—Secret committee in France in 1788—The Duc de la Rochefoucauld—Destruction of the *noblesse* contemplated—Murder of Rochefoucauld 397

Proposal to rescue Louis XVI. 398

Mr. Miles to M. Le Brun. December 21.
    Le Brun on Maret's interview with Pitt, December 2—Origin of the conference explained—Maret substituted for Mourgue—Le Brun advised to satisfy the English Government . . 400

Mr. Miles to M. Maret. December 22.
    France and the Scheldt—War should be avoided—Peace in Europe would be beneficial to France 403

Decree of the National Convention. December 15, 1792 . 405

Extract from the Register of the Executive Council. December 16 409

M. Scipion Mourgue to Mr. Miles. Paris, December 17.

Return of Maret expected—The Executive Council uninformed on English affairs Deception by Chauvelin The Scheldt—War will end in despotism—The control of religion necessary . 410

General Dampierre to Mr. Miles. Paris, December 17.

Intrigues of Walckiers—Acknowledgment of the Republic in the person of Chauvelin—The Abbé Noël and Chauvelin—Le Brun and Maret—Excitement in Paris—Influence of the Jacobins 412

Mr. Miles to M. Noël. December 23.

Maret opposed in Paris—Chauvelin without character. . 414

Mr. Miles to Lord Fortescue. December 23.

Suggestion on the Alien Bill—Landing of foreigners with arms—The English Cabinet should explain itself to France Peace still possible—Mr. Burke under the dominion of passion - Peace with honour 415

Mr. Miles to M. Scipion Mourgue. December 24.

The despatch of Le Brun causes uneasiness—Chauvelin—The French must not trust to the Opposition in England—The Revolution has lost ground in England—Danger of anarchy—The reason why Mourgue's father withdrew from the French Cabinet 418

Mr. Miles to Mr. Aust. December 26.

Report that Spain has acknowledged the French Republic—Lord Lansdowne—D'Aranda and Bourgoing—Chauvelin insists on being acknowledged in London—Noël gone to the Hague . 421

Mr. Miles to Mr. Pitt. December 27.

Noël blamed by Le Brun—The Scheldt—Le Brun's report to the National Convention—Threatened appeal to the English people 422

M. Scipion Mourgue to Mr. Miles. Paris, December 24.

Arrival of Maret—Ungenerous language in the House of Commons—Mr. Windham—Le Brun desires political relations with Miles 423

General Dampierre to Mr. Miles. Paris, December 24.

War inevitable—Despotism must be destroyed. . . 425

General Wimpffen to Mr. Miles. Paris, December 28.
 Louis XVI. and the Queen will perish—Hébert at the Convention—Terror in Paris 426

Extracts from Papers forwarded by General Wimpffen . 427

Mr. Miles to M. Le Brun. January 2, 1793.
 Erroneous conception of the interview of Maret with Pitt—The Executive Council misled by the success of the army—The Republic reproduces the despotism of the monarchy—Peace is still possible—The decrees of November 19 and December 15 cause irritation—Lord Hawkesbury, Mr. Dundas—The Belgians and the Liégeois 430

Mr. Miles to Lord Fortescue. January 2.
 Hope of peace still cherished—War would injure Mr. Pitt—Bland Burgess and Maret—Timidity of Clavière—Danton, Robespierre, and Marat—The Revolution was necessary—Burke misled—England cannot steer a middle course . . . 434

Minute of Conference between M. Reinhard and Mr. Miles . 438

Mr. Miles to Mr. Long. January 4.
 Mr. Pitt and the cabal at Buckingham House—No good possible from union with the Powers on the Continent—Fox, not Burke, is the prescient statesman 443

Minute of Conference between M. Reinhard and Mr. Miles . 445

Mr. Miles to Mr. Long. January 4.
 M. Chauvelin desires a private audience with Mr. Pitt. . 448

M. Maret to Mr. Miles. Paris, December 31, 1792.
 The dispositions of the English Ministry not pacific—Treaty of commerce—Disregard of stipulations by England . . 448

Mr. Miles to M. Maret. January 4, 1793.
 Intrigues of the French in England and Ireland provoked the Alien Bill—Obstinacy of Le Brun—The Executive Council must abandon the Scheldt 451

INDEX TO THE CORRESPONDENCE

PAGES

I. From Miles *to* Aust 350, 351, 355, 421
" Buckingham . 150, 160, 178, 208, 213, 317, 370. 375
" Cocks . 127, 130, 214, 224, 232. 246, 272, 338, 341
" D'Aremberg 184
" Edwards 185
" Fabry 378
" Fortescue . . . 316, 346, 415, 434
" Latude 256
" Le Brun . . . 366, 389, 393, 400, 430
" Leeds 121, 122, 123, 124, 125, 128, 133, 135, 140, 141
" Long . 333, 344, 354, 358, 361, 377, 382, 443, 448
" Maret 366, 403, 451
" Mourgue 356, 372, 418
" Newenham 171, 182, 209, 258, 280, 292, 311, 312, 337
" Noël 391, 414
" Pitt . 298, 308, 354, 359, 360, 381, 389. 392, 422
" Pye 194, 202, 239
" Rodney . . . 146, 153, 236, 253, 270
" Rose 170, 176
" Smith 310
" Talleyrand 152

II. To Miles *from* Aust . . 320, 329, 332, 335, 350, 352, 372
" Buckingham 374
" Cocks 138
" Crelet (*la Société de* 1789) . . . 170
" Dampierre 412, 425
" De Chartres 223
" Fabry 132
" Fortescue . . . 287, 309, 315, 334
" Gower 310
" Huskisson . . . 202, 313. 314, 329
" Lafayette, Madame de . . . 252
" Le Brun . . . . . 1"9

		PAGES
II. To Miles *from* Lodge		332
,,	Long	364, 376
,,	Maret	448
,,	Member of the National Assembly	305, 315, 385
,,	Miles, Miss	277, 284, 288, 289, 295, 301, 303
,,	Mirabeau	169
,,	Monsieur ——	337
,,	Mourgue	321, 325, 330
,,	Mourgue, Scipion	328, 387, 410, 423
,,	Newenham	335
,,	Pétion (*la Société des Amis de la Constitution*)	169
,,	Rich	136
,,	Rodney	311
,,	Talleyrand	153
,,	Wimpffen	149, 299, 426

THE CORRESPONDENCE

OF

WILLIAM AUGUSTUS MILES

ON THE

FRENCH REVOLUTION

INTRODUCTION

ON February 5, 1832, the 'Age' newspaper contained the following paragraph: 'Sir Charles Flint was Under-Secretary of State for Ireland. He resigned more from private than political causes. Sir Charles is, we believe, the surviving trustee for the security of the papers of the late William Augustus Miles, of whom and his papers we may have much to say hereafter.' The trustees surviving at the above date, and to whose care the correspondence of Mr. Miles had been committed, were Sir Charles Flint and Captain Digby Willoughby, R.N. (afterwards Lord Middleton). The intimation given by the London journal is explained by the fact that Mr. Miles, as was then well known, had been in close political relations with Mr. Pitt; that he had maintained during many years literary intercourse with some of the leading men of the day; and that, although a considerable number of the productions of his pen had appeared in print, there still remained letters and memoranda hitherto unpublished. In fact, the manuscripts extant date from the year 1776 to 1817, covering, therefore, a period of intense interest and importance in English history. In reference to some portions of these papers, Herbert Marsh observes that 'Perhaps the documents of which Mr. Miles speaks will hereafter be laid before the public.'[1]

The delay in the publication has been unavoidable, the trustees, in the first instance, objecting, on political grounds, to the letters being printed during the lifetime of certain prominent statesmen; and, subsequently, the three elder sons of Mr. Miles, obtaining commissions in the army at the age of sixteen, joined their respective regiments in India, and either never possessed the opportunity, or did not realise the desirableness, of examining the voluminous manuscripts bequeathed by their father. The junior of these three sons, Captain Rawdon Muir Miles, fell at Junga Fareekee, in the disastrous retreat of the British forces from Cabul, January, 1842; another son, Major Frederick Alexander, after having commanded a battery of field artillery during the Punjab campaign of 1848–49, resigned soon afterwards, and expired almost immediately on his return to England; and the eldest, Lieutenant-Colonel Robert Henry, died whilst on a visit to Malta, in the spring of 1867.[2] The youngest member of the family, Thomas

---

[1] *The History of the Politicks of Great Britain and France from the time of the Conference at Pillnitz to the Declaration of War against Great Britain*, by Herbert Marsh, Fellow of St. John's College, Cambridge (London, 1800), ii. 114. Dr. Marsh had been Private Secretary to Mr. Pitt, and became Bishop of Peterborough.

[2] Very soon after their arrival in India, in 1825, Frederick and Rawdon Miles, having passed the necessary examination at Fort William in the Oriental languages, were placed on the regimental staff as Persian interpreters. The former translated Pinnock's *Catechism of Astronomy* into Oordoo, and it was printed, 'For the use of the Lucknow College, by Order of the King of Oude, at His Majesty's Lithographic Press,' in

Willoughby, was accidentally drowned in his boyhood. It has, therefore, devolved on the fourth and last surviving son—the editor of these volumes—to arrange for the press the several letters, despatches, and minutes now presented to the public. They have been in his custody since the decease of his mother, in 1872; but he found it impracticable to enter upon the literary labour necessarily associated with the undertaking until he could conscientiously resign his living as Vicar of Monkwearmouth, and thereby procure the required leisure in absolute retirement. His ministry, dating back to 1837, has been connected with some of the most populous of the metropolitan and provincial spheres of pastoral work—Whitechapel, Limehouse, Chelsea, Sunderland, Glasgow, and, at a more recent date, as Principal of the Protestant College, Malta, where the incessant demand upon his time and thoughts put the contemplated task entirely out of the question. Perhaps, however, no previous period could have been more opportune than the present, so closely allied as it is with the centenary of the French Revolution.

At a very early age Mr. Miles, having inherited property sufficient for his independence, crossed the Atlantic in search of information or pleasure. He was actually on his way to Mount Vernon, in Virginia—as the young travelling companion and guest of Governor Eden—to pay a visit to General Washington, but, not

1832; and the latter completed a translation of Voltaire's *Life of Charles the Twelfth* into Persian for publication, but, unhappily, having taken his MS. into Affghanistan for final revision, the work was lost in the midst of the Cabul disasters in 1842. The elder brother, Robert Henry, contributed to Colburn's *New Monthly Magazine*, in 1866-7, a series of articles descriptive of a 'Journey to Palestine, viâ Mount Sinai and Petra.' During his tour in Egypt, Colonel Miles accompanied Monsieur Ferdinand de Lesseps, as his guest, on an inspection of the Suez Canal preparatory to its being opened for traffic.

foreseeing the eminent position which Washington was destined to obtain among statesmen, changed his mind and returned to England. He was then only in his nineteenth year; he married, and, as shown by his papers, embarked at once upon a literary and political life—a devoted admirer of Wilkes, soon afterwards an ardent supporter of Pitt, and a frequent contributor of articles, as a pastime, to periodicals and journals. He was thus brought under the notice of public men. In 1773 there appeared the first of his productions in the pamphlet form.[1] His earlier correspondents included David Garrick, Lord Rodney, Horne Tooke, Oliver Goldsmith, Lord Fortescue, Sir Edward Newenham, Somers Cocks, and Lord Temple. The topics that came under review, among a variety of domestic and foreign matters, were Parliamentary Reform, Catholic Emancipation, and the state of Ireland. But the letters here selected are almost entirely restricted to the affairs of the French Revolution, and to the conduct of the war between France and England, embracing the period from 1789 to the close of hostilities in 1815.

The circumstances under which Mr. Miles first entered into political relations with the Government are narrated by himself in the subjoined minute, preserved among his papers:—'In March, 1782, Lord North was driven from power by the united strength of the Rockingham and Shelburne parties. I congratulated Lord Shelburne on his being appointed one of His Majesty's principal Secretaries of State. He asked me if he could be useful to me. I declined his favour from the project I had conceived of retiring to France, in order to live

---

[1] *A Letter to Sir John Fielding, Knt. Occasioned by his extraordinary Request to Mr. Garrick for a suppression of the 'Beggar's Opera.'*

within the limits of my income—too scanty for this
metropolis—and complete the education of my only
child. I had already taken leave of my friends—among
the rest, Mr. Fortescue, who had just married a sister
of Lord Temple, but the death of Lord Rockingham
having occasioned another change in the ministry, by
which Lord Shelburne became First Lord of the Treasury,
and Earl Temple appointed Lord Lieutenant of Ireland,
my friend, Sir Edward Newenham, Member for the
County of Dublin, wrote to me in pressing terms to get
some appointment under Government and go over to
Ireland, assuring me that he would serve Administration
so far as possible, if Administration would serve me. In
consequence of this letter I waited on Lord Shelburne,
at his house in Berkeley Square, and, after a long conference, his Lordship insisted on my writing to Lord
Temple and using his name, telling me that he also
would write.' The following letter shows that he then
decided to apply for employment.

MR. MILES TO THE HON. MR. FORTESCUE

London: July 16, 1782

Upon mature consideration I have deferred my
journey into France until Louis XVI. and George III.
have made up their quarrel, for, in the present situation of affairs, it is very possible that the French
Ministry may provide me with apartments in the
Bastille should I, as I am very apt to do, let my tongue
run before my wit, and condemn the impertinence of the
Court of Versailles for interfering in our contest with
Messieurs les Américains. I have had it in contemplation to retire to a cheaper country than England, so as
to live within the limits of my small fortune, and, at
the same time, educate my daughter in Paris. But the

death of the Marquis of Rockingham having called Lord Temple into public life, I feel an inclination to accompany his Lordship to Ireland. I would really like to go over to Dublin, where, from my intimacy with Sir Edward Newenham, I venture to assert that I could be useful to Administration.

Mr. Miles had an interview with Lord Temple, August 24, when the promise was given of an appointment connected with the Irish Government, subject, however, to political conditions to be determined on their arrival at Dublin Castle. He left London September 1, and after being nearly a week on the road, including a day and night of amusing adventure at sea when traversing St. George's Channel, he reached the Irish capital. 'My old acquaintance, Sir Frederick Flood,' he notes in a minute of that date, 'whom I had met some years before at Hagley, the seat of Lord Lyttelton, wrote to me a warm invitation to go to his town house in Merrion Square, and make it my own. Lord Temple arrived on the 15th, and on Tuesday the 17th I attended the Levee. On Thursday I went to the private audience. It being likely that I shall be called into scenes in which the conduct of ministers will be brought nearer to my vision, and in which, perhaps, the purity I profess at present may relax and give way to the distemper of the times, *I shall henceforward preserve, if possible, my correspondence, so far as it relates to public affairs*, until I retire from the bustle of politics, or the curtain falls and closes this strange eventful history of life for ever.'

It was unfortunate that Sir Edward Newenham was now absent on the Continent. The following letter may be read with interest.

Sir Edward Newenham to Mr. Miles.

Paris: October 9, 1782.

Dear Miles,—I had much pleasure this day in receiving your letter, and, as you took my former offer of advising you just as it was intended, I shall preface this short note with a continuation of the same liberty. Do not take any house or apartments in Dublin, suddenly, for more than three months, or you will repent it; do not be displeased with the Viceroy for these six months to come; keep your mind to yourself, even before Mr. Graydon; do not let any human being into your own cabinet; take care of the Lord Mayor. At present I most heartily condemn the Fencibles, and approve of the resolutions against them. But my great objects are the Revenue Bill and the more equal representation of the people. If I gain these points I shall then contentedly retire for ever from the field of politics.

I never write about politics in this kingdom, though I have visited and been visited by all parties and nations. I have dined, breakfasted, and been in company several times with his Excellency Dr. Franklin, who is really an honour to the age he lives in. His grandson is an amiable young man. I have dined several times with Mr. Jay, ambassador from America to Spain, and the Marquis de Lafayette. I have been often in company with the Oppositionists of Ireland. I see and hear all opinions, but never have once given my own, except that of my heart, which is for freedom to America in its full extent.

It is not possible for me to write to you either a long or an entertaining letter. To recapitulate the amusements of this city would be only reviving your desire of travelling, which does not correspond with your present views, and must not be thought on. We were highly honoured at the Royal dinner at Marly, as a place near the Queen was reserved for us, and the Marquis de Lafayette drank separately to each of us, which is deemed a particular honour. My son was invited most particularly to a Royal hunt, where he was much surprised to see the first ladies of the Court equipped in breeches and boots, in the exact form of an overgrown Newmarket jockey. Plays, operas, the drolleries of the boulevards, Chinese Ridotto, &c., have deprived me of many pounds. The cheapest articles are claret and Burgundy. As to apartments, we have a truly superb suite for four louis a week—four bed-chambers, and a hall, with a noble parlour. On Saturday or Sunday we set off upon a zig-zag tour, viz., Fontainebleau, Tours, Bordeaux, Lyons, Avignon, and Marseilles, to which last place all my letters are to be directed, à la poste-restante. I have got a smart touch of the rheumatism in my shoulders by getting cold at the Church of St. Geneviève, which has been twenty-five years building, after the model of St. Peter's at Rome, and is not yet quite finished. All my family here send their sincere regards to you, Mrs. and Miss Miles—whom I suppose by this time safely landed at Eblana, on Anna's Banks. Take no house—do not lay out your money in Ireland. Adieu, my dear Miles, and believe me to be most sincerely and unalterably yours.

But before the above letter was received political difficulties had arrested further progress in respect to the relations of Mr. Miles with the Irish Executive. On Sunday, September 29, he attended the Levee as usual. The next day he had a lengthened conference with the Secretary at the Castle, the purport and result of which are explained by himself:—' Mr. Grenville [1] assured me that his brother owned that I had been encouraged by him to come over, but that it was idle to be reserved upon the business. He would, therefore, communicate to me without hesitation that his Excellency had anticipated that Sir Edward Newenham would give his whole and unqualified support to Government, in which case he would have a very great right to expect that an appointment would be provided for me; but, so far from giving his support, he had taken a decided part against it, and, in particular, by insisting on a Bill of Rights and approving of Mr. Flood's opposition. That this conduct had put it out of the power of the Lord Lieutenant to do anything for me without giving offence to all the friends of Government, who were already open-mouthed for more appointments than he had at his disposal, and whom he dared not disoblige; that my connections and political sentiments were well known, and that a clamour would instantly be excited against him if he offered a place to me. Mr. Grenville added that perhaps my friend, on being written to, would see the difficulty that lay in my way, and the impropriety of supporting Mr. Flood if it was expected that Government should support me. Astonished that such an opinion should be openly avowed, I exclaimed, with some warmth, What! Is it thus that Lord Temple and yourself intend to commence your political career? Is it that, coming into office on professed Whig principles, you would preface your reign by an endeavour to corrupt the representative integrity of the country? I am sure that you would not desire any fact so injurious to be proclaimed. But, if it is meant that I should state to Sir

---

[1] Brother of Lord Temple, and, as Lord Grenville, Secretary of State for Foreign Affairs from 1791 to 1801.

Edward Newenham that he is expected to support, right or wrong, every measure of Government, I must decline; and allow me to assure you that if my friend should pledge himself to such a condition, I would despise him and renounce his acquaintance for ever. Mr. Grenville replied that he must refer me to his brother for an *éclaircissement*.'

At a private audience with the Lord Lieutenant, October 3, the question of an appointment was discussed at considerable length. 'His Excellency then observed'—so the minute concludes—'that he had a personal wish to serve me, but the situation of Ireland was such as obliged him to exert and to strain every nerve in his power to secure a majority, in order to obtain a point which he was determined to carry if possible, and if not, he would resign, and be off in twenty-four hours; that with respect to my friend, he had, since he had written to me, taken a decided part against Government in publishing a string of resolutions declaratory of fully supporting Mr. Flood, and insisting on a Bill of Rights from England, renouncing all legislative authority over Ireland; that this violence was the very reverse of what he had expected, and which prevented him from doing what he really wished, and had intended. He submitted it to me whether, connected as I was, it would not be countenancing the measure he reprobated, and which he was resolved to oppose, if he provided for me. His Lordship then entered largely into the state of Irish politics, and revealed to me the true character of its senate, adding that, if anyone in England had told him the condition of affairs, he would not have believed it, and that he was sure that I must also have seen sufficient to surprise me and excite my indignation. The corruption of the British Parliament, he said, great as it was, seems as nothing when compared to that of Ireland. His Lordship protested he had witnessed enough to puzzle the faith of the most credulous, nor had he in his whole experience, or in the course of his reading, discovered so much infamy. He then expressed his great uneasiness at not having it in his power, from the situation in which he found himself, to do as he wished towards me. From the whole tenor of Lord Temple's conversation, from the agitation and visible distress of his mind, and the extreme anxiety to discharge his duty to this country, and yet stand well with the people of Ireland, I felt that it was unreasonable to press his Lordship any further. I therefore desired to know whether his embarrassment would be diminished by my withdrawing from the Castle, assuring him that, if it would leave him more at liberty, I would from that instant waive and relinquish every claim that I had on his attention. His Excellency declared that I had given him great relief, and that my frank manner had made him more at a loss how to act by me than with the mercenary applicants who came to sell their votes. He added, after paying me many compliments, that I might depend upon his friendship wherever he may be. Thus ended my expedition to Ireland.'[1]

By the course thus adopted Mr. Miles cemented, at the same moment, the attachment of Sir Edward Newenham and the esteem of Lord Temple, which, as will appear in the perusal of the correspondence now published, endured throughout life. He wrote to Lord

[1] In the *Correspondence between the Right Honourable William Pitt and Charles Duke of Rutland, Lord Lieutenant of Ireland*, lately published, the Duke, in his letter to Pitt, August 15, 1784, alludes to letters that passed between Sir Edward Newenham and Mr. Miles, and in which Lord Temple is mentioned by the latter with some severity, not justified by subsequent circumstances.

Shelburne: 'My friend having been compelled to decide in favour of Mr. Flood, the Lord Lieutenant thinks that he is released from the assurances he held out to me in London, and, to confess the truth, his Excellency is really in a very perplexed situation. In waiving my claim I have consulted the repose of Government, and in this light, I trust, it will be considered.' Before leaving Dublin on a tour he addressed the following letter to the Lord Lieutenant.

Mr. Miles to His Excellency the Earl Temple

October 5, 1782

My Lord,—In waiving my pretensions to the favour of Government, I have considered equally the convenience of your Administration and your own personal repose, and, after paying some visits in the western part of this kingdom, I shall return to England. Your Excellency may be assured that I shall take a decided part against every question that may have the remotest tendency to any further abridgement of the supremacy of Great Britain. While the people retain their ardour for military associations, bold and enterprising men will perpetually embarrass Government by starting what they call constitutional questions; but if a different direction could possibly be given to the minds of the former, it would be one of the means for restoring public peace. I shall do myself the honour to appear at the Levee to-morrow, in case your Excellency should have anything further to state; and, as Lord Shelburne will certainly be surprised at my leaving Ireland, I trust to your communicating to his lordship the occasion of my departure. In congratulating you on the safe arrival of Lady Temple, allow me to wish you and your family the full enjoyment of every happiness this fleeting life affords, and, with sentiments of unaffected regard and respect, I remain, &c. &c.

After a sojourn of two months in the southern counties, Mr. Miles communicated to Lord Shelburne a concise narrative of what he had seen and heard. His letter, December 6, concludes thus:—'Since my arrival in Ireland I have had frequent opportunities of conversing with all descriptions of men, and believe me when I assure you that the number who are friendly to Administration are very few when compared with those who are clamorous for renunciation. I could mention several other particulars which tend to prove the hostile spirit of Ireland. I shall reserve myself until I return to London. It is my sincere wish that your Lordship may preserve the unity of the British Empire, and restore peace and confidence to a distracted people.'

Lord Shelburne to Mr. Miles

London: December 13, 1782

Sir,—I am much flattered by your letter from Carrick-on-Suir, and beg you to accept of my best thanks for the very important communications which it contains. I shall hope, from your former letter, to have the honour of personally assuring you how sensible I am of your obliging attentions to me.

I am, Sir, your most obedient, &c. &c.

Resolved on retirement from political strife, Mr. Miles directed his thoughts towards the Ardennes, and, finally, fixed his residence at Seraing, a quiet spot in those days, situate on the Meuse, and about four miles distant from the City of Liège, where stood the ancient château of the bishops of the principality.

'Let me call to your remembrance,' he says, when writing to Newenham at a later period, 'the delightful hermitage in which you found me on your return from Italy in the year 1783—on the banks of a river, in a fertile and romantic vale, where the mountains on one side, abounding in vines, and cultivated to their very summit, exhibited a striking and beautiful contrast to the bleak and barren hills on the opposite shore, condemned by their incorrigible sterility to remain in the wild and ruthless state in which they were left by the hand of nature. The Meuse, whose constant ebbing stream presented a faithful but melancholy picture of human life, watered in its silent passage to the sea an extensive garden, equally adapted for recreation and convenience, whilst an incessant navigation, animating the rural scene, dissipated even the gloom of winter. The late Prince Bishop, who to a graceful and elegant person added the accomplishments of the gentleman and the scholar, having his country residence within a few yards of my house, received me with that gracious condescension which rendered him the idol of those who had the honour of his acquaintance. It was thus in my power to vary the scene, and to partake of the pleasures of the palace, whenever the solitude of the cottage ceased to amuse me. This Prince died a few months after my arrival, and, desiring to remain in the tranquil obscurity of domestic life, I declined waiting on his successor; but he seduced me from my retirement by attentions which could not fail to leave an impression, and, won by the advances he made, I cultivated his acquaintance, and an intimacy ensued which augmented the pleasures of my retreat.'

In 1784 and 1785 a series of letters appeared in a London newspaper under the signature of 'Neptune.'

The subjects treated were both moral and political. Animadversions in strong language were addressed direct to the heir of the British throne on the irregularities and extravagances practised at Carlton House, the conduct of prominent public men was reviewed and condemned in incisive terms, and the measures of the Administration were in general supported. These letters were written by Mr. Miles during his solitude on the banks of the Meuse. They excited considerable attention among political and literary men.[1] In his diary he speaks of them as follows :—' The letters under the signature of "Neptune," dictated by a love of freedom and of my country, were written on the Continent, on the destruction of the Coalition, and transmitted in confidence, under cover, to the Reverend Howell Howell Edwards, at that time a student at Christ Church, Oxford, with the request that he would send them to one of the daily papers, but not to communicate his name or mine to the printer. He was as ignorant as myself of the mode by which our public prints are conducted. Neither of us knew that one set was in the pay of Ministry and the other hired by Opposition. Chance decided him to address these essays to the ' Morning Post '—they became popular, and a communication was desired with the author. I declined revealing myself;

[1] '*Letters of Neptune and Gracchus.* These letters, originally published in the *Morning Post*, are addressed to the Prince of Wales and other distinguished characters. They contain strong expostulations on particular occasions, and are evidently framed, in point of style, upon the model of Junius.'—*Critical Review*, November 1784. ' The editor of the *Morning Post* understands that he is indebted to Mr. Miles for the elegant and sensible letters which have lately appeared in this paper under the signature of " Dramaticus." Whenever Mr. Miles thinks proper to honour the editor with his contributions, they shall always have a conspicuous insertion.' Thackeray, in a note not published, says : ' When I wrote my *Lectures on the Four Georges*, a copy of *Neptune's Letters* was lying upon my table.'

offers were made for the payment of my services, but I answered that, while Mr. Pitt, whose youth and the part he had taken inspired me with confidence, adhered to the Constitution, I would support the minister, without any pecuniary recompense, from a sense of duty to my country.'[1]

An extract from one of these letters may not inaptly be given here. Thus, in September 1785 'Neptune' says: 'The right of investigating the measures of Government is perhaps the most valuable privilege annexed to the British Constitution. It is a security against despotism which no other nation enjoys; and I am willing it should be preserved in its fullest latitude. But when the exercise of it degenerates into a mercenary opposition—when it has no other object than the aggrandisement of party or the private interest of individuals, it loses its value, and becomes a vice of the most pernicious tendency. . . . Let me ask you what possible good can be expected from our echoing the clamours of Opposition? Their object, it is certain, is to excite discontent in this kingdom and in Ireland, in the hope that it may ripen into revolt, and the latter be provoked to follow the example of America. But who is there among us so little skilled in the politics of this country as not to know that, if Ireland should be amputated from us, we bleed to death?'

[1] The means through which Mr. Miles became known as the writer of these letters is described by himself. 'I had addressed a letter to his Majesty, signed "Legion," and enjoined my Oxonian friend to transcribe it for the *Morning Post* as usual. Unfortunately he sent the MS. exactly as he had received it, and the editor, astonished at the boldness of the language, took it to the Treasury to inquire whether it would be advisable to print it. On seeing the handwriting Mr. Pitt exclaimed, "I know the author, it is Miles's hand." Mr. Rose thereupon revealed my name to the editor, whom he had before directed to purchase me on any terms.'—*Letter to Lord Moira*, May 6, 1812.

As the result of the most friendly intercourse with the Prince Bishop of Liège and his court, it had become possible to obtain important information as to affairs on the Continent, which, having been transmitted to the Marquis of Buckingham,[1] led to the formation of political relations between the Chancellor of the Exchequer and Mr. Miles, as shown in the subjoined letters.

MR. MILES TO THE MARQUIS OF BUCKINGHAM

Liège: August 5, 1785

My Lord,—I am this instant returned from dining with the Prince, where I had a long conversation with the Marquis de Cordon,[2] who assured me that he was warmly interested in the prosperity of the present Ministry, and still more so in that of England. I made acquaintance with him last year, and on his arrival this summer at Liège I renewed it and mean to cultivate it. I was much pleased to find that he had communicated to Lord Carmarthen the very same intelligence respecting the intrigues of France in Ireland that I had the honour to transmit to your Lordship the year before last. He purposes to pass the winter here, and from his friendship and connections I have no doubt of occasionally deriving useful intelligence. In case it should be resolved to fix me here, I may enter upon business, as it were, directly, and I shall not hesitate to ask the Prince to procure me from his ministers at foreign courts all the information in his power. My intimacy with him will justify this freedom.

Foreigners think they do us ample justice in acknowledging we are a great nation; but they hold themselves

---

[1] Lord Temple, who became Marquis of Buckingham in Dec. 1784.

[2] Lately arrived from London, where he had resided ten years as Envoy Plenipotentiary from the King of Sardinia.

VOL. I.

at liberty to censure our manners while they extol our magnanimity. It has been my endeavour to convince them that we are not less amiable than our neighbours, and that our aversion to receive strangers with open arms at first sight is rather an argument in favour of our prudence than a proof of want of courtesy. I cannot, however, but wish that our countrymen were more affable, and less reserved with foreigners. The address and affability of the French have a wonderful effect on the minds of men. They even procure them a favourable reception among people who suspect them, and which they never fail to turn to a good account either to themselves or their country.

I have presumed to inclose a letter for the press. Your Lordship, I trust, will have the goodness to seal it, and send it to the post. You will perceive that at this distance, and without facts to go upon, I am restricted in my information on home politics. Like the spider, I spin from myself: would to Heaven I could resemble it farther, and entangle the factious fly in my patriotic web!

I have the honour to be, &c.

THE MARQUIS OF BUCKINGHAM TO MR. MILES

Margate: September 1, 1785

Sir,—Your letter to me by the King's messenger, who passed by Ostend, came very quickly to my hands; that by the packet was forwarded to London, and from thence to me at Margate. I must send your letter to Mr. Pitt. He will write to you, and the nature of the correspondence requires that, in future, it should be addressed to him. I cannot and ought not to omit the satisfaction I feel in seeing the zeal and activity with which you have endeavoured to make yourself useful. Mr. Pitt will give you his orders.

As to the nature of your appointments, you certainly are right in stating the expenses which you are likely to incur, and, if Mr. Pitt avails himself of the channel which you have so ably opened, he will certainly take care to reward your services; but upon all this he will give you his orders, and my distance from London prevents my speaking to him on the subject, but this letter passes through his hands.

I am, Sir, &c., &c.

Mr. Pitt to Mr. Miles

Brighthelmstone: September 11, 1785

Sir,—I am very sorry that amidst a variety of business before I left town it escaped me to transmit to you the inclosed letter which I had received from Lord Buckingham, together with the papers you had sent his Lordship. I flatter myself that the line of information which you have opened may be of material use, and if you can render it so you will find me sincerely happy to acknowledge your services. In the meantime I am desirous to learn from you what allowance you think necessary, in order to enable you to try the experiment. I shall then be able to judge how far the prospect of advantage is adequate to it. Though it is not any large sum that can be allotted to these purposes at present, you may be assured that your rewards shall keep pace with the degree of service which you may be able to render to Government. I send this letter to his Majesty's Consul at Ostend, that it may be forwarded to you if you have left that place.

I was much flattered with the compliments which you conveyed to me from the Marquis de Cordon, and will beg you to make my acknowledgments to him.

I am, Sir, &c. &c.

On receipt of the above letter, Mr. Miles, acting on the advice of the Prince Bishop, set off for England, the bearer of a special message from his Highness to Mr. Pitt. One result of that journey may be given in his own words: 'London, October 11.—Found that the Minister had left town for Burton Pynsent;[1] took post horses, and arrived in time to breakfast with him this morning. When speaking on the subject of finance, I suggested the alternative of a tax on legacies. Mr. Pitt took out his pocket-book, and, whilst observing that there was no occasion to introduce such a tax at present, made an entry of my suggestion.'[2] Immediately after his return to the Continent, the communications from Liège to Downing Street were frequent and direct, copies of the letters being still extant.

Before the Court of Versailles had even suspected the possible *bouleversement* of its regal and ancient grandeur, several of the European states had become involved in revolutionary measures, which, although restricted, or even suppressed for the moment, necessitated vigilance on the part of the great powers. Whether influenced by patriotic motives of spontaneous growth, or stimulated into active force by the successful issue of the American struggle, popular opinion made itself felt in the Republic of Holland, in the Principality of Liège, and in the Empire of Austria, in

---

[1] Burton Pynsent, in Somersetshire, the seat of the first Earl of Chatham.

[2] The Legacy Tax was adopted by Mr. Pitt in 1796, without any recognition of the fact that it had originated at his own breakfast table from Mr. Miles. 'His mind was very receptive to the ideas of others, and he was accused of not always acknowledging his obligations. This was specially true of his sinking fund, the main idea of which was taken without acknowledgment from Dr. Price.'—Lecky, *History of England in the Eighteenth Century*, v. 24. See *Letter to the Prince of Wales* (London, 1808), by Mr. Miles, p. 138.

which several territories the people, rising in opposition to the constituted authorities, entered upon a determined conflict on behalf of political independence. The Prince of Orange as Stadtholder of the United Provinces, the Prince Bishop as sovereign over the Liégeois, and the Emperor Joseph II., whose dominion embraced the Low Countries, were the parties more immediately concerned in the revolutions now initiated; but also Prussia, from her geographical position, could not avoid becoming entangled in the disturbances, and France, ever on the alert, was already well to the front in the direction of Liège at this critical juncture in the affairs of Europe. Whilst, then, the Courts of Vienna, Berlin, and Versailles respectively were operating each for its own interests, each regardless of the Dutch, it had not escaped the attention of Mr. Miles, resident on the spot, that the city of Liège had become the centre of political intrigues on behalf of all the disputants. At Liège there had been no representative of the English Government. Hence arose the decision of Mr. Pitt to place an agent in this desirable locality, where, as the subjoined letter shows, the interests of Great Britain would for the moment at least receive cordial support; whilst, at the same time, the opportunity was afforded for the transmission of important statistical information to the Chancellor of the Exchequer connected with the Commercial Treaty.

THE PRINCE BISHOP TO MR. PITT

Liège: le 26 janvier, 1786

Monsieur,—L'amitié dont Monsieur Miles m'a inspiré me fait désirer de partager son zèle pour le bien de sa patrie et pour la gloire d'un Ministre qui a étonné l'univers par ses talens à un âge que l'esprit des autres est à

peine formé, et qu'on préfère souvent le plaisir aux
affaires. Vous nous avez donné un tel exemple de grands
talens et d'une application si assidue, qu'il est impossible
d'en être témoin sans prendre le plus vif intérêt à votre
succès. Permettez, Monsieur, de vous assurer du profond
respect que j'ai toujours eu pour sa Majesté Britannique,
votre souverain, et que le plus fidèle des sujets de sa
Majesté ne peut désirer plus ardemment que moi que son
règne soit heureux. Permettez que je vous répète les
sentimens d'estime qu'une conduite non moins glorieuse
pour vous-même qu'utile pour la nation qui a confié
ses intérêts à vos soins m'a inspirés, et soyez persuadé
que je saisirai avec empressement toute occasion qui se
présentera pour vous prouver de la sincérité et de la
haute considération avec lesquelles j'ai l'honneur d'être,
  Monsieur, votre très-humble
    et très-obéissant serviteur,
      L'Evêque et Prince de Liège.

But at this date the Commercial Treaty between
England and France interested Mr. Pitt incomparably
more than did the disputes in the neighbourhood of the
Meuse, although these latter were pregnant with forebodings of danger to the tranquillity of Europe. The
letter from the Prince was not even acknowledged—an
unfortunate circumstance, as the want of courtesy gave
great offence, and eventually diverted the friendship of
the Bishop from the interests of England.

Mr. Miles forwarded to the Minister ample statistics
on the imports and exports connected with trade, both
in the Pays de Liège and in the Austrian Netherlands.
In some instances details were supplied which Lord Torrington, Minister at Brussels, had reported to the Treasury
he could not possibly obtain. Through the whole of

this year, 1786, the information transmitted to London was both commercial and political. The following letter concludes with the mention of an individual, resident at that time in Liège, who some few years later acted an important part in Paris during the French Revolution.

MR. MILES TO MR. PITT

Liège: November 13, 1786.

Sir,—It is with the highest satisfaction I acquaint you that it will be in my power to furnish you with the information you desire by the meeting of Parliament, and I am encouraged to believe it will be not only ample and authentic, but will contain the details for some two or three years past.

Allow me to submit to your consideration the idea of an article in the Treaty of Commerce to the effect that pacquet boats carrying the mail, especially in the Narrow Seas, be exempted from capture in the event of war between the two kingdoms. It is with the utmost deference that I offer my opinion on this matter, but, as it strikes me as being practicable and highly beneficial to commerce and society, I have ventured to suggest it to you.[1]

[1] 'Pitt revived the idea of a close commercial treaty with France. Eden was selected as the English negotiator in Paris, and the treaty was signed in September 1786. It was to continue in force for twelve years. It established between the two countries complete liberty of navigation and commerce in all articles that were not specially excepted. . . . The war of the French Revolution a few years later tore to shreds the Commercial Treaty of Pitt, and by a strangely unfortunate fate the Minister who had laboured so assiduously to lay the foundations of a lasting friendship between the two great nations which had been for centuries divided was afterwards regarded by France as the most inveterate of her enemies. The merit of the conception of the French treaty belongs chiefly to Shelburne, but Pitt deserves much credit for the skill and courage with which he carried it into effect. . . The Commercial Treaty was probably the most valuable result of the legislation of Pitt.'—Lecky, v. 36–46.

'The French talk with some freedom on politics. I have heard them

The editor of the 'Journal Général de l'Europe,' Monsieur Le Brun, having frequently depreciated our public funds, I wrote to him, and, informing him of his error, requested he would render justice to a nation that has never yet failed in any of her engagements. I should not have given myself this trouble if I did not know the very great influence which this gazette has on the minds of the people here, for, their Breviary excepted, the whole of their reading is confined to it. The fugitive editor of this paper thinks to pay his court to France, which spurns him, by his libels on England.[1]

in their coffee-houses, which are beset with spies, give their opinion without the least reserve on the Treaty of Commerce: they unanimously declare that their negotiators have been outwitted, that the treaty must operate very much to their disadvantage, and consequently to the advantage of England. The ground they go upon is that, if the duty upon articles be equal in both countries, English goods must necessarily have a greater sale, not only from their superior excellence, but also from the populous condition of France, which, of course, occasions a more extensive consumption. The French are not a little surprised at the idea of an English Minister possessing more finesse than one of their own country, as they look upon France as the seat of political adroitness.'— *Letter from Mr. Fitzsimmons to Mr. Miles*, Paris, December 8, 1786. See also *Travels of Arthur Young in France and Italy*, 1787-1789, p. 73.

[1] 'M. Le Brun is a proscribed man. M. de Vergennes ordered him out of France for having spoken too warmly in favour of the American Revolution at the conclusion of the war. As he is an able man, I judged it advisable to win him to the interests of his Majesty's Government.'— *Miles to Pitt*, December 14, 1787.

'As I now confine myself solely to the business, or rather the no business of this place, I must keep my knowledge to myself at the expense of my feelings and of my duty to my country at large. You, not being in a similar predicament, act very properly in warning Government of what is the opinion of the most enlightened politicians on the Continent. In respect to Le Brun, the same narrow line of conduct I have found myself obliged to adopt deprives me of the ability of serving him further than in taking his journal. If our Government attended to the useful *minutiæ* of France in such instances as you very properly mention, they would do right to have such a man in their pay to insert proper articles in favour of Great Britain in his journal, for it is not to be conceived the benefit France derives from public papers, and the injury these papers do to us. Why not mention this man to Mr. Pitt?'—*Lord Torrington to Mr. Miles*, Bruxelles. November 20, 1787.

In June, 1787, Mr. Miles was brought into diplomatic relations with the Foreign Office, being entrusted with a confidential mission to the Prince Bishop of Liège, or, in the words of Lord Carmarthen,[1] 'as a public agent, acting under the official authority of the executive Government, in the same manner as Mr. T. Walpole had been appointed some time before on a special commission at the Court of Deux-Ponts.' It had been contemplated to send him to Bonn to succeed Mr. Heathcote as Minister at the Court of the Elector of Cologne; but public affairs indicated that he should remain at his post, whence, as from a centre, he was able to communicate important intelligence. 'The continuance of your correspondence whilst the troubles in your neighbourhood subsist,' wrote Sir Robert Murray Keith from Vienna to Mr. Miles, 'will be of advantage to the King's service and add to my personal obligation. I am glad to find that the latest accounts from Bruxelles give some hope of seeing the affairs of that country brought to an amicable adjustment. It will give me great pleasure to learn that you have succeeded in your confidential mission to the Prince Bishop.'

Any peaceful settlement, however, under the existing governments, had become hopeless. Liège, disturbed originally by some gambling transactions at Spa in 1785, full particulars of which were transmitted by Mr. Miles to Lord Carmarthen, was now involved in an insurrectionary upheaval, and Brabant, irritated by arbitrary misrule on the part of the Emperor, had resolved to throw off its allegiance. The conflagration was general. The North of Europe was in a state of ferment. And all this disquietude—all this revolutionary contention for enfranchisement, it may here be

[1] The Marquis of Carmarthen, afterwards Duke of Leeds, Secretary of State for Foreign Affairs.

observed, was the precursor of the analogous struggle on the part of France in search of political liberty.

It was at this period that a singular incident occurred to Monsieur Le Brun. Four men arrived at Liège from Brussels, in disguise, provided with power to seize him, on account of the advocacy of liberal principles in the columns of his gazette, but, being warned by a friend, he escaped, and fled to Vienna. Mr. Miles, on hearing that he had departed with only *six livres* in his possession, forwarded to the fugitive a cheque for twenty louis-d'or. The original letter in acknowledgment has been preserved.

Monsieur Le Brun to Mr. Miles

Ratisbonne : le 7 Juillet, 1787

Monsieur,—Ah ! Sans doute vous êtes Anglois, et vous méritez de l'être. Ce trait généreux et la noblesse dont vous l'accompagnez annoncent une âme toute brûlante de l'amour de la vérité et de sensibilité pour les infortunés, et vous craignez encore, homme incomparable, et vous avez la délicatesse de craindre, que je ne prenne en mauvaise part le bienfait que vous m'offrez. Non, Monsieur, j'en suis, au contraire, tout pénétré de reconnoissance, et j'accepte votre don avec plaisir, quand ce ne seroit que pour ne pas priver votre âme de la seule récompense digne d'elle, c'est-à-dire, de cette jouissance délicieuse qu'on éprouve en faisant le bien. Nous comptons être à Vienne sur la fin de la semaine, et je ne doute pas que nous ne trouvions toute la satisfaction qui nous est due auprès du souverain. J'aurai soin et je m'en ferai un devoir de vous informer des progrès de nos sollicitations, ne désirant rien tant que de pouvoir reprendre au plutôt nos travaux, et vous prouver d'une manière plus éclatante les sentimens d'estime,

d'admiration, et de reconnoissance que vous m'avez inspirés, et avec lesquels j'ai l'honneur d'être, Monsieur,
Votre très-humble, très-obéissant serviteur,
                                                  Le Brun.

The insurrection among the Liégeois and the Brabançons continued to spread. The leaders of the revolutionary party, which included Monsieur Fabry, Burgomaster of Liège, were gaining the ascendant, and under the impression that the protection of England might be secured, the friendship of Mr. Miles was sought on the side of the people. 'I do not see how extremities can be avoided,' he observes in a letter to Lord Buckingham, July 16, ' and, in case of revolt, they intend to possess themselves of the Citadel, which commands the Meuse, and of Maestricht, and, if they are supported by our Government, the whole country would be devoted to us. I wrote yesterday to Mr. Pitt, and expressed my regret at his having neglected to cultivate the friendship of the Prince Bishop of Liège, who, at this moment, might have been useful to us. The insult he has received disposes him to incline towards France. This trifling circumstance shows by how curious a chain the events of this life, both great and small, are connected, and how necessary and profitable it is to be civil and polite to everybody.[1] I am becoming uneasy at being kept here, for I am without instructions. Unfortunately, our Ministers of late are forced to attend more to the intrigues and cabals of the House of Commons than to affairs abroad, and, of course, they pay little or no regard to foreign

[1] 'During my short residence in this world I have observed that address wins more than force, and one civil word from you to the Prince Bishop might be of the utmost advantage to his Majesty's interests.'— *Miles to Pitt*, December 6, 1785.

politics.'[1] Somewhat later on (July 30) he wrote to Sir Robert Murray Keith, at Vienna: 'In this principality matters are tending, though slowly, to a crisis. The Prince Bishop, whose obstinacy is strengthened by a provisional sentence from Wetzlar, irritates the people, and the mischief may extend further than his Highness suspects. The Austrian troops in the Low Countries, amounting to about 12,000 men, are disaffected to the Court of Vienna, and the people seem resolved to persevere. I dare not be more explicit at this distance.' But, in fact, Mr. Miles had received an offer from the insurgents to place the Citadel under his charge, pending negotiations with the English Government. It was his opinion that the Liégeois and the Brabançons were being carried forward with unadvisable haste, and that grave danger might be anticipated from the suppressive measures known to be in contemplation; but he was convinced that, notwithstanding the obvious need of reflection and caution, the popular sentiment could not be controlled by the laws of prudence or justice, that, on the contrary, the resolution of the people was becoming more intense, and more manifest from day to day, and that it would certainly precipitate the conflict between the opposing forces. The question occurred whether, on the termination of a struggle which he plainly foresaw

---

[1] 'I have kept myself aloof—I have lived retired, and have scarcely seen anybody—expressly to avoid all discourse upon the subject of affairs, *as I have received no instructions from my Court*, and therefore I was determined to be silent as much as I could with common decency.'—*Lord Torrington to Mr. Miles*, July 20, 1787.

'Our principals at home are too much occupied with the House of Commons to attend to what passes on the Continent; and if any good is ever done there, it must be effected through the King's ministers abroad, and not by those about his person. Long experience has taught me this, and I never yet received an instruction that was worth reading.'—*Malmesbury Diaries*, ii. 112.

was inevitable, the Court of St. James or the Court of Versailles should dominate in that quarter of Europe. In the interests of England, he considered that the Brabançons and the Liégeois, instead of being allowed to waste their strength in separate strife, bringing disaster upon themselves, should, with the concurrence of the British Cabinet, be welded into a united and strong republic, and so constitute a barrier against any possible advance of a French army.

Sensible of the extraordinary position in which he was unexpectedly placed, and fully aware of the inutility of waiting for definite instructions from home, Mr. Miles proceeded to London, and obtained at once interviews with Lord Carmarthen and Mr. Pitt, August 11. Lord Buckingham had already written to him: 'Your information seems very material.' The following minute explains the subject discussed on that occasion with his Majesty's Ministers: 'It related to the state of public affairs in Liége and in the Low Countries, also to the measures to be pursued by England towards both, and to the advantage that would be derived from friendship with Liége in the event of the French marching into Holland. The papers transmitted to me from the principality were of the utmost importance, and, in compliance with Lord Buckingham's advice, I gave them to the Marquis of Carmarthen. I was asked what sum would be sufficient to ripen the revolt, in case of necessity, into action. A loan of 20,000 florins would be required, but one half that sum would suffice to put the insurgents in motion and answer our purpose.'

Some months later, writing from Brussels to a private friend,[1] he says, 'I went over to England, charged with an offer from the popular party in Liége to wrest

[1] Charles Jackson, Esq., Comptroller-General, Post Office, London.

that principality from the Bishop, and give it to the Emperor by adding it to Brabant and Limburg, which arrangement would have served as a barrier to the Dutch on the side of Maestricht against the French. When I proposed this to Lord Carmarthen, I was told that it would be going great lengths. The remark convinced me that his Lordship is opposed to any interference on an extensive scale. But there never was a moment so favourable to restrain France as the present: she has no money, few resources, and a distracted Government. She is labouring with all her art to gain the Emperor, and for that purpose is endeavouring to restore peace to the Turks and Russia. Things cannot go on long in this manner. The Archduke complained to me of the ignorance of both clergy and people. All this is true. But Joseph is rash and imprudent; his head is filled with crude ideas, which he has not the ingenuity or patience to methodise, and while he exists Belgium can have no repose.' In connection with these affairs, one more letter, written a year later, may suffice at present for this introductory notice.

Mr. Miles to Lord Carmarthen

Bruxelles: December 20, 1788

I shall always leave to the King's Minister [1] at this Court to inform your Lordship of the transactions in the Austrian Flanders, and of the progress of public opinion in favour of a revolution, which imperial force cannot subdue nor imperial ingenuity prevent, after the vexations that have been imposed by imperial folly; but, as it was your Lordship's express desire that I should preserve my intercourse with Liége, and with the popular party there, I beg to inform you that my efforts are

[1] Lord Torrington.

directed to retain in our interests the persons possessing the most power and credit in that principality, and who are in opposition to the Prince Bishop, against whom an inveterate war will be held, as both parties have gone too far for any hope of reconciliation. Fabry and Chestret are for secularising the bishopric. Regnier, Bassenge, and the two Donceels, are of the same opinion; and, if the Netherlands should be provoked to revolt again, I beg leave to submit to your Lordship the measure which I mentioned at the interview with which you honoured me, of incorporating the two countries under the same government. Men of very active minds here are disposed to second such a measure. It is probable that my zeal has been too prompt and active on this occasion. But your Lordship seemed to consider that events on the Continent might render a revolt necessary as a measure of diversion, and, being on the spot, and observing the general disposition and the great changes in preparation, it has been impressed on me that the measure of revolt, should it be necessary for diversion, must go further, and ripen and consolidate itself into a permanent revolution, in order to be beneficial to the people of Liège or useful to our country. If I have ventured beyond the object of Government, I must offer as an excuse my certain knowledge that, if we do not attach the people to us by rescuing them from a despotism become intolerable, the principality of Liège and the whole of Brabant and Flanders will fall under the dominion of France. I assure you that France has her eye upon the Low Countries, and, if we are not active, she will certainly possess them. I am authorised to say that Liège is ready to put itself under our protection, and I believe it will not be difficult to engage the Austrian Netherlands to follow the example of the

Liégeois and unite with them. France at this moment could not prevent the junction. Nor can a revolution of some sort be prevented here. Zeal to render it favourable to us may have led me to exceed my instructions. But, *as the change must inevitably occur*, I will beg to conclude these remarks in the words of the Duc d'Epernon, addressed to the Parliament in Paris on the death of Henry IV. : 'Ce qui peut se faire aujourd'hui sans péril, ne se fera peut-être pas demain sans carnage.'

On the development of these revolutionary disturbances—including the unrest in Holland and Prussia—there are still preserved copies of many despatches, written from the midst of the events enacted, and addressed by Mr. Miles either to Mr. Pitt or Lord Carmarthen. There are also many letters that he wrote to Lord Buckingham or to ambassadors and private friends on the same subject. But further quotations here may be considered as out of place. And yet the part taken by France in the popular excitement among the Dutch —her interference at a later period in the question of the open navigation of the Escaut or Scheldt, the subsequent invasion of Belgium by her armies, and, lastly, the close connection between these several incidents and the war declared by the Convention against England and Holland in the winter of 1793, signify that the political movements in the Pays de Liège and the Austrian Netherlands had a close connection in their future with the progress of the French Revolution. The full information forwarded to the English Cabinet from Liège—of which the quotations above given are only examples—was sufficient to indicate the imminent approach of danger; and, when it was known, not many years later, that the French had been victorious at Jemmapes, that Dumouriez had entered Belgium, and that the Dutch and the Scheldt were imperilled, it was perceived, and indeed the Duke of Leeds acknowledged, that the policy so persistently placed before the British Government by their confidential and indefatigable Envoy at Liège would have been found judicious in its adoption and advantageous in its results.[1]

Mr. Miles, who had left Liège on account of the insurrection in that Principality, resided in Brussels during the year 1788, still holding confidential relations with the English Cabinet; but when 'the signs of the times' became more and more threatening on the Continent, he was sent by Lord Carmarthen on special service to Frankfort, and left London to take up his appointment at the end of March 1789. 'I most sincerely wish that your mission to Frankfort may answer your expectations,' wrote Lord Fortescue to him on the eve of his departure, 'and I have no doubt of your fully answering those of the Government. I wish you health and success in your embassy, and no Bishop of Liège to dispute with you.'

The letters despatched to the Foreign Office during April, May, and June give a general report of events current in that part of Europe, and are interspersed with anecdotes gathered from the political society in which he moved. The French, for example, were purchasing corn in the Duchies of Juliers and Berg, and in the neighbourhood of Frankfort, 'not for the purpose of

---

[1] 'England,' Leeds said, 'fully admitted the pernicious consequences that would ensue if the Austrian Netherlands became absolutely dependent on France, and she was quite prepared to co-operate with Prussia and Holland in preventing it. But it was necessary that this danger should be clear and imminent.'—Lecky, v. 241. See *Letter to the Prince of Wales*, by Mr. Miles, London, 1808, Appendix, p. 180; also *Histoire des Belges à la Fin du XVIIIe Siècle*, par M. Borgnet; and Ernouf's *Maret, Duc de Bassano*, p. 42, &c.

forming magazines on the Rhine, but in consequence of the extreme scarcity of grain in Dauphiny and Provence.' The inhabitants of Franche-Comté were said to be almost reduced to famine; all the corn obtained was forwarded with the utmost expedition to Strasburg under the urgent directions of the French Resident at Frankfort. Among the local affairs narrated was a festival given by the English community on the day that George III. went to St. Paul's Cathedral, April 23, to return thanks for his recovery, when the health of his Majesty 'was drank with loud huzzas, to the astonishment and no less admiration of the phlegmatic Germans, who, catching the virtuous enthusiasm of our countrymen, entered fully into the spirit of the meeting, and did not break up until six the next morning.' Another incident was the arrival of the Duke of Sussex. 'I have had the honour to pay my respects to his Majesty's sixth son, Prince Augustus Frederick, who alighted here last night on his way to Gottingen, in good spirits, and apparently recovered from his late indisposition. I accompanied his Royal Highness to the Town House,' continues Mr. Miles in his letter to the Duke of Leeds,[1] May 18, 'where he was received by the magistrates, who were enchanted no less with his affability than with his pertinent questions. It is my intention to proceed with him to-morrow as far as Hanau, which will enable me to judge whether his coach, which broke down between Heidelberg and Frankfort, is in a condition to proceed, for, otherwise, I shall employ every argument in my power to persuade him to accept mine.' The next day he passed several hours with the Prince, and afterwards accompanied him to Wilhelmsbad and Hanau, the conversation during dinner

[1] The Marquis of Carmarthen succeeded, March 24, to the title of Duke of Leeds.

being directed towards home politics. 'His Royal Highness spoke of the Opposition with ill-humour, and particularly of Mr. Burke, whom he reprobated in the strongest language. He lamented that Mr. Pitt, for whom he professed the greatest regard, should have declared that the Prince of Wales had no more right than any of the King's subjects to the Regency, observing that, although his brother had properly no more right, yet his claim was stronger than that of any other man.' The report of this conversation is given at some length in this letter.[1]

Frankfort, at the above date, seems to have been a centre for political talk and intrigue. 'The Corps Diplomatique,' Mr. Miles remarks, 'are as numerous as if they had to regulate the complicated interests of the whole world. Every sovereign on the Upper Rhine makes it a point to send his representative here.' But, writing to the Duke of Leeds, he observes: 'I have been six years on the Continent, and have not met with one foreigner who has a correct idea of the British Constitution or of the character of the English people. Count Romanzow, the Russian Minister, and his brother, who was Minister at Berlin, dined with me last Monday, and in a long conversation with the latter, in which he endeavoured to prove that it was the interest of the Court of London to ally itself to that of St. Petersburg, he inquired if I thought it was possible to engage a member of the House of Commons in the interest of the Empress—" un homme de talent pour échauffer les esprits, et par ce moyen et celui des brochures de forcer Monsieur Pitt d'écouter la raison et d'adopter les principes

---

[1] The question of the Regency had been already discussed by Mr. Miles, under the signature of 'Neptune,' through the Press, and in support of the views maintained by Mr. Pitt. It is fully treated by Mr. Lecky, v. 100, &c.

de milord Stormont sur ce sujet." When he mentioned the probability of success from the notorious venality of some men, as from the necessitous circumstances of others, who—to use his own words—creep into Parliament on all fours, I assured him that, whatever truth there might be in what he had advanced, I was firmly convinced that there was not a member in either House of Parliament corrupt and abandoned enough to dispose of his voice to any foreign court whatever, and that, even if an individual so lost to every sense of honour existed, the dread of the thing being discovered would deter him. Yet, Romanzow continued to maintain that, in his opinion, the idea of pensioning a member of the English House of Commons in the interests of Russia was both practicable and justifiable.'[1]

In the third week of July 1789 the news of the fall of the Bastille reached Frankfort, which being quickly followed by the arrival of *émigrés* in their hurried flight from Paris, caused much consternation throughout Germany. At the close of the year, Mr. Miles, after having transmitted to the Foreign Office all possible in-

---

[1] In 1791 Mr. Miles sent forth his pamphlet entitled *The Expediency and Justice of Prescribing Bounds to the Russian Empire*. This *brochure* is still carefully preserved in the Imperial Library at St. Petersburg. The writer, in his protest against the advance of Russia towards India, revived the suggestion of a *Suez Canal*. His words are: 'A canal of little more than a hundred miles in length will connect the Red Sea with the Mediterranean. The commerce of Asia will revert into the channels through which it passed into Europe before the discovery of the Cape of Good Hope, and under circumstances infinitely more advantageous than ever Venice or Genoa possessed.' Some forty years elapsed before Waghorn practically opened up the route to India *via* Egypt. But it was not until 1854, or *sixty-three years later than the published prediction of Mr. Miles*, that the intelligent and indefatigable Ferdinand de Lesseps conceived 'le projet d'un canal entièrement maritime.' The inauguration of this canal took place on November 20, 1869.—See *Authentic Correspondence with M. Le Brun*, &c., by Mr. Mi'es, London, 1796, pp. 125-129.

formation connected with his mission, and having paid several visits to the Elector of Mayence at his palace, Aschaffenburg, acquainted the Duke of Leeds that, unless he heard to the contrary, it was his intention to return to England by way of Liège and Brussels.

The revolutionary demonstrations among the Liégeois and the Brabançons still engaged his thoughts: 'Il y a deux ans et demi,' he wrote to M. Fabry, December 31, 'que j'ai proposé à ma Cour l'affranchissement du Pays de Liège et des Païs-Bas Autrichiens. Je suis toujours décidément de l'avis que c'est le meilleur parti à prendre.' On January 9, 1790, he arrived at Liège, and immediately called upon M. Fabry, with whom he had a long consultation on public affairs. His letter of that date to the Duke of Leeds, replete with details on the intensity and expansion of the insurrectionary uprising, concludes as follows: 'As this principality, from its geographical position, must be interesting to your Grace, and as you may from the exigencies of the moment, as also from the communications and suggestions which I had the honour to make at my conferences with your Grace in 1787 and 1788, deem it necessary for his Majesty's service that I should continue here, I shall remain a sufficient time to receive your instructions, after which I shall proceed to Bruxelles and thence to London. I have promised M. Fabry that no efforts on my part shall be wanting to impress most strongly on the minds of his Majesty's Ministers the policy of incorporating this principality with the Austrian Netherlands, and insuring to them all the rights of an independent nation. The actual situation of France is an additional motive for my presuming to recommend the Liégeois and Brabançons to the protection of your Grace, and, as the times are pregnant with great and serious events, I need not add that I shall wait with the utmost impatience for an answer to this despatch and for further instructions.'

Mr. Miles arrived in London at the beginning of February, and, as recorded in the following memorandum, lost not a moment in the endeavour to support in person the opinions unfolded in his previous correspondence.

'I obtained an early interview with the Duke of Leeds. I had been entrusted with proposals from the popular party at Liège and from the Vonckistes at Bruxelles that the Austrian Netherlands and the principality of Liège should be erected into an independent republic under the guarantee of Great Britain, Prussia, and Holland. I detailed at length to his Grace the advantages that would result from such an arrangement. In my correspondence with the Foreign Secretary I had stated even in 1787 the mischiefs that would ensue to our commerce and dominion if the French should ever become masters of the Low Countries, for that, in possession of the Scheldt at the east, and of Brest at the west of the British Channel, they would be in a condition to contest with us, and perhaps to ravish from us, the empire of the Narrow Seas. Then again, on Wednesday last, I drew the attention of his Grace most earnestly to this important and pressing question. I stated, among other facts, that the French already looked forward to a union with the Austrian Netherlands, and, with the view of engaging the latter in the interest of France, M. Sémonville had arrived from Paris with considerable offers; that, under the arrangement I proposed, the Low Countries would become a formidable barrier to Holland, and, being declared independent, would render any application to the French for protection unnecessary, and would also secure themselves from invasion in case of rupture between France and the Emperor—a contingency which it is easy to foresee is unavoidable—and, further, that the party in whose name and at whose request I made this offer would rather enter into an alliance with England than with France; and, since the emancipation of these provinces is an event which must sooner or later take place, I entreated his Grace to consider whether it would not be safer for this country that the Austrian Netherlands should be independent than that they should fall under the dominion of France. The Duke of Leeds, after observing a profound silence for several minutes, remarked, as on a former occasion, that it would be going great lengths. After assuring him that it is the only measure this country can adopt to prevent the Low Countries from coming under the protection of France, the conference terminated.'

'What I dreaded in 1785,' wrote Mr. Miles a few years later, 'and predicted in 1787, actually happened in 1792. The French had rendered themselves masters of the Low Countries, and even of Liége and Aix-la-Chapelle, and, if they had been less intoxicated with their victories, and more attentive to the obligations of morality, or even to the suggestions of policy, they would have preserved their conquests against all the force of Europe. Sensible of the importance of the Scheldt, whose silent and indignant waters had been chained—if I dare hazard the metaphor—to the walls of Antwerp for a century, they instantly declared it should be free, and would have gone to war for that object alone, not from affection to the people of Brabant, but with a view to acquire ultimately the entire sovereignty of the Narrow Seas. If the project I suggested could have been realized, Holland would have been secured from invasion. The French would have had no excuse for overrunning the Low Countries, rescued, as they were, from the mischief and ignorance of a bad government; and the Flemings, in possession of rational freedom, would have resisted the contagion of French licentiousness, nor would their fertile and emancipated provinces have been desolated by rapine and the sword, or have become the theatre of incessant and remorseless carnage.'[1]

In the autumn of 1789 unforeseen intelligence reached London from the North Pacific Ocean. During the previous April, two English vessels trading in furs and other articles indigenous to the sea-board of California were seized by two Spanish war-ships whilst at anchor in Nootka Sound, on the western side of Vancouver's Island; the British ensign was hauled down, and, among other insults, the crews were subjected to ill-treatment, under the pretence that the American shores in those far-west meridians were subject to the flag of Spain. Some months later, when the news was confirmed, the English Cabinet adopted peremptory measures at Madrid; the restoration of the merchantmen, together with indemnification, was demanded, and the dispute soon assumed alarming dimensions. An amicable arrangement was happily effected. But during the crisis there existed an element of disturbance, which, in the event of hostilities, might have proved detrimental or even fatal to the interests of England. A treaty had been concluded for the third time between France and Spain, known as the 'Pacte de Famille,' or Family Compact, signed at Paris, August 15, 1761, by which the French and the Spanish branches of the Bourbons

---

[1] *The Conduct of France towards Great Britain Examined*, by Mr. Miles, London, 1793, p. 82.

were bound to afford mutual support in case of either nation coming into collision with any other Power. The desire on the part of the British Government was the abrogation of this perplexing treaty, or to obtain at least the neutrality of France should England become involved in war with Spain.[1]

The above state of affairs brought Mr. Miles again into diplomatic employment. On March 4, 1790, he received a note from the private secretary of Mr. Pitt, requesting him to call in Downing Street on the next day. The subject under consideration was the treaty between France and Spain. Some uncertainty existed as to the course to be pursued. During this interval Mr. Miles, writing to Lord Buckingham, says: 'It has been proposed to bring me into Parliament at the general election at a trifling expense to myself, but, as the offer comes from the dissenting interest, and I would be expected to support the party, I have declined. I shall much prefer being employed abroad.' It was at last decided that he should proceed on a special mission to Paris, but it was July before the completion of arrangements enabled him to leave for his destination. The purport of his mission was precise: *he was to exert his personal influence with the view of inducing the National Assembly to annul the Family Compact*; and, although not included in the official instructions, it was understood that the occasion would be used to promote permanent relations between the two countries. 'I was sent to Paris,' he himself remarks, 'with the hope that the idea of an alliance between France and England, which I had

---

[1] '"Pacte de Famille," signed August 15, 1761, during the most disastrous crisis of the Seven Years' War, when Spanish intervention alone saved France from the most crushing defeat.'—*Edinburgh Review*, July to October, 1887, p. 192. See Lecky, v. 206-209, and Sybel, i. 206, 216.

long cherished, and which the late Duc d'Aiguillon had reduced to form, would be accomplished. It was under this impression, and well aware that my political sentiments were fully known to Mr. Pitt, from my correspondence with him for several years, that I returned to the Continent in the summer of 1790.'[1]

It must be regretted that the letters from Mr. Miles to Mr. Pitt between August 1790 and April 1791, that is, during his residence in Paris, are not extant, nor are there any copies of these letters known to exist. That there should not be found the slightest trace of the official communications sent direct to the Minister is remarkable. It forms an exceptional and unaccountable gap in the voluminous correspondence that has been carefully copied and preserved. The despatches addressed to Mr. Pitt on that occasion, as gathered from contemporaneous sources, were very numerous, and, as may be well believed, were full of interest, for they reported in detail the several topics discussed, and the results obtained, during more than eight months of friendly and frequent intercourse with Mirabeau, Lafayette, and other men of influence in the French metropolis.

Abundant information, however, lies scattered through a multitude of private letters. 'I was sent confidentially to Paris in 1790, on a secret mission,' he wrote to Sir Home Popham, 'as was also my friend Hugh Elliot, and precisely for the same object.' 'I was despatched to Paris,' he reminded Mr. Rose,[2] ' to accomplish an object of great national import by means that never could have entered into the head of any man

---

[1] On the treaty projected by the Duc d'Aiguillon when Minister in 1771, and intended for presentation by the Marquis de Joviac to the Court of St. James, see *Letter to the Prince of Wales*, by Mr. Miles, London, 1808, p. 135.

[2] Mr. George Rose, Joint Secretary to the Treasury.

conversant only with politics.' To Lord Buckingham he wrote: 'In September 1790, Mr. Pitt knew from me that monarchy would be abolished in France.' And in a long letter to Lafayette he refers to this particular mission as follows: 'Mr. Elliot, who has been in the Corps Diplomatique ever since 1773, was at Paris when I was there in 1790 and 1791, and we were the only two who did not humour the erroneous wishes of our Court by assuring ministers that a counter-revolution was on the point of being declared. On the contrary, we respectively wrote—not in concert, for we were ignorant of each other's letters at the time—that the Revolution would not be interrupted in its march, that any attempt to stay it would only enrage an immense population broken loose from all restraint, and that, ignorant of the force and resources of a nation which had sprung a mine of intellect, we should wait patiently the course of events, and seize the first favourable calm moment to propose an alliance with so powerful a neighbour. In this sense I wrote to Mr. Pitt; so did Mr. Elliot.'[1]

So early as October 11, 1790, or little more than two months after his arrival in Paris, Mr. Miles sent the

[1] 'In 1790 Mr. Elliot came home on leave, and was sent by Mr. Pitt on a secret mission to Paris in 1790–1791. Beyond the bare fact that he was so sent, the correspondence tells nothing of this mission. In one letter only is there an allusion which throws a light upon its nature and success. A brother-diplomatist, writing to him some years afterwards concerning a delicate negotiation then pending, says: "If you could have been sent to conduct it as successfully as you did your mission to Mirabeau," &c.—*Memoir of the Right Honourable Hugh Elliot*, by the Countess of Minto, Edinburgh, 1868, p. 335.

The *official instructions* given to Elliot seem, like the letters on the same subject from Miles to Pitt, to have disappeared. 'I have inquired of Sir Edward Hertslet, and am told that no paper of this kind exists in the Foreign Office. I am also informed by Mr. Kingston that no direct trace of Mr. Elliot's mission exists in the Public Record Office, although search has often been made for it.'—*Despatches of Earl Gower*, p. 38. Note by Mr. Oscar Browning.

following notice to the Treasury: 'The great object of my mission is in general much liked. The business is realised. Mr. Pitt may, if he follows it up, secure its accomplishment, and thereby lay the foundation for a union between the two kingdoms.' Soon afterwards, November 30, he further reported to Mr. Rose: 'I have very great pleasure in assuring you that my mission is likely to have a fortunate issue, and that no difficulty will be made to dissolve the Family Compact, provided that France can reckon upon the friendship of England in exchange. Mr. Pitt may count to a certainty on the concurrence of the people with this his favourite object. Mirabeau, Barnave, Lafayette, Frochot, and several other members of the National Assembly, are well disposed to dissolve the compact, but they require, if not an equivalent for the loss of Spain, a something to substitute in its place, so as to fill the vacuum in the foreign political relations of France.'

About the same time, October 22, 1790, Lord Gower, his Majesty's Minister at Paris,[1] wrote to the Duke of Leeds: 'I think it my duty to inform your Grace that that party has signified to me, through Mr. Elliot, their earnest desire to use their influence with the Court of Madrid in order to bring it to accede to the just demands of his Majesty, and, if supported by us, I am induced to believe they will readily prefer an English alliance to a Spanish compact.' A few days later, October 26, Lord Gower reports: 'Mr. Elliot

[1] The Duke of Dorset 'concluded by proposing to take leave of absence, and it is evident that his position had become untenable. In point of fact he did not return (he continued from England to supply Marie Antoinette with English gloves), and Lord Robert Fitzgerald acted as Chargé d'Affaires till May 1790, when Earl Gower, afterwards Duke of Sutherland, was appointed Ambassador.'—*Edinburgh Review*, 1888, p. 141.

being very anxious that your Grace should be informed, without loss of time, of the disposition of the leading men of the prevailing party with whom he has had communication, I shall send Morley to London to-night, who will be the bearer of this dispatch. I must observe to your Grace that the opportunities which Mr. Elliot has had of conversing with the members of the Comité Diplomatique, and which from my situation it was not in my power to have, have enabled him to convince them of the pacific intentions of his Majesty; and I can add with pleasure that they seem anxiously inclined to co-operate with his Majesty's Ministers in order to induce Spain to comply with his just demands.'[1]

The original cause of the quarrel between England and Spain had been removed at an earlier date. On June 16 the Spanish Ambassador in Paris wrote to M. Montmorin, the French Secretary of State for Foreign Affairs, ' que le roi, mon maître, a approuvé la conduite du Vice-roi, qui a relâché les bâtiments entrés dans le port de Nootka. C'est donc par suite de ses droits, et dans l'espoir de conserver la paix, que sa Majesté catholique a commencé des négociations amicales avec l'Angleterre.' The letter continues : ' L'accomplissement prompt et exact du traité signé à Paris le 15 Août 1761, sous titre de Pacte de Famille, devient donc un préliminaire indispensable pour pouvoir traiter avec succès. C'est d'après cette nécessité absolue, dans laquelle l'Espagne se trouve malgré elle d'avoir recours au secours de la France, que le roi, mon maître, m'ordonne de demander expressément ce que la France pourra faire

---

[1] *The Despatches of Earl Gower.* It may be explained here that, whilst Mr. Elliot transmitted *his* information through the *British Embassy* to the Foreign Office, Mr. Miles had been enjoined to act independent of Lord Gower, and to forward *his* intelligence *direct* to the Treasury. See *Letter of Mr. Miles to Lord Buckingham*, July 15, 1790.

dans la circonstance actuelle pour venir au secours de l'Espagne.' On August 2 the President of the National Assembly announced the receipt of an important despatch from M. Montmorin. It commences as follows: 'Le roi m'a ordonné, au milieu du mois dernier, d'informer l'Assemblée Nationale des motifs qui nécessitaient un armement de 14 vaisseaux; cet armement est à la veille d'être complété. Le roi me charge de prévenir l'Assemblée que les armements de l'Angleterre continuent, quoique la bonne intelligence subsiste toujours entre les deux nations. Sa Majesté pense qu'il est prudent et utile d'augmenter nos armements. Le roi d'Espagne réclame, de la manière la plus positive, l'exécution des traités, dans le cas où la négociation de la cour de Madrid avec celle de Londres n'aurait pas l'issue qu'on en espère.' M. Montmorin concludes: 'Ma lettre a donc deux objets—le premier de prévenir l'Assemblée de la nécessité d'augmenter les armements; le second de provoquer la délibération de l'Assemblée sur la demande de la cour de Madrid: le roi pense qu'il serait convenable de charger un comité de conférer avec le Ministre des Affaires Étrangères.'[1]

On the next day, August 3, M. Dupont, député de Nemours, spoke as follows in the National Assembly: 'Il s'agit de savoir s'il est utile aux Français et aux Espagnols d'être alliés, de se garantir mutuellement leurs possessions, de jouir les uns chez les autres de tous les avantages civils et commerciaux qu'il est possible d'accorder dans son propre pays, à ses propres concitoyens. Ces conventions réciproques sont la base d'un traité solennel, fidèlement exécuté depuis trente

---

[1] See *Lettre de son Excellence M. le Comte de Fernan Nunez à M. de Montmorin*; also *Lettre de M. de Montmorin*; *Archives Parlementaires*, tome xvii. p. 503; and *The Despatches of Earl Gower*, Paris, August 6, 1790.

ans.'[1] And Mirabeau, when speaking as a member of the Comité Diplomatique, on the report drawn up by the Committee, August 25, said: 'Nous ne pouvons balancer le nombre des vaisseaux anglais qu'avec ceux de notre allié. L'intérêt nous oblige donc de confirmer notre alliance avec l'Espagne, et le seul moyen de la conserver, c'est de remplir fidèlement nos traités. . . . D'ailleurs, s'il est certain que l'abandon de nos engagements forcerait l'Espagne à négocier plus promptement la paix avec l'Angleterre, il n'est que trop facile de prévoir quelle pourrait être dans ce cas la nature de cet accommodement, et le tort irréparable qu'une semblable négociation ferait à notre crédit, à notre commerce.'[2]

Such was the uncertain state of this untoward business at the close of August 1790. Before the end of October important advantages had been gained as the result of the confidential mission to Paris; the public mind had been in some measure reassured with respect to the attitude of England, and there no longer existed any immediate apprehension of Spain receiving material assistance from France. 'There was indeed no more question of a Spanish war; the Minister, Florida Blanca, was greatly dispirited, and announced his submission to the English Ambassador, not, he said, because the claims of England were just, but because Spain was compelled to make a sacrifice. If France, he added, would support us, I should hold out, but alone we are too weak and must give way.'[3]

The family compact with Spain, however, was not

---

[1] *Archives Parlementaires*, xvii. 586.
[2] *Ibid.*, xviii. 263-293. See 'Réflexions sur le projet de décret proposé le 25 de ce mois, Août 1790, par M. de Mirabeau l'aîné,' with the accompanying notes, inserted immediately after Letter to Lord Buckingham, September 6, 1790, in this volume.
[3] *History of Europe*, by Professor von Sybel, i. 216.

dissolved on the part of France, nor was any negotiation encouraged towards an alliance with France on the part of England. Why was this? The fact is, at this important juncture Mr. Pitt had suddenly changed his mind or had become totally indifferent as to either of these points. 'Two months have elapsed since I dispatched my first letter to Mr. Rose on the subject of my mission;' such was the complaint forwarded by Mr. Miles to Lord Buckingham from Paris, December 13; 'I have not received any answer, and, doubtful of my own judgment in a matter of equal delicacy and importance, it is painful to be left to my own guidance, without advice, communication, or any kind of instructions whatever. The matter, however, confided to me has been happily executed. France is well disposed to come in to the measure, and the friends of liberty, I may venture to assert, are for it to a man. I took the liberty to start the idea of an alliance, and to urge it several times in London to Mr. Rose before I came here; but he seemed to throw cold water on it. If Mr. Pitt would propose it, I am sure he would be as popular in this country as he is in his own, and be enabled to do as he pleases. The *family compact* would be dissolved directly, and no power on earth would dare even to think of disturbing the repose or of attacking either nation.'

The correspondence still extant shows that the English Minister had been urged, urged frequently and in vain, to adhere to his original wishes and intentions —the same intentions and wishes that had developed the Paris mission.[1] Every political occurrence of im-

---

[1] 'Pitt had seldom shown more political courage than when he introduced his commercial treaty with France, and maintained that the two great nations which confronted each other across the Channel were intended by Nature to be friends and not enemies.'—Lecky, v. 445.

portance—every political sentiment expressed by men of influence in the French capital, had been transmitted to the Treasury in order to persuade the Government to *avow* a positive decision in favour, not indeed of any immediate treaty of alliance, but of an amicable understanding with France. 'All these facts,' Mr. Miles said to Mr. Pitt a few years later in his retrospect of events, 'were fully and repeatedly stated to you in my letters from Paris, accompanied by suggestions which would probably have ensured success to the enterprise. Every obstacle to your wish seemed as if it were removed, and a very little more—a very small advance on the part of this country—would have detached France from Spain, and perhaps have preserved a hapless monarch and his throne from destruction. Little more was required from you than to have been explicit as to the conduct that this country meant to observe towards France in her then perilous and distracted state. It has ever been matter of surprise to me, and no less so of serious regret, that this little was not accomplished, and that a measure so wise in itself, so beneficial in its consequences, and so admirably well-timed, with a train of circumstances so decisively in its favour, should have been *unaccountably abandoned* almost as soon as it was adopted —the fatal renunciation, I must repeat, of your project for detaching France from Spain at the very moment when its completion was within your grasp.'[1]

[1] The letter from which the above extract is taken will be found under date of December 30, 1795. It enters into the question of the Family Compact and the mission to Paris. See also Letters to Lord Buckingham, September 6, 1790, and December 25, 1795. Writing to Mr. Long, November 19, 1808, Mr. Miles observes: 'Mr. Hugh Elliot, who is now in town, saw the French Revolution at that period precisely, I think, as I saw it, and I have reason to believe that he gave Mr. Pitt much the same information and good counsel. This I know, that his information was not well received.' The only written communication extant from Elliot

Mr. Miles wrote upon this subject in impassioned language from the deep conviction that, if Mr. Pitt had not departed from the policy that dictated the mission to Paris, the conference at Pilnitz, which at least excited suspicion and provoked annoyance, would not have been called into existence. If the National Assembly, by abrogating the treaty with Spain, had secured the sympathies of England, so he argued, Austria would not have dreamed of crossing the French frontier, nor would there have been any motive for intervention, since the royal family of France would not have been exposed to peril; there would have been no need for a coalition among the European powers, and, in the absence of the irritating causes which exasperated the French people beyond control, the influence of England might have directed or tempered the revolutionary movement. The excesses committed during the upheavals and impulses of the period might then have been unknown in history. 'On my return to London,' Mr. Miles observes in a letter to Mr. Long, 'I told Mr. Pitt that he could not stop the Revolution, but that, with a little address, he might guide it.' It might, perhaps, have been guided at its dawn. But events which unfolded with remarkable rapidity soon threw dark shades over the entire Continent. 'Look where you will, immeasurable obscurantism is girdling this fair France, which, again, will not be girdled by it. Europe is in travail; pang after pang; what a shriek was that of Pilnitz! The birth will be war.' [1]

to Miles is the following note, dated Paris, October 27, 1790: 'Mr. Elliot presents his compliments to Mr. Miles, and will take care of the letters committed to his charge. Mr. E. will not fail to write to Mr. Miles from England.' Mr. Charles Long, above mentioned, was appointed Joint-Secretary of the Treasury in 1791. He 'was an attached friend of Mr. Pitt,' and was raised to the Peerage in 1826 as Lord Farnborough. The title became extinct. See Stanhope's *Life of Pitt*. ii. 123.

[1] *The French Revolution*, by Thomas Carlyle. ii. 64.

The declaration of Pilnitz was signed on August 27, 1791. It concludes thus: 'Alors, et dans ce cas, leurs dites Majestés l'Empereur et le Roi de Prusse sont résolus d'agir promptement, d'un mutuel accord, avec les forces nécessaires pour obtenir le but proposé et commun. En attendant, elles donneront à leurs troupes les ordres convenables pour qu'elles soient en état de se mettre en activité.' Now the *end* contemplated at Pilnitz was the maintenance of Louis XVI. on his throne by the *enforced* volition of foreign powers—'pour mettre le Roi de France en état d'affermir, dans la plus parfaite liberté, les bases d'un gouvernement monarchique également convenable aux droits des souverains et au bien-être de la nation française.' Soon afterwards the Emperor of Austria remarked to the Marquis de Bouillé: 'Je suis assuré de la co-opération de toutes ces puissances, à l'exception de l'Angleterre, qui est déterminée à observer la plus stricte neutralité.'[1] But the mischief was already effected. It was not the avowal of *neutrality* after hostile action had been inaugurated in 1791, but the manifestation of *friendship* in 1790 on the part of England, that might have restrained the terrible forces then generating in France; and the opportunity for any beneficial action was supplanted by an ill-conceived and unhappy attempt to intermeddle by an armed demonstration in the affairs of a neighbour. 'No doubt can now exist that the interference of the Allies augmented the horrors, and added to the duration of the Revolution. All its bloodiest excesses were committed during or after an alarming but unsuccessful invasion by the allied forces.'[2]

[1] *Mémoires du Marquis de Bouillé*, pp. 294, 300. See Herbert Marsh, i. 2.
[2] Alison, *History of Europe*, v. 129. It may be remarked here that, although the Family Compact died a natural death on the downfall of monarchy in France, the idea of a similar treaty was revived on the

On April 9 Mr. Miles started on his own account for England to obtain from Mr. Pitt some directions as to his future course, and, with the expectation that he would soon return to Paris, he left his wife and daughter under the roof of the Duchesse de Richelieu in the Faubourg Saint-Honoré. It was the end of May before anything definite was suggested. He then heard from Lord Buckingham in conversation that the Minister was postponing his decision until the recess of Parliament, but that, instead of his returning to France, the proposal would be made to retain him in London, to give support to the Administration. This unexpected change of views, involving the total collapse of the family compact negotiations, caused some embarrassment. Mr. Miles refused to promise his unqualified support to any Administration whatsoever, and represented that, as the Duke of Leeds, when in office, had promised him a foreign embassy, he hoped for continued employment on the Continent.

But on June 25 he wrote to Lord Buckingham: 'I am this instant returned from having an interview with Mr. Pitt, whose reception of me was very gracious and flattering. I find it is his wish that I should remain in England; my wish is to go abroad, from a conviction that the diplomatic line is the best adapted to my talents, and the only one to which I feel myself fully equal. His idea is to give me a pension in com-

restoration of the Bourbons in the person of Louis XVIII. 'The Duke added that he traced back the present politics of France to their chagrin at the dissolution of the Family Compact. At the general pacification the Duke, on the part of the English Government, insisted upon that treaty not being renewed, and made a journey to Madrid for the purpose of determining the Spanish Government. Talleyrand and the King of France made great efforts to induce the Duke to desist from his opposition to the renewal of the treaty, and both were exceedingly mortified at being unable to shake the determination of our Government on this point.' —*The Greville Memoirs*, i. 72.

pensation for expenses incurred by me in the public service. I assured him that, as my wish was really to render myself serviceable to my country, I should think it my duty to conform to any arrangement he might make. Mr. Pitt seemed pleased with this declaration, for the point which he appeared to have most at heart was to obtain my consent to remain in this country, and, when he had obtained it, although it was reluctantly given, he expressed his obligations and seemed much gratified. It is his hope that I will uphold the Government by my literary exertions. It is this I most dread and hold in abhorrence. It has ever been my pride to exert my abilities in favour of good men and honourable measures; but further I cannot go. In saying this I do not mean to decline supporting Government to the very extent of my zeal and talents, whenever it can be done consistently with the principles I have uniformly advocated through life. The love of letters is my favourite passion; all I contend for is that I must feel what I write, and then I am vain enough to believe that my pen may have some influence on the public mind. A man writes best when he writes from conviction. No honest man writes otherwise.' The conjecture may be hazarded, or rather it may be frankly stated. that the persistent opinion, as conveyed in his letters from Paris, that an alliance between France and England would be a better guarantee for the peace of Europe than any coalition of European powers against France, influenced Mr. Pitt in his strong desire to keep Mr. Miles at home; the foreign policy of the Minister being no longer in harmony with the avowed bias of his irrepressible agent. It was the autumn of 1792 before he took again any prominent part in the affairs of France, although, indeed, correspondence with political men on the Continent and literary contributions to the press in England were sustained without interruption.[1]

In March 1792 a change in the Cabinet placed Dumouriez at the head of Foreign Affairs, Roland accepted office as Minister of the Interior, Clavière became Finance Minister, and somewhat later Servan received the portfolio of the War Department. On April 20 the King, no longer a free agent, proposed to the Legislative Assembly, 'with tears in his eyes,' that war should be declared against the Emperor Francis II. as King of Hungary and Bohemia, and, notwithstanding the wretched state of their soldiery and the exhausted condition of the public treasury at that crisis, the proposition was accepted with applause. Thus there was kindled a fire destined to burn with increasing intensity for many years throughout the civilised world. In Paris, agitation among all classes, with disorder and riot among the lower orders, accompanied by arbitrary imprisonments both in the capital and in the departments, augmented the general alarm and discontent. The action of the Assembly did not tend to diminish the embarrassment. On May 24 a law was passed for the banishment of non-jurors, or those who, like the refractory priests—*prêtres non-assermentés*—might decline to take the oath of fidelity. The King resolved to exercise his *veto* on this decree, and, still further to mark his displeasure, summarily

[1] During his interval of suspense in London, and whilst waiting for the return of his family from Paris, Mr. Miles wrote on *The Expediency and Justice of Prescribing Bounds to the Russian Empire*. The first leading article in the *Times*, November 16, 1855, is supported by reference to this publication. 'We have before us,' says the writer, 'a pamphlet by no ordinary hand, which shows that in the year 1791, on the very eve of the French Revolution, Russia presented just the same aspect to English vigilance as she did in 1853. Yes, sixty-four years ago our more observant politicians saw and denounced her restless ambition.'

dismissed, on June 13, Servan, Roland, and Clavière, the *Patriot* ministers, as for the moment they were called by the people. M. Mourgue, formerly director of the public works at Cherbourg, and a personal friend of Dumouriez, filled the place vacated by Roland as Minister of the Interior.[1] Soon afterwards Dumouriez, dissatisfied with the outlook, resigned, and proceeded to join the army now gathering in haste on the northern frontier. There also Lafayette, who had retired during the previous autumn from his position as commandant of the Parisian National Guards, had already established himself, having been named in December to the command of one of the three armies mustered in the vicinity of Sedan to repel the advancing foreign invasion. M. Bailly was no longer Mayor of Paris. This worthy man, eminent in his career of science, unfortunate in his association with the municipality and politics, feeble in the maintenance of authority, and murdered at last in the streets of the capital, had fallen into popular disrepute for the part he took in the Champ de Mars, July 17, 1791, when the demoralised crowds, shouting for the *déchéance* of Louis, were forcibly dispersed by Lafayette. In November the office of Mayor had been conferred upon Pétion. Such was the distracted situation in the summer of 1792.[2]

[1] See *Despatches of Earl Gower*, p. 190. M. Mourgue, on receiving the seals as Secretary of State for the Home Department, wrote immediately to Mr. Miles on the critical condition of affairs. This communication was forwarded at once to the Foreign Office. Mr. Aust, in his acknowledgment, June 20, says : ' Lord Grenville having been out of town, I had no opportunity of showing him Mourgue's letter, and perhaps it is now rendered less important by the late events in Paris, of which we have the detail by our express to-day.' This letter was never returned from the Foreign Office. Its purport, however, is stated by Mr. Miles in a ' minute,' where it is mentioned as ' addressed to me. *praying my good office with Ministers to avert the calamities of war.*' Other letters from M. Mourgue will be found in this volume.

[2] M. Bailly was guillotined, November 11, 1793. For a touching

The morning of June 20 was the witness of another insurrectionary and disgraceful scene. Paris, grown familiar with popular commotions, was early on the move. Prominent among the more advanced demagogues were Santerre, a wealthy brewer of the Faubourg St. Antoine, and Legendre,[1] a butcher, who adopted the revolutionary programme at its birth and in its most fiery type. The incidents that occasioned the present *émeute* were, specially, the *Veto* and the dismissal of the Ministers. Santerre headed the mob that marched from St. Antoine to the Legislative Assembly, where a petition was presented for the recall of Roland, Clavière, and Servan. This ungovernable crowd, excited to the utmost pitch, and armed with pikes and other weapons, pressed forward and encompassed the Tuileries, forced an entrance into the royal apartments, and insulted both the King and Queen in person with their clamorous demands. '"A bas M. Veto! Au diable le veto! Le rappel des ministres patriotes! Il faut qu'il signe; nous ne sortirons pas d'ici qu'il ne l'ait fait!" En avant de tous, Legendre, plus déterminé que Santerre, se déclare l'orateur et le fondé de pouvoir du peuple souverain. "Monsieur," dit-il au roi, et, voyant que celui-ci fait un geste de surprise, "Oui, monsieur, écoutez-nous; vous êtes fait pour nous écouter. Vous êtes un perfide, vous nous avez toujours trompés, vous nous trompez encore—mais prenez garde, la mesure est à son comble, le peuple est las de se voir votre jouet." "Sire, sire," crie un autre énergumène, "je vous demande au nom de cent mille âmes qui m'entourent le rappel des ministres patriotes. Je demande la sanction du décret sur les prêtres et les 20,000 hommes.

narrative of the execution, see *Histoire de la Révolution Française*, par M. Thiers, tome v. p. 170.

[1] 'A member of the National Convention, 1793-1795, and a butcher by trade. He served me with meat while I was in Paris.'— MS. note by Mr. Milos.

La sanction ou vous périrez."[1] It was not until the King, at the instigation of Legendre, placed a red cap as the emblem of liberty upon his head, and presented himself at an open window for public gaze, that this brutal exhibition of an unrestrained and vulgar mob was brought to a fortunate close.

But no substantial or immediate signs of relief were visible anywhere. Alarming rumours, on the contrary, continued as rife in the departments as in the capital; and, indeed, the dark clouds discernible far above the horizon gave warning of imminent peril both at home and abroad. The next few weeks were characterised by incidents of significant import: the Jacobins denounced by Lafayette as the promoters of trouble; Lafayette, in his turn, accused of treason by his political enemies, but acquitted by the verdict of the Assembly; the continued emigration of the more moderate or more timid citizens; the appearance in Paris of numerous bands of soldiers, hastily recruited, and hurried forward on their march to the threatened frontier; the excitement produced by the arrival of some 500 accoutred men sent by the municipality of Marseilles to intensify, as it would seem, the disorder in the metropolis; the demand of the Jacobins for the deposition of the King; and the proclamation by the Assembly that the country was in danger. News had reached Paris that the Prussians and Austrians were entering French territory, and that the Duke of Brunswick, on moving forward from Coblentz, had issued a manifesto (July 25), in which the maintenance of Louis XVI. on his throne was declared to be the object of the Allies; and, further, it was asserted in language the most imperative that any opposition on

---

[1] *Les Origines de la France Contemporaine—La Révolution*, ii. 206, par M. Taine.

the part of the Assembly or municipality would involve the punishment of death as soon as the foreign troops marched into the capital. At this terrible moment the authorities were paralysed, or, at least, they were incapable of arresting the general fermentation. No waterlogged vessel drifting with the storm was ever more helpless than was the Legislative Assembly or the Executive to check the ever-rising tide of indiscriminate violence and passion. Every event at the close of the month of July was pregnant with danger. Each subsequent day increased the agitation. On Friday, August 10, the tocsin sounded and the roll of the drum was heard long before sunrise; the Faubourg St. Antoine once again poured forth its angry swarms of armed men; and, as the first fruits of the day, Mandat, the commandant of the National Guards, was summoned to the Hôtel de Ville, where, on account of his preparations against the meditated attack, he, suspecting no harm to himself, was condemned and assassinated on the spot. The royal family, whilst the surging mass was moving towards and pressing on the Tuileries, crossed the garden leading to the Salle de Manége, and found shelter under the protection of the Assembly. The Swiss Guard behaved nobly on the occasion. The defence was heroic and effective. But the King had commanded that their fire should cease. The direful result of that mistaken order was instantaneous. The mob forced an entrance into the palace; the Swiss were either shot down at their posts, or else, with few exceptions, massacred during their retreat; their mutilated bodies, stripped and exposed, to the number of one hundred and eighty, affording a spectacle that will never be forgotten.[1]

[1] See *Histoire de la Révolution*, par Deux Amis de la Liberté, tome viii. p. 186.

It was inevitable that the catastrophe of August 10 would lead to important political changes. It was almost equally certain that disturbances in an aggravated form would follow. Thus the functions of the monarch were placed in abeyance without delay. Louis, Marie Antoinette, the Dauphin, and the other members of the royal family, helpless and hopeless, were conveyed to the Temple for security on the third day after the insurrection; Roland, Clavière, and Servan returned to office; Danton, a pronounced demagogue, entered the Cabinet as Minister of Justice; Le Brun, already mentioned as destined to become a prominent figure, received the portfolio as Secretary of State for Foreign Affairs; Santerre, who had directed the mob in their attack on the Tuileries, was appointed by the Commune to the command of the National Guards; Pétion retained his post as Mayor, to which he had been restored after his suspension in June; Robespierre and Marat, the uncompromising advocates of an advanced democracy, obtained positions more dominant than ever in effecting the development of their principles; and the municipality, representing the forty-eight sections into which the capital had been divided, having lost all civic control on the night of August 9, found itself soon afterwards superseded in authority by the self-constituted Commune of Paris. From no part of France did news arrive to compensate for the disquietude felt in the metropolis. La Vendée, a maritime department in the south-west, and a centre of royalist and clerical activity, showed towards the end of August unmistakable signs of revolt against the actual Government. On the 23rd of the month, Longwy, in the north-east, had succumbed to the Prussians. The fall of Verdun was supposed to be imminent. Dumouriez was now in command of the army on that frontier. Lafayette, threatened with death by the Jacobins, and convinced that disaffection towards himself pervaded his troops, realizing that he could no longer hope to avert the gathering storm which hung over his country, had already thrown up the command (August 18), and, in the expectation of escaping into Holland, sought to pass through the lines of the Prussians under the promise of a safe escort. But, on the contrary, he was arrested, and sent in the first instance to the fortress of Magdebourg, from which he was afterwards transferred to the Austrians, and confined in the citadel of Olmütz, in Moldavia.[1]

Scarcely was it possible that so many clouds surcharged with elements of danger could pass over Paris without precipitating their contents. Towards the end of August the prisons rapidly filled with suspected persons—royalists, aristocrats, priests—and, at the instigation of Danton, the Assembly passed a decree authorising domiciliary visits for the search of arms. The greatest activity was also promoted in the extemporised manipulation of weapons and munitions of war from every available material. The barriers of the city were closed by order of the Commune, and the

---

[1] 'Les journaux donnaient les détails de la résistance de mon père à Sedan. On vit bientôt que tout était inutile, et rien n'est comparable aux angoisses de ma mère pendant les jours qui suivirent. Les gazettes étaient pleines de décrets sanguinaires auxquels on se soumettait partout, excepté sur le point où mon père commandait. On mit sa tête à prix. On vint promettre à la barre de l'Assemblée de l'amener mort ou vif. Enfin, le Dimanche, 24 Août, elle reçut une lettre de sa sœur, Mme. de Noailles, qui lui apprit que mon père était hors de France.'—*Vie de Madame Lafayette*, par Mme. de Lasteyrie, sa Fille, p. 231.

The Marquis de Latour-Maubourg, M. Bureaux de Pusy, and Alexandre de Lameth, were arrested at the same time, and shared the long and cruel captivity at Olmütz. Colonel De La Colombe, a near relative of Lafayette, and on his staff at Sedan, also crossed the frontier, but, more fortunate than his companions, escaped to Antwerp, and so reached England.

panic was increased from day to day by the continued arrest of individuals, without distinction of rank, or age, or sex, who, apart from any legal authorisation, were suddenly seized in their own homes and hurried off to places of public detention. Terror, anarchy, brutality, as the case might be, were conspicuous everywhere; 'men's hearts failing them for fear,' whether they gazed upon their near surroundings or cast their eyes abroad for consolation or relief. The first week in September witnessed an outburst of violence unparalleled among civilised nations—'si déshonorante pour notre siècle, et dont la postérité concevra difficilement toutes les horreurs.'[1]

The second of September was on Sunday. The several prisons—Châtelet, Bicêtre, Conciergerie, Abbaye, La Force—were now crowded. At that moment rumours ran through Paris, even before the event occurred, that Verdun had fallen; apprehensions for the safety of Thionville were then felt, and the alarm spread that the Austrians and Prussians could advance on the city without encountering any effective opposition. The consternation among all classes rose to the highest pitch, and, as was natural, the panic assumed a sanguinary form when once it had seized upon the more ferocious members of the community. 'Toutes les haines se réveillèrent, et nul homme de bien ne fut à l'abri de la suspicion.' An awful narrative is thus handed down from generation to generation. About 1,050 persons were summarily murdered in Paris during these early September days; deeds of unsurpassed horror were perpetrated on defenceless men, women, and children; nor was there a ray of hope or comfort to support or cheer the affrighted citizens; not a voice

[1] The Abbé Sicard. See *Histoire Parlementaire*, xviii. 72.

raised to stop the wholesale and indiscriminate massacre. The details of these tragic scenes are not without instruction. They are the palpable and incontrovertible evidence of the depravity and brutal tendency natural to man, when, 'being without God in the world,' there exists no innate power to control or regulate the passions of the mere animal—no acknowledgment of any law except individual volition, derived and fostered, it may be, at the passing moment, out of the noxious and contagious materials of the immediate environment.

It had been resolved after August 10, 1792, that a National Convention should take the place of the Legislative Assembly, not yet twelve months old. This decision came into force on September 21; and it was then ordered, as the initiatory decree of the Convention, that the French Republic should be proclaimed over the ruins of abolished royalty. The monarchical form of government, paralysed in 1789, did not cease to breathe until the autumn of 1792. But, forasmuch as Louis XVI. was totally deprived of the functions of sovereignty on August 10, or immediately after the assault on the Tuileries, the Court of St. James recalled its ambassador, Lord Gower, as soon as practicable. His lordship quitted Paris, August 21, on his return to England. In the previous spring, Louis, still holding nominally the reins of revived power, as guaranteed by the Constitution of September 1791, had appointed the Marquis de Chauvelin his Minister Plenipotentiary to George III., and it was further arranged that Prince Talleyrand, Bishop of Autun, endowed with a shrewd and vigorous mind, should cross the Channel as the Ambassador's adviser and friend.¹

---

¹ 'Mais comme il [Talleyrand] ne pouvait, en sa qualité d'ancien Constituant, remplir ostensiblement aucune fonction publique avant un

Chauvelin left Paris on April 21, and Talleyrand followed in a few days. But the circumstances which induced the recall of Lord Gower applied equally to the French Minister in London, the English Cabinet considering that the credentials of the latter were cancelled at the moment when the authority from which they were derived was destroyed, and thenceforward, as Chauvelin ceased to be acknowledged at the British Court, diplomatic relations between the two countries were peremptorily and inconveniently interrupted. In this dilemma, Le Brun, Minister for Foreign Affairs, had recourse to an expedient whereby he might still be in touch with English opinion, and provide, if possible, that access to the Government, however indirect or informal, should, in some measure, be maintained; the first object of the French Executive being to secure from England the recognition of the Republic in the person of Chauvelin.[1]

Among the agents employed for the above purpose were the Abbé Noël, M. Scipion Mourgue, son of the late Minister of the Interior, and M. Reinhard, these two latter gentlemen being officially attached to the embassy in London. On the same business M. Maret also occupied at this anxious period a prominent position. It is interesting to observe the course they adopted.

laps de deux années, il fut convenu que l'ex-Marquis de Chauvelin aurait jusque-là le titre d'ambassadeur, avec Talleyrand pour mentor. Cette singulière combinaison était indiquée dans une lettre d'introduction auprès du roi d'Angleterre, que Dumouriez avait fait signer à Louis XVI. le 1er Mai. Chauvelin, fils d'un favori de Louis XV., et remplissant lui-même à la cour un office important, s'était néanmoins prononcé avec énergie pour la Révolution.'—Ernouf, p. 77. On the mission of Talleyrand, see note to Letter, Mr. Miles to Lord Fortescue, January 2, 1793.

[1] 'Lebrun était souvent raisonnable, quand on lui permettait de l'être. Il n'osait éliminer Chauvelin, qui s'était fait des protections redoutables par ses exagérations de patriotisme.'—Ernouf, p. 79.

The influence of both political parties in England was eagerly sought. Mourgue and Noël, who were the first on the spot, placed themselves in close intercourse with Mr. Miles, whom they knew to be in confidential relation with the Treasury. 'C'est un homme à ménager,' wrote Noël to Le Brun, September 26, 'en ce qu'il est fort lié avec le frère de my Lord Grenville.' But they were likewise indefatigable in courting the support of the Opposition, Mr. William Smith, member for Norwich, the well-known philanthropist, being the friend specially selected. 'C'est un homme qui jouit ici d'une grande considération,' wrote Noël to Le Brun, October 29. 'Je suis invité dans leurs différentes possessions, et je suis certain que cette liaison me sera très utile.' The Abbé had already applied to Mr. Miles to procure for him an audience with Mr. Pitt, and was assured that he should 'be furnished with the means of obtaining the interview he desired as soon as he had secured from the Executive Council its authority.' [1]

As the autumn advanced affairs took a still more serious turn. The victory of Dumouriez over the Austrians at Jemmapes, November 6, and the dangers which thereby threatened Belgium, the Scheldt, and Holland, introduced grave complications. On that battle-field Maret had taken leave of Dumouriez, and, travelling through Flanders, arrived in London on the evening of November 8. This mission, it is stated, was simply on private matters connected with the Orleans family, but the opportunity was readily seized to watch the political horizon. 'J'aurai eu le temps, cher citoyen,' he wrote to Le Brun, November 10, 'de causer

---

[1] Letter, Miles to Le Brun, December 18, 1792. Also *Authentic Correspondence with M. Le Brun.* &c., by W. A. Miles, London, 1796, p. 87.

à fond sur nos affaires avec vos agents et les autres personnes qui peuvent me donner des notions exactes de notre situation politique avec l'Angleterre. Je vous reporterai tout ce que j'aurai recueilli, et je le déposerai dans votre sein comme dans un terrain fertile où cette semence fructifiera pour le bien de la République.'

It was doubtless the serious wish of Le Brun to procure positive information as to the opinions and intentions of the British Government in respect to the military movements on the Continent. Mourgue, accordingly, informed Mr. Miles that he would soon be authorised to request through him an interview with the Minister, that 'many unsuccessful efforts had been made to get access both to Lord Grenville and Mr. Pitt,' and that, 'discouraged, he urged him to use his interest in consideration of the great stake at issue.'[1] This formal application, proposed on November 13, and immediately communicated to the Treasury, prepared the way for an animated correspondence. There now no longer remained any difficulty as to the consent to grant the coveted audience, but some uncertainty respecting the official character of the agent prolonged the negotiations. In this sense Maret wrote to Le Brun, November 29 : 'Alors il me paraîtrait nécessaire d'autoriser à agir pour préparer toute cette affaire l'homme, quel qu'il fût, que vous vous détermineriez à envoyer ici comme agent sous l'ambassadeur extraordinaire qui serait nommé. J'entre dans ce détail parce que je sais que dans cette supposition le Ministère anglois désirerait ne traiter qu'avec une personne destinée à occuper ici une poste diplomatique. On l'a dit formellement à Mourgue, et il n'est pas sans vraisemblance, que M. Pitt se soit expliqué lui-même à

---

[1] *Authentic Correspondence with Le Brun, &c.,* pp. 89, 90.

cet égard.' Mr. Miles had insisted on being assured positively by Mourgue that he was acting on the authority of the French Executive preparatory to his being received by the English Minister. 'Dans le même moment,' Maret reports to Le Brun, 'la personne très influente qui est en relation avec Mourgue devient très pressante dans ses mouvemens.' This despatch continues: 'Au même instant M. William Smith, ce membre du parlement, ami de M. Pitt, et qui avait déjà eu une conférence avec Noël, demande avec instance à parler à quelqu'un qui tienne au gouvernement français. On m'a proposé de le voir. . . . J'irai donc demain chez M. Smith. Je me tiendrai dans la réserve qui convient à ma position et j'engagerai à la confiance en fesant sentir que ma place près de vous donne l'assurance que rien ne sera perdu des confidences qu'on pourrait me faire et des dispositions qu'on aurait envie de me témoigner. Mourgue agira de son côté. J'unirai mes conseils et mon zèle à l'activité du sien, et peut-être avant deux jours serons-nous entièrement délivrés des incertitudes d'où nous commençons à sortir.' On this same day (November 29) Mr. Long wrote to Mr. Miles: 'Will you introduce me to M. Mourgue this forenoon? If you can do so, I will call upon you for that purpose, provided you think he will make his communication to *me*. It seems the best channel, for you must see how impossible it is for Mr. Pitt or Lord Grenville to admit him to an audience as things stand.' On the previous day Miles had written to Mourgue: 'Mr. Pitt has asked for your name. You have failed to inform me whether you are fully authorised by the executive power to treat with the Court of London.' Hence the significance of the above note from the Treasury. On November 30,

Maret held his conference with Smith. On the following morning, Long had his interview with Mourgue, and Pitt, waiving his objection to receive a *non-accredited* agent, arranged that, on the evening of the same day (December 1), he would give an audience to Maret. The fact is, Mourgue had intended all the while (acting, no doubt, under secret instructions from Le Brun) to slip out, and so allow Maret to slip in, as soon as access to the Minister had been assured. 'When the parties met, it was not *this* man, but *another*, that was deputed to treat. That other was M. Maret; and when he was produced from behind the curtain, it appeared that he had as little to say as his friend, and that neither was instructed to open any negotiation or to offer any propositions whatever to Government. Maret, having nothing to say, contented himself with expressing the happiness he should feel in being instrumental in preserving a good understanding between the two nations, and, after a few general expressions of a similar nature, he retired. This was his frank acknowledgment to me at the time, and he has declared it to me in his correspondence.'[1]

The reception of Maret was postponed until the next day, Sunday, December 2. No time was lost in transmitting to Le Brun a full narrative of the interview.[2] Another despatch, bearing the same date, and giving an account of his previous conference with Smith, concludes thus : ' J'ai quitté M. Smith assez rassuré, fort bien disposé pour nous, et se préparant, je

[1] *Letter to Earl Stanhope*, by W. A. Miles, London 1794, p. 147. Herbert Marsh discusses fully this substitution of Maret for Mourgue, ii. 6-17, chap. xiii. See also Ernouf, pp. 82, 86.

[2] This despatch, December 2, 1792, will be found among the archives at the Foreign Office, Quai d'Orsay, Paris, vol. 584, p. 19. The *Annual Register* for 1792 reproduces it in English. *State Papers*, p. 190.

n'en pouvais douter, à rendre compte à M. Pitt de notre conversation, qui a probablement facilité l'entrevue dont je vais vous occuper.' It may be stated that Noël, not Maret, would have been the agent introduced at the Treasury on this occasion if he had not been absent on a mission to Dumouriez. He returned to London too late. 'En arrivant,' he wrote to Le Brun, December 13, 'j'ai trouvé que la glace avait été rompue. Je n'ai vu dans cette première communication que le bien de la chose, et je suis loin d'en être fâché, d'autant plus qu'il paraît que mon absence seule m'a privé de l'avantage de recueillir le fruit de toutes les peines et de tous les dégoûts que j'ai essuyés. C'est du moins ce que Miles m'a assuré, et c'est lui qui a aplani toutes les difficultés qui pouvaient s'opposer à l'entrevue qui a eu lieu entre Pitt et Maret.'

This letter of Noël conveyed to Le Brun the particulars of a lengthened discussion between Mr. Miles and himself on the political divergence which at that moment agitated the two Governments. 'Nous commençames,' he said, 'à conférer ensemble sur les moyens de rapprochement entre la France et l'Angleterre.' The conduct of the English Minister, as represented in this report, was severely attacked by Noël. The rejoinder of Miles was also frankly transmitted to Le Brun. 'Il faut que je vous détrompe, s'écria-t-il. Jamais, jamais M. Pitt n'a contribué ni directement ni indirectement à vos troubles intérieurs. Il a constamment refusé d'y prendre part. . . . Au nom de l'humanité, me dit-il, sauvons à nos pays les malheurs qui les menacent—réunissons nos efforts, vous auprès du gouvernement français, moi auprès de M. Pitt, dont je suis beaucoup plus content que de Grenville. Pitt ne veut point la guerre. Ne craignez rien de notre armement. Je me fais part de vous faire avoir satisfaction.' The French agents in London did not cease to search for information through the medium of the Opposition also. 'Ce soir,' continues Noël, 'étoit pris pour un rendez-vous avec M. Smith chez M. Wilberforce. Ce dernier ne s'y trouva pas. Les interlocuteurs étoient M. Smith, Maret, Labouadière et moi. La substance de la conversation fut la même '—that is, the same as maintained a few hours before between Miles and Noël.[1]

On the following day, December 14, Maret communicated to Miles a despatch received that morning from Le Brun. It commences: 'J'ai reçu, citoyen, la dépêche que vous m'avez adressée le 2 de ce mois, et j'ai lu avec beaucoup de satisfaction les détails intéressants qu'elle contient. Il résulte tant des avis que vous nous donnez, que de ceux qui nous sont transmis par le Citoyen Chauvelin, que le Ministère britannique, et surtout M. Pitt, sont disposés à saisir les moyens d'éviter une guerre avec la France ; mais qu'ils ne croyent pas pouvoir s'en dispenser, s'ils ne reçoivent pas des explications satisfaisantes sur l'ouverture de l'Escaut, sur le décret du 19 Novembre dernier relativement à la fraternité et à la protection promise aux peuples qui voudront s'affranchir du joug du despotisme, et sur les intentions actuelles du Gouvernement par rapport à la Hollande. Il paraît au reste que la reconnaissance de la République française par l'Angleterre ne forme pas actuellement une difficulté insurmontable.' This despatch instructs Maret that he must restrict himself to assuring Pitt 'que la République de France est prête à faire des déclarations qui prouveront au Ministère britannique combien elle est disposée à saisir tous les moyens propres à se tenir en bonne intelligence avec la nation anglaise.'

[1] Archives, Paris, vol. 584, p. 185.

Unhappily the goodwill here expressed was vitiated by the sentence which follows—'qu'elle a chargé le Citoyen Chauvelin, son Ministre à Londres, de faire sur cet objet toutes les déclarations convenables aussitôt qu'il en sera requis par le Ministère britannique, qui dès lors se trouve le maître d'obtenir de la manière la plus solennelle et la plus authentique tous les éclaircissements qu'il peut désirer sur les objets sur lesquels il a paru montrer quelque inquiétude.' The affair of August 10, it will be remembered, had thrown the Ambassador at the English Court into the shade. Le Brun, although assured of the embarrassment which such an impolitic decision would occasion, persisted in upholding the diplomatic character of Chauvelin, and, moreover, denied to Maret all power to act except on his personal responsibility. 'Vous ajouterez,' he finally adds, 'que vos pouvoirs ne s'étendent pas plus loin, et vous résisterez à tous les efforts qui pourraient être faits pour vous engager à vous expliquer plus en détail.'[1] The importance of this despatch induced Mr. Miles to advise Maret to request an immediate interview with Mr. Pitt, Miles also forwarding a note to the Minister under the same cover. The audience was granted, but, like the former one, it terminated without any useful result. Maret and Noël forwarded to Paris at once their respective opinions on what had transpired. The latter concludes his report with the following passage: 'Nous devons de la reconnoissance à Miles. Il a mis dans toutes ces ouvertures autant de bonne foi et de philanthropie que de zèle et de bonne volonté.'[2]

[1] This letter to Maret is dated Paris, December 9. On the same day Le Brun wrote a long despatch to Chauvelin, with full instructions for his guidance, and confirming his diplomatic character at the British Court. See note, Letter, *Dampierre to Miles*, December 17, 1792.

[2] Ernouf states: 'Dans la nuit du 13 au 14 décembre Maret et Noël

Le Brun, in the *Mémoire*[1] he prepared for the Convention, and in allusion to the naval preparations in England, states the controversy in the following succinct terms :—

'Il en résulte encore que les griefs qui servent de prétexte à ces armements se réduisent à trois principaux, savoir :—

'1e. L'ouverture de l'Escaut.

'2e. Votre décret du 19 novembre.[2]

'3e. Les intentions que l'on suppose à la République française relativement à la Hollande.'

On December 27 M. Chauvelin communicated to Lord Grenville the instructions received from the Executive Council with respect to the above points in dispute. The assurance was given that France desired to preserve peace with England, that she never intended to employ the decree of November 19 as an instrument for the promotion of insurrection, that she would not attack Holland so long as that power remained neutral, and that she could not believe that England would consider the opening of the Scheldt a sufficient pretext for hostilities; but, on the other hand, any aggression on her dignity as a free and powerful nation would be repelled with energy, and would throw upon England the respon-

eurent une conférence avec Miles et Smith. Les deux Anglais furent consternés de la décision du conseil exécutif de France. Smith consentit pourtant à faire demander pour Maret une nouvelle entrevue, bien qu'il n'en augurât rien de favorable dans de telles conditions' (p. 103). Mr. Miles, however, was *not* present at this conference with Mr. Smith. Nor was it until the arrival of Le Brun's despatch on the forenoon of the next day that, as shown above, the proposal was made for a second interview with Mr. Pitt. Ernouf may have been misled by the following passage in Noël's letter of December 13 : 'Miles est venu deux fois aujourd'hui : la 2e fois il m'a trouvé. Il a vu Pitt ce matin. *Rendez-vous pour ce soir.*'

[1] 'Mémoire, Commune de Paris, du 19 décembre,' *Gazette Nationale ou le Moniteur Universel*, No. 356, du Vendredi, 21 Xbre, 1792.

[2] The Decree of November 19 will be found after the Letter, *Miles to Aust*, November 26, 1792.

sibility in the event of a declaration of war. Chauvelin added that he was enjoined to demand a written answer to this note. Lord Grenville replied on December 31. 'You are not ignorant,' he wrote, 'that since the unhappy events of August 10 the King has thought proper to suspend all *official* communications with France. You are yourself no otherwise accredited to the King than in the name of his most Christian Majesty. . . . I am therefore to inform you, Sir, in express and formal terms that I acknowledge you in no other public character than that of Minister from his most Christian Majesty, and that, consequently, you cannot be admitted to treat with the King's Ministers in the quality and under the form stated in your note.' In this communication the chief objections of the English Cabinet to the policy of France are stated and argued. 'England will never consent,' his Lordship added, 'that France shall arrogate the power of annulling at her pleasure, and under pretence of a pretended natural right of which she makes herself the only judge, the political system of Europe established by treaties and guaranteed by the consent of all the powers. This Government, adhering to the maxims which it has followed for more than a century, will also never see with indifference that France shall make herself, either directly or indirectly, sovereign of the Low Countries or general arbitress of the rights and liberties of Europe. If France is really desirous of maintaining friendship and peace with England, she must show herself disposed to renounce her views of aggression and aggrandisement, and to confine herself within her territory, without insulting other governments, without disturbing their tranquillity, without violating their rights.'[1]

[1] 'Two days after Lord Grenville had communicated this answer to M. Chauvelin, Mr. Miles wrote a letter to Le Brun, the French Minister

The year 1793 opened with undiminished forebodings of war. On January 12 the answer of Le Brun to the despatch of December 31 arrived at the French Embassy in Portman Square. Lord Grenville was informed of the fact during the afternoon of the same day. A copy of the despatch was in the possession of the Foreign Office on the following morning. It is simply a review of the political position, and certainly did not contribute to calm the troubled waters. It concluded as follows: 'Après une explication aussi franche, dictée par un désir aussi pur de la paix, il ne devrait rester au Ministère de S. M. B. aucune nuage sur les intentions de la France. Mais si ces explications lui paraissent insuffisantes, si nous sommes encore obligés d'entendre le langage de la hauteur, si les préparatifs hostiles se continuent dans les ports d'Angleterre, après avoir tout épuisé pour le maintien de la paix, nous nous disposerions à la guerre avec le sentiment du moins de la justice de notre cause, et des efforts que nous aurons faits pour éviter cette extrémité; et nous combattrons à regret les Anglais que nous estimons, mais nous les combattrons sans crainte.' That this letter was intended as an *ultimatum* may be inferred from the injunction given to Chauvelin in the postscript: 'Voilà, citoyen, la réponse à M. Grenville toute faite, et vous la remettrés telle qu'elle est à commencer par le paragraphe —*le Conseil, &c.*, que vous ferés seulement précéder par les deux ou trois lignes de préambule nécessaire.'[1]

for Foreign Affairs, on the subject of the pending negotiation; and, as this letter is a document of some importance, and throws considerable light on the history of French politics, it will be necessary to make from it a few extracts.'—Herbert Marsh, ii. 152. See this letter, *Miles to Le Brun*, January 2, 1793. The letters, *Chauvelin to Grenville* and *Grenville to Chauvelin*, are produced by Marsh in full, and are accompanied by notes, ii. 18-51. See *Annual Register.*

[1] See *Moniteur*, January 14, 1793: 'Note officielle du pouvoir exécutif de France, en réponse à celle du Ministère britannique. Paris, le 7 Janvier,

Maret, who had quitted London on December 19, wrote to Miles by the same courier that left Paris on January 8. His letter was dictated by order of the Executive Council, and bears the same date as the note from Le Brun to Chauvelin. The various questions at issue are therein discussed in detail. It contains, in fact, a summary of the entire controversy between the two nations. Mr. Miles placed this document in the hands of Mr. Pitt without delay—namely, on Sunday, January 13. The effect produced on the Cabinet by its perusal —for the Cabinet was sitting at that moment—seems to have been an aggravation of the difficulties.[1]

Nor did the tardy acknowledgment of the note from Le Brun improve the strained condition. No movement on either side tended to alleviate or diminish the tension. It was thus that the friction between the two nations became more and more alarming. Both parties asserted an ardent desire for amicable relations—both deprecated war with equal fervour—but, instead of closing to embrace, each side receded, and, with the recoil, the

---

1793, l'an deuxième de la République.' A translation of this letter is given in the *Annual Register, State Papers*, p. 119, also by Marsh, ii. 56 88.

[1] 'Nous avons trouvé la preuve certaine de la démarche préalable faite par Maret dès le 7 janvier auprès de cet ami qui lui avait déjà servi d'intermédiaire, c'est-à-dire, auprès de Miles. Sous une forme intime et cordiale, cette lettre était un véritable mémoire destiné à passer sous les yeux de Pitt. Maret y abordait tous les points litigieux. La fin de ce mémoire laisse entrevoir combien Maret avait su se rendre important et utile dans ces graves circonstances.'—Ernouf, p. 113.

'The attitude of Chauvelin was so hostile, and his connection with disaffected Englishmen so notorious, that the English Government would hold no confidential communication with him; but through the instrumentality of Miles some correspondence was still kept with Maret, who had now become Chef de Département at the Foreign Office under Le Brun, and even with Le Brun himself. In a very earnest though very amicable letter dated January 11, Miles had warned Maret that, unless the French Convention could be induced to recede from its present policy, war was absolutely inevitable.'—Lecky, vi. 112.

situation became more precarious and complicated. Full five days elapsed before Grenville replied to Chauvelin. On the next day, January 19, 'le samedi à trois heures du matin,' Reinhard, Secretary to the French Legation, wrote to Miles: 'La réponse de Lord Grenville est arrivée. Elle paraît rendre impossible tout moyen de s'entendre. Le Gouvernement anglais nous méprise. Voilà sur quoi je fonde encore mon espoir. Je n'aurais pas le tems de vous attendre. Je vous écris les mains roides de froid, et le cœur bouillant d'indignation. La dépêche du 8 n'a point été satisfaisante en aucun point.[1] Si la notification en eût été faite dans une forme régulière et officielle, on auroit répondu que la déclaration de la rupture du traité de commerce et la manière dont on répondait sur l'Escaut n'étaient que des nouvelles offenses. On a ajouté qu'il serait inutile de converser avec M. Chauvelin sur des points particuliers, mais qu'on se prêterait cependant encore volontiers à l'entendre, s'il avait dans la même forme à proposer quelque chose qui embrassât le système général des affaires relativement à la crise actuelle, et qui concernât en même temps l'Angleterre, ses alliés, et la sûreté générale de l'Europe. *M. Chauvelin part!*'

Events of portentous significance soon occurred in quick succession. On January 21 Louis XVI. was executed. The startling news reached London on the afternoon of the 23rd; the excitement throughout England, and especially in the metropolis, was intense, and the war fever among certain classes ran its course with great rapidity.[2] Not more than twenty-

[1] 'I have examined, sir, with the utmost attention, the paper you remitted to me on the 18th of this month. I cannot help remarking that I have found nothing satisfactory in the result of it.'—*Grenville to Chauvelin*, January 18.

[2] See Lecky, vi. 122; Ernouf, p. 119. For a touching narrative of the execution of Louis XVI., see Carlyle, ii. 210, &c.

four hours elapsed before Chauvelin was summarily enjoined to quit the kingdom within eight days. The official order, as preserved in the Archives at Paris, is as follows: [1]—

'Sa Majesté en conseil a bien voulu ordonner, et elle ordonne par ces présentes, que Monsieur Chauvelin, qui fut reçu par sa Majesté le 2 Mai, 1792, comme Ministre Plénipotentiaire accrédité par feu sa Majesté très chrétienne, sorte de ce royaume avant le premier jour de février prochain, et que le très honorable Lord Grenville, principal Secrétaire d'Etat de sa Majesté pour les Affaires Etrangères, fasse connaître cet ordre de sa Majesté au susdit Monsieur Chauvelin.'

This document, dated January 24, was accompanied by a letter from Lord Grenville. 'The character with which you have been invested at this Court,' his Lordship observes, 'and the functions of which have been so long suspended, being now entirely terminated by the fatal death of his late most Christian Majesty, you have no more any public character here. The King can no longer, after such an event, permit your residence here.' The reply of Chauvelin was prompt: 'J'ai reçu, il y a une heure, par M. Aust, la lettre que vous avez été chargé de m'écrire, avec les pièces qui y étaient jointes. Je compte partir demain matin pour la France.'[2] On the same day Chauvelin reported the crisis to Le Brun: 'Je partirai demain, citoyen, et serai peut-être à Paris en même temps que cette lettre. Je vous adresse la copie de la lettre que j'adresse à Lord Grenville. Vous verrez, citoyen, qu'en vous laissant la possibilité de caractériser ainsi que vous le jugerez convenable la démarche du Gouvernement britannique, j'ai indiqué que

---

[1] 'Traduction de l'Ordre du Roi d'Angleterre communiqué au Citoyen Chauvelin.'

[2] See *Parliamentary History*, xxx. 269, 270.

je cédais à la force en me soumettant à un ordre auquel je ne me connais à moi seul aucun moyen de résister.' He added the following postscript: 'La démarche du Ministère anglais sera certainement regardée ici comme une déclaration de guerre. On s'attendait peu à cette démarche.' It was not, however, the *Order in Council* that was solely responsible for the flight of the Ambassador. It served only to accelerate his steps and increase his hostile disposition. The letter of Reinhard shows that he had *previously* resolved to leave England.[1]

Facts connected with the above unhappy event, although familiar to the historian, command special attention here from their importance; and, as they receive additional interest when narrated by a French writer of our own times, it is from the work of Baron Ernouf that the following passage is taken: 'Le même jour, 24 janvier, dès le matin, Chauvelin avait reçu l'invitation de quitter l'Angleterre dans un délai de huit jours. Il s'en alla dès le lendemain, et rendit encore un mauvais service à son pays par ce départ précipité. S'il était resté seulement quelques heures de plus, il aurait reçu à temps une importante dépêche, expédiée le 22. Cette dépêche, rédigée par Maret, répondait aux lettres dans lesquelles l'ex-ambassadeur avait dépeint sa position comme absolument intolérable. On lui donnait en conséquence l'ordre de partir, *mais* après avoir remis une dernière note dont on lui indiquait les termes : "Vous ferez sentir que si le Ministère britannique, rendu à des sentiments plus convenables, désirait un rapprochement, il nous y trouverait encore disposés; combien il serait douloureux pour nous de porter les armes contre un peuple qui était entré le premier dans la carrière de

---

[1] See an article on the expulsion of Chauvelin, &c., in the *Fortnightly Review*, February 1883.

la régénération sociale ; que cette guerre, ne fût-elle qu'une suite de victoires, nous paraîtrait encore funeste, s'il en résultait le réveil de ces haines nationales que de longues années ne suffisent plus à détruire. . . ." Cette remarquable dépêche, inconnue jusqu'ici à tous les historiens, se terminait ainsi : " Le Citoyen Maret va partir incessamment comme chargé d'affaires. . . . *Vous en préviendrez Lord Grenville*, et, dans le cas où vous jugeriez convenable de revenir avant que Maret soit arrivé, vous laisserez votre premier secrétaire pour faire la remise des archives." Le courrier porteur de cette dépêche rencontra Chauvelin entre Douvres et Londres.[1] L'ex-ambassadeur se crut autorisé par les circonstances à considérer ces derniers ordres comme non avenus. Son amour-propre n'admettait pas qu'il eût laissé derrière lui quelque tentative d'arrangement possible par un autre. Il pensa aussi que, depuis l'expédition de ce courrier, on avait dû apprendre l'exaspération produite en Angleterre par la mort de Louis XVI., et que ce projet d'envoi d'un nouvel agent était abandonné. Il poursuivit donc sa route, et ne songea pas même, en débarquant à Calais, à y laisser un mot d'avertissement pour Maret. Il ne réfléchit pas que cette négligence pouvait avoir pour celui-ci des conséquences fort désagréables, peut-être dangereuses, si par impossible Maret était parti de Paris dans cet intervalle, et si, voyageant par une longue et sombre nuit d'hiver, ils se croisaient sans se voir. Ce fut précisément ce qui arriva. Malgré la violente impression produite à Londres par la catastrophe du 21 janvier, la guerre n'était pas encore inévitable. Telle est l'opinion nettement exprimée dans une lettre écrite le 28 par le secrétaire de légation Reinhard, lettre qui suffirait pour justifier l'hommage public que Talleyrand

[1] At Blackheath.

et Bignon ont rendu de concert, quarante-cinq ans plus tard, à la sagacité de ce diplomate.'[1]

On the same day that Chauvelin left London (January 25), Le Brun had given instructions to Maret to proceed to the British metropolis in a diplomatic character. His nomination was signified in the following terms: 'Les circonstances où nous nous trouvons, citoyen, vis à vis de l'Angleterre, exigent qu'en l'absence du Ministre de la République à cette cour nous ayons un chargé d'affaires qui joigne au talent de négocier avec autant de sagesse que de prudence, le patriotisme le plus pur et beaucoup de zèle pour la chose publique. Connaissant en vous, citoyen, toutes ces qualités, je ne puis mettre en meilleures mains les intérêts de la République et faire un choix qui remplisse mieux son objet. Je vous nomme donc son Chargé d'Affaires à Londres, où vous voudrez bien vous rendre le plus tôt possible.' The tentative measure to reopen negotiations with the English Cabinet was not made without deliberation. Thus, two days before the appointment was definitively announced (January 23), Maret wrote to Miles: 'Vous apprendrez avec quelque surprise que je pars bientôt pour Londres. Vous serez instruit de mon arrivée à l'instant même où je mettrai le pied dans votre ville. Si vous avez quelque chose à me mander, écrivez-moi

---

[1] *Maret, Duc de Bassano*, Paris, 1884, p. 119. The letter of Reinhard, January 28, 1793, is preserved in the Archives at the Quai d'Orsay, Paris. It contains the following passage: 'Je suis loin de penser, citoyen, que le moment est déjà venu où il faut rompre toute mesure de paix. La dignité nationale ne saurait être blessée des démarches qui tendraient encore à éviter la guerre, ou à montrer que la France a tout fait pour l'éviter. La prudence et la politique nous les conseillent. Nous les devons à la France et à l'Angleterre. Il paraît évident que le Cabinet britannique, sans exception d'aucun de ses membres, est décidé à nous faire la guerre; que l'opinion nationale nous est entièrement défavorable; et que même dans le moins d'unanimité nous ne pouvons prudemment séparer le gouvernement de la nation.'

à Douvres posté restante. Je prendrai votre lettre en passant. J'espère qu'on ne me défendra pas de vous voir—assurément on ne pourra jamais m'empêcher de vous aimer.' This letter reached the French Embassy on the 27th. It was immediately forwarded by Reinhard to Mr. Miles, whom the French Executive had been constrained by circumstances to regard as a 'mediator between them and the British Ministry,'[1] and who transmitted it at once to the Treasury as the earliest intimation of the approaching arrival of Maret. The next day Long wrote to Miles: 'I am desired by Mr. Pitt to say to you, in answer to your note accompanying a letter from M. Maret, that he thinks you should not answer M. Maret, and he wishes you to decline making yourself the channel of any verbal or written communication from him upon the subject of French affairs. Mr. Pitt desires me to return his thanks to you for the communication you have made.' The observations of Mr. Miles upon the above request will be found under their proper date. It suffices to remark here that the wishes of the Minister as conveyed to him were loyally respected. For want of information, however, as to the state of affairs, Maret, on landing in England, was not without embarrassment. 'J'apprends, citoyen,' he wrote to Le Brun from Dover, January 29, 'en arrivant ici la manière dont Chauvelin a quitté l'Angleterre.[2] Je crois devoir ne rien changer à ma marche et aller attendre à Londres les instructions qu'il est nécessaire que je reçoive prompte-

---

[1] Herbert Marsh, i. 141.
[2] 'Il est sans doute fâcheux que vous n'ayés pu rencontrer Chauvelin sur votre route. Ce Ministre avait demandé des informations sur votre compte depuis Calais, mais ce n'est qu'à Abbeville qu'il a appris que vous aviés passé. Il était trop tard de vous rejoindre.'—*Le Brun to Maret*, February 2, 1793.

ment de vous dans de telles circonstances. Il ne me paraît pas convenable qu'avant de les avoir reçues je cherche à voir les Ministres, mais je profiterai du tems pour me mettre en mesure sur ce point et pour recueillir des notions précises sur notre position actuelle avec l'Angleterre.' Unfounded rumours as to an immediate declaration of war on the part of England were rife on the sea-coast. Hence Maret adds in a postscript: 'On assure que la guerre sera proposée ce soir au Parlement. Dans ce cas seulement je partirai de Londres pour vous en porter sur le champ la nouvelle.' And his anxiety to be accurately instructed at the present crisis is further shown in the following note, dated from Portman Square, January 30: 'J'arrive à l'instant, mon cher Miles. Je désire vous voir le plutôt possible. Faites-moi dire à quelle heure je vous trouverai chez vous ce soir.'

The interviews which ensued between Maret and Miles could not possibly have had any practical result in the circumstances under which they occurred. Whether France, in sending at the eleventh hour a Chargé d'Affaires to London, was honest in the interests of peace, or insincere in adopting a measure of procrastination, it is certain that, as indicated above, the English Cabinet were then averse to receive any communication from Maret, or even to hear anything about the mission with which he was intrusted. At all events, the proposed channel—the only channel available for the transmission of an exchange of thought between the two countries at that momentous period—was obstructed by the express desire of Pitt himself. The possible bridge between the dissentient parties was gratuitously barricaded. Maret, indeed, lost no time in authorising Miles to assure the Minister that the intentions of the

French Executive were pacific; that the propositions he had to offer would include the relinquishment of the Scheldt and the Netherlands, the French troops would also be withdrawn from the Belgic provinces, and all conquests made upon the Rhine would be abandoned; that the terms on which the above arrangements would be based could not be otherwise than acceptable to England; and that, finally, in the event of a friendly policy being entertained by the Court of St. James, Dumouriez would come over invested with power to sign and exchange. The commendatory letter which Maret brought over from his Government was couched in language equally reassuring. 'Je vous prie, Monsieur,' wrote Le Brun to Lord Grenville, 'de vouloir bien l'accueillir avec bonté. Je suis convaincu d'avance qu'il s'empressera de vous témoigner le désir qu'il a de mériter votre estime et votre confiance. Il ne sera pas moins attentif à exprimer à votre Excellence le vœu sincère de la République et de son Gouvernement pour le maintien de la plus parfaite harmonie entre les deux nations.' Mr. Miles explained the reason why he declined forwarding this information to the Treasury; but, at the same time, he advised Maret to send it direct to Pitt, and without delay. The motive assigned by Maret for postponement deserves notice. He demurred, he said, until he should hear further from Paris, for, as the departure of Chauvelin was not known when he left that city, 'he was apprehensive that the circumstance of the late Ambassador having been ordered to quit the kingdom, and the manner in which he would represent the matter, might change the position, and precipitate a rupture which it was the *ardent* and *unanimous* wish of the Executive Council to avoid.' Maret acknowledged the inconvenience of remaining in

London as Chargé d'Affaires from the French Executive, whilst he delayed all official communication with the British Government, but, in consequence of the peculiarity of the situation, he resolved merely to announce to the Foreign Office his presence, and then wait for final instructions, 'before he applied for the honour of an interview with Mr. Pitt.' He realised his embarrassment from the moment of his arrival. 'J'ai cherché sur le champ Miles,' he wrote to Le Brun, 'pour le prévenir de tous ces détails, et l'engager à dire, dans le cas où on s'étonnerait que je ne demandasse pas à voir les Ministres, la véritable raison de cette réserve.' He continues: 'Il m'a laissé entrevoir des espérances de paix et de succès, et je dois conclure des ouvertures qu'il m'a faites que le Ministère britannique ne répugnerait pas à des négotiations qui seraient concurremment suivies par un grand personnage et moi.' He adds that Lord Lansdowne, 'avec plusieurs personnes que j'ai déjà eu l'occasion d'entretenir,' agreed with Miles in the opinion that as yet peace was not impossible. That letter was written on January 31.[1]

However, all thought of negotiation was dissipated with remarkable celerity. The question of receiving the French agent was indeed mooted in the Cabinet. But, on February 4, Aust sent word to Miles that he had just seen an order issued from the Home Department for Maret to quit the kingdom in three days; 'the circumstances of the times having rendered it improper that his stay in this country should be prolonged.' The next afternoon Maret wrote: 'Nous partons dans

---

[1] A *summary* of the important parts of this very long letter from Maret to Le Brun is given by Mr. Lecky, who observes: 'For the past fortnight the English Government seemed to have given up all hopes of peace, and on neither side was there now any real disposition to make sacrifices for it' (vi. 125-128). See also Ernouf, pp. 125-129.

quelques heures. Venez nous voir, mon cher Miles, que nous ayons encore le plaisir de vous embrasser.' At seven o'clock on the following morning (Wednesday, February 6), Maret and Mourgue left the Embassy *en route* for France, and, after some detention at Dover from the difficulty of obtaining transport, they landed at Calais on the 8th. The musket-fire on their packet-boat, by two corsairs when within sight of port, conveyed the first intimation that war was already declared![1]

Maret found waiting for him a letter from Le Brun, the first he had received since he set out on his mission; it is dated February 2, and explains the political crisis in the following terms: 'Depuis votre départ de Paris les choses ont bien changé de face. L'embargo mis en Angleterre sur plusieurs bâtiments français, l'ordre qui a été signifié à Chauvelin, et la proposition faite au Parlement d'augmenter les forces navales et de terre, ne laissent plus de doute sur les intentions du Roi d'Angleterre. Pour repousser cette aggression injuste d'une manière digne de la République française, la Convention nationale a adopté unanimement le Décret dont je joins ici la copie.'[2]

[1] Ernouf was misled by the *Annual Register* into the supposition 'que Maret était resté, dans ce second voyage, huit jours entiers à Londres.' He was only *six* whole days in London. His sudden expulsion Ernouf explains as follows: 'L'ordre de partir lui avait été envoyé par le Ministère anglais, après que la nouvelle fut parvenue à Londres de l'embargo mis dans les ports de France sur tous les navires anglais' (pp. 129, 130). Maret, writing to Miles from Dover, remarks: 'Les matelots ont une grande répugnance à passer à Calais, où par une étrange violation des droits établis, et des égards que se doivent les nations, on retient six paquebots, entre autres ceux qui ont porté Reinhard et les gens de Chauvelin. Je ne connois aucun motif qui puisse légitimer un semblable procédé, et je me propose, quelque chose qui puisse m'en arriver, de réclamer contre cette incroyable conduite que l'opinion publique n'approuvera pas sans doute.'

[2] 'Décret qui déclare que la République française est en guerre avec le Roi d'Angleterre et le Stathouder des Provinces-Unies. 1ᵉʳ Février, 1793.' See *Annual Register, State Papers*, p. 139, and *Hist. Europe*, p. 234.

It had been expected that the above intelligence would reach Maret whilst in London. The letter contains his recall. But there had been no mail communication between the two countries for a week. Maret attributed to that fact the delay of the expected instructions from Le Brun, and, before he was aware of the unhappy turn of events in Paris, deplored the prolonged silence as the proximate cause of the predicament in which he had found himself. 'Depuis vendredi,' he wrote to Miles from Dover, ' aucune lettre de France n'est arrivée ici—aucune lettre d'Angleterre n'est passée à France. De là vient, mon cher, le manque absolu où je me trouvais d'ordre du Gouvernement. Il faut nous affliger de cette circonstance, qui a plus qu'on ne peut croire influé sur le sort réservé aux deux nations.' But, in fact, the Minister for Foreign Affairs had left his agent absolutely without directions until he announced the outbreak of hostilities. The force of circumstances had now become beyond control. A private letter received by Mr. Miles from Paris at that time says: 'The intrigues of Chauvelin have triumphed; all hopes of peace are vanished; the Convention was unanimous in its vote for war against England; while horror, silence, and despair mark each countenance of those who wished for peace. Maret will now return only to experience ingratitude and disgrace.' It is sufficiently apparent that the two nations were *allowed* to drift into conflict. No honest or sustained effort was ever made either by the French Executive or the English Cabinet to forestall and counteract the evolution of so direful a calamity. The sequel justifies the application of the text: 'All they that take the sword shall perish with the sword.'[1]

[1] ' Le Brun and Chauvelin contributed by their misrepresentations and

The condition of France from the moment when she declared war against Great Britain and Holland became more and more critical. Her armies under Dumouriez and Custine, after their first successes in Belgium and on the Rhine, were soon entangled with serious difficulties; the subsequent defeat of the former general by the Prince of Coburg at the battle of Neerwinden, March 18, 1793, intensified the gravity of the position, whilst bitter dissensions between the advanced political parties, the Girondists and the Montagnards, paralysed all thought of united action on the part of the Convention in defence of the Republic. The capital, thrown into a 'convulsion of despair,' as represented in a private letter to Mr. Miles dated from Paris in that same month, was still further agitated by the fear of civil war or an immediate insurrection among the inhabitants of La Vendée. Everywhere on the horizon

exaggerations to fire the public mind in France even to phrenzy, and they are the principal cause of war being declared against Great Britain by the National Convention.'—W. A. M.

'Pendant ce temps, le brusque retour de Chauvelin produisait à Paris le résultat qu'appréhendait son successeur. Ce *coup de tête* était digne du reste. Il devenait à son insu, par cette dernière esclandre, l'auxiliaire de ceux des ministres anglais qui, tout en désirant la guerre, craignaient d'en prendre l'initiative. Il les mit pleinement à leur aise en contraignant, par l'exagération du scandale, la Convention à rompre la première.' Ernouf, p. 129; also pp. 76, 187.

The following curious account of the immediate origin of the outbreak was given by Maret himself, in August 1797, to Lord Malmesbury : 'The failure of his negotiation,' he said, 'could be attributed to the then French Government, who were bent on that war; that the great and decisive cause of the war was *quelque vingtaine d'individus marquans et en place, qui avoient joués à la baisse dans les fonds, et là ils avaient porté la nation à nous déclarer la guerre. Ainsi,*' said he, '*nous devons tous nos malheurs à un principe d'agiotage.* He said, on his return to France, he was informed of this, and was considered as in possession of so dangerous a secret, that they wanted first to send him to Portugal, which he refused; then to Naples, which he was *forced to accept*; and that he had every reason to believe that his arrest and confinement were settled and concerted at Paris before he left.'—*Malmesbury Diaries*, 1844, iii. 502.

the outlook was overcast. Nor were the apprehensions
delusive. The sudden flight of Dumouriez across the
northern territory into the Austrian camp, chased from
France by his own troops (April 4), increased the
universal alarm, and the revolt in the western department
was a veritable factor with which the Convention
would have to contend at an early period.

It was at this juncture, when stability in the
governing power at Paris had no existence, and when
the least possible obstruction could have been exhibited
against monarchical reaction, that, on March 11, M. De
La Colombe, commissioned by his fellow-countrymen
in the Auvergne, communicated to Mr. Miles an organised
plan for creating a diversion in favour of a
counter-revolution in the southern departments. M. De
La Colombe, it will be remembered, held the rank of
colonel in the French service, and was a near relative
of Lafayette; he had escaped from the Prussians, in
the previous August, to Antwerp, and thence, before
emigrating to America as the last resort in search of
personal security, visited London for the purpose just
specified. This communication, in a written form, was
immediately taken to the Foreign Office by Mr. Miles.
It was to the effect that, on certain specified conditions,
the inhabitants of the Cévennes, Auvergne, Dauphiny,
and the adjacent country—including the whole of five
departments—were ready to arm, march on Paris, and
proclaim Louis XVII. King of France; and, further,
the engagement was given to equip, at their own
expense, from 24,000 to 30,000 men, with artillery and
ammunition. The only stipulations annexed were that
Lafayette and his companions should be released from
their captivity, it being intended that Lafayette should
command the Royalist forces, and that the coalesced

powers should be satisfied with the establishment in France of a *limited* monarchy. The details of this proposition, made to the English Government as a practicable and immediate measure for the restoration of order and peace, will be found under their own date. Lord Grenville took no notice of the proposal.

The months of April, May, and June witnessed the continuous spread of disorder and terror in Paris, as shown in the appointment of the Revolutionary Tribunal for the speedy disposal of suspected persons, the arraignment and acquittal of Marat before that arbitrary court, the organisation of a committee of public safety, the triumph of the Montagnards over their political opponents, the waning power of the Convention subordinated to exterior influences—the insurrectionary manifestations in the streets of the capital (May 31), the final collapse of the Girondists, involving the arrest of twenty-nine of their deputies (June 2), and the rapid ascendency of Robespierre and the reign of terror. Such were the disintegrating forces at work within and around the Tuileries.[1] In La Vendée, Calvados, Brittany, the popular commotion against the Government showed no symptoms of voluntary decline, nor could the rebellion in those localities be suppressed by any available force; whilst further south, as at Lyons, the courage of the Royalists at that critical moment was absolutely irrepressible.

M. De La Colombe, with twelve of his expatriated friends, all eager to return and assist in the restoration of a limited monarchy, as the easiest and surest antidote for the troubles that harassed their country, and hoping against hope for the timely countenance of Great Britain, were still in London; and, realising how

---

[1] On May 10 the Convention, abandoning the Salle de Manège, removed to a spacious hall within the Tuileries for its future sittings.

opportune was the moment for action, sought a second time through the mediation of Mr. Miles to approach and influence the Cabinet. In the memorial signed by La Colombe, July 10, it is maintained that the military interference of the Allies served only to augment the enthusiasm of the French soldiers in the defence 'd'une liberté mal entendue;' and that, in short, ni le rétablissement de la monarchie, ni le retour de l'ordre, ne peuvent s'opérer par la force des armes étrangères. L'intérieur peut seul, par un mouvement bien dirigé, abattre l'anarchie et relever le trône.' It was added that, during the enforced absence of Lafayette, success in the proposed enterprise would be less certain; 'tandis que s'il était libre, si l'on avait cette preuve non équivoque à donner des intentions pacifiques des Puissances, je réponds alors, et sur ma tête, d'opérer dans les Montagnes d'Auvergne—dont lui et moi sommes originaires—les Cévennes, le Vélay, le Gévaudan, et le Languedoc, une diversion telle que bientôt on verrait le Gouvernement reprendre en France une nouvelle force, et les efforts des Anarchistes anéantis pour jamais.' This reiterated proposal was sent to the Treasury without success.

Early in September, Mr. Pitt was informed that 15,000 of the Mountaineers, known to be favourable to limited monarchy, but losing all heart in their cause, would be sent against Lyons. Even after the Convention had rallied its strength in the south, and secured a crushing victory over the Lyonnais and the Royalists in Toulon, Mr. Miles intimated to the Minister (December 16) that La Colombe, instead of embarking for America, would, at his own expense, proceed instantly to Auvergne and engage for an army of 24,000 men assembling and proclaiming the child, or, in case of the death of the young prince, his uncle, Monsieur, as King of France, provided that the combined powers would consent to the limitation of the royal prerogatives. He was 'charged to add that, if such a promise had been made previous to the siege of Lyons, that city would have been saved from destruction.' In despair La Colombe sailed for America. It was, indeed, in this same month of December 1793 that an expedition was sent under Lord Moira to support the Vendéens in their struggle with the Convention, but, before the succour could be made available, the Republican forces under Kléber and Marceau had almost destroyed the Royalist army in the fierce battles of Le Mans and Savenay. The Vendéens failed in their attempt to possess Granville. The arrival of Lord Moira had been deferred too long.[1] At a later period, too late by far, the English Government moved in the same direction. 'It has been determined,' Lord Grenville informed Mr. Wickham, June 8, 1795, 'to collect a pretty large supply of military stores of various kinds and attempt to land this in Brittany, under the escort of about three thousand men, being the whole of the *émigré* corps of different descriptions which are now in England.' The expedition to Quiberon under the command of D'Hervilly and Puisaye, fitted out in British waters and convoyed by British war ships, as were the troops under Moira, was conceived and planned after the opportunity for success had slipped away; and the heterogeneous assembly embarked on that ill-contrived enterprise was annihilated by the Republican battalions under Hoche in the month of July, almost as soon as it landed on the French coast.[2] The costly mission of Mr. Wickham,

---

[1] See *Guerres des Vendéens et des Chouans contre la République française*, tome iv. pp. 279-281. Also Alison's *Hist. of Europe*, iii. 375.

[2] 'Mr. Windham was the man who planned the Quiberon expedition, and Mr. Pitt, against his judgment, acceded to it in order to preserve Mr. Windham.'— Note by Mr. Miles.

designed to promote a counter-revolution at that procrastinated date, was, in like manner, barren of any practical results. About the same time, August 12, Mr. Windham consulted Wickham on the merits of a memorial which an 'ecclesiastic' had presented to him, 'the object of which was to recommend the exciting of an insurrection in the Cevennes.' It is curious to notice that, whereas in 1793 the proposal of La Colombe, which would have placed Lafayette in command of an enthusiastic Royalist army in the southern departments, was not appreciated, the Secretary of State for War in 1795 listened with deference to an analogous suggestion from a clerical *émigré*, and without any guarantee, as it would appear, that the people of the Cévennes, under their altered circumstances, would or could respond to the summons. The attempt made by Austria at this crisis to seduce the French general, Pichegru, from his allegiance to the Republic, and divert his troops towards the restoration of monarchy, whether justifiable or not, failed also as to the main object contemplated. It is true that there was then a reactionary movement among the French in favour of monarchy. But the Republic had already asserted its strength. The Allies had lost their chance. 'It was absolutely indispensable,' as Von Sybel writes, 'if they looked for aid from the internal disturbances in France, to support the opponents of the Convention, and not to allow Lyons and La Vendée to bleed to death unaided.' This remark points to the year 1793. 'But the Courts of Vienna and London, unwilling to connect themselves with any French party, rejected every idea of this kind with perfect indifference; nor did they understand that in this case nothing but an immediate advance upon Paris and the Convention could save them. And thus they gave the enemy time and opportunity to develop an overwhelming force in the midst of the most fearful dangers.'[1] This was the opinion held by Mr. Miles at the time when the effect of the inaction or hesitation of the Government was only too evident.

Appalling events in Paris had marked the closing months of 1793. It is a terrible and painful story. The deposed Queen Marie Antoinette, removed from the Temple to the Conciergerie, August 2, insulted as well as degraded, was driven in a cart to the Place de la Révolution, where, like her unfortunate husband, she expired under the axe of the guillotine, October 16. On the 31st of the same month the twenty-two Deputies from the Gironde, arrested in June, were hurried to the scaffold. M. Roland died by his own hand in despair. Madame Roland, Clavière, and the ex-Mayor, M. Bailly, are included in the death-roll of this period. 'Ainsi, dans cet épouvantable délire qui rendait suspects et le génie, et la vertu, et le courage, tout ce qu'il y avait de plus noble, de plus généreux en France, périssait ou par le suicide ou par le fer des bourreaux.'[2] It was at this delirious moment that the Christian religion was publicly proscribed in France, and the worship of the Goddess of Reason proclaimed and inaugurated (November 10) within the cathedral of Notre Dame.[3] The Duke of

---

[1] Sybel, iii. 137. See *Wickham Correspondence*, i. 82, 125, 105. 'Nor had the Government of England shown any superabundance of sagacity or skill. How deplorably had it neglected to support La Vendée and to make use of Toulon!'—Sybel, iii. 356.

[2] *Histoire de la Révolution française*, par M. A. Thiers, tome v. p. 170.

[3] 'It was observed a short time ago by a revolutionary publicist, in words the terseness of which translation would mar, "La Révolution démolit Dieu, démolit tout le vieux monde, et une chose seule reste— l'évolution scientifique." "Others may occupy themselves, if they will," said M. Paul Bert, " in seeking a nostrum to destroy the phylloxera; be it mine to find

Orléans had already perished, and the death of Le Brun is among the last scenes enacted in this year. 'Dans un moment où le peuple appelle la justice nationale sur la tête de tous les coupables,' exclaimed Billaud-Varennes, Deputy for Paris, 'il est un homme bien criminel que vos décrets n'ont pas encore atteint. Je veux parler de l'ex-ministre Le Brun, de cet homme qui nous a brouillés avec toutes les puissances de l'Europe, de cet homme qui a eu l'impudeur d'appeler Dumouriez un grand homme après sa trahison. Si la Convention avait ouvert les yeux sur les crimes de ce traître, il aurait déjà payé de sa tête toutes ses perfidies.'[1] Le Brun, who concealed himself under the name of Lebrasseur Liégeois in the house of a friend, was discovered by the police, arrested, and brought to the guillotine on December 27. But this sad history need not be pursued here in detail. The Reign of Terror followed swiftly on the ostentatious avowal of atheism, nor could the subsequent decree of the Convention, acknowledging the existence of the Supreme Being and the immortality of the soul, arrest the advancing flood of cruelty and death. All personal liberty was destroyed or suspended. People were brought up to the tribunals and transferred thence direct to the guillotine in batches. Thus disappeared the notable individuals—Hébert (le Père Duchêne), Hérault de Séchelles, Camille Desmoulins, Danton, and, finally, Robespierre, whose miserable death by the hand of the executioner, July 28, 1794, brought this unparalleled tragedy to an end. 'Envisagée en dehors de son caractère grandiose et fatal,' said M. Ernest Renan in his recent address before the Académie Française, 'la

---

one that shall destroy the Christian religion."'—*A Century of Revolution*, by William Samuel Lilly, London, 1889.

[1] *Le Département des Affaires Étrangères pendant la Révolution, 1787-1804*, par Fred. Masson, Bibliothécaire du Ministère, pp. 281-283.

Révolution n'est qu'odieuse et horrible. À la surface, c'est une orgie sans nom. Les hommes, dans cette bataille étrange, valent en proportion de leur laideur. Tout y sert, excepté le bon sens et la modération. Les fous, les incapables, les scélérats y sont attirés par le sentiment instinctif que leur moment d'être utile est venu. Le succès des journées de la Révolution semble obtenu par la collaboration de tous les crimes et de toutes les insanités. Le misérable qui ne sait que tuer a de beaux jours.'[1]

During the years 1794–1799, Mr. Miles maintained his communication with the Continent, receiving through the medium of a variety of sources authentic intelligence from Paris, Dunkirk, and the Hague, also from Vienna, Florence, Naples, Venice, and Madrid. These letters, with scarcely any exception, will now appear in print for the first time. Important intelligence so obtained was conveyed to Mr. Pitt, too often without any useful result, because the Minister was incredulous as to foreign news whenever it was at variance with his hope or expectation. Thus he was advised that Spain was veering round towards France several weeks before he could realise the correctness of the information by the accomplishment of the fact. The correspondence will be found to contain criticisms on the mismanagement and calamities of the war—on the respective characters of Danton and Robespierre, and on the impolicy of the European coalition against the French Republic. Mr. Miles had often forewarned Mr. Pitt, in 1792–1793, of the danger of attempting any such combination of incompatible forces. But the object he kept specially

---

[1] *Discours de M. Ernest Renan, Réception de M. Jules Claretie, élu en remplacement de M. Cuvillier, Supplément au journal 'Le Temps' du 22 Février,* 1889.

in view was the arrest of the war. His natural aversion to the shedding of blood was intense. He insisted that all wars, except for self-protection, were impolitic, indefensible, and criminal. Hence, as the correspondence shows, he sought to bring private influence to bear on Danton and Robespierre, and was sanguine enough to hope that, considering the difficulties with which France was then beset, the Convention might be induced to take the initiative and propose to the British Government overtures in the direction of a general peace. His efforts were not unknown to the Cabinet. The Abbé Noël, Minister Plenipotentiary from the French Republic at Venice, was the medium through which this pacific attempt was hazarded. Later on he is found in direct communication with M. Barthélemy, Minister Plenipotentiary at Bâle. Several letters passed on this occasion. An opening for negotiation seemed probable. In December 1794 Barthélemy replied as follows: 'La Convention est prête à recevoir des propositions pour la paix, pourvu qu'elles soient convenables à la dignité, à la sûreté et aux intérêts de la République française.' It was by the express order of the Convention that the above note was transmitted to Mr. Miles from Bâle, with the understanding that it would be placed under the eyes of the English Government. It was entirely disregarded by Lord Grenville and Mr. Pitt. The laudable hope so warmly cherished was but a momentary illusion. 'In March 1795,' Mr. Miles remarks, 'I received an assurance from a person in power at Paris that I must no longer hope for peace; that France was resolved, under the persuasion that the rancour of this country was inextinguishable, to prosecute the war until Great Britain was crushed, and that she would shut us out from the Elbe and the Mediterranean. The person to whom I allude is the Abbé Sieyès.'[1] The conviction, however, remained that, if the British Cabinet had favourably regarded the conciliatory message sent through M. Barthélemy, peace might have ensued from *immediate* action.[2] The missions of Lord Malmesbury—Paris, October 1796, and Lisle, July–September 1797—did indeed signally fail, as did the mission of Mr. Wickham, for they had been conceived or organised too late for any successful issue. The military power of France was then in the ascendant, and the Directory,[3] elated by the victories of its armies, demanded more from England than could be conceded.

> 'There is a tide in the affairs of men
> Which taken at the flood leads on to fortune:
> Omitted, all the voyage of their lives
> Is bound in shallows and in miseries.'

Mr. Miles now foresaw a protracted struggle disastrous alike to all engaged, and he deplored the enormous sacrifices that would be demanded in life and treasure. His recoil, as it were, from the vision of 'garments rolled in blood,' is conspicuous throughout his writings at this anxious period; and, conscious that he could not serve the cause of humanity or the interests of his country by any further political exertions—dissatisfied and disheartened, he resolved to withdraw from the immediate arena and agitations of public life. His early enthusiastic admiration of Pitt, 1784–1790, was rapidly on the wane. He could place no reliance on the Government. It was suggested that he should

---

[1] MS. note by Mr. Miles.

[2] 'I am certain that, from the disastrous issue of the contest, you must feel regret at having declined the overture to peace which M. Barthélemy transmitted to me *by direction of the Convention* for the purpose of being communicated to you.'—*Miles to Pitt*, May 18, 1797.

[3] The Directory, which superseded the National Convention, was installed. October 27, 1795.

now give support to Fox. But he also distrusted the Opposition. He adhered, therefore, for some time longer to the actual Administration, and, in his intercourse with the admirers of Fox, was careful to justify rather than depreciate Pitt. 'I do not despair of making you a convert to the opinion I have uniformly supported,' he wrote to Sheridan, 'namely, that Mr. Pitt could not have avoided hostilities but on terms at once dangerous and dishonourable. With respect to the *conduct* and lately avowed *object* of the war, the difference in opinion between us, if any, cannot be great.' At the close of the year 1795 he left London, and during the remainder of the century resided at Froyle, near Alton, in Hampshire. It was sheer vexation at the untoward course of events that drove him into the country. 'You are not the only man,' he observed to the member for Bridport, 'that is in possession of my sentiments respecting the King's servants, nor are the King's servants ignorant of the conviction I feel of their incapacity to govern the country, nor of my severe condemnation of the principles they have manifested both in respect to foreign and domestic affairs. The printer of the 'Times' has three or four letters on this subject, much stronger than any you have written to me, in answer to repeated applications that I would come forward with my pen in support of measures proposed by Government. My friends, Erskine and Aust—the latter of whom was displaced to make room for Mr. Canning—and Stephen Rolleston, who is related to Fox, have volumes of my letters explanatory of my resolve to keep aloof at present from politics.'[1]

[1] Letter to Mr. Charles Sturt, February 22, 1798. Mr. Henry Gerard Sturt, grandson of Charles Sturt, was created Lord Alington of Crichel January 15, 1876.

About this time Mr. Miles published as follows:—'An Exculpation

In the spring of 1800 Mr. Miles returned to town, and, resuming his position among literary and political men, showed no abatement of interest in the progress of public affairs. Early in 1801 it was considered possible that corn might be imported from Brabant, and, for this purpose, he was to proceed to Paris to obtain the necessary permission, whilst Mr. Garland, member for Poole, was to undertake the commercial part of the transaction. No objection whatever arose on the part of the Government in Paris. 'I have been assured by Talleyrand,' Lafayette wrote to Mr. Miles, 'that he never conceived, nor did he ever express, an objection to your coming over to France. The Minister told me that M. Otto had his powers to settle passport matters in London, and you will find in him the disposition to which you are so well entitled.' But the enterprise was abandoned from an apprehension that, possibly, the arrival of Mr. Miles in the French capital at this juncture might be interpreted as a tentative mission under the direction of the English Cabinet. The letters will give further particulars. In February of this year Mr. Pitt withdrew temporarily from office, and was succeeded as Prime Minister by Mr. Addington.

It has been stated that Mr. Miles, in 1795, published

of M. de Lafayette from the Charges unjustly advanced and indecently urged against him by Mr. Burke in the House of Commons on March 17, 1794;' 'Letter to the Duke of Grafton;' 'The Author of the Letter to the Duke of Grafton vindicated from the Charges of Democracy,' London, 1794; 'Letter to Earl Stanhope,' London, 1794; 'Letter to the Prince of Wales on a Second Application to Parliament to discharge Debts wantonly contracted since May 1787,' London, 1795 (this publication passed through thirteen editions under the signature of 'Neptune'); 'Letter to Henry Duncombe, Esq., Member for the County of York, on the subject of the very extraordinary Pamphlet lately addressed by Mr. Burke to a noble Lord,' London, 1796; 'A Vindication of M. de Lafayette from the Libellous Aspersions of the Right Honourable Edmund Burke,' London, 1796; and 'Authentic Correspondence with M. Le Brun, the French Minister, and others, to February, 1793,' London, 1796.

a letter addressed to the Prince of Wales on the subject of the debts contracted by his Royal Highness since 1787. The rumour became current that the Minister had suggested this publication. Mr. Rose had already been urgent in pressing for an authoritative denial of the unfounded charge. 'On Mr. Pitt being accused of having employed me to run the Prince down,' Mr. Miles observes, 'I desired Sir John Morshead and Lord Moira to assure the Prince that Mr. Pitt knew nothing of my intention of writing the letter, or of my being the author, until all the world knew it, which was when the eighth edition was on sale.'[1] The discussion terminated as follows:—

Mr. Miles to Lord Moira

May 18, 1801

I beg you to be persuaded that I am fully sensible of your Lordship's great kindness in mentioning to the Prince of Wales the impression under which the letter addressed to him in 1795 was written. I felt it due to my own character to rescue Mr. Pitt from the imputation involved in the slander that he had employed me to degrade the Heir-Apparent in public opinion. Even if the Minister had been disposed to stab the Prince through the agency of the pen, I am the last man in the world to whom he would have hazarded such a proposal. You have already been informed of my motives for writing the letter. You know the impulse under which it was written, and that neither Mr. Pitt nor any one connected with his Administration were apprised, directly or indirectly, of my intentions. My motives were pure, however intemperate my manner may have

---

[1] 'Some very curious anecdotes respecting the Letter addressed to the Prince of Wales will be found among my MS. papers, selected and noted as such.'—MS. note by Mr. Miles.

been, and his Royal Highness has rendered me in this instance the justice I deserve. The gracious message which the Prince has condescended to transmit to me through your Lordship has made an impression on my mind not easily to be effaced; and the assurance that he harbours no unkind feeling on account of the severity of my remarks on his conduct has given an earnest of what may be expected from a mind generous enough to take no offence at well-meant admonition, and to pardon in its own warmth—to use his own expression—the warmth of others.

On October 1, 1801, the preliminaries for the suspension of hostilities between France and England were signed in London, and the definitive treaty of peace, or rather the truce, was completed at Amiens on March 27, 1802. During the negotiation, Mr. Miles forwarded to Lord Hawkesbury some interesting notices connected with the Newfoundland fishery. These papers are produced in their proper place. Among the foreign complications that embarrassed the English Government was the political position of Malta. In the spring of 1802 a deputation of gentlemen arrived in London from the islands of Malta and Gozo, the object being to secure the friendship and assistance of Great Britain. Some interesting details on this question appear under their respective dates. At this period Napoleon Bonaparte, who had overthrown the Directory on the famous day of November 9, 1799—18 Brumaire, an VIII.—and named himself First Consul, had attained a military position dangerous to the liberties of Europe.[1]

Among domestic questions Parliamentary reform

---

[1] On the resumption of hostilities in the summer of 1803, and the difficulties connected with the British retention of Malta, see 'England and Napoleon in 1803; being the Despatches of Lord Whitworth and others,'

continued to agitate the public mind. The following letter explains the position in a few words.

MR. STURT TO MR. MILES

Crichel, Dorset: November 29, 1801

I arrived last night after some days of fatigue and worry, and I mean to return next Tuesday or Wednesday. I am quite safe. To talk of the independence of Parliament is too absurd when we recollect how we are elected. We purchase our seats as you do your beef and mutton. It is lamentable—it is an evil that has brought our calamities upon us. God bless you, my worthy, my honest friend, and may you live to see reform—may you be one of the leading instruments to bring it about, for I am satisfied that the country cannot be saved without it. But the opposition of vested interests will occasion a struggle and delay.

In 1803 Mr. Miles again sought retirement, and for the next three years resided at Brownsea Castle, situate on an island about five miles in circumference near Poole, the property of Mr. Charles Sturt, who, during an absence on the Continent, had placed it at his service. 'I consider myself your deputy,' he wrote to his friend, 'and, as Lord of Brownsea *et Roi de lapins*, I would not exchange this delegated sceptre for the acquired diadem of Bonaparte. He is welcome to his sovereignty; all I covet is that I may be allowed to retain mine and left to enjoy it in repose. So much for the reveries of your Viceroy, which, whether they are sane or insane, are the reveries of an honest man, who loves his country, and prefers peace to war. Would to God that he could in-

---

edited by Oscar Browning, London, 1887, pp. 78, 79, &c. A copy of the Treaty of Amiens will be found in Cobbett's *Political Register*, i. 323.

fuse similar sentiments into the bosoms of all mankind!'
This same year Mr. Sturt was a prisoner of war in France.[1]

Mr. Miles, who had been a widower since May 1792, now married Harriet, daughter of Mr. Watkinson, solicitor, Bristol; her mother being a first cousin, on the maternal side, of Hannah More. She was educated at the establishment of the Misses Mills, Park Street, Bristol. It may be remembered that Selina Mills married Zachary Macaulay, and became the mother of the future Lord Macaulay.

In April 1804, Mr. Pitt received his Majesty's commands to form a new Administration. During this year Mr. Miles published 'A Letter to the Earl of Wycombe on the present state of Ireland,' in which were advocated religious toleration, impartiality in the execution of the laws as applied to the Irish people, and that 'the Catholic laity should be released from the offensive and intolerable burden of supporting two churches.' Mr. Erskine, in acknowledging the receipt of this pamphlet, wrote: 'Your subject is deeply interesting, and you have treated it with your usual ability, and with the most obvious good intention. Alas, poor Ireland! I see nothing good approaching her. Mr. Pitt has given himself up unconditionally, I suppose, to the King, and his Majesty's opinions militate against the only redress for that unhappy country.' The tranquil life at Brownsea was brought to a close by the death of Mr. Pitt, January 23, 1806. In the previous year Mr. Addington had been raised to the peerage as Viscount Sidmouth.

[1] Mr. Talbot, writing to Lord Whitworth, May 30, 1803, in allusion to his own arrest at St. Denis, says: 'The same soldier conducted Mr. Charles Sturt as a prisoner, whom, he informed me on his return, he had deposited in the Temple.'—*Whitworth Despatches*, London, 1887. In 1806 Mr. Miles appealed to the Foreign Office, Paris, for the release of Mr. Sturt on parole.

The preceding pages have shown that Mr. Miles, who, through the medium of the press, had warmly supported Mr. Pitt from 1784 to 1793, held, from 1793 to 1806, an opinion adverse to the administrative genius of the Minister. 'The tide on which Mr. Pitt's fortunes were embarked,' he wrote in 1796, ' flowed rapidly and triumphantly. It was, indeed, a most full and glorious sea; and, if he had taken the current as it served, he would have saved his ventures; but, harassed and assailed by faction at home, and little versed in foreign politics, he was compelled to follow as he was led in all matters that related to the latter, while his whole strength, vigour, and attention were necessarily engaged to defend his wise and beneficent measures of domestic polity from the artful attacks of his angry and disappointed opponents. But for the fatal troubles that broke out in France, and shook the repose of nations, Mr. Pitt would have continued the idol of his country and the admiration of the world; but his inexperience, or rather his ignorance of the Continent and its people, rendered it an easy matter to impose upon his understanding and mislead his judgment.'[1] Mr. Miles insisted that, although the Convention and the Executive Power in Paris were alone responsible for the course of events which, subsequent to August 10, 1792, led to the declaration of war against England, February 1, 1793, the Cabinet of St. James—if it had only discerned the imminent peril

[1] *Authentic Correspondence with Le Brun, &c.*, p. 130. 'And now came the French Revolution. This was a new event; the old routine of reasoning, the common trade of politics, were to become obsolete. Mr. Pitt appeared wholly unprepared for it; half favouring, half condemning, ignorant of what he favoured and why he condemned, he neither displayed the honest enthusiasm and fixed principle of Mr. Fox nor the intimate acquaintance with the general nature of man, and the consequent prescience of Mr. Burke.'—*Essays on his own Times*, by Samuel Taylor Coleridge, London, 1850, ii. 325.

of the situation—might, in 1790–1791, have so far controlled the French Revolution as to have prevented the outbreak of hostilities everywhere in Europe; and he attributed the disregard for an amicable policy to the intense passion for political power that was wont to overrule the better judgment and the peaceful aspirations of Mr. Pitt. 'I call to mind,' he observed to Lord Lansdowne, 'the peals I incessantly rang in the Minister's ears from 1790 to 1793. I foresaw and forewarned him in all my correspondence with him from Paris what the result would be of a war with France. Events have verified my predictions. But Mr. Pitt preferred war, or rather, on being required in 1791 to war with France or resign, he preferred to retain his place, and thereby sacrificed his own opinion.'[1] Two years later the above statement, as communicated in a private letter, was reiterated through a public channel: 'I speak from a perfect knowledge of the circumstance; and, as those who had a share in giving that mischievous advice, and those who were concerned in communicating to the Minister the alternative of war with France or resignation, are yet in existence, I dare them to deny the fact. At the period when it was intimated to Mr. Pitt that he must war with France or resign, the French Revolution was in its cradle; it had scarcely peeped over the boulevards at Paris; and Mirabeau, the ablest of its leaders, the most likely to look beyond the Rhine, the Channel, or the Pyrenees, and whose mind was as comprehensive as it was enterprising, was decidedly for

---

[1] Letter from Mr. Miles to the Marquis of Lansdowne, dated Brownsea, January 3, 1806. 'Mr. Pitt preferred flinging his country into a contest, which he and his great antagonist by uniting their forces might have prevented; but then he must also have shared with Mr. Fox the power which he was determined to enjoy alone and supreme.'—Brougham's *Statesmen of George III.*, quoted by Cobden in his *Three Letters.*

preserving, if I may use the diplomatic jargon of Lord Grenville, *the relations of peace and amity.* As Mirabeau swayed public opinion in France and was hailed for the moment as one of her deliverers, he aimed, and I speak from a knowledge of the fact, being then on the spot, and in the habit of daily intercourse with him, to preserve peace, and to avoid everything, even in public debate, that might give offence to foreign powers. Consequently the intimation to war or resign was made to Mr. Pitt before any umbrage could possibly have been given to our Government.'[1]

The new Cabinet[2] had not been long settled before Lord Moira proposed to Mr. Fox that, from the grave importance attached to the critical situation of the Ionian Islands, Mr. Miles should be sent as Consul-General to Corfu. This occurred on his arrival in town from Brownsea in May 1806. Such an arrangement was considered opportune for his immediate return to public employment. The illness of Mr. Fox, however, retarded the efforts of Lord Moira, and, on the decease of the

---

[1] *Letter to his Royal Highness the Prince of Wales,* by W. A. Miles, London, 1808, p. 132. 'In 1791, Mr. Pitt received a message from the King by Lord Hawkesbury that he must war with France or resign, and Lord Moira was actually sent for express to town in order to be at the head of a new Administration had Mr. Pitt resigned.'—MS. note by Mr. Miles. See Letter from Miles to Sturt, December 8, 1795.

[2] The Cabinet, known as 'All Talents,' was composed as follows:

Lord Erskine	Lord Chancellor.
Earl Fitzwilliam	President of the Council.
Viscount Sidmouth	Lord Privy Seal.
Lord Grenville	First Lord of the Treasury.
Lord Howick	First Lord of the Admiralty.
Earl Moira	Master-General of the Ordnance.
Earl Spencer	Secretary of State for Home Affairs.
Mr. Fox	Secretary of State for Foreign Affairs.
Mr. Windham	Secretary at War.
Lord Henry Petty	Chancellor of the Exchequer.
Lord Ellenborough	Chief Justice, with a seat in the Cabinet.

—*Annual Register,* 1806.

Minister for Foreign Affairs, September 13, less than eight months after the death of Pitt, the appointment to Corfu was abandoned.

On November 28, Mr. Miles wrote the following minute: 'I am just returned from a conference with Lord Moira. An infatuation as deplorable as it is incomprehensible yet pervades our Councils. A proposition was made to me so very impracticable that I now almost despair of our country being rescued from its difficulties. We yet look for salvation from the Continent. What could not be accomplished by immense and well-appointed armies of kingdoms we vainly expect may be produced by miserable insurrections in small provinces kept in subjection by well-disciplined garrisons in towns strongly fortified. We think France is drained of men. I told Lord Moira that he was mistaken. And I conjured him to be assured that no insurrection of any avail to Europe could possibly take place in Liège or Brabant, unless, indeed, Holland would set an example and be enabled to expel Bonaparte, or that a general revolt in France, fatigued by perpetual war, should be brought about. Measures might have been taken during the short interval of peace. We ill employed that interval. We have been as lavish of our time as of our means, and I am afraid that the opportunity of doing anything on the Continent is lost. Advice was thrown away upon Lord Hawkesbury, who then held the foreign seals. He still remembers the severity with which I had arraigned and reprobated the pernicious influence of his father behind the throne. I declined the mission proposed to me this day by Lord Moira. He desired to see me on Tuesday, saying that he would ask Mr. Windham to place me where I could be useful to my country. Knowing what I know, and seeing what I see, I am not very desirous of being employed, and, if I were, common sense would forbid my being sanguine. These men have not the special talent necessary to save the country at the point she has now reached.'

Not a week seems to have passed without some contribution from his pen appearing in the London newspapers, either as leading articles or as correspondence, under the signatures of 'Hampden,' 'Coponius,' 'Regulus,' 'Obadiah,' 'Tiberius Gracchus,' 'Civis,' 'Amicus Justiciæ,' &c. The 'Independent Whig,' whose columns in some instances are almost entirely filled with his writings, reproduced at this time the 'Letters addressed by "Neptune" to the House of Commons on Parliamentary Reform,' which he first published through the 'Morning Post' in 1785.[1] A series of letters appear from the same hand on the Westminster election, in favour of Sir Francis Burdett. The 'Statesman' also shows the activity of his pen during the early years of this century. Nor was he less occupied in his private correspondence with influential men. Many letters passed at this time between Lord Moira and himself on foreign politics—as, for example, on the affairs of Sweden and Denmark, including the bombardment of Copenhagen—and on the intentions and progress of Bonaparte. Either through the one channel or the other, the mismanagement, as he thought, of public affairs was often minutely criticised.

On the formation of the Cabinet, March 1807, in

[1] 'In consequence of the letters of "Neptune," which we have republished in our paper, and the manner in which we have been induced to speak of Mr. Miles, who is well known to have been the author of them, from the respect that we cannot but feel for a gentleman who has so ably distinguished himself, it has been very currently reported, during the last week, that Mr. Miles has some connection with this paper. We notice the report only to give it the most flat contradiction.'—*The Independent Whig*, May 17. 1806.

which Mr. Canning held the seals of the Foreign Office, the 'Independent Whig' gave the following announcement: 'We hear that Mr. Miles has arrived in town to be sent on an important foreign mission to the Continent. We wish it may be so, for we believe him to be very capable; but we rather suspect it is for the purpose of supporting with his powerful pen the pretensions of the present junto to the situation they have wriggled themselves into by intrigue. Estimating as we do the talents and manly conduct which Mr. Miles has in all his publications displayed, we should be sorry to see him fall in public opinion, and forfeit the character he has long since established in the world as an honest and independent man—a friend to his country and to liberty—by his upholding an unprincipled faction.' The suspicions of the editor of this journal were ill founded. Mr. Miles, who through the whole of his political career had declined to be bound by party ties or to be associated with intrigues, would have accepted, as a harbinger of peace, a mission on the Continent from Canning as readily as from Fox, provided only that its object was to terminate hostilities; but in other respects his 'powerful pen' was directed rather against than in favour of the Administration then recently constituted. The efforts of Lord Moira to have him employed on the Continent were indefatigable. The question was submitted to the Prince of Wales, and soon afterwards it was arranged that his Royal Highness would receive Mr. Miles at a private audience.

Lord Moira to Mr. Miles

July 3, 1807

If you will have the goodness to meet me at Carlton House a little before one to-morrow, I shall have the pleasure of presenting you to the Prince, and in the meantime have the honour to remain, &c.

It was the expectation that he would be sent in a public character to initiate on the Continent dispositions favourable to peace that had brought Mr. Miles to the metropolis; his occupation as a political contributor to the public journals was mere pastime; but the difficulties in the way seem to have been insurmountable so long as the Administration then in office existed. In 1808 he published 'A Letter to his Royal Highness the Prince of Wales, with a Sketch of the Prospect before him'—a pamphlet of 264 pages, in which the policy of England from 1791 is considered at some length.

Towards the close of 1810 the mental trouble that had afflicted the King in 1788 returned, and the Minister, Mr. Perceval, brought the embarrassing circumstance under the consideration of Parliament. In January 1811 a bill was passed assigning to the Prince of Wales the title of Prince Regent, who, as soon as the necessary formalities were completed (February 6), assumed the functions of the sovereign. It was at once anticipated that, as the Prince had associated himself with the Whig party, the Tories would be replaced by a new Administration. On the contrary, Mr. Perceval was retained in power. The Opposition, disappointed at the apparent slight of Lord Moira, manifested considerable trouble and displeasure, especially those members of the party who were expecting to benefit by the overthrow of the Ministry. About the same time, Lord Wellesley resigned his office as Secretary of State for Foreign Affairs, being dissatisfied with the want of energy or the hesitation shown by the Perceval Cabinet in the conduct of the Peninsular war. He was succeeded by Lord Castlereagh. The question of the political emancipation of Catholics was also now being agitated. On May 11, 1812, Mr. Perceval was assassinated in the lobby of the House of Commons—shot through the heart by a man named Bellingham, and soon afterwards expired. The death of Perceval was followed by some embarrassment. Lord Wellesley failed in his attempt to form a Cabinet. The Regent then empowered Lord Moira to reconstitute the Whig Ministry. But, as the result of certain disputes, it was finally arranged that Lord Liverpool should be First Lord of the Treasury, whilst Lord Castlereagh resumed his post at the Foreign Office. Lord Moira was appointed Governor-General of India. This brief notice of the unsettled state of public affairs will be sufficient to explain certain events as unfolded in the correspondence now published.

Mr. Miles abandoned the long-cherished hope that he would be sent to the Continent on a pacific mission, a hope which would have been realised if Lord Moira had returned to political power. Public employment under Lord Liverpool was so entirely out of the question, that he retired finally to Hythe, a secluded spot on the margin of the Southampton Water, and not far from the borders of the New Forest. There his family had already resided during the last few years. He maintained as active a correspondence as ever on the momentous events of the day; Whitbread, Waithman, and Wood being now prominent among the politicians whom he knew and esteemed.[1] The personal

[1] Mr. Samuel Whitbread, M.P. for Bedford; Mr. Robert Waithman, Alderman, and M.P. for the City of London in 1819; and Sir Matthew Wood, Lord Mayor of London in 1815 and 1816, and M.P. for the City in 1817.

friendship of Lord Moira, as appears from the following
letters, was now directed towards the private interests
of Mr. Miles as the only channel left through which he
could manifest his regard.

LORD MOIRA TO MR. MILES

London: December 28, 1812

I have applied to the India Directors in favour of
your eldest son. Whether I can get a writership for
him is very doubtful. But apprize me, in case I should
find it in my power, if you would like it for him. I do
not give up hopes of getting you employed.

Ministers have really deluded themselves to such a
degree with the notion that Bonaparte's army was
annihilated, and himself devoid of all chance to escape,
as to have thought it superfluous to take any ulterior
measures. I believe they now suspect that their
utmost activity will be requisite to provide against the
probable renovation of his strength.

LORD MOIRA TO MR. MILES

March 31, 1813

It gives me much pleasure to tell you that your
son's appointment is announced to me from the Court
of Directors, so that you may now take what steps you
please respecting him. The state of the crew of the
'Stirling Castle' must delay me still two or three days
in town. This prolongation of time will not be inconvenient to persons employed in making arrangements
for me, but it is really most uncomfortable for myself
to be detained here in the present condition of affairs.

Mr. Miles wrote to Lord Moira in warm acknowledgment of his friendship, and accepted for his eldest son the nomination to Haileybury College, as the preparatory step for the Civil Service in India. His attachment to the new Governor-General—better known at a later date as the Marquis of Hastings—continued until his death undiminished. They met for the last time when his Excellency embarked for Calcutta.

Mr. Miles to his Wife

Portsmouth: April 4, 1813

I have seen Lord Moira. Lady Loudoun[1] arrives to-morrow evening, and I shall look out for her Ladyship at Gosport. I was asked by Sir Home Popham to meet his Excellency at dinner last evening, but being previously engaged to Craven I was unable to accept the invitation. As soon, however, as I landed at Point, I posted to Government House, and, instead of walking in *sans cérémonie*, as usual, I desired the servant to announce me. Lord Moira got up instantly, and seemed, by his affectionate greeting, as glad to see me as I was to see him. Indeed, I am most sincerely attached to him. He invited me to breakfast with him to-morrow at the 'Crown,' and unless his Lordship wishes me to stay till he sails I will be with you on Monday evening. *Saturday.*—I am just returned from Lord Moira, who, on my taking leave of him, expressed a wish to see me on board the 'Stirling Castle.' I have, therefore, consented to stay till Tuesday. He was very kind, and at parting desired me to send William out to him as soon as I could. I could scarcely refrain from tears, although his staff was present. I told his Lordship that his going was like a dream, and that I could

---

[1] In 1804 the Earl of Moira married Flora Muir Campbell, Countess of Loudoun in her own right.

scarcely credit my senses. He assured me it was precisely the same with him. The Cravens are angry with me for not having brought you to Portsmouth, and I beg you will not in future get me into these kind of scrapes by staying at home.

The flood tide in the reign of Napoleon had already turned. His retreat from Moscow in 1812 had been most disastrous, whilst the war in the Peninsula had discomfited his plans nearer home. Battle after battle failed to restore his ascendency. On March 31, 1814, the Allies, with the sovereigns of Russia and Prussia at their head, entered Paris. The dynasty of the Bourbons was restored in the person of Louis XVIII. Soult could no longer arrest the advance of Wellington into French territory; and Napoleon, unable to resist the shock of adversity, signed at Fontainebleau, April 11, his abdication of the throne, and was conveyed on board the 'Undaunted,' an English frigate, to the island of Elba, as his future residence. Peace was thus apparently secured, to the joy of all Europe.[1] Mr. Miles now communicated to the Marquis de Lafayette and M. Reinhard his intention to revisit Paris. Reinhard, it will be remembered, was Secretary of the French Legation in London at the period of the outbreak of hostilities. It is interesting to observe how mutual esteem had remained undiminished throughout the twenty years of conflict between the two nations.

[1] 'Not having the gift of prescience, I could not foresee that the powers of Europe, having lost their character and almost their authority in 1803, would redeem the one and recover the other in 1814. The change in the fortunes of Europe is almost as miraculous as it is brilliant.'—MS. note by Mr. Miles.

Monsieur Reinhard to Mr. Miles

Paris : ce 6 Août, 1814.

J'ai été très agréablement surpris par la lettre que vous m'avés fait l'honneur de m'écrire, et par la perspective que vous m'offrés du plaisir que j'aurai de vous revoir. Soyés bien sûr que je n'ai jamais oublié l'obligeance que vous m'avés montrée à Londres, et les preuves que vous m'avés données de votre bienveillant souvenir, et je m'estimerai vraiment heureux de trouver des occasions pour vous prouver ma reconnaissance et mon amitié.

Pour répondre immédiatement aux questions et aux démarches concernant votre projet de débarquement au Hâvre, j'aurai l'honneur de vous dire que je n'y connais à la vérité personne, mais que j'écrirai à M. le Comte de Girardin, Préfet à Rouen, dès que j'aurai été informé de votre résolution définitive; que pour le passeport et la faculté de vous rendre à Paris, il n'y aura aucune démarche à faire ici, et que rien ne s'opposera au Hâvre à ce que vous continuiés votre voyage; que si vous vouliés passer quelques jours au Hâvre, ou si vous éprouviés le moindre retard, vous n'auriés qu'à vous adresser à M. le Sous-Préfet, auquel je prierai M. de Girardin de parler de votre arrivée; que, quant à vos effets, le mieux sera, dans le cas où au Hâvre l'on vous ferait la moindre difficulté, ce que je ne crois pas, de les y faire plomber pour leur expédition au dépôt général des douanes à Paris, et que là il me sera aisé d'obtenir pour eux la franchise que vous desirés. Il est entendu que ce qui se trouvera dans votre voiture ou sera nécessaire à votre usage immédiat, restera à votre disposition probablement sans visite.

Je ne manquerai pas de vous rappeler au souvenir de M. le Prince de Benevento,[1] qui, aimable pour tous, l'est surtout pour les Anglais, et pour les hommes de votre mérite. Quant à M. le Duc de Bassano, il est à la campagne, et son règne est fini.

Je vous ai dit que pour écrire à M. de Girardin j'attendais une seconde lettre de vous; cependant, comme vous fixés au mois courant l'époque de votre arrivée au Hâvre, et qu'avant tout je désire que vous ne changiés ni ne retardiés votre résolution, je pense qu'il vaut mieux lui écrire immédiatement. J'attens, Monsieur, avec impatience de vos nouvelles ultérieures. Ne doutés pas, je vous prie, de l'extrême plaisir que j'aurai à vous revoir, et à vous renouveler l'impression de tous les sentimens d'estime et de reconnaissance par lesquels je vous suis attaché.[2]

Europe was again thrown into excitement by the probability of renewed war. Napoleon, having escaped from Elba, landed at Cannes, March 1, 1815, and, rallying the army to his standard amidst the cries of 'Vive l'Empereur!' arrived in Paris on the 20th day of that

[1] Talleyrand.
[2] 'It has been erroneously inserted in some of our public prints that Baron Reinhard, who was at the head of the Foreign Department in France under Prince Talleyrand, had attached himself to the fortunes of Bonaparte, and that, having engaged in some mission, he had been arrested at Frankfort by the allied troops. It may be stated on unquestionable authority that he resigned his official situation immediately on the return of Bonaparte, and quitted Paris to retire on his estate near Dusseldorf, resolved to pass the remainder of his days in that seclusion which is congenial to his habits and disposition. It was in this retreat that he received a pressing invitation from Bonaparte to enter into his service. An answer in the negative was instantly returned, and, being intercepted by the Prussians, a different construction was given to it, and he was arrested and conducted to Mayence. His papers were seized and sent to Vienna; but, as they were all perfectly innocent, there is no doubt but that he will soon be released.'—MS. note by Mr. Miles.

month. At the same date, Louis XVIII. fled from the metropolis for refuge in Ghent. Events unfolded themselves with rapidity. Napoleon encountered Blücher at Ligny, June 16, when the Prussians were compelled for the moment to retire; Wellington held his position at Quatre Bras during a fearful struggle with Marshal Ney; and, finally, Napoleon, vanquished on the field of Waterloo, June 18, accomplished a precipitate retreat upon Paris. He signed his abdication at the Elysée. The Allies, under Wellington and Blücher, entered Paris, July 7, and next day Louis XVIII. returned to his capital and re-established the monarchy. Napoleon had been proclaimed Emperor in 1804; hence the republic, dating from 1792, had endured for only twelve years. The anxious interval between March 13 and June 22 is known as the *Cent Jours*, or Hundred Days.[1]

Mr. Miles embarked with his family at Southampton, April 23, 1816, and crossed to Havre *en route* to Paris, where he expected to be well furnished with authentic materials for his contemplated history of the French Revolution. Soon after their arrival, they passed a month at the Château Lagrange, where, as the guests of Lafayette and his daughters, Madame de Maubourg and Madame de Lasteyrie, they received the most affectionate attentions.[2] Madame de Lafayette had died, December 25, 1807, from an illness aggravated by the cruel imprisonment of her husband at Olmütz. Towards the close of an active public life, extending from 1780 to 1815, vexed and disappointed as to his early and ingenuous estimate of public men, he resolved on absolute retirement during his temporary absence from England.

---

[1] Or, according to others, dating from the arrival of Napoleon in Paris, March 20, to his departure on June 29.

[2] Lagrange-Bleneau, département de Seine-et-Marne.

'I feel no inconvenience in leading an isolated life in Paris,' he wrote to Lafayette, August 18, 1816; 'I have wished to be near you, and to have some friend to whom I may unburden my mind on public affairs when overcharged with anxiety, *qui arrive assez souvent*; but, as to going out to parties, I shall refuse all invitations. Yet I love mankind, and my manners to all prove that I take an interest in their happiness. Such men as Humboldt[1] and yourself are worth seeking; their acquaintance is desirable, and their friendship invaluable. It is in this manner that I estimate mankind, not by their acres, for wealth and authority, independent of intellect and integrity, furnish no passport to my heart, and I would rather pass my life in one of the cottages near your vineyard, with such men as Washington and Franklin, than luxuriate in a palace where these higher mental and moral qualities are disregarded. I avail myself, dear General, of the departure of M. de Lasteyrie for Lagrange to send you a pacquet of correspondence, which will prove to you how firmly I am attached to those principles which have so long endeared you to me. Read them at your leisure.'

Notwithstanding his desire for rest, Mr. Miles kept up a vigorous correspondence with his political friends at home. The agitation in England on the subject of Parliamentary reform, which he had persistently urged through the press for several years, and the retrospect of the sufferings and loss of life occasioned by the war, dominated his thoughts to the end. Health already broken now rapidly failed. A few more letters—and these written from his bed to attached friends, among whom were Sir Matthew Wood, Lord Mayor of London,

---

[1] Humboldt was on a visit at Lagrange at the same time with Mr. Miles.

and Sir Robert Liston, Ambassador at Constantinople—and all was over. Mr. Miles expired, April 23, 1817, after a short illness, at the age of sixty-three. He was interred in the cemetery of Père la Chaise. Among the mourners were the Marquis de Lafayette and his son, M. George Lafayette. The bereaved family soon afterwards returned to England. His widow, who survived him for fifty-five years, departed this life February 27, 1872, aged ninety, at Monkwearmouth Vicarage, Sunderland.[1]

This review of the political life of Mr. Miles demands a brief allusion to a curious statement published in recent years. Mr. George Rose, the intimate friend of Mr. Pitt, is reported to have received from 'a Parliamentary supporter' information that 'a conspiracy against the Church' was already organised in 1807. 'The conspirators,' says the Rev. Leveson Vernon Harcourt, 'were Mr. Miles and Lord Wycombe, afterwards Lord Lansdowne. The former begged the latter to inquire what was the value of the Deanery of Durham and its prebends, and how many there were.' Reference is next made to the desire of Mr. Miles to see tithes abolished. 'This rapid excursion to the contemplated ruin of the Established Church indicates a mind very much in harmony with the prediction of Talleyrand, that Christianity would go into the grave without a struggle, . . . but the Power above, which never entered into his thoughts, and the religious principle which he ignored, have defeated all his speculations, and saved the

---

[1] At the same vicarage, March 21, 1880, died Mrs. Collison, the mother-in-law of the editor of these volumes, at the age of ninety-four. Her father, Captain Portlock, R.N., was with Captain Cook, at Owhyhee, when the latter was killed by the natives, February 14, 1779, and was the officer chosen to take home the despatch announcing to Government the untimely death of the celebrated navigator.

Church of England under the control of a superintending Providence.'[1] The inferences here drawn are absolutely inaccurate. In 1795 Mr. Miles published 'An Address to the Bishops on the Danger to be apprehended to our Ecclesiastical Establishments from the Profligate Example of some of the Non-Resident Parochial Clergy, and the Necessity of Ordering every Incumbent to reside on his Living, and to act in conformity with his Station.' It is probable that the very title of this pamphlet may have given offence, at the close of the last century, in certain quarters. In 1804 he wrote as follows: 'I profess myself to be the decided friend of religion; it is man's best consolation in this world, and fairest hope in the next: but it must be religion; it must neither be the semblance, nor the mockery of it; it must not be statecraft on one side, nor bigotry or fanaticism on the other.' His contention against tithes arose, not from any objection inherent in the principle of tithes, but from the conviction that, *as the law then stood*, they were injurious to religion, and that, with respect to Ireland, the enforcement of them was detrimental to the common weal. 'Any measure,' he observed, 'that tends to do away this fatal, this ruinous cause of perpetual misunderstanding and warfare between clergy and laity will not only tend to the improvement of the landed interest, but benefit morals and fortify religion—the great object of which I conceive to be to make bad men good and good men better.'[2] These sentiments publicly recorded do not indicate a mind void of religious thought. 'The objection that has been made to tithes,'

---

[1] *The Diaries and Correspondence of the Right Hon. George Rose*, &c., edited by the Rev. Leveson Vernon Harcourt, London, 1860, ii. 309.

[2] *A Letter to the Earl of Wycombe on the Present State of Ireland*, by W. A. Miles, London, 1804, pp. 52, 67.

Mr. Miles observed to Lord Stanhope, 'does not in fact proceed from a wish to ease the industrious farmer of what seditious and interested men would persuade him is a burthen, but from a rancorous and criminal hatred to all ecclesiastical establishments whatever. The Dissenters are a numerous, learned, and certainly a very respectable body of men; but they do not perceive that they are in danger of being made the tools and instruments of faction. The abolition of episcopacy would be followed by the subversion of presbytery in Scotland and of toleration in England. It is not the mitre and crozier that these modern reformers would demolish. It is faith and good morals that they wish to extirpate. Their aim is the general ruin and extinction of all religion; and the Dissenters, for aiding them in this diabolical enterprise, will only have the miserable consolation of being the last sacrificed.'[1]

[1] *A Letter to Earl Stanhope*, by W. A. Miles, London, 1794, p. 23.

CORRESPONDENCE

MR. MILES TO THE DUKE OF LEEDS[1]

Franckfort: July 12, 1789

The most perfect tranquillity reigns in this part of Europe, and, but for the ill state of the Emperor's health and the fermentation in France which is rapidly approaching a crisis, the politicians in Franckfort would have no topic for conversation. Count Romanzow's brother, who desired to know whether it was not practicable to secure some of the members of the House of Commons,[2] in the interest of his sovereign, has left this place with an intention to visit London. He has already been in England, and, as he will possibly open himself with the same freedom to your Grace as he has done to me, you will be able to discover whether his journey is on pleasure or business. I have it in contemplation to go and pay my respects to the Elector of Mayence, who is at his Château at Aschaffenburg, and from thence to Deux Ponts, accompanied by General de Wimpffen.[3] Should this project be realised, I shall not fail to give you an account of my reception.

[1] The letters to the Duke of Leeds in this series are selections from Official Despatches addressed to his Grace as Secretary of State for Foreign Affairs.
[2] See Introduction, p. 35.
[3] 'The Baron de Wimpffen, a General in the French army, and whose

MR. MILES TO THE DUKE OF LEEDS

Franckfort : July 30, 1789

A private letter from Basle mentions that Monsieur Necker, accompanied by his wife and daughter, passed through that place on his return to Paris at half-past seven last Saturday morning. *C'est un charlatan enivré qui va se perdre dans une Révolution dont il ne peut pas voir les suites.* Marshal de Broglio is at Hesse-Darmstadt. The Count d'Artois is expected every moment at the Hôtel de l'Empereur in this town. That the Count should have taken this route occasions much speculation, and equally so that Marshal de Broglio should be in the neighbourhood. Monsieur de Francks, the first banker in Strasburg, was obliged to seek safety in flight from the fury of the populace, and is here with his wife. It is conjectured that the Count d'Artois and the late Commander-in-Chief are sent to negotiate for foreign troops to support the tottering throne of his Most Christian Majesty. All France seems convulsed, and is likely to convulse all Europe, for the

younger brother, Felix, is one of the Deputies for Caen. No man has seen more vicissitudes than Wimpffen. Born in Alsace, he entered at an early age into the service of France, whence he passed by the King's consent into that of the Duke of Württemberg for the purpose of serving as a spy for the Court of Versailles. The Duke sent him to Madrid to arrange a treaty with Spain. He returned by London to Germany, settled at Stuttgart, had a regiment given to him which bore his name—made a fortune, lost it by his extravagance, and forfeited his regiment by imprudence. He endeavoured to attach himself to the Emperor, and to the late King of Prussia; went to Warsaw, was sent on an Embassy to Constantinople, lived afterwards by his industry. In 1787-1790 he wanted bread to eat. A personal quarrel with M. Necker last November occasioned his being ordered to quit Paris, and he complains bitterly of the ingratitude of the French Government. In 1791 he was sent by the National Assembly to command at Colmar, and was allowed 20,000 livres a year. Felix Wimpffen distinguished himself by his heroic and successful defence of Thionville in 1792.'— W. A. M.

panic has extended beyond Paris and Versailles, and has already passed the frontiers on every side. It is my duty to watch the progress of this Revolution, and no efforts on my part shall be wanting to procure for your Grace full intelligence of an event so great and so unexpected, an event which cannot fail to exercise a very serious effect on the general system of European politics, and to become either a calamity or a blessing to this quarter of the world.[1]

MR. MILES TO THE DUKE OF LEEDS

Franckfort: August 1, 1789

You may judge of the impression which the recent Revolution in France has made in this town when every carriage that arrives from the Limburg side of the country is supposed to contain fugitives from Paris or Versailles. It was last night reported that the Queen of France had arrived; on inquiry I found it to be the Countess de Kinsky, on her road to Vienna. The tumult at Würtzburg among the blacksmiths has been suppressed without bloodshed. Three battalions of the Regiment of Bender descend the Rhine on their way to the Austrian Low Countries. It is still asserted that Marshal de Broglio is at Hesse-Darmstadt. Messrs. Neufville, the bankers here, have received directions to

---

[1] 'News at the *table d'hôte* at Colmar curious. There was a little coterie in one corner listening to an officer's detail of leaving Paris; that the Count d'Artois, and all the princes of the blood, except Monsieur and the Duc d'Orléans, the whole connection of Polignac, the Maréchal de Broglio, and an infinite number of the first nobility had fled the kingdom, and were daily followed by others; and lastly, that the King, Queen, and Royal Family, were in a situation at Versailles really dangerous and alarming, without any dependence on the troops near them, and, in fact, more like prisoners than free.'—*Travels of Arthur Young*, London, 1792, pp. 142–144.

supply the Count d'Artois with money. He has not yet arrived—and it is now Saturday morning—but he will be here this day. It is asserted that a coronation will take place in spring.

Mr. Miles to the Duke of Leeds

Franckfort: August 6, 1789

Letters from Basle mention that a mob consisting of 1,000 persons had assembled and destroyed several buildings in the neighbourhood. Prince George of Hesse-Darmstadt has arrived at Hesse-Darmstadt from Paris, whence he escaped, disguised, and travelled a considerable part of the road on foot. The Prince of Württemberg left this yesterday for Mayence; he also came from Paris, and owes his escape to the great presence of mind of his porter, who, on being questioned by the mob as to whether any German princes were lodged in the hotel, answered in the affirmative, but added that they had changed their apartments the night before. His Highness with great difficulty obtained a passport. A stranger of rank arrived here at the Maison Rouge two days since, and keeps constantly in his room. The master of the house and his servants are forbid to enter his apartment. His domestic alone serves him. The Regiment of Bender does not embark before the 10th instant. M. Neufville has received an order to pay the Count d'Artois 400,000 livres. It is said he is at Namur. Madame de Polignac was at Basle. Franckfort is not judged to be an asylum for the fugitives, as it is said the magistrates would deliver them up on the first requisition. Marshal de Broglio is not at Darmstadt. The gazettes say he is at Verdun, where he is besieged. It is the Prince de Conti who is at the Maison Rouge.

Mr. Miles to the Duke of Leeds

Franckfort: August 11, 1789

The Regency at Freyberg has opposed the departure of the Regiment of Bender. The Governor declared he must obey the orders of the Emperor. An express was immediately sent to Vienna requesting the regiment might remain—or at least a battalion—to overawe the rabble who had already committed several depredations in that neighbourhood. The peasants in the Bishopric of Spires drive back the French who seek refuge there. The Duke of Württemberg has sent troops to quell a disturbance at Montbéliard, whence the insurgents had compelled the Prince, brother of the Duke de Württemberg, to escape for his life. I am this instant informed all is quiet again. The gazettes mention that the Count d'Artois and the Prince de Condé passed through Mayence last Monday on their way to Mannheim. Your Grace must have long since heard of the terrible revolt at Strasburg from which Prince Maximilian of Deux-Ponts has been obliged to fly. The Princess of Deux-Ponts is at Hesse-Darmstadt, but the Prince Maximilian, her husband, has returned to Strasburg and peace is restored. The Landgrave of Hesse-Cassel is expected at Wilhelmsbadt on the 23rd instant.

Mr. Miles to the Duke of Leeds

Franckfort: August 17, 1789

A private letter from Vienna mentions a victory obtained by the Prince of Coburg, in which the Turks lost 1,500 men killed, besides a considerable number wounded and taken prisoners. The frontiers on the French side of the Margravate of Baden have been patrolled since the troubles commenced, and admission is denied to the fugitives, who fly in all directions from the merciless rage of their countrymen. It is apprehended by the numerous princes in the Empire that the spirit of revolt will become general—that their subjects will follow the example of the French, and, in consequence of this impression, a visible change has taken place in their conduct. This neighbourhood would have been in flames if the disturbances had not subsided on the other side of the Rhine. It was reported that a revolt had happened at Cassel, that orders had been given that citizens conversing together in the street should be seized; but, although the extreme detestation in which the Landgrave is held both by the civil and military population gave force to the probability of an insurrection, the report proves to have originated from a dispute between the soldiery and the bakers on the subject of bread.

Our political relations with Hesse render it necessary to be attentive to the transactions of a Government whose people are so discontented; and, therefore, considering the distance of the King's Minister,[1] who resides constantly at Bonn, and the indifferent state of his health, which prevents that active vigilance so necessary in the diplomatic service, I have presumed to submit to your Grace the propriety of my occasionally residing at Cassel, especially during the winter months, when this town ceases to be a thoroughfare. The Landgrave of Hesse-Cassel is expected at Wilhelmsbadt on the 26th inst. I intend to pay my respects to him, and to proceed afterwards to wait on the Elector of Mayence, who is at Aschaffenburg. On Sunday last I was presented by the Countess of Athlone to the Prince and the Princess of

---

[1] Mr. Heathcote.

Nassau-Weilburg, who pressed me very much to pass some days with them. As the Hereditary Prince of Orange is expected at their château at Kirchberg next month, I have some thoughts of accepting their invitation, and will contrive to be there, if possible, at the same time with his Highness. The Duke of Württemberg, it is thought, will be the new Elector in preference to the Landgrave of Hesse-Cassel. The report which prevailed for some days past that the Duke of Deux-Ponts was shot by the father of a child whom he had ordered to be cruelly beaten is void of foundation.[1] His situation, however, is far from pleasant. Mr. Walpole dined with me last Saturday on his way to Aschaffenburg. The Margrave of Baden is hourly expected here on his way home through Mannheim.

Mr. T. Somers Cocks to Mr. Miles

Charing Cross: August 25, 1789

We enjoy perfect tranquillity in this country, and are not at all afflicted by the troubles, either foreign or domestic, which disturb the rest of Europe. Our funds and our commerce flourish, and, which is not the least happy event, our King enjoys perfect health and now pursues a course which is most likely to preserve it, while the young princes are doing everything to destroy theirs. We are crowded with Frenchmen, who come every week from their own country to enjoy the freedom of ours, many of whom rejoice when they are safely landed. I used to look upon France as a more civilized nation, and could not have conceived they would have been guilty of such barbarities and cruelty. Although the French, by a most wonderful and sudden revolution,

---

[1] 'This titled miscreant had a negro baked in an oven till he died for a trifling misdemeanour.'—W. A. M.

have overset their former Government, they seem very far from settling a new one—at present, indeed, they have none at all—and I cannot believe that the King, the ancient nobility, and the clergy, will long submit to be controlled by the mob, but rather are only waiting for a favourable moment to exert themselves to regain their former power and influence. I expect there will be a good deal of bloodshed before the business is entirely arranged. I see by your accounts that troubles are breaking out in other parts of Europe. I dare say the spirit of liberty which has broken out in France will extend itself to other countries. The King of France must now be sensible of his mistake in having intermeddled in the American war. It has come home to him.

Mr. Miles to the Duke of Leeds

Franckfort: September, 1, 1789

Were I not sensible of the importance of your time, I would attempt to give your Grace an idea of the situation of Aschaffenburg—naturally beautiful and picturesque, in which the refined taste and patient industry of the Elector appear conspicuous at every point of view. My reception has been most cordial. I intended to have paid my respects to his Highness and to return immediately, but he insisted on my staying, nor was I permitted to depart at the expiration of five days, until I had given my promise to revisit him in a fortnight, and afterwards to spend part of the winter at Mayence. A *déjeuner champêtre* was given to me every morning, at a different place, by a different party belonging to his household; and the whole Court vied in showing me the most flattering attentions, particularly Madame de Condenhoff and Madame de Ferrette, the latter of whom did me the honour to accompany me in my morning excursions on horseback. These two ladies are distantly related to the Elector, and enjoy his entire confidence. To the former he has entrusted the management of all foreign relations; she is in fact his Secretary of State for Foreign Affairs; she is in correspondence with the Count of Herzberg and with other Ministers; she has great quickness and discernment, appears to be very intelligent—a shrewd and remarkable woman, *bien éveillée*, with a turn for business—the perfect gentlewoman, and from her influence with the Elector has much weight. I endeavoured to interest her on behalf of the Liégeois, but the Prince Bishop had forestalled me.

The Elector did me the honour to converse with me every day after my morning and evening excursions till dinner or supper was announced. He was very inquisitive about the King's health, spoke with enthusiasm of his Majesty, and assured me that no man rejoiced more warmly and sincerely in his recovery than he had done. He was interested in my description of the illuminations in England, and of our humble demonstration at Franckfort.

I met the Imperial and Prussian Ministers at Aschaffenburg, with the former of whom—Count de Schlick—I became intimate, but saw little of the latter, as he is a sportsman. I also met the Prince de Galitzin, who appeared extremely anxious to convince me that he had not been hostile to England during his embassy at the Hague, and that the armed neutrality was intended eventually to serve the British interests. I replied that I had never heard that he was a foe to England. He has an idea that Lord Dover has so represented him. He returns to the Hague, where he lives in a private character, and appears to be really a good-hearted man—an affable and well-bred man he certainly is—and he will no doubt be restored to favour in Russia whenever the Grand Duke ascends the throne. A gentleman from the Duc de Deux-Ponts has been some time on a visit to the Elector. It is said that the Duke is soliciting the suffrage of his Highness to be elected King of the Romans.[1] The Elector means to assemble a synod next winter, in which it will be proposed that the clergy shall be permitted to marry.

I left Aschaffenburg last Friday with great regret. The Landgrave of Hesse-Cassel arrived the day after at Wilhelmsbadt, where I had the honour to be introduced to him, after which I returned to Franckfort. The Duke of Saxe-Meiningen called yesterday and remained to supper with me. To-morrow I shall accompany him to dinner at the Landgrave's.

The Elector has promised me the head of a wild boar which, being prepared in the German fashion, will keep good for a year. It is my intention to forward it to your Grace.

Mr. Miles to Mr. T. Somers Cocks

Franckfort: September 1, 1789

I have just returned from a visit to the Elector of Mayence. He is at his château at Aschaffenburg—a most delightful spot, where the grounds are laid out in the English taste, and almost equal Stowe for their beauty and extent. His Court is a paradise to visitors, provided they do not meddle with its intrigues. He is an excellent man, lives in magnificent style, seldom less than thirty at dinner and supper; both plenty and elegance reign at his table. I was introduced last Saturday to the Landgrave of Hesse-Cassel; to-morrow

[1] Moldavia.

I dine with him. The Duke of Saxe-Meiningen supped with me last night, and stayed till almost two o'clock in the morning. The fair brings a number of the *bon ton* to Franckfort, and renders the place cheerful, after which it will sink into its native insignificance and become almost intolerable to all except those whose minds are absorbed in the pursuit of commerce. Germany begins now to amuse me. When the Count d'Artois was at Mannheim, the river Neck*ar* overflowed the country, upon which the Count observed that, wherever he went, he saw nothing but ruin and devastation occasioned by Neck*er*! You forget to send me the comedy of 'The Liar.' Many thanks for your letter. I was playing chess with the Duke of Saxe-Meiningen when it arrived, and read to him the passage which mentions the perfect re-establishment of the King's health. I go frequently to Wilhemsbadt, which is a public place in this neighbourhood. I persuade the band to play 'God save the King.'

You have heard of the revolution in Liége, at which I rejoice, from the conviction that all ecclesiastical governments ought to be secularised, and that temporal concerns do not in policy or right appertain to the Church. What does great credit to those who accomplished this revolution is, that by their wisdom and unremitting attention no blood has been spilt. Not so the French. They have run wild, and gone into all the horrible excesses of riot and revolt. They are displaying a fickle and frivolous temperament—*tout se fait chez eux à la mode*—and, no matter what the fashion is, whether it is to dance at a ball or to overthrow a Government, they do either with the same alacrity and in the same spirit, and will laugh at the overthrow or the dance in an epigram or an *ariette*. Yet, with all this frivolity and caprice, they are really a scientific and gallant people.

M. Fabry to Mr. Miles

Liège: August 26, 1789

Since your letter, my dear friend, in which you informed me that you were going to see Chestret at Wetzlar, I have had no news from you. Chestret has not seen you, and I think you have left Franckfort without knowing in what corner of the world you might be found.

Yes, the revolution is true! Since the 17th instant I have not had a minute to myself. The work is immense. We must watch day and night. It is impossible for me to give you the details; it is a miracle that this operation has been effected without a drop of blood, without a scratch. On the 16th and 17th we sported the cockade; we carried it to Chestret, who returned from the country. We re-entered the town together amidst the acclamations of 30,000 people, who lined the faubourgs and the streets; they took out the horses and drew our carriage. At ten o'clock in the evening the Patriot-Chiefs assembled at my house; we agreed on the operations for the next day; we negotiated, however, with The Highness, whom we had made acquainted with the danger. The Chancellor and the Count Charles de Gelöes left at midnight for Seraing; they brought back assurances that the Prince would yield everything, but they wished to insure the work. On the 18th they repaired to the Hôtel de Ville, dismissed the magistracy, proclaimed Chestret and myself Burgomasters. We took possession. The burgesses occupied the citadel and all the posts. The regiment was disarmed. Chestret went to Seraing and brought back The Highness: I approached his carriage to receive him; I gave him my arm to walk up to the great hall of the Hôtel de Ville, where he signed the proclamation and the abolition of the settlement of 1684. I again gave him my arm, and re-conducted him on foot to the Palace—this scene would have made you laugh —the acclamations of four thousand men made us giddy. Next day we escorted The Highness back as far as the Chapel on the Avroi; we were admitted into his coach, and one of his carriages brought us back to the Hôtel de Ville. At the demand of the people the Count de Lannoy is named Grand Mayeur. The infamous Fréron is discarded. In the cathedral a 'Te Deum' was sung at our request. All the towns have imitated the capital in dismissing from their magistracies the party named by the Prince; they all came to compliment us by deputations—all the corporations did the same. The insurrection is general. *Voilà le beau, voici le laid!* I am tired to death; all is not yet settled. Our cowardly enemies, whom we leave free, work underhand; they stir up the people. We were forced yesterday to suppress the taxes. Notwithstanding, whenever I move from one place to another, it is always amidst the acclamations of the people intoxicated with joy! We form corps—the burgesses are armed. If I was sole master, I will dare to say that all would go well; but I have a terrible task in controlling the effervescence of patriotism. *Bon jour, mon cher; je vous embrasse bien en hâte.* I am obliged to take this moment—four o'clock in the morning—to write to you.

Mr. Miles to the Duke of Leeds

Aschaffenburg: September 25, 1789

The Circle of the Upper Rhine will assemble in this town on Friday next; it is a sudden and extraordinary meeting, the object being, it is said, to take efficacious measures against that part of the Empire bordering on Alsace being inundated by French emigrants. Monsieur de Breteuil,[1] his daughter, and several families of distinction, passed through Franckfort last week on their way to Switzerland; they had forty-four post-horses. An exchange of territory between the Landgrave of Hesse and the Elector of Mayence, in which the county of Hanau is to be ceded to the latter, is again mentioned: if such an event be likely to happen, your Grace shall have the earliest information. The enclosed is a copy of a letter from Liège; it gives a perfect idea of the situation of affairs in that principality.[2]

The following anecdote is a fact. The Prince de Salm was in a bookseller's shop here with M. O'Kelly, the French Envoy at Mayence, conversing on the affairs of France, whilst M. de Breteuil and several others were at the door. The Prince exclaimed: 'The man who deserved the most to be hanged at Paris has unfortunately escaped, and is at this moment in Franckfort.' O'Kelly entreated him not to speak so loud. The Prince replied that all the world knew it to be a fact, and all the world might hear him! No notice was taken of this pointed affront, but the *motive* of it was instantly explained by M. de Breteuil informing his friends that, after having repeatedly prevented the creditors of the Prince from proceeding to extremities at Paris, he was finally obliged to let the law take its course against him by refusing any longer delay.

The Elector of Mayence has given directions that in the winter some young boars' heads shall be prepared as a present to his Majesty. I shall address them to our Consul at Ostend.

[1] Minister of the Interior, Paris.   [2] Letter from M. Fabry to Mr. Miles.

The Hereditary Prince of Saxe-Cobourg and the Princess, with some ladies from Aschaffenburg, dined with me at Franckfort on the 17th instant, after which I returned to this place to pass some days with the Elector of Mayence.

Mr. Miles to the Duke of Leeds
Franckfort: November 9, 1789

Although the spirit of liberty has not manifested itself in this neighbourhood with the degree of violence exhibited in France and in the Low Countries, the farmers in some parts of the electorate of Mayence, on being commanded to repair the roads, laconically answered that *they had not time,* and, accordingly, *corvées* were dispensed with *until they were at leisure.* The Elector has also judged it prudent to postpone those grand hunts, which require from 800 to 1,200 peasants, declaring that at this moment *il faut les laisser tranquilles.* If the *corvées* had been refused last year, a detachment of Hussars would have compelled the farmers to obey the summons, and, as the indulgence of Government on this occasion is visibly the effect of fear, it is possible that concessions of greater magnitude may be exacted, since the people do not hesitate to express their discontent.

The British Court is strongly suspected at Mayence of having fomented the disturbances in France by means of money, although the impossibility of the Minister's disposing of the public wealth without the authority of Parliament was fully explained by me to his Electoral Highness; and it is still more strongly believed that it countenances the revolt in the Belgic Provinces, which, however, would give no displeasure on account of personal ill-will towards the Emperor if they were not apprehensive that the contagion may extend to the Rhine.

The French interest is very strong at Mayence. I have been constantly under the painful necessity of refuting various reports respecting the conduct of my Court towards France, some of which are too absurd, I should have thought, to have been credited. Indeed, I have gone so far as to say that, if my country were capable of availing herself of the deplorable state of France to excite a civil war amongst her people, I would forswear the name of Englishman for ever. However, the part which the Court of Versailles took in the American war may be thought to justify such a proceeding—a proceeding so atrocious that no injury whatever could authorise it. I had no mental reserve in holding this language to the Elector and his Court. It is my wish to impress foreigners with the idea that we are incapable of profiting by the internal distresses of even a rival and hostile kingdom, or wishing to revenge a wrong or triumph over its ruin.

His Royal Highness the Duke of Sussex set off from this town in good health and spirits yesterday morning for Pisa.

ADMIRAL SIR THOMAS RICH TO MR. MILES

London: November 13, 1789

Your favour found me here, no longer a mighty man of war, but a very peaceable and humble-minded sort of person, knowing little how the world goes further than the 'Herald' informs him at breakfast, and, though not caring much which end of this unaccountable machine goes foremost, the news of the day is a kind of salt and seasoning to my muffins, which I cannot well dispense with. A genius like you will always find amusement wherever there are living souls, be they heavy Germans or the more volatile French; whereas a dull, stupid fellow like myself, instead of learning a new A B C, has nearly forgot the alphabet of my native tongue, and has substituted nothing in lieu, except the knowledge that all that I have done hitherto has been unwise and unprofitable, and that I am advancing to the period of doing nothing to please myself, and of course very little to please anybody else. Still, I enjoy life, and if I can keep in motion, ward off duns from the door, and leave a little for those that are to take up the cudgels when a *hic jacet* shall point out the spot of Sir Thomas Rich, I care not, as I am growing too old to be ambitious, and hope I am too generous to become avaricious.

Egotism, for want of other matter, is all I can deal in; it is a never-failing mark of the barrenness of the soil; for, in short, I have no anecdotes of any of your acquaintances to relate, and, were I to enter upon politics, I should write about what I know nothing of, and you would most likely confront me with lies of my own invention in my own handwriting, so that I shall leave you to the public prints—my only source of information —to select such matter as best suits your palate, instead of sending you extracts therefrom, and spurting them as if they were my own received from great men who sometimes deign me a significant nod and a friendly squeeze by the hand. Whenever you quit your German Embassy, or whatever you may style your Excellency's diplomatic appointment, and revisit these kingdoms, I shall always be glad to see you. Perchance you may find me turning up the clods in Berkshire with my swords and hangers hammered into plowshares, rusticated and retired from the alarms of war and from the

sophistry of the Senate, singing lullaby to a squalling cross child in a rocking chair, and my flitch shall be offered to your knife. Be assured that in all situations
I am very truly, &c., &c.

Mr. T. Somers Cocks to Mr. Miles
London: November 24, 1789

The new under-secretaries to the Duke of Leeds are Mr. Ryder and Mr. Bland Burgess. I am glad you have spent your time so pleasantly, and have received so many civilities from the different princes. I expect to hear of many other revolutions; the spirit of liberty seems likely to break forth throughout Europe. The French have begun at the wrong end, and seem to have come to a sudden stop; for there is nothing to be done without money, and they have got none, nor do they seem to have power enough to raise any; they are on the brink of national bankruptcy, by which many private people will lose their whole incomes, and, of course, be much out of humour. By-and-by the public in general will find themselves so distressed that they will be glad to have recourse to their old Government, or the consequence will be that it must at last end in a civil war; it seems to have arrived nearly at a crisis. This country in the meantime is increasing in power and wealth.

The King has returned from Weymouth in good health, and has had two Levées, where he appeared as well as ever, and again goes hunting. He went to the play last week, for the first time since his illness. Not one fifth of the people that crowded there could get into the house; 'God save the King' was repeated three times, the whole house joined in chorus, and many were so affected with his reception as to burst into tears. The Parliament will certainly not be dissolved till after next session. Mr. Pitt remains in full power, and the country in general is so conscious of the great things he has done and of his abilities still to do more, that there is no doubt but he will have as many friends in the next Parliament as he has in the present.

Though I am as great a friend to liberty as you can be, I cannot say I approve of the present proceedings either in France or Brabant. I do not like these mobility governments; they bring everything into confusion, by means of which the French have brought themselves into a more desperate situation than ever; the lives and property of people are totally at the mercy of the populace, and the poor King is quite a State prisoner, and cannot eat, drink, or sleep without the permission of his worthy governors. The idea of putting all persons upon an equality can never do; no government can be carried on in that manner, and I am apprehensive that the general plan of *Liberty,* which seems to pervade almost all ranks, may be attended with great disorder and extend even to this country, which I look upon as possessing the happiest government on earth. People here, seeing other nations destroy all government, may fancy they have as good a right to overthrow ours. As for the King of France, I cannot help pitying him; but the Emperor deserves the worst that can happen to him. I dare say we shall keep clear from meddling either with the French or German troubles, for, as you justly observe, it is for our advantage that, however much they may quarrel and fight with each other, we should remain neuter. By means of our alliance with Prussia and Holland we are become a respectable Power.

The weather has been so wet lately that the farmers have been obliged to leave a great deal of wheat-ground unsown, by which means corn is risen to a great price.

Mr. Miles to the Duke of Leeds.

Franckfort: December 5, 1789.

The apprehensions of a general revolt occasioned the Circles of the Upper Rhine to forbid the public prints in their respective districts from inserting anything in favour of the Brabançons.

The disturbances in the Electorate of Trèves are likely to require a greater force to suppress them than the Elector of Mayence has sent. It was yesterday reported that the Regiment of Hartsfeld was ordered to march. The success of the Brabançons, and the happy issue which, as is said, the affairs at Liège have obtained, make a great sensation in this neighbourhood, and it is not improbable but next year may produce in Germany scenes of riot and desolation similar to those with which France is afflicted.

My information of tumults and insurrections happening at any distance from Franckfort will necessarily be late and imperfect—late from the pains taken to suppress the intelligence, and imperfect from the exaggerated accounts which men from fear or malevolence retail on these occasions. Last autumn, for example, it was current, and generally believed, that the Landgrave had been driven from the metropolis and would be compelled to seek safety in flight! As insurrections of great magnitude are expected, I take the liberty to request permission to transport myself nearer to the scene of action, so that my information may be less liable to error. It is my opinion that, if I were to divide my time between Franckfort, Coblentz, Mayence, and Mannheim—as Mr. Walpole is at Munich—it might tend to the public service.

The Prince de Conti arrived some days since, and, it

is said, means to pass the winter here, or at least a portion of it. There is to be a party this evening at the Princess de Holstein Beck's, who has arrived from Russia, and I shall probably meet him there.

My aversion to eat the 'bread of idleness' has induced me in this inactive situation to write a pamphlet entitled 'Cursory Reflections on Public Men and Public Measures;' it is of considerable length, and I trust it will do no discredit to the pen of 'Neptune.' I have desired my publisher, Stockdale of Piccadilly, to send a copy to your Grace as soon as it is printed.[1]

Mr. Miles to the Duke of Leeds

Franckfort: December 30, 1789

The disturbances in the Electorate of Trèves, I am told, are suppressed, but terrible apprehensions are entertained by all the little despots in the empire should the Brabançons succeed. The Elector of Mayence is highly offended with the Courts of Berlin

---

[1] '"Cursory Reflections on Public Men and Public Measures" I wrote at Aschaffenburg during the preceding autumn, in consequence of the revolution that had happened in France, and with the view of inducing Mr. Pitt to avail himself of that great event as an opportunity to efface for ever the unhappy enmity and jealousy which the two Governments of England and France had, contrary to true policy, not to say wickedly, encouraged by all kinds of arts—on the same principle that the ferocity of two bulldogs, when fighting, is inflamed to madness by the greater ferocity of their cruel bystanders. From the conviction that the union of these two warlike nations would contribute to the general good of the human race, I sent such an idea into the world to prepare men's minds for such an event, whilst, in my private letters and conversations addressed to those through whose agency the change could be accomplished, I earnestly and most pathetically recommend the measure; but it is out of the ordinary course of things, and men are content to travel in old ruts. Our politicians lack either the skill or the disposition to improve, or even to repair the old track, however beaten down or worn-out it may be, and so, I am afraid, all my suggestions for an alliance with France will be of no avail.'—W. A. M.

and of London for their supposed secret support of the revolt in the Pays-Bas, and, particularly, with the former for refusing to act with vigour against the Liégeois. I am sorry to find that his Electoral Highness is outrageous at the decree of Wetzlar not having been enforced agreeably to the wishes of the Electors of Bavaria and Cologne, and my concern is augmented by his employing all the resources in his power to that effect. He is still further stimulated by the clamours of Mesdames la Baronne de Ferrette et de Veningen, whose losses in Alsace since the revolution in France have rendered them furious.

Some of the foreign prints have the insolence to attribute the recent insurrections to the secret intrigues of the British Court—reports which I wish your Grace would authorise me to contradict. The Prince de Conti still remains here, but, as the Marshal de Broglio, should he recover from his present illness, is expected, and the Prince de Lambesc,[1] with whom it is said the Prince de Conti is not upon good terms, it is thought he will remove. He sighs impatiently to return to Paris, and inquires of almost every one if they think he may venture to go back. He says he has nothing to reproach himself with, but he cannot venture into a country where the King and Queen are held, as it were, in bondage. He appears much dejected, avoids society, and complains that he is *ennuyé*.

The ecclesiastical princes in the empire, and particularly those in the neighbourhood of the Rhine, who have long been apprehensive of a revolt, tremble at the approach of the Brabançons, lest the spirit of liberty

---

[1] The Prince de Lambesc, at the head of the Royal Allemand Regiment, charged the mob in the Tuileries during the procession with the bust of Necker, July 13, 1789.

should infect their respective subjects. The *chasse* and the *corvées* have been in a manner given up in some parts of the Electorate of Mayence, where the peasants have appeared discontented, and in the Electorate of Trèves. My letters from Liège announce a disposition in some people to unite with the Pays-Bas, but Fabry assures me he will engage that his country shall keep its word with the King of Prussia, if the King of Prussia will keep his word with it, and not execute the decree of Wetzlar. The Emperor was this day reported to be dead, but a letter I received from Vienna makes no mention of such an event. Preparations are making for a coronation in the spring, though some are of opinion that a war is by far more probable. General D'Alton passed through on his way to Vienna by Franckfort. Count Trauttmansdorff is forbid to come to Vienna. Zwierling, the agent of the Bishop of Liège, arrived from Wetzlar with his son, most graciously and cordially received by the Elector, and proceeded thence to Trèves. Expresses continually passing and repassing from Vienna, Dresden, Prussia, and Munich. A revolt near Strasburg in the territory belonging to Cardinal Rohan: 200 Palatines and 200 of the Mayence troops sent to restore public order, but the peasants refuse to pay, and dare the military. Regiment of Hartsfeld is under orders to march. Soldiers declare they will not fire on their fellow-citizens in case of a tumult. The first week in January, 600 men march from Coblentz to reinforce the garrison of Trèves.

Should I receive no instructions from your Grace to the contrary, it is my intention to leave Franckfort on the 8th of next month, and to take Liège, Bruxelles, Ghent, and Ostend, on my way to England.

M. Le Brun to Mr. Miles

Liège: 13 Janvier, 1790

Je ne puis qu'approuver votre résolution, et je me chargerai avec un vrai plaisir de la traduction et de l'impression de votre excellente lettre. Elle est intéressante à tous égards, et par les circonstances et par la profondeur et la justesse des idées. Je ne doute pas qu'elle ne soit fort accueillie du public. Je puis dès demain m'occuper de la traduction.[1]

M. Le Brun to Mr. Miles

Liège: 15 Janvier, 1790

Je vous serai obligé de m'envoyer la partie de votre manuscrit qui parle d'une séparation de la Bretagne et de la Normandie pour en faire une province séparée du reste de la France. Je crois avoir occasion de faire usage dans le journal de demain des réflexions très judicieuses que vous m'avez lues à ce sujet.

Oserai-je profiter de l'occasion pour vous prier, monsieur, de me rendre un service qui dans ce moment seroit pour moi très essentiel ? Il me manque dix-huit louis pour l'acquittement d'une lettre de change qui écheoit aujourd'hui, et qui me jette dans une grande peine. Ne pourriez-vous pas joindre à tous les sujets de gratitude que je vous dois ce nouveau bienfait ? Je vous remettrai cet argent sans faute à la fin du mois. A tout autre qu'à un Anglois, et à tout autre Anglois qu'à Monsieur Miles, je n'osai faire une semblable proposition. Mais vous m'avez inspiré depuis longtemps des sentimens de confiance et d'estime. Vous m'avez témoigné une amitié dont je tâcherai de me rendre digne. J'ai

---

[1] The translation into French of 'Cursory Reflections on Public Men and Public Measures.'

fait en vain le tour de tous ceux qui me doivent, et je n'ai trouvé partout que des délais. Les révolutions actuelles sont en grande partie cause de cette pénurie de numéraire. Ces tracasseries me chagrinent extrêmement, et nuisent beaucoup à mon travail, qui n'avance qu'autant que l'esprit est libre d'inquiétude. Je vous prie de me faire savoir par le porteur de cette lettre si je puis vous aller voir cette après-midi vers les trois heures.

La traduction et l'impression de votre manuscrit iront, j'espère, très promptement.

J'ai l'honneur d'être, avec la plus profonde vénération, monsieur, votre &c., &c.

Minute by Mr. Miles.—I have preserved this original letter written by a man most miserably indigent. Le Brun, exiled from France for having wished that the land of his nativity should be as free as America, took refuge in Liège, where he became a journalist. He was driven thence at the instigation of Catherine, and established himself in the Duchy of Limburg. In 1787 he came into conflict with the States of Brabant, at that time in revolt against Joseph II., and, eluding the order for his arrest, fled to Vienna to obtain protection. He succeeded, and resumed his business at Bruxelles. The Emperor, after having lowered himself to employ the journalist to defend tyranny, was mean enough to dispute with him for a few *liards* of pay. His Majesty refused to give more than a hundred pistoles, and the scribe would not prostitute his pen to Cæsar for less than a hundred louis. Le Brun, now embroiled with Joseph, fled to Paris, and was enrolled as a member of the Jacobin Club, where I saw him. He then proposed to write in a political newspaper, but, becoming acquainted with Dumouriez, who at that time was master of Louis XVI., and for the moment of France, he attached himself to the fortunes of the general; became afterwards Minister for Foreign Affairs; induced the Convention to declare war against England; signed the order for the death of his sovereign; and finished his singular career by being decapitated six months afterwards. Such was the fate of a man whom I had twice relieved, whom I had endeavoured to serve, and whose wife has since asked for bread from the legislators of France—the accomplices of her husband—on behalf of herself and children without obtaining it. *Sic transit gloria mundi!*

[The above memorandum is written on the back of the original letter of Le Brun.] [1]

Mr. Miles to Lord Rodney

Liège: January 28, 1790

Your very friendly letter reached me at Aschaffenburg, where, whilst partaking of the hospitalities of an Electoral Court, I endeavoured by those attentions to everybody which are so acceptable to all, but which the general run of our countrymen refuse almost to everybody, to convey a favourable impression of the English character, and so win by courtesy the interchange of civility which, if our own people could only understand it, is due from all to all. The opposite line of conduct argues want of feeling as well as want of knowledge, and is attributed by foreigners to an excess of pride amounting at times to insolence, and is founded on an arrogant opinion of our superiority over other nations. I am not disposed to discuss the origin of manners, but the unsocial demeanour and *hauteur* which Englishmen too often exhibit on the Continent do us

---

[1] See Introduction pages 24, 26.

no good service, nor do they add one atom to our power, but, on the contrary, they act as repellents everywhere. Let a Frenchman and an Englishman be ushered at the same moment into a fashionable circle at any part of the Continent, the former will receive attentions which would perhaps be cheerfully accorded in preference to the latter, if only his sterling qualities could be discovered through the cold and distant exterior in which he envelopes and conceals himself, as it were, from the rest of the world. The mischiefs resulting from this behaviour are beyond all estimate. They throw us in the rear of all political negotiations in which British gold, in the shape of subsidies, does not atone for British presumption. At the Courts of Versailles or Madrid, for example, where no undignified mixture of personal pride throws ridicule on the pomp and pageantry with which the sovereign is surrounded, the stiffness which marks our national character is offensive and prejudicial. It indisposes foreign powers towards us, and creates enemies where it is our interest to have friends. I remarked to Lord Torrington[1] that an Englishman ought so to conduct himself abroad that the fact of his being a native of England should be a sufficient letter of credit, without anything of the kind from his banker. He held the same views as myself, and lamented that in too many cases the very reverse is the fact. I wish, my dear Lord Rodney, that I could impress upon our fellow-countrymen the infinite satisfaction they would derive to themselves, and the infinite advantage they would obtain for their nation, by adopting the maxim by which I have endeavoured to steer my own course through life, that in this world we are fellow-passengers, and we should strive to render the journey

---

[1] Minister from the Court of St. James at Brussels.

as agreeable as possible. If Ministers, in their selection of men for foreign missions, would choose those who are familiar without being vulgar, and gracious without being lifted up by pride—endowed with a ready and obliging disposition—they would find their account in it. The diamond in the rough, as for immediate use, is without value, and lies as in a dormant state, whilst the Bristol stone blazes at the ball and dazzles the multitude. Your Lordship can make the application of this simile.

Now for news. The dissensions which unhappily prevail at Bruxelles give much uneasiness to the leading people in opposition at Liége, whose fate depends upon that of the Low Countries. The mansion is in flames, and the blockheads are disputing whether they shall extinguish the fire with spring or river water. The Elector of Cologne wished to have sent 15,000 sacks of flour to Luxemburg, but he was opposed by his chapter; a subsequent attempt was made for a smaller quantity, which was also refused. Recruits arrive daily to reinforce that garrison in small parties from Suabia, and, as they are disciplined, the veteran troops are sent out to join the imperial army at Marche-en-Famène. The garrison at Luxemburg consists of only 9,000 men, and the province itself is tolerably well affected to the Emperor, as is also that of Limburg.

I have recently sent, under cover to my bankers, the manuscript of a pamphlet,[1] which I wrote whilst at Aschaffenburg, and Stockdale the publisher has instructions to forward a copy to you. *Je ne suis pas un écrivain aux gages*—I write neither for fame nor profit—my sole wish is to serve our country and humanity, and the motive is good, however unsuccessful the attempt

[1] 'Cursory Reflections on Public Men and Public Measures.'

may be. I have earnestly recommended the Governments of France and England to lay aside their long-nurtured hatred and to enter into an alliance; the moment is favourable for such a purpose, and, if realised, it would ensure the happiness of both nations and the peace of the world. This publication will appear to-morrow in a French dress. Le Brun, the editor of 'La Feuille de Hervé,' translates it. The French, I have reason to believe, are well disposed to the measure, and I hope Mr. Pitt will see the wisdom and utility of it as clearly as I do. On Sunday last I was in some personal danger at this place, arising out of the political state of affairs; but, as I seldom travel without my wits, I escaped for the present. I hope soon to have the pleasure of seeing your Lordship.

General Wimpffen to Mr. Miles

Paris: February 3, 1790

Mirabeau, who, you will remember, was complimented in some elegant lines by Bassenge at Liège, is again in France, *où il joue le premier rôle, car le Roi n'est pas si grand que lui.* He set up a journal in Paris on his arrival from exile, and, as is said, all the extracts of letters from London inserted in the 'Moniteur' are penned by him or by his secretary and a man in their pay. Since writing the above I hear that you are acquainted with each other, and, if so, I rely on your friendship not to mention to him what I told you of his adventures. I hear that he related to you the anecdote of himself with Count Kelly, the French Minister at Mayence. It is true that the Count lamented that M. Mirabeau did not make a friend of the Queen when she offered to serve him, and that he replied to the French Minister: 'Bah! elle aura plus besoin de moi dans trois mois d'ici que moi d'elle.' His prophecy is verified, for, between you and me, the Court cannot do without him.[1]

Mr. Miles to Lord Buckingham

London: July 15, 1790

I had an interview yesterday by appointment with Mr. Rose, and the matter which I had the honour to communicate to your Lordship before you left town was again proposed. As it is meant to carry this idea into immediate execution, I was directed to write instantly and prevent the return of my family from the Continent. It having been judged advisable by Mr. Pitt that I should have no communication whatever, either directly or indirectly, with the King's Minister[2] at Paris, I have thought it my duty to apprise you of this arrangement, that you need not have the trouble to send the introduction which you kindly promised. Everything being finally settled, I shall leave town the latter end of next week. I wish your Lordship the full enjoyment of health and happiness.

Mr. Miles to Lord Buckingham

Paris: August 16, 1790

The wonderful events that daily occur, the still more wonderful changes in preparation, and the grandeur of

---

[1] '*Liège, July* 30, 1785.—Breakfasted at Court, also dined with the Prince. Heard that the Emperor had totally lost himself in the opinion of all the world by his contemptible conduct towards the Dutch. Inquired for a book written against the Emperor by the Count de Mirabeau upon the subject of his claims on Holland. It is so severe that it is prohibited throughout the imperial dominions, and even the booksellers' shops have been examined at Liège by the Mayor. When Mirabeau was asked by the French Minister how he could venture to put his name to a publication so offensive, he replied: ' I know it is in your power to send me to the Bastille, but my papers are in the hands of a friend in a neutral country, and I shall not be in prison four and twenty hours before the world will be informed from whom I received the facts which I have stated.'—*Diary of Mr. Miles.*

[2] Lord Gower.

the scene before me, engross my thoughts since my
arrival here. I have dined three days in succession
with Monsieur de Lafayette. We last met in America in
1781; he is extremely amiable, and certainly a friend
to liberty. But he has a powerful rival for popularity,
or rather an enemy, in the Duke of Orleans, and, secure
as he fancies himself in the affections of the National
Guards and of the municipalities, he will fall, I fear, a
victim to his confidence and to the depravity of those
he is endeavouring to serve. The days I dined with
him we were disturbed by addresses from all the districts,
also from the battalions of National Guards, who came
in procession to his hotel to assure him of their eternal
attachment. He took me from table into the street—we
walked arm in arm until they all filed off after having
harangued him—and some of the privates, stepping
aside from the ranks, after the address had been read,
added: 'Ne craignez rien, mon général; nous mourrons
tous pour vous s'il faut.' Their enthusiasm was certainly great, and I believe sincere, but it is the nature
of enthusiasm of that description to be of short duration;
it is certainly not blessed with longevity. All these
addresses were in opposition to the Orleans faction, who
wish to place one of the Lameths at the head of the
National Guards. Lafayette has great facility, and, at
times, much presence of mind. He answered every
address in a different manner with great fluency and
elegance, and I conceive him to be rather a man of
pleasing and conciliatory manners, with great personal
courage, than of vigorous mind and great resources—I
mean, of course, in the Cabinet, not in the field. When
these numerous processions were over, he asked me
what I thought of the state of parties, and whether he
had anything to fear from the Duke of Orleans. I

answered: Yes, everything; that his wealth and high birth would always procure him partisans, but that, if he was liberal as well as ambitious, he would be suspected as dangerous; that nothing was so fluctuating as popularity; that the people, although meaning well, yet, not possessing discriminating powers in proportion to their zeal and promptitude, were very frequently hurried into error, and liable to have their minds poisoned; that his post was perilous as well as difficult; and that he must not consider himself secure, or the glorious work of liberty accomplished, until he had silenced faction. He assured me that they were endeavouring to do this, and that the police would soon be enabled to act with vigour. I concluded a long conversation with the remark that, having eradicated despotism, he must now destroy the very spirit of cabal and intrigue, or the business of the Revolution was only half done. He agreed with me. Yet I find he thinks himself perfectly secure. I shall not forget to repeat to him at every interview that he will fall a victim unless he suppresses the vile spirit of intrigue which I perceive reigns here, and mars or endangers everything.

MR. MILES TO MONSIEUR TALLEYRAND

Paris: August 20, 1790

I had hoped to place in your hands the enclosed letter from Sir Thomas Miller, but, notwithstanding the decree of the National Assembly that no person can be arrested unless accused of high treason or charged with misdemeanour, I have been detained a prisoner for more than a week at the Hôtel de la République de Gênes by an attack of the gout. This is the reason why I have been prevented from assuring you in person how deeply I am interested in all that can contribute to the prosperity of a nation worthy of the high position to which it has just raised itself by breaking into pieces the shackles of despotism. I pray you to accept my apology for having so long detained the letter of the Chevalier. It will soon be in my power, I hope, to assure you *vivâ voce* of my high consideration.

Monsieur Talleyrand à Monsieur Miles

Paris : Lundi, 23 Août, 1790

L'Evêque d'Autun regrette de ne s'être pas trouvé chez lui quand M. Miles lui a fait l'honneur d'y passer. Il est très empressé de faire connoissance avec lui, et il ira le trouver au premier moment qu'il aura libre. Il le prie de recevoir ses sincères complimens.

Mr. Miles to Lord Rodney

Paris : August 23, 1790

If I continue an *itinerant* much longer, rambling over Europe, I shall pick up a budget of information, stories, and anecdotes sufficient for a book-maker's fortune, were he as avaricious as old Pultney, and enrich all Paternoster Row with my writings. This place abounds with matter to fill quarto volumes. It is no uncommon thing to be stopped in the street by an entire stranger, who asks your opinion of the measure under consideration in the National Assembly, and he asks it with a gravity that would lead you to believe he is interested in the answer, and really wished your opinion; but before you are recovered from the surprise at being so abruptly accosted, he is off, chaunting 'Malbruck' or some other popular ballad, and leaving you all amazement at such inconceivable levity in times of so much danger and general calamity.

It is a vice peculiar to the nation, but, what is most remarkable, it is accompanied by talents, and belongs no less to the man of science, the man of letters, and the statesman, than to the hairdresser or to the street-sweeper. Ether is not half so volatile as a Frenchman. The German is the reverse, and can as little move from his own impulse as an oyster. Paris, at all times interesting, both to the libertine and the philosopher, is more so now than ever, and the man who is fond of scrutinising the human character, and of developing the most secret recesses of the heart and mind, will find ample employment for his talents at research, and will discover every moment new matter to excite his admiration or provoke his abhorrence. I am wonderfully amused at times, and, having seen this place under the stern rigour of absolute monarchy, everything appears in its present disorganised state as in masquerade. I fancy myself in the midst of a grand Carnival, and would enter *de bon cœur* into all the mirth and ridicule of the diversified characters that jostle me and each other perpetually in the street were it not that I am frequently called from the folly of the actors to a commiseration of their sufferings and to a horror of their crimes. They do not, however, suffer or feel disgusted at atrocities that would freeze our blood; they will mount the scaffold on which they are to perish with a hop, step, and a jump, take a pinch of snuff, crack a joke with the executioner, and die with a *bon-mot* or a pleasantry in their mouths.[1]

---

[1] On arriving at Aire, a town between St. Omer and Lille, Dr. Moore addressed a grave-looking man who was smoking his pipe at the door. 'He asked where I lodged. I answered, "*Aux Trois Rois*." "Aux Trois Rois!" he repeated with a grimace. "Ma foi, monsieur, vous avez choisi là des hôtes qui ne sont plus à la mode." The maid of the inn, after giving a terrible account of the devastation and destruction occa-

It may perhaps be matter of information and of merriment to your Lordship, as it has been to me, that on the continent of Europe the office of executioner is, like monarchy, an hereditary prerogative. It descends from father to son, with this advantage over royalty—that it is not so often liable to suffer from the convulsion of the times or to be subverted by revolutions. Their marriages, like those of kings and princes, are always confined to the same rank, without being exposed to the chance of being dishonoured by misalliance. The overture, and, indeed, the whole business, is even negotiated in much the same manner, and occasions have occurred where the ceremony has been solemnised by proxy. The parties are often strangers to each other, and the extent of practice in the one instance, as the extent of power and dominion in the other, is generally the criterion by which the propriety of the overture is judged. I should suppose that if the daughter of the executioner at Paris was demanded in marriage by the hereditary hangman of the Principality of Liège, it would be received with as much disdain as an overture from the Gonfalonier of Lucca to one of our princesses. I cannot take upon me to affirm that the law of primogeniture is in force among them, but, as I am assured, the dignity of the office cannot be declined, nor is abdication allowed except in favour of the offspring, or of some member of

sioned by the pillaging in the villages, said it was not easy to tell whether the Hulans or the red-hot bullets were the most mischievous, but, continued she: "Ce qui est certain, monsieur, est, que le sang coule dans ce pauvre Lille depuis huit jours comme l'eau coule dans les rues d'Aire. Ah! monsieur, cela déchire le cœur." Having pronounced this with a sympathising accent, she went out of the room, and I heard her singing a very gay tune as she went downstairs.'—*Journal during a Residence in France from the beginning of August to the middle of December* 1792, by Dr. Moore, iii. 225.

the fraternity; nor would they be allowed to fly from
their post, like our second James, and live upon the
precarious bounty of a brother-hangman, as that ill-
advised monarch did on the ostentatious generosity of
Louis XIV. The public executioner on the Continent
is also entitled to certain privileges of another kind,
and which were brought under my notice whilst I
resided on the banks of the Meuse, near Liège, in 1786.
The stream had floated a dead dog, with a rope about
its neck, and left it on the shore near my garden wall.
On giving directions to my servant to push it off, I
received a positive refusal, and on my remonstrating I
was informed that no domestic would degrade himself
by touching the dead body of the beast—that it was
the business of the *hangman*. I inquired what other
functions belonged to that profession. I was at once
told that these gentlemen are frequently excellent
surgeons. The customs and prejudices of this world
have very often an abundance of ridicule in them. It
would be well for us if they never had anything worse,
but, unhappily, they have at times *that* in them which
excites horror—not laughter—and which appertains
more to guilt than to pleasantry.

It was when I lived in the vicinity of Liège that I
became acquainted with that most terrible punishment
of death by 'breaking on the wheel,' which, among
other tortures sanctioned under the monarchy, and
practised within the Bastille as elsewhere, has only
ceased to be tolerated in France since the Revolution.
A priest named Pierlot, at Vervier, near Spa, having
ruined himself at the gambling-table, conceived the
horrible idea of retrieving his circumstances by assassinating an entire family. He had murdered three of
them, but, his strength failing him on attempting the

fourth, he made his escape, and, if he had succeeded, he would not even have been suspected, for he was regarded more as a saint than a sinner. He took refuge in a house of Capuchin Friars in the country of Luxembourg, from which he was transferred to the jail at Liège. Hitherto, perpetual confinement had been the only punishment inflicted on reverend criminals for the most enormous offences, but this man, it was said, must be publicly executed, for the dread of the Emperor interfering if they did not execute him, and the probability of a revolt among the people, decided the clergy to abandon their *confrère* to the rigour of his fate. There had been only one instance in the principality of a priest having been punished with death by the forms of justice, and that was a deacon, for presuming to say mass and to administer the sacrament. His offence was deemed more criminal than the assassination committed by the priest at Vervier. On entering the jail, Pierlot called for his breviary, and, with the greatest *sang-froid*, declared that he would say masses for the souls of those whom he had murdered, and that, as he would only be imprisoned, he would say the offices of the Church to the other prisoners. But he was sentenced to die. It was on a Monday morning in the month of February that this priest was degraded. I saw the ceremony. The criminal felt less than I did. The whole town of Liège was assembled in the marketplace, where a temporary altar had been erected, and where the troops were formed in an extended circle, into which the prisoner was conducted in a cart. He descended immediately of his own accord, undaunted, put on the different vestments of his several ordinations with a degree of composure that provoked the indignation of the most phlegmatic observer. The Suffragan Bishop, Count François de Mean, in all the mystic pageantry of the Church, and attended by two abbots no less gaudily arrayed, walked in procession in the rear of the intrepid criminal, who, unawed by the solemnity of the occasion or by the impatient curiosity of an indignant people, advanced to the Bishop, kneeled, and received from the altar his final dismission—the Suffragan informing him that, having profaned the sacred office, it was his duty to degrade him, and deliver him to the civil power. He was then divested of his ecclesiastical dress. I saw him get into the cart on his return to the dungeon with as much alacrity as if he had been going to an entertainment. His fate was decided the day after. His sentence was, that he should be carried from Liège to St. Giles on the following Saturday; that on the road his flesh should be torn eight times with red-hot irons; that his arms, legs, and thighs should be broken on the wheel; that he should be left in that dislocated state for four hours before he received the *coup-de-grâce*, or final stroke, which was to terminate at once his sufferings and his existence. I had no desire to witness that part of the punishment. Those who can patiently behold such an execution could perform it as well as the hangman. But I was assured that he bore the burning of his flesh and the breaking of his limbs with the most perfect composure; that he neither appeared alarmed at the horrid preparations for his violent death nor expressed the least anguish under his accumulated tortures. That part of the sentence which ordered that he was to be exposed for four hours with his dislocated limbs on the wheel had been remitted by the Prince-Bishop. When the executioner advanced to give him the *coup-de-grâce*, the wretched criminal exclaimed: 'Laissez-moi souffrir. Je n'ai pas encore expié mon crime.' He never uttered a groan. It is a lamentable reflection that a mind capable of such firmness, and so resolved as that of Pierlot appears to have been, had not received a better direction.

A miserable wretch at St. Petersburg, who had pledged himself to sell some stolen plate with the vow that not even torture would induce him to betray the thieves, showed, on detection, similar *sang-froid*. He endured the punishment calmly, without making any confession. The judge, enraged at the obstinacy shown, threatened to have the culprit burned alive, and, when the faggots were brought and the fire kindled, the man recanted, and made the required disclosure, on the ground that he had bound himself to suffer any amount of 'torture,' ordinary or extraordinary, but that, as *burning alive* was not in the bargain, he thought himself released from the obligation of his oath.

The inhabitants of Paris are so changed that you would scarcely acknowledge them to be the people whom you formerly knew. That attention to dress which once characterised the natives of this country, and forbade a Frenchman to appear after dinner except in full dress, or with a sword, prevails no more. I find a revolution in their manners as well as in their government; and, although their prejudices will not be totally removed for some time, there is little doubt but the succeeding generation will be relieved from all that frivolity which marked their ancestors. The share which every individual now has in the Legislature gives him a turn for thinking more consonant to manhood. It is inconceivable the change that has taken place in the minds of men. The Palais Royal, the Tuileries, the bridges, and all the public places, are inundated with newsvenders and politicians; all ranks of men begin to reason on the principles of government, and the Minister who would dare to divert the current into another channel would risk something more than his place or character. We mistake these people very much in England by imagining that their manners will remain the same as they were under the despotism of their ancient Government. Whoever feels a pleasure in contemplating the progress of human knowledge, or whoever admits that governments are established for the good of the whole and not for the aggrandisement of a few, will be delighted at the change that has taken place in France, and will look with impatience to a similar revolution in those states where an individual raised above his equals by the accident of birth and decorated with the title of sovereign considers himself absolute master of the lives and fortunes of those whom he has the temerity to consider as his dependent subjects. Thank Heaven! we are in England subject only to the laws. The laws alone are sovereign. And it is to this circumstance that we are indebted for being the greatest nation in the world.

Mr. Miles to Lord Buckingham

September 6, 1790

The anarchy and distraction that unhappily prevail in this country afford arguments in favour of despotism of which the partisans of tyranny will not fail to avail themselves. Fourteen months have elapsed since the Revolution was accomplished, and yet the Government is without credit, and its authority is so precarious that its very existence depends upon the zeal and activity of the National Guard, whose patriotism, firmness, and discretion in all probability preserved the populace last Thursday night from dictating the law and renewing those excesses which were committed in the beginning of the Revolution. The drums beat to arms through every street in Paris, the infantry were drawn up three deep, the cavalry and cannon were out, and 40,000 of the people, it is said, had assembled in the Tuileries clamorous for the dismission of the Minister,[1] whilst some of them insisted, not only on the death of the Marquis de Bouillé for his heroic conduct at Nancy, but on that of the Marquis de Lafayette. Since that period the patrols have been doubled, and M. Necker, alarmed for his life, has given in his resignation, assigning the two millions of livres due to him from the nation, and his houses, to answer any demand that may be brought against him. Public report says that he is off. The fact is, he went in a *fiacre* to sleep out of town on Friday night, but he returned on Saturday, and in a few days he will quit the kingdom for ever. His vanity must be too much humbled to allow him to return, should even the people be inconsistent enough to desire it. Thus ends the political career of a man whom I pronounced to be a charlatan when he succeeded the Archbishop of Sens,[2] and whoever succeeds him must have great talents to repair the finances of the King, and still greater courage to attempt it, for he will be exposed to the caprice of an ill-judging multitude ready to assassinate the object they have deified only the moment before.

I am sorry to find amidst all these internal distractions a spirit of jealousy excited against England, which,

---

[1] The War Minister, M. Latour Dupin.
[2] Loménie de Brienne, formerly Archbishop of Toulouse.

exclusive of its injustice, must retard and perhaps endanger the re-establishment of the Government in France. The press teems with libels. If the populace should read and believe them, the English here will be exposed to insult and risk. Mr. Pitt is declared to be the greatest enemy to his country. Monsieur Dupont, a member of the National Assembly, introduced in his published observations on the ' Family Compact ' the expression—' Les amis de l'Angleterre et du trouble.'[1] His rank and education should inspire him with sentiments of justice and moderation. These falsehoods propagated, and this animosity encouraged, may eventually prevent the final establishment of that freedom which the nation has acquired, and which, as a friend to humanity, I should rejoice to see secured. The more shortsighted politicians here do not perceive that, if they madly plunge their country into war in order to protect the ill-founded and extravagant claims of Spain, they risk not only possessions in the East and West Indies, but the possibility of an army invading France from the banks of the Rhine to recover the possessions of the German Princes, which, although secured to them by the Treaty of Westphalia, the National Assembly lately offered by Commissaries sent to Darmstadt to compromise, but which the Princes insisted on preserving fully

[1] ' Que font en France les amis de l'Angleterre et du trouble, ceux qui veulent nous précipiter dans l'isolement au dehors, ceux qui veulent entretenir l'anarchie au dedans, ceux qui veulent nous conduire, comme la Pologne, au démembrement de l'état ? Ils s'attachent aux expressions, ils négligent l'essentiel, ils nous crient: " Rompez le traité ; abandonnez vos alliés ; engagez-vous dans une discussion très embrouillée ; en attendant qu'elle soit éclaircie, laissez accabler la seule puissance qui vous ait jamais efficacement prêté son secours, ou laissez-la s'unir avec la seule puissance qui ait constamment montré l'intention de vous nuire, et qui croit avoir des intérêts opposés aux vôtres: vous verrez ensuite ce que vous aurez à faire." '—*Archives Parlementaires*, 3 Août, 1790, tome xvii. p. 587.

and entire. Should such an event ever happen, a civil war will follow of course. The nobility dispersed would reassemble and revenge the pretended wrongs they have received. The idea industriously circulated in Paris by the enemies of the Revolution is that the English wantonly quarrel with the Court of Madrid either to crush Spain or force her into a treaty of commerce with us, so that, in the one case, England would then fall upon France and destroy her marine, and in the other the most valuable part of French commerce would be lost. To prevent this latter result, the necessity of *confirming* the 'Family Compact' is urged.

The people seem to be on the point of undoing all that their courage and patriotism have hitherto effected. From infancy I have been an advocate for a free government, but little thought I should ever become its champion on Gallic ground. The dissipations of this metropolis do not suit my manners. Paris must be dreadfully *ennuyant* for any rational being without suitable companions, and terribly dangerous for young men without conduct or experience. The people have their resource in the Palais Royal, that sink of infamy, where the depravity of the passions has full scope. I have happily made acquaintance with the Maréchale de Richelieu, who is very civil to me, and the Duke and Duchess d'Aremberg, whom I had seen at Bruxelles, very politely sent to invite me to dinner the instant they heard I was in town. Good company is a most desirable thing here. In addition to their society, the Duke has undertaken to get me introduced into the club at the Jacobins, also into that of 1789, into which Lord Clive has been lately received. My known attachment to liberty will secure me, I trust, a welcome reception; and if I could inspire those two societies with the same rational zeal for the real prosperity of their country which I possess for my own, I should have an additional reason to rejoice in the honour of being admitted a member. I shall not despair of seeing France and England in alliance. Such a result from the Revolution would render that great event a blessing to the world.

RÉFLEXIONS SUR LE PROJET DE DÉCRET PROPOSÉ LE 25 *DE CE MOIS, AOÛT,* 1790, *PAR M. DE MIRABEAU L'AÎNÉ.*

La saison est avancée ; dans trois semaines les vents de l'équinoxe vont forcer les escadres de Suède, de Russie, d'Espagne, et d'Angleterre de rentrer dans leurs ports, et cependant le comité diplomatique nous propose à l'improviste, dans le cinquième article de son projet de décret, de porter en ce moment jusqu'à quarante-cinq vaisseaux de ligne nos flottes en commission.[1] Je n'examinerai point l'état actuel de nos finances. Je dirai seulement, de quoi s'agit-il donc ? Sommes-nous attaqués ? Nos colonies, sont-elles en danger ? Non, c'est toujours de l'affaire du Nootka-sund dont il s'agit ; c'est toujours sous le prétexte frivole et insidieux de quelques peaux de loutre achetées par les Anglois sur les côtes de la Californie, à quatre ou cinq mille lieues d'ici, qu'on veut absolument nous engager dans une guerre destructive de notre liberté. On veut que, dans la crainte de risquer pour un an ou deux notre commerce avec l'Espagne, nous hasardions réellement notre commerce général ailleurs, celui du Levant surtout, nos colonies, le reste de nos finances, notre sang, et notre constitution. Remarquez bien que c'est sous la prési-

[1] 'Décrète que le Roi sera prié de donner des ordres pour que les escadres françaises en commission puissent être portées à 45 vaisseaux de ligne, avec un nombre proportionné de frégates et autres bâtiments.' —*Archives Parlementaires*, xviii. 293.

dence de M. Dupont que cette proposition est faite. Mais ce n'est pas tout ; cette fois-ci le piége est complet ; il nous enveloppe dans tous les sens. Lisons les deux premiers articles du projet proposé :

'L'Assemblée Nationale décrète :

'1°. Que tous les traités précédemment conclus' (les traités avec la maison d'Autriche et avec la Russie) 'continueront à être respectés par la nation française, jusqu'au moment où elle aura revu ou modifié ces divers actes, d'après le travail qui sera fait à cet égard, et les instructions que le Roi sera prié de donner à ses agens auprès des puissances de l'Europe'—c'est-à-dire, jusqu'au moment où l'Europe entière sera en feu, et où le Ministère françois aura dissous l'Assemblée Nationale et renversé notre constitution.

'2°. Que, préliminairement à ce travail, et à l'examen approfondi des traités que la nation croira devoir conserver ou changer, le Roi sera prié de faire connaître à toutes les puissances avec lesquelles la France a des engagemens, que, la justice et l'amour de la paix étant la base de la Constitution française, la nation ne peut, en aucun cas, reconnaître, dans les traités, que les stipulations purement défensives et commerciales.'

Remarquez bien que la première phrase du premier article—'tous les traités précédemment conclus continueront à être respectés'—rend offensives dans le fait les stipulations déclarées à la fin du second article purement défensives et commerciales. C'est dans cette équivoque que le Ministère françois saura bien interpréter à sa fantaisie lorsqu'il aura les armes à la main, que nous voyons avec une profonde douleur l'influence absolue de ce même Ministère sur la bonhomie du comité diplomatique, et le mystère de toutes les combinaisons du comité autrichien de Saint-Cloud. A Dieu ne plaise que nous soupçonnions la pureté d'âme de M. Mirabeau l'aîné, ni d'aucun des membres du comité diplomatique, mais nous pourrions dire que quand même l'Espagne, l'Autriche, et la Russie auroient payé mille piastres, mille ducats de Kremnitz, et mille roubles, chaque lettre des deux articles que nous venons de citer, ces puissances n'auroient pas mieux réussi pour nous attacher à leur destinée et nous faire servir d'instrumens à leur ambition. En effet, comment se persuader que l'Autriche et la Russie, liées par des traités secrets et très récents avec l'Espagne, ne profiteroient pas de l'alliance, prétendue défensive seulement, mais offensive en effet, de la France avec cette dernière pour forcer même la France par des ruses et des négociations instantes à prendre un parti général en Europe, non seulement contre l'Angleterre, mais contre la Hollande, la Suède, et le Roi de Prusse surtout, qui vient d'humilier si complètement Léopold à Reichenbach, et qui met en ce moment Catherine dans la nécessité d'accepter toutes les conditions qu'il veut lui imposer ? Comment ne pas voir que les véritables motifs des efforts incroyables du comité autrichien de S.-Cloud, dans cette circonstance, sont de relever l'Autriche et la Russie de leur humiliation en nous engageant dans une guerre qui détruira en même temps notre commerce, notre constitution, notre liberté, et dévorera les ressources que nous promet la vente des biens ecclésiastiques ? Voilà les deux buts combinés de la cour. Je le prédis d'avance et le consigne dans cette feuille, si l'Assemblée Nationale adopte le plan du comité diplomatique en tout, ou même en partie, nous sommes entièrement perdus, ou bien une guerre générale en Europe produira une révolution générale dans ce continent ; il n'y a pas de milieu : tout ce que nous pourrons faire en faveur de cette dernière chance sera de charger nos troupes de mer et de terre d'un grand nombre d'exemplaires de quelques bonnes brochures traduites en différentes langues, sur la déclaration des droits de l'homme et des nations pour les semer dans les pays étrangers, et d'inviter ces mêmes troupes à chercher l'occasion de boire avec les Anglois, les Prussiens, les Hollandais et les Suédois, et de s'embrasser bien fraternellement, au lieu de s'égorger comme des bêtes féroces pour le bon plaisir et la fantaisie de Léopold ou de Catherine. Si l'Assemblée Nationale y réfléchit bien, quoiqu'on ne lui ait donné que vingt-quatre heures pour la réflexion à la plus grande question qu'on puisse proposer, elle se contentera de se porter purement du côté de l'Angleterre, c'est le parti le plus sage et le plus prudent.[1]

[*Extracts from the Speech of M. Mirabeau in the National Assembly on August* 25, 1790

M. le Président : L'ordre du jour est un rapport du comité diplomatique sur l'affaire d'Espagne.[2]

M. de Mirabeau l'aîné : 'Messieurs, un décret de l'Assemblée Nationale, en date du premier Août, a chargé votre comité diplomatique de lui présenter son avis sur la réponse que demande l'Espagne. Le désir et le besoin de la paix, l'espérance, presque certaine, qu'elle ne sera pas troublée, les principes de notre Constitution nouvelle, nous ont seuls guidé dans l'examen de cette importante question.

. . . .

Supposons donc que l'Angleterre prévoie avec inquiétude l'accroissement qu'une Constitution libre doit

---

[1] See Introduction, pp. 45-47.
[2] The members of the Diplomatic Committee, elected as *le résultat du scrutin*, were MM. Fréteau, De Mirabeau l'aîné, Du Châtelet, Barnave, De Menou, D'André.—*Archives Parlementaires*. xvii. 489.

un jour donner à nos forces, à notre commerce, à notre crédit ; qu'elle lise dans propre histoire l'avenir de nos destinées, et que, par une fausse politique, elle veuille profiter des circonstances pour rompre une alliance formidable dont elle a souvent senti tout le poids : quelles sont les mesures qu'une telle supposition doit nous inspirer ? Nous ne pouvons balancer le nombre des vaisseaux anglais qu'avec ceux de notre allié. L'intérêt nous oblige donc de confirmer notre alliance avec l'Espagne, et le seul moyen de la conserver, c'est de remplir fidèlement nos traités.

. . . . . .

On pensera, peut-être, que l'Espagne, sûre de notre appui, se rendra difficile dans la négociation de la paix ; au lieu, dira-t-on, qu'en ne nous mêlant pas de cette querelle, l'accommodement que nous désirons n'éprouverait ni lenteurs, ni difficultés. Nous avons déjà repoussé cette objection ; les principes que nous vous proposons de reconnaître ne laisseront aucun doute à la Grande-Bretagne sur nos intentions, et manifesteront à l'Espagne que notre Constitution regarde seulement les engagements défensifs comme obligatoires ; notre conduite ne la portera donc à aucune démarche hostile que ne nécessiterait pas une juste défense ; elle ne pourra non plus contrarier les Anglais que dans le cas où ils voudraient être agresseurs. D'ailleurs, s'il est certain que l'abandon de nos engagements forcerait l'Espagne à négocier plus promptement la paix avec l'Angleterre, il n'est que trop facile de prévoir quelle pourrait être dans ce cas la nature de cet accommodement, et le tort irréparable qu'une semblable négociation ferait à notre crédit, à notre commerce. Enfin, messieurs, ce n'est point le pacte de famille entier que nous vous proposons de ratifier. Conclu dans un temps où les rois parlaient

seuls au nom des peuples, comme si les pays qu'ils
gouvernaient n'étaient que leur patrimoine, ou que la
volonté d'un monarque pût décider de leurs destinées,
ce traité porte le nom singulier de *Pacte de famille*, et il
n'existe aucun de nos décrets qui n'ait annoncé à
l'Europe entière que nous ne reconnaîtrons désormais
que des *Pactes de nation*.

. . . .

C'est pour réunir les différents objets annoncés dans
son rapport que votre comité vous propose le décret
suivant, comme le plus propre à remplir vos engagements
sans imprudence, à changer l'ancien système sans se-
cousses, à éviter la guerre sans faiblesse. L'Assemblée
Nationale décrète, &c., &c.']¹

Monsieur Mirabeau to Mr. Miles

17 Septembre, 1790

Des circonstances imprévues empêchent M. de Mirabeau de dîner demain chez lui, et d'y recevoir Monsieur
Miles. Il le prie de recevoir son excuse et de trouver
bon que la partie soit remise à Samedi prochain toutes
affaires cessantes.

Monsieur Pétion to Mr. Miles

Paris: 17 Septembre, 1790

M.,—Vous êtes prévenu que la Société des Amis de
la Constitution, séante aux Jacobins de la rue Saint-
Honoré, vous a admis au nombre de ses membres. Vous
êtes prié en conséquence de venir prendre votre carte
d'entrée au bureau du secrétariat, qui sera ouvert, pour
cet objet, les jours d'Assemblée, depuis six jusqu'à sept
heures du soir. PÉTION.

[1] *Archives Parlementaires*, xviii. 263–266; also 291, 293; *Histoire
Parlementaire*, vii. 119-122. See *Despatches of Earl Gower*, August 27,
1790.

Monsieur Crelet to Mr. Miles

Au Palais Royal, No. 105:
ce 24 Septembre, 1790

Monsieur,—J'ai l'honneur de vous prévenir que la Société de 1789, dans son assemblée générale du 19 de ce mois, vous a nommé pour l'un de ses membres. Elle a suivi en cela votre vœu, qui lui a été porté par M. Godin, et elle désire que vous partagiez l'empressement qu'elle a de vous recevoir.

J'ai l'honneur d'être, avec le plus sincère attachement, monsieur, votre très humble et très obéissant serviteur,

CRELET,

Commissaire de la Société.

Le concierge est chargé de votre quittance pour la cotisation, qui est de 120 liv. pour la première année.

Mr. Miles to Mr. Rose

Paris: October 11, 1790

You will be astonished when I tell you it is my intention to harangue an assembly of Frenchmen in their native language. The multiplicity of atrocious libels daily published against England, and the indefatigable pains taken by the friends of the ancient Government to excite, or rather to inflame, the populace against us, have determined me to address the Jacobins, of which society I am a member, and endeavour to engage the National Assembly to decree that those writings which tend to inflame the two nations are infamous. I have tried to soothe the different prints into good temper by describing the real state of the dispute between our Court and that of Spain—appealing to their justice—and this, not only from the love of truth, but for the personal security of our countrymen in Paris; for, if the reports in circulation are once believed by the populace, that the British Ministry have by their emissaries in France excited the insurrection that rages yet with increasing violence at Brest,[1] every Englishman holds his life at the mercy of the mob. Warm in whatever concerns my country or liberty and truth, I hope my zeal will be justified by the motives, and that the two nations, one of which I love and the other respect, will understand their interests, and despise the cabals that would inspire them with rancour and hatred towards each other.

The great object of my mission is in general much liked. The business is realised. Mr. Pitt may, if he follows it up, secure its accomplishment, and thereby lay the foundation for a union between the two kingdoms —an issue which I have long had at heart, and which, emancipated as the French people are from despotism, is the wisest course the British Minister can pursue. With France in our close neighbourhood, its citizens in possession of conscious freedom, active, warlike, and enterprising, we shall have no other alternative than either to cherish amity or else, like gamecocks, live in perpetual hostility until one or the other succumbs and falls.

MR. MILES TO SIR EDWARD NEWENHAM

Paris: November 27, 1790

As a friend to liberty, I rejoice in the Revolution that destroyed the systematic tyranny by which France

---

[1] 'All discipline and subordination seemed to have disappeared from the ranks, and when directions were given to arm the fleet at Brest, in consequence of the English preparations for war with Spain, the alarming fact was disclosed that the same spirit of mutiny was equally prevalent among the sailors, and that the French fleet was entirely unfit for a serious war.'—*Lecky's History*, v. 537.

had been oppressed for ages; but as an enemy to anarchy, dissimulation, and public rapine, I detest the conduct of those whose temporary popularity alone preserves them from the halter, and who do not appear disposed to restore public tranquillity until every creature that displeases them is banished or massacred. Everything is in a state of confusion; nor do I see any prospect of the return of order without a violent contest, not only between proscribed aristocracy and reigning democracy, but between those who subverted the ancient Government. Mirabeau, more distinguished by his crimes than by his abilities, and whose character in any other country would exclude him from all public and private confidence, aspires to govern this distracted kingdom; but the principle on which he wishes to carry his point is ill adapted to the character of the nation, and is to the full as barbarous as it is happily impracticable. There are more than the Queen in his way. You may imagine what a deluge of blood must flow before this man can get himself declared protector, or the monarchy annihilated, for such are his views; and, as he is not without his *adorateurs*, I leave you to judge of the virtues and principles of a people who can elevate so despicable and so profligate a vagabond into power and dignity. Mirabeau is the declared enemy of your friend the Marquis de Lafayette, whom I firmly believe to be a good citizen, and to possess as much moral rectitude and to be as sincere as it is possible for mankind to be. The contest for superiority is between these two men; and, when I tell you that the former has rendered it current that the latter is gone over to the Court, you will not be surprised whenever you hear that Lafayette has fallen a sacrifice to a mob more brutal and ferocious and less governable than any that England ever produced in the worst of times. I am convinced that Lafayette wishes to see France free for the sake of his fellow-citizens more than for his own, whilst Mirabeau wishes to see his country emancipated from the shackles of monarchy merely to enslave it more effectually and more disgracefully by those of a turbulent and remorseless democracy. Such is the state of parties in France, and you who know my sentiments will not be at a loss to guess to whom my voice will be given. Believe me, the French are not so enlightened as is generally thought; there is a great deal of intellectual capacity in the nation, but there is very little knowledge and still less principle.[1] I know no people so corrupt as the higher orders of Frenchmen; and it is the extreme profligacy of the clergy and nobility that retards the completion of the work in hand. The peace with Spain is fortunate for France; but Spain, I am

[1] 'The generality of foreigners, excepting the French, know little more of other nations than what they read in the public prints. If the truth is contested, the only answer they give is, "Il faut que cela soit vrai, car il est imprimé." A person in high rank and in high official situation, on being told that almost every house in London had a lamp at its door, expressed his astonishment, and, addressing himself to me, demanded: "Est-il vrai, monsieur, que les rues de Londres sont si bien éclairées?" "Oui, monsieur," I answered, "les rues et *les hommes* y sont très eclairés." The same person could not easily believe that Mr. Pitt was not a lord.'— *Authentic Correspondence with M. Le Brun and Others, &c.*, by W. A. Miles, London, 1796, p. 18.

'I met to-day with an instance of ignorance in a well-dressed French merchant that surprised me. He had plagued me with abundance of tiresome foolish questions, and then asked for the third or fourth time what country I was of. I told him I was a Chinese. How far off is that country? I replied 200 leagues. "Deux cents lieues! Diable! c'est un grand chemin!" The other day a Frenchman asked me, after telling him I was an Englishman, if we had any trees in England. I replied that we had a few. Had we any rivers? Oh, none at all. "Ah, ma foi, c'est bien triste!" This incredible ignorance is to be attributed, like everything else, to Government.'— *Travels of Arthur Young in France and Italy*, 1787-1789, p. 37.

assured, would not have made peace if the revolt had not happened among the seamen at Brest. This treaty does credit to Mr. Pitt's Administration; there is one provision in the Convention which former Ministers never thought of, which is that, in case of infraction, the commanding officers on the spot are to transmit an account to their respective Governments, and not to offer any outrage. This will put it out of the power of subaltern authority to plunge the two nations into war; and, as this provision is new as well as salutary, I trust you will not forget to render the homage due to the fidelity and vigilance of the British Minister. Should this letter arrive late, I wish you to recall the circumstance to the memory of the House of Commons.

I met, my dear Newenham, with Madame de Tarente again at dinner at the Duc d'Aremberg's some days since, and had a long conversation with her on the deplorable condition of the royal family, and on the very little interest which the Queen seems to inspire the people with at this moment. I am sure that her Majesty is ill advised, and that her ambition, mortified not humbled, seeks to recover the stupendous height from which she has fallen. She soars at impossibilities. I am sure that she will rue the facility with which she listens to weak and wicked minds, who imagine it is as safe and as easy to climb a precipice as to fall from it. Mark my words, she will fall a victim in the attempt, and perish in the midst of tumult and general carnage. I requested Madame de Tarente to assure the Queen that, if her Majesty would condescend to trust herself to me, I would pledge myself to take her safe to England; adding that I had no instructions from anyone in my own country to embark on such an enterprise, nor had it been suggested to me by anyone else, but it was the mere dictate of my own distressed feelings on beholding her Majesty exposed to daily insult, which, from the ferment that prevailed at Paris, might have a fatal issue. I was very sensible of the hazard of the attempt, and of the consequences to myself in the event of its failure; yet I would cheerfully encounter the risk to rescue her Majesty from her very perilous situation, if she would commit her person to my care. Madame de Tarente executed her mission without delay, and delivered to me at the Duc d'Aremberg's the following answer from the Queen: 'Her Majesty is fully sensible of the generosity and magnanimity of your offer, but as she is resolved to share the fate of the King, and never to separate herself from him, her Majesty is under the necessity of declining your offer, whilst thanking you at the same time for the interest which you take in her safety.' You will say that this is perfectly consistent with my romantic character; but who would not do as much to rescue a woman from insult and from danger? She has great fortitude of mind; but as she is resolved to share the fortunes of her husband, I wish I had the power to persuade her to desist altogether from *political* intrigue. The clergy and nobility are digging both her grave and their own. I compare France to a horse that has got the bit out of his mouth and run away with his rider. In that case prudence says the rider should either sit quiet or throw himself off. Do you know Lord Kerry? He is here, and in my neighbourhood. I am told he is extremely social. I should like to make his acquaintance. Let me hear if you have received all my letters. This is the fifth I have written to you from Paris. Direct to me in future at No. 113 Rue du Faubourg St. Honoré, à Paris.

Mr. Miles to Mr. Rose

Paris: November 30, 1790

I have very great pleasure in assuring you that my mission is likely to have a fortunate issue, and that no difficulty will be made to dissolve the 'Family Compact,' provided that France can count upon the friendship of England in exchange. I have been obliged to observe the utmost circumspection in broaching this subject, and to break ground, as it were, at a considerable distance from the matter itself, *mais toujours sur le chemin qui y mène*. I always contrived to avoid all mention of Spain, preferring to have her brought into discussion by the person in conversation with me. The very title of the treaty between France and Spain is held in abhorrence by all the middle and lower orders of men in France. The 'Family Compact' they consider as nothing else than a league or agreement between the two sovereigns for their own personal advantage or aggrandisement, in which the people have no interest, from which they can derive no benefit, but for which they are to pay and to bleed. The national prejudice against Spain fortifies this opinion, and Mr. Pitt may count to a certainty on the concurrence of the people with this his favourite object. Mirabeau, Barnave, Lafayette, Frochot, and several other members of the National Assembly, are well disposed to dissolve the 'Family Compact,' but they require, if not an equivalent for the loss of Spain, a something to substitute in its place—to fill the vacuum in the foreign political relations of France. And now, if I dare presume to offer an opinion upon State affairs, I would say to you that this is a most happy conjuncture for proposing that alliance between the two countries which I took the liberty to request you would mention to Mr. Pitt in May and June last. I can take upon me positively to assure you that such a proposition would be joyfully received by all the popular party, and by the great bulk of the nation. I am even authorised to say as much to you by those who are most likely to carry such a measure into a decree of the National Assembly, and who will propose it, if Mr. Pitt will come forward. The King's party will oppose, for they dread an alliance between France and England. They look upon us as the authors of the Revolution—as having disseminated the seeds of liberty in this country—and consider that while any amicable connection or intercourse exists between the two peoples a counter-revolution, on which this party are fatally bent, will never take place. To put an end to this intercourse they propagate tales and falsehoods against us hourly, in order to force their country into a war with us. God forbid that their wicked efforts should succeed; God send that France may be free, and that wars between her and England may be put an end to for ever! I remember your saying to me, when I proposed the alliance, that it would not be advisable to think of it at present; that it would be better to wait and see what turn matters would take in France before such a measure was proposed. Believe me, Mr. Pitt could not choose a better, happier moment than the present. I am on the spot. I know the temper and feeling of the French nation. They are at this moment most cordially disposed to such a union. They would accede to it in raptures; and, if in the vile publications which daily appear here you sometimes by chance see a contrary sentiment, it is that the fears of the people are worked upon by the aristocratic party, and the former are taught to consider us as their bitter enemies. The proposition of an alliance from the British Minister would do away this suspicion. It would diffuse a general joy throughout this distracted country, accomplish the great object they have in view of a *free* Government, and do away all fear, all jealousy of parties and of foreign powers, and bind France to us for ever. It is even the interest of the royal family to accede to this plan, for, in the agitated state, or rather frenzy, of men's minds from the uncertainty of what issue their efforts in favour of liberty will have, it is possible that this fallen, degraded, hapless monarch may become a victim to popular fury and alarm, and be torn to pieces by the multitude. France is more afraid of us than of any nation, or of all the nations of Europe put together, and if Mr. Pitt is anxious to have the alliance with Spain dissolved he has the means of carrying it into immediate execution and of securing the repose of the world.

MR. MILES TO LORD BUCKINGHAM

Paris: December 13, 1790

Two months have elapsed since I despatched my first letter to Mr. Rose on the subject of my mission. I have not received any answer; and, doubtful of my own judgment in a matter of equal delicacy and importance, it is painful to be left to my own guidance, without advice, communication, or any kind of instructions whatever. The matter, however, confided to me has been happily executed. France is well-disposed to come into the measure; and the friends of liberty, I may venture to assert, are for it to a man. I have presumed to go a step farther than I was authorised, and have felt the general pulse as to an *alliance* with England. Every man I conversed with on the subject was in rapture at the idea. It struck them in the same point of view as it did me, and they behold in it a confirmation, not only of their revolution, and of an assurance of *freedom* to themselves and posterity, but of perpetual peace with us, which, believe me, is the general wish of the country, and the very idea of it intoxicates every man with joy to whom it has been mentioned. The moment is favourable. The critical situation of the kingdom conspires to ensure a reception to the measure which would be the more acceptable as coming from a nation represented as hostile even to inveteracy, with whom France has been almost always at war, and which is alone formidable to her. I took the liberty to start the idea of an alliance, and to urge it several times in London to Mr. Rose before I came here; but he seemed to throw cold water on it. If Mr. Pitt would propose it, I am sure he would be as popular in this country as he is in his own, and be enabled to do as he pleases. The 'Family Compact' would be dissolved directly, and no power on earth would dare even to think of disturbing the repose or of attacking either nation.

Although your Lordship derives your information of foreign politics from sources superior to any that I can pretend to, I may venture to inform you that I was this morning assured by a person, whose rank and veracity entitle him to credit, and whose situation furnishes him with the means of early and authentic information, that there is a negotiation carrying on between France and Prussia; that the Emperor will have an army of 80,000 men in the Netherlands, 30,000 of which are actually on the march, and the report here is that Mr. Pitt is dissatisfied with the Court of Vienna. An attempt is being made to unite the *côté gauche avec le côté droit* in the National Assembly, eight members of the former excepted; and this coalition is considered by the moderate as the only means of preventing a civil war. I am assured that, if the Emperor or any other potentate should declare war against France, a reward of from two to four millions of livres will be offered for their heads. Such a proposal has been suggested in the Jacobin Club. I was present when it was made. The person had been in conversation some time in what is called the President's box with Robespierre, and the secretaries to the club—he was afterwards with Danton; but who he was I do not know. He soon mounted the tribune and proposed that a number of patriots should enrol themselves for the purpose of putting those kings to death who should declare war against France. The proposition was received with great applause, and this frenzy, which for the sake of *Liberty* I wish could be moderated, is increasing daily. When it will end, and to what extent it will be carried, it is impossible to foresee; but as it is evidently the result of fear—of an apprehension that despotism will again resume her authority, and that the Revolution will be marred by foreign powers—nothing would so much contribute to quiet men's minds in this country, and to the return of order, as a solemn assurance from our Cabinet of a pacific disposition towards France. She certainly watches with jealousy, alarm, and anxiety every measure of our Government; she knows our force, and our influence on the Continent; and, although I believe Lord Gower, during the whole of the Spanish negotiation, breathed nothing but the language of peace towards this country, the French are suspicious of us, and there would be policy, and something better than policy, even magnanimity, my Lord, in our coming forward and doing away this jealousy before it propagates itself throughout the nation and infects the public mind. The *Royal party* most infamously endeavour, by their conversation, by the press, and by every way they can devise, to excite and confirm this suspicion. They avail themselves of every opportunity to assure an inflamed populace that we meditate their destruction in order to revenge ourselves for the part which France took in the American war. The people are daily lectured to distrust us; and, if measures are not taken to counteract this cruel calumny, the National Assembly, which cannot move but in unison with the public voice, may be forced to abet the diabolical views of the red-hot Royalists by declaring against us. When Mr. Pitt was making the commercial treaty, I took the liberty to applaud the wisdom of approaching France as a *friend*, and to hope that it would lead to an alliance. If ever a moment for so desirable an event was more propitious than another, it is the present. Your Lordship has assured me that Mr. Pitt is pacific in his temper, and that war would mar his projects for the welfare of our country. He is at present in some sort the master of the destiny of both nations, and he has it in his power to unite them, and to banish warfare from Europe and the world. France is well-disposed to unite with us. I am authorised to say as much by Mirabeau, by Lafayette, and by several members of the National Assembly, who would be proud to have a share in accomplishing an alliance between France and England.

I am sure that, if we were to come forward with such a proposal at this moment, when France is menaced by the Emperor, by the King of Sardinia, and by all the King's friends, as they call themselves, who are forming regiments on the banks of the Rhine to wage war against their own country, the English nation would be adored, and calm restored to the public mind throughout France. An offer to protect her, should she be attacked in the moment of her internal confusion and distress, or even a declaration of neutrality on our part, would endear us to the French; and, in the former instance, our magnanimity would be the general theme of grateful and joyful exultation. It would quiet men's fears here, and tend to the restoration of order, whereas at present, as our intentions are not known, we are feared, and to be feared is to be hated. An avowal of friendship at this moment would make us beloved.

It is asserted that the deputies from the States of Flanders offered to submit under the guarantee of the three Powers, but the Baron de Bender effaced that condition. The clemency and discipline, however, observed by the Austrian troops and by the Government announce a disposition on the part of the Emperor to conciliate the affections of the people.

I find that Mr. Elliot is going as Minister to America. Your Lordship will have received by the last post my two letters. I mentioned a visit from that gentleman on the eve of his departure from Paris. It will be great satisfaction to my mind to hear that you possess the various letters and pacquets I took the liberty to send you. As Lord Gower has my address, I shall beg the favour, in case you should honour me with a line, to transmit it under cover to his Lordship.

Mr. Miles to Sir Edward Newenham.

Paris: December 13, 1790.

I mean to answer you more fully by the messenger on his return from Marseilles. The Marquis de Lafayette has also promised to write by the same opportunity.

Your letter dated the 29th of last month proves that our correspondence is interrupted somewhere. I have been in my present lodging two months, yet you direct to me Rue de Grenelle. This is the fourth letter I have written to you since November 1. There is no police here. In the moment of revolution, authority acts on the emergency; forms are as much dispensed with as under despotism itself; and it cannot be otherwise, for the violence of contending factions prevents the establishment of order. Believe me, nothing has been done as yet in this country worthy of being imitated in yours. There is much intellectual capacity in France, but not so much acquired knowledge, and still less principle. The National Assembly commits blunders, and acts so oppressively and ignorantly that they provoke contempt. Burke's book makes a great noise in Paris. It is upon the whole a poor performance. The Duke d'Aremberg desired me to give my opinion of it in a letter to him, which I did, and of which several copies are in circulation. If I had been in London, I would have answered and refuted this apostle of despotism. Do not be so sanguine as to the affairs of this country. The National Assembly contains too much profligacy and ignorance to do much good to their fellow-citizens. It wants as much purgation as ever did the Court of Versailles. But the whole of the clergy and *noblesse* in the kingdom is one mass of corruption, and will continue so till the rising generation reaches manhood.[1] I am vexed to see the cause of humanity so ill conducted; and the greatest

---

[1] 'The clergy in France have been supposed by many persons in England to merit their fate from their peculiar profligacy. But the idea is not accurate. That so large a body of men, possessed of great revenues, should be free from vice would be improbable or rather impossible, but they preserved, what is not always preserved in England, an exterior decency of behaviour.'—*Arthur Young's Travels.* p. 543.

curse that could befall your country and mine would be to imitate the conduct of France since July 15, 1789. The 14th was a glorious day. Since that they have terribly mistaken the road. In short, how could men whose talent is intrigue alone become legislators and politicians in an instant?

MR. MILES TO THE DUC D'AREMBERG

Paris: 24 Décembre, 1790

Un auteur, Monseigneur, qui enveloppe ses idées d'un verbiage épais et difficile fera toujours tort au sujet qu'il traite, quelque important qu'il soit ; et voilà un des principaux défauts de l'ouvrage sur lequel votre Altesse m'a fait l'honneur de demander mon avis ; un défaut qui empêchera les paresseux d'en achever la lecture, et qui ne permettra pas aux gens peu instruits d'en approfondir les raisonnements. Tout homme impartial conviendra que l'ouvrage de M. Burke contient des vérités et des observations très justes et très spirituelles. Le malheur est que pour les découvrir, et encore plus pour les apprécier, il faut traverser une foule de mots inutiles dont elles sont ensevelies, pour ainsi dire, et qui me paraissent plus propres à grossir la brochure que d'en embellir le sujet ou en éclaircir le sens.[1] Je crois connaître ma langue à fond. Je crois avoir la faculté de comprendre assez généralement ce que je lis ; cependant, je me suis trouvé obligé de lire et de relire plusieurs passages, et cela avec si peu de profit au commencement que je fus tenté plus d'une fois d'en abandonner la lecture. Mais, si je fus offensé de la

---

[1] 'Burke, who was in some respects an immeasurably greater man [than Pitt], often emptied the House by his discursiveness, and excited ridicule or disgust by extravagances of passion, taste, and metaphor, which seemed scarcely compatible with sanity.'—Lecky, v. 10.

manière dont M. Burke s'est expliqué sur la Révolution
arrivée en Angleterre l'année 1688 ; si je fus dégoûté
d'un verbiage qui fatigue l'esprit et la patience, j'en fus
bien dédommagé dès qu'il commençait de parler des
affaires de ce malheureux pays, et de s'expliquer sur
les moyens que les révolutionnaires auraient dû adopter
au lieu de ceux qu'ils ont employés. C'est ici que M.
Burke s'est élevé au-dessus de lui-même en mettant au
jour toutes les bévues, toutes les fourberies, et toutes les
atrocités qu'on a faites en France depuis le 14 Juillet,
1789. La Révolution prise en elle-même est une char-
mante chose ; elle étoit même indispensable. J'en fus
enchanté. Je croyais voir la liberté et la justice des-
cendre du ciel en France pour faire le tour de l'Europe ;
mais les Français, enivrés de ce qu'ils ont fait, semblent
avoir perdu la vue de l'objet qu'ils cherchaient, et au
lieu d'établir un gouvernement équitable ils sont tombés
dans une anarchie affreuse, d'où je défie l'homme le plus
clairvoyant de voir une sortie, sinon que par une
guerre civile, ou par une explosion funeste, et à ceux
qui veulent et à ceux qui ne veulent pas la nouvelle
constitution.

J'ai l'honneur d'être, Monseigneur, &c., &c.

Mr. Miles to the Rev. Howell H. Edwards

Paris : December 24, 1790.

Much occupation, much chagrin, and much indisposition have hitherto prevented my writing to you, or
rather finishing the many letters I have commenced.
Nor do I believe that in the ease and security of
cloistered indolence I could have written three coherent
lines for the last three months. The extraordinary
events which occur in rapid succession, and set even

conjecture at defiance as to their issue, afford constant and laborious exercise to the inquisitive mind. The Revolution in France appeared to me at a distance to be one of those magnificent events which rouse even the most torpid into admiration and enthusiasm. Being, at the time it happened, on a visit at a German Court, where pride and ignorance contended for dominion, and where habitual servitude and degradation seemed rather a condition of existence than the effect of human policy, I formed the most extravagant expectations from the change, and, in the wildness of an imagination which sober men like you call distempered, I fancied that my favourite divinities—Liberty and Justice—resolved on a visit to this sublunary globe, had descended in Paris, and would make the tour of at least the continent of Europe. The Revolution, considered solely by itself, without its contingencies, and without any reference to the multifarious causes that accelerated it, had certainly something in it at once awful, instructive, and consolatory. I am positive that it must have impressed such ideas on all those who did not recur to the minutiæ of manners, morals, and politics, or whose indolence or incapacity rendered them indifferent or insensible to the various combinations by which the wonderful superstructure of civil society is raised and preserved. To those who see nothing in the destruction of the ancient Government but the subversion of despotism, the Revolution must have appeared glorious and worthy of example; and if courage had been aided by wisdom in the perilous enterprise, the spirit of freedom would probably have extended itself to Petersburg and Constantinople. The shores of the Baltic and Hellespont would have reverberated the animating cry of Liberty, and the despots of the earth would have fallen prostrate at the sound. A contrary conduct has served the cause of despotism by showing how immediate and almost inevitable the transition is from tyranny to anarchy, and how preferable is even the lawless dominion of one man to the wild, ungovernable, and capricious fury of millions! This country exhibits a melancholy proof of these woeful truths. Eighteen months have elapsed since the regal sceptre was violently torn from the imperfect grasp of its weak and deluded sovereign, and from that period to the present moment every kind of savage enormity—every possible plunder that the most confirmed ignorance could commit—have stained with sable spots the annals of this wretched, impoverished, and distracted kingdom. The nation is without revenue and government, its metropolis and provincial towns are without police, its legislature without talents, without probity, and without credit, except with a senseless and sanguinary rabble who would suspend their representatives from a 'lantern' with as little motive, and with as much facility, as they applaud their tumultuous and indecent harangues in the Senate. There is no prospect, not even the most distant, of public tranquillity being restored; no measures are taken, or in appearance thought on, to conciliate the disaffected, relieve the injured, or establish order; and, enamoured with confusion, they wish to render the evil contagious, and spread the horrible mischief over the habitable globe. Committees are formed and correspondences opened for this diabolical purpose with the firebrands of all nations and of all complexions; and in their nocturnal assemblies they seem to emulate each other in their indefatigable zeal for the extinction of all those virtues of the heart and mind which unite us together in social life.

I have been present when foreign letters were produced expressive of the impatience of their authors for the subversion of all order and decency in their respective countries. A letter from London was read last Friday to a heterogeneous assembly of near two thousand persons[1]—men, women, and children, at which the audience was gravely assured that, owing to the patriotism and perseverance of Mr. Sheridan, Great Britain was on the eve of following the *glorious* example of France; that already the populace, supported by that virtuous and intrepid Senator, had compelled the Minister to consent to a reform in Parliament; that the Prince of Wales, persuaded by Mrs. Fitzherbert, had consented to the measure, and even to the abolition of hereditary distinctions; that the nation had received every assurance of support and protection from that lady, and that no doubt whatever remained but that the English would soon give themselves a constitution as free and as perfect as that of France! The senseless herd made the concave ceiling resound with their vulgar and criminal applause at this coarse and sorry compliment, and with a ferocious joy in their countenance they cast their eager eyes around to see if they could discover a native of the country that had been so scandalously libelled. Credulous and infatuated people! They believe that the vagabonds in London, in imitation of those in Paris, have usurped the employment and abused the office of the hangman by exterminating truth and virtue and driving all that is great or good into exile. Contradiction, injustice, or stupidity, marks their every action. They are erecting churches, while they are tearing up religion by the roots; and the profligacy and vices practised in the interior of convents are represented on the stage. The massacre of the Protestants

[1] At the Jacobin Club.

in the reign of Charles IX. and the destruction of a Protestant family in 1762 at Toulouse—the story of Calas—have produced three affecting tragedies well calculated to give the *coup-de-grâce* to an expiring and proscribed clergy. In one word, the pale of the Roman Church is thrown down, not for the fraternal admission of any other sect, not for a generous and indiscriminate reception of the human species—a wide, benevolent, and equitable toleration, but to become a wild and sterile heath, affording neither hope nor consolation of any kind to the wayworn and dejected wanderer! You know the extreme liberality of my sentiments on religion, and will be astonished, perhaps, at the concern I feel for ecclesiastics; but, whatever my opinion may be on a matter which has so long divided mankind, I am hostile to every species of violence and injustice, and, therefore, I respect the rights of the priesthood equally with my own; and, believe me, averse as I am to all the pantomimic performances of Rome, I should be sorry to see even her vices give place to an insolent and unprincipled spirit of irreligion, which extinguishes all sentiment as well as all reverence, and gives to the crimes it engenders a permanent and triumphant existence. God alone knows when, and in what manner, this country will be extricated from the lamentable state of legalised anarchy into which it has fallen!

The paper money issued by the State, on the security of the Church lands, cannot be converted into cash, even in the metropolis, without a discount of near six per cent., and yet they are fully persuaded they are the freest people on earth, though their freedom consists in little else than the power of libelling and assassinating each other with impunity.

We are kept in constant alarms of counter-revolutions. Victims are almost daily sacrificed in the distant provinces to what is called the public safety; discontents prevail and increase in all parts of the kingdom, and, if they could be collected into one mass, the explosion would be terrible. A beggarly clergy and banished nobility complain loudly of oppression, and seek by means not only inadequate but frivolous to avenge themselves. Their folly and their madness, or rather their crimes, may cost the Queen and her infant family their lives, for the first formidable effort of the aristocratic party will be followed by the destruction of the royal family, and this will be its fate should any foreign power interfere. Nor would the sovereign who attempted to restore degraded majesty to the splendour and authority of the throne live to accomplish his work, for it is resolved to offer from two to four millions of French livres for the head of whoever orders his troops to invade this country. Little insurrections happen daily, and I am apprehensive that all these distractions will terminate in a civil war. The National Assembly suspects it, and accordingly prepares. Regular troops 152,000, and Militia 130,000, with the distribution of 50,000 muskets throughout the kingdom, are some of the measures already adopted to repel the threatened danger, whilst four millions have been issued to put the frontiers in a state of defence, *et le Général de Rochambeau, pour tranquilliser les esprits, est parti pour son commandement.*

M. de Lafayette, with whom I often dine, is in an awkward, and I think a dangerous situation. The Orleans party vote him to destruction, and will accomplish it should a commotion ensue! The Royal party pay court to the marquis, and his vanity, flattered by attentions, will probably accelerate his fall. This is what he may well fear, *mais, aveuglé par l'amour propre, il ne voit rien.* To give you an idea of the impotency and abject condition of this odd compounded and vitiated Government, I transcribe some passages from one of the many libels hourly circulated in this corrupt and execrable metropolis, the sink of every vice and the receptacle of adventurers and villains from all nations :

'Voilà donc un commencement de guerre civile, et c'est le Roi, chef des conspirateurs, que l'Assemblée Nationale, traîtresse, supplie de pourvoir à la défense des enfans de la patrie, des amis de la constitution ! Aveugles et lâches citoyens! vous touchez au moment de votre ruine. L'alarme est générale d'un bout à l'autre du royaume. Tous les bons citoyens voyent que leur perte est jurée. Commencez donc par vous assurer du Roi, du Dauphin, et de la famille royale ; mettez-les sous une forte garde, et que leurs têtes vous répondent de tous les événemens. Abattez ensuite, sans hésiter, la tête du général,[1] celles des ministres et des ex-ministres ; celles des maires et des municipaux ; passez au fil de l'épée tout l'état-major Parisien, tous les noirs, et les ministériels de l'Assemblée Nationale, tous les suppôts connus du despotisme. Je vous le répète, il ne vous reste que ce moyen de sauver la patrie. Il y a six mois que cinq à six cents têtes eussent suffi pour vous retirer de l'abime. Aujourd'hui que vous avez laissé stupidement vos ennemis implacables former des conjurations et se mettre en force, peut-être faudra-t-il en abattre cinq à six mille, mais fallût-il en abattre vingt mille, il n'y a pas à balancer un instant!' How can my pen describe the anguish I feel in reading the bloody scroll ? From this sample of premeditated murder I leave you

[1] M. Lafayette.

to judge of Gallic freedom and Gallic urbanity. This extreme licentiousness of the press proves either the savage and remorseless profligacy of Government or its impotency.

I was last night at the Jacobins, which I never saw so fully attended. M. Mirabeau took his leave; accused by his constituents, he has solicited permission to go into Provence, from whence he came, to justify himself. I never saw affliction of mind so visible on any face before. He appeared depressed even to despair; all that boldness that hitherto characterised every word he uttered, and which a guilty security alone could produce, seemed to have forsaken him; hopeless and fallen, he appeared to have a presentiment of his approaching destiny, and he quitted the room as if he was to enter it no more. I followed him downstairs, and read him as he descended. Two months are almost elapsed since I vowed to myself never to exchange another word with him. If he returns again to the National Assembly, you may add another wonder to the existing seven. He is publicly reproached as the cause of the massacre lately committed at Aix, one of the murdered people being the lawyer of Madame de Mirabeau in a process against her husband. Vengeance was also pronounced against the Minister for Home Affairs, M. de St. Priest. A schism has taken place between the civil and military guardians of the new constitution. In short, the fermentation increases. Navarre yet persists in refusing to pay any of the new taxes, and has no Deputies in the National Assembly, and consequently the Legislature is imperfect. The people are become suspicious of the national troops. A battalion in Paris, hostile to one of the measures of the National Assembly, asked their brethren in the provinces to federate with them, whereupon last night a motion was made to vote them useless, burdensome, and dangerous. All these dissensions amongst themselves augur no good to the commonwealth, and I foresee much serious mischief and calamity to the nation.

This long epistle will enable you to hold forth in confidence, for, as no man is more in the way of seeing and hearing than myself, you may depend on my information. In return I wish you would call on Lord Buckingham in Pall Mall, and inquire if his Lordship has received the many letters and French pamphlets I sent him. His silence makes me very uneasy, as I wrote with great freedom on public affairs. I have no objection to your submitting this letter to his perusal. It may be acceptable to him, and, as I am anxious to know the fate of my correspondence, I rely on your friendship to solicit the honour of an interview with the Marquis for the purpose of communicating to him my fears. Mrs. and Miss Miles remained at Franckfort till the coronation, and did not arrive here until the 13th of last month. They both wish you the compliments of the season, and wish themselves anywhere but where they are. The Duke and Duchess d'Aremberg are here, with their charming daughter, and are extremely attentive to us. I dine there whenever I please, and his horses are at my service. He deplores with me the wildness with which the French are managing the Revolution, and talks of going to Italy. I shall be sorry when his Grace leaves Paris, for I feel much friendship for him, great resource in his conversation, and I meet good company at his house. The Duchess is a charming woman, her daughter is very amiable and, I think, handsome; and it is to this family more than to any other in all the Austrian Netherlands that our countrymen are indebted for uncommon hospitality. But all our countrymen are not always sensible of the kindness they receive from foreigners, and they are sometimes apt to consider it, not as a favour, but as what they are entitled to.

MR. MILES TO MR. HENRY JAMES PYE [1]

Paris: January 5, 1791

Indisposition will account for my not having written to you since I left England. A temper naturally ardent and impatient is ill calculated to contend with the variety of evils with which this life under all its advantages, is perpetually assailed, and, unhappily for my repose, *trifles light as air* are wont to throw a damp upon my spirits, and render me very often indifferent in my choice to live or die. How far our pleasures are augmented by this extreme sensibility, or whether their being enhanced on such terms is desirable, I will not inquire. I mean nothing more by touching the string on which depends our joys and woes than to apologise for a silence of six months, the guilt of which, however, does not entirely belong to ill-humour and ill-health. These rather indisposed than incapacitated me from fulfilling the promise I made to you in July; and if I could have written with any tolerable accuracy on the lamentable condition of this distracted country my impatience to cultivate your friendship would long since have triumphed over the gout and spleen. Your becoming *Laureat* is a proof that you did not totally renounce *politics* when you renounced a seat in Parliament; on the contrary, you obtained a kind of prescriptive right to touch the high-sounding chord of

[1] Poet Laureat, and late member for the county of Berks.

State affairs once a year. Both Whitehead and Wharton, I think, always alluded in their annual odes to any great event that diminished or increased the prosperity of their country. Their pliant muse adapting her song to occurrences was complimentary, consolatory, or prophetic, as the times were happy or calamitous; nor did the former, during the whole of our disastrous and ill-conducted contest with America, chaunt one desponding note. How far either of your predecessors were quidnuncs in themselves I know not. Poetry and politics, I know, *ne s'accordent pas bien ensemble*, and the classic elegance of your mind, as well as the natural rectitude and benevolence of your heart, but ill correspond with the harshness, dissimulation, violence, and injustice which abound more or less in all systems of government, *et qui entrent toujours pour quelque chose dans le caractère de ceux qui se mêlent des affaires publiques*. I am so fully convinced of this melancholy truth that I pity every man whose ambition or necessities plunge him into the bustle of politics; and I would much rather live humble and obscure in the New Forest on 300*l.* a year than blaze ambassador extraordinary at the first Court in Europe. The members of the National Assembly in France are of a different opinion, and so fond are they of legislating that they work double tides—they have morning and evening service; and 'Sunday shines no Sabbath day on them.' God knows what will be the final result of their indefatigable labours! The joint efforts of their zeal, talent, and industry have hitherto produced little to admire, and nothing worthy of imitation, at least in England. Believe me when I assure you that the misfortunes of this country are far from their height, and of course distant from their conclusion. The Bastille will never be permitted to raise its terrific battlements above the surface of the earth again, but the power that laid it prostrate must also give place in its turn to something like order, or else both king and kingdom will fall a sacrifice to anarchy and to all its attendant mischiefs. The despotism of the Court has been succeeded by that of an ignorant and ferocious mob void of all principle, and destitute of all humanity. Decency and respect for public opinion ameliorated the ancient authority of the Crown, but these restraints are unknown to the populace of this corrupt metropolis; and, acting from the caprice of the moment, the objects of their present idolatry may possibly fall victims to their sanguinary licentiousness and indiscriminate fury. They can plead the authority of example for whatever excesses they commit. The principles of justice, moderation, and decency are as little understood, or at least as little practised, within the National Assembly as they are without. A system of vexation appears to have been adopted, and the sovereign, nobility, and clergy alternately experience the little equity and indulgence they are to expect while this wild spirit of democracy rides lord paramount in the nation. The imbecility of the royal mind renders the King incapable of any wise or vigorous effort to recover what he has lost; and to the same cause may be attributed his insensibility to the affronts that are daily offered to him with impunity. Those who are disposed to emancipate him from the abject state into which he is fallen are forbidden even to think on a scheme of the kind; to those who are the most attached to him he says the least, and, when he speaks, it is to desire that they will be quiet. The Queen, whatever her guilt may have been, has more than atoned for all the offences she could possibly have committed. Her degradation alone is a punishment beyond the measure of her vices, if she had any, and gives her a claim to the admiration, compassion, and affection of every man awake to a sense of justice or humanity. But the vulgar, insolent and unjust, triumph in her disgrace and insult her in misfortune. The people of this country have become brutal, nor were the cruelties exercised in the worst of times in England so atrocious as are those committed by the rabble at Paris since the Revolution. The *people* by their representatives are absolute. Their decrees, indeed, must have the sanction of the King, but, as he dare not refuse, it is an additional insult to degraded majesty to require the royal assent. An instance of this occurred last November, when a decree was passed against the whole body of the clergy. The King wished to decline giving his assent, and evaded it for a month, at the expiration of which it was in a manner extorted from him; and, if he had refused, or delayed compliance, it is not improbable that by this time the Seine would have ebbed a crimson current to the sea. The bishops are placed in an awkward dilemma, for, by refusing the oath prescribed, they not only forfeit their bishoprics, but become objects of popular resentment. If religion has yet any hold on the minds of the people in the provinces, the clergy will become a formidable phalanx, and perhaps resist the capital. There is great fermentation throughout the whole country. Happily for the popular party, there is neither union nor correspondence among the discontented, who, distributed throughout the kingdom, have no chief to head them against their adversaries, and, satisfied with general invective and abuse, although not without the means of resistance, they submit to insult and oppression, venting their griefs to every stranger that will condescend to listen to their sad tale of woe.

Mr. Burke is in raptures with the French *noblesse*. If he speaks from what he has seen, his vision is imperfect; if from what he has heard, he has been deceived. In the one instance he has mistaken deformities for perfections, and gazed at them through a magnifying glass; in the other he has been unpardonably credulous. The man who publishes what he writes should be authentic, and particularly so if he writes for posterity. The innocent and ingenious fictions of poetry can alone justify a deviation from truth; philosophers and historians should never take things upon trust. I do not know a more despicable class of men than the French nobility. Under the ancient form of government they were insolent and oppressive, deserting their châteaux and their tenants, submitting to dance attendance in the ante-chamber of ministers, and content to become the instruments of their exactions, of their despotism, and of their pleasures. Parasites at Court, in the country tyrants, and in all situations infamous. Such was the character of the scattered, beggared, and banished *noblesse* of France.[1] Nor were the higher orders of the clergy much better. Their profligacy and avowed neglect, not to say contempt, of the sacerdotal character, first shook the faith of the rabble, and paved the way for that immorality, dissoluteness, and practical atheism which have extirpated all that is valuable or desirable in religion, and rendered the priesthood objects of mockery and detestation. Men are at all times apt to fly from one extreme to the other. From believing everything, they now reject everything. The Roman

[1] See Arthur Young's *Travels*, 1787, p. 66.

ritual has not given place to any other; but the pale of the Church is thrown down, and the whole is become a dreary, sterile waste, affording neither hope nor consolation to the wayworn traveller.

I am no friend to Mirabeau. I have conversed with him enough to know him, and it is impossible to know him and not despise him. I am scarcely acquainted with one amiable character in the whole patriot party; but, however vain, vicious, and contemptible they may be, they are not the primary cause of the extensive ruin into which their country is fallen. They are mere subalterns in the dreadful havoc, plunder, and dissolution of the French monarchy, and are only entitled to half the odium of so much guilt. They found everything in disorder, and they have increased the general confusion. The power they possess is an usurpation, for it was never delegated to them; it is far from being permanent, for they now hold it at the pleasure of the Jacobins, who, on the slightest provocation, will perhaps dismiss them with as little ceremony as Cromwell dismissed the Parliament in the middle of the last century. This club, composed of men of all ranks and of every climate, faith, and description, has no bond of union—no common relation, and, meeting tumultuously four days in the week to give their orders to another club, superior to them in name but inferior in authority, they separate, and become as distinct and as detached as the sand on the beach. From such an assemblage, from such a piebald crew of nobles, plebeians, priests, beggars, thieves, and assassins, what good can possibly be expected! The Jacobins govern the kingdom, or rather, they carry everything before them. Louis XVI. retains the title of king; he is allowed to live in the Palace at the Tuileries, and is indulged with an income worthy of the rank he formerly held; but not an iota of the regal authority remains to him, not even the pageantry of royalty. For my part, I do not see any termination to the confusion that prevails but in a civil war; and, from all that I see and from all that I hear, everything tends to accelerate that direful calamity. At Bayonne the national cockade has been thrown into the canal. Navarre has no deputies in the Assembly, and peremptorily refuses to pay any taxes; a spirit of disaffection prevails, but, being equalled by a spirit of distrust, ever vigilant and vindictive, it remains disaffected.

Next Sunday will be a day of much sorrow, perhaps of bloodshed. The clergy are required to take the oath decreed by the National Convention last November, and Sunday is the limited time for Paris. The bishops in general have refused, the inferior clergy, I am assured, will follow their example, and, of course, will be deprived of their preferments.

There is something atrociously cruel in putting a man's subsistence and conscience at variance; the clergy have been robbed, they are now to be persecuted. Violent *motions*[1] by itinerants, unprincipled and mercenary politicians, have been made in the Palais Royal and in other sinks of infamy, in which the million are invited to assassinate the clergy. Woe be to the Legislature that employs a senseless, profligate rabble to enforce its laws! Lanterns are arguments in this country, and they are likely to continue so until some superior genius happily *wills* order to this dreadful chaos. Fifteen years' profession of the sacerdotal office was necessary and indispensable to obtain a bishopric; the Solons of France, I am told, propose *de revenir sur leurs pas*, and to decree

---

[1] The *questions* moved and debated in clubs respecting the measures of Government were called *Motions*.

that *five years* will be sufficient. This is for the purpose of more readily supplying the place of those who prove refractory.[1] It is Mirabeau, I am told, who is to propose this alteration in the Church discipline to the Senate, and the King will also be obliged to make a retrograde motion. Thus they do and undo; and the great business of the constitution, like Penelope's web, will never be finished.

Mr. Burke is certainly right in the picture he has drawn of men and things in this kingdom. He has, however, only taken a view of one side. He feels, and very justly, for insulted and degraded majesty, but he should also feel for suffering millions during a series of ages under the rod of despotism. Impartiality is a duty in every author. Neither am I pleased with Mr. Burke in his poor attempt to explain away the principles of the Revolution in England in 1688.

Fonthill Beckford is here. He has an entire hotel —30,000 livres per annum—keeps three cooks, has every day *le monde à dîner, mais jamais plus que huit personnes*. His hobby at present is the formation of a great library, *et qu'il aime actuellement la lecture à la folie*. After having studied men, he studies books; no wonder if he becomes wise, since he explores every avenue to knowledge.

[1] 'Tandis que la mort était à l'ordre du jour par le ministère de ce tribunal de sang, les accusés, parmi lesquels étaient des religieuses et des prêtres, y paraissaient avec cette intrépidité qui sait braver la mort et les bourreaux. Si votre devoir, disait un d'eux, est de nous condamner, obéissez à votre loi: j'obéis aussi à la mienne; elle m'ordonne de mourir et de pardonner à mes ennemis. Crois-tu à l'enfer, demandaient les juges au curé d'Amplepuis ? Comment en douter, dit-il, en vous voyant ? Un autre prêtre croit échapper au trépas par l'athéisme. Crois-tu en Dieu ? lui demande-t-on. Très peu, répondit-il. Meurs, infâme, dit aussitôt le Président, et va le reconnaître.'—Prudhomme, *Révolution Française*, vi. 44; *Crimes commis à Lyon sous les Proconsuls conventionnels*, Octobre 1793.

MR. HUSKISSON[1] TO MR. MILES

Paris: January 28, 1791

The enclosed letter came yesterday by our courier. I was very much concerned to hear that the letters you had sent by him had not been delivered. The people at the office say they are very exact, and therefore I hope they are received. If not, your friends must send to Whitehall to enquire after them. I mean to call upon you soon, for I have many things to say.

MR. MILES TO MR. PYE

Paris: January 30, 1791

I have long suspected that my letters were intercepted, and yours of the 23rd instant proves at least that they have been detained somewhere—perhaps each Post Office is authorised to examine all correspondence. The extreme discontents that prevail in this country require the utmost vigilance to prevent the introduction of principles which tend to the dissolution of civil society and of all the obligations of religion and morality. *Les deux comités de recherches dans la rue de la Plâtrière à Paris et dans Lombard Street à Londres font très bien* to open and ramble over the letters that pass through their hands, and thus stop the poison in its source. I little suspected two years since that I should virtually become a legislator in France and have a right to deliberate on the most important points of foreign and domestic policy, and that, too, in a country where despotism has degraded mankind to a mere animal

---

[1] Private Secretary to Lord Gower in Paris at the above date. He became Cabinet Minister as Secretary of State for the Colonies. On September 15, 1830, he was accidentally killed by a locomotive engine on the opening of the Liverpool and Manchester Railway.

existence. And yet, strange and almost impossible as such an event appeared to be, it has happened, and my feeble voice and still more feeble talents have been exerted in the Jacobin Club to temper that wild and dangerous effervescence, so common to men broken loose from confinement and in possession of power and rights of which they could have had no adequate idea, and which it was more than probable they would abuse. The Jacobins are a society open to men of all nations, professions, and persuasions, where every individual has a right to vote, deliberate, and deliver his opinion, where he may propose any measure for adoption, and point out any absurdity or danger he may discover in the decrees of the National Assembly, and where he may even impeach any man from the sovereign to the constable. The principle of this extreme latitude and the ostensible motives for this indulgence to foreigners are plausible. The one is calculated to defeat every attempt to restore the ancient system by rendering every man vigilant and attentive to the common interest, whilst the other is a tacit acknowledgment of ignorance and incapacity for public affairs, and a direct invitation to men of information and talents to communicate their knowledge. There is something liberal in this confession, and this should lessen our severity against a body of men who, unaccustomed to public affairs and scarcely acquainted with even the first principles of civil government, are happy to obtain instruction from any source, and even at the expense of their vanity, which, joking apart, is a great sacrifice for a Frenchman. Like bewildered travellers on a pathless common, they are ready to ask the road and explore their way home by foreign aid. Mirabeau, who is certainly the best informed man in France, and possessed of a very considerable portion of intellect, did not disdain to ask my opinion on the subject of the assignats, and the principle of this condescension cannot be disputed—*que les lumières sortent du choque des opinions.* Hence it is that strangers are admitted into the Jacobins and other political clubs in France. The Prince Charles de Hesse, who is also a Jacobin, remarked to me this day week *qu'il était assez singulier qu'un Anglais et un Allemand se trouvassent dans une telle société. Je lui répondis, qu'il y avoit de quoi s'étonner d'y voir un Allemand, mais pas d'y voir un Anglais, puisque celui-ci, sachant apprécier la liberté, aime voir les hommes libres, tandis que les Allemands, étant ou despotes ou esclaves, ne peuvent guère se plaire dans une société d'où la tyrannie fût proscrite.* The force of my answer was understood by those who were near to us, for they instantly remarked, 'Oui, monsieur, vous avez raison, car les Anglais sont libres et aiment les pays libres.'[1]

I do not know a class of men more insolent or ignorant than the German nobility. I have lived much among them, and they have scarce an idea beyond eating and drinking and hunting. Prince Charles de Hesse—or *Monsieur Hesse*, as he is called here—having served in France and travelled much, does not want for that general knowledge which any man may pick up who lives in the world and does not shut his eyes and his ears.

[1] 'Prince Charles, or, as he at that time called himself, Citizen General Hesse, was about thirty-five years of age, had a long gaunt form, a pale face, with remarkably high cheek-bones, large but dull blue eyes, and very light hair. He spoke much and rapidly, and accompanied his speech with incessant convulsive gesticulations, concluding every sentence by gnashing his teeth, the sound of which was more or less loud according to the state of his mind. "If," said one of his auditors, " his deeds are as wild as his words, one might imagine him to be a wild cat endowed with human speech." '—Sybel's *History of the French Revolution,* ii. 100.

You will now understand the *original* institution of the club at the Jacobin Convent. Its present character —or at least, the principles of those who control a society which now masters the kingdom by its violence and injustice—may soon provoke a spirit that will deluge the country in blood. The Duke of Orleans, whose son is a constant attendant, seems to place his entire security in the support of this club, courts its protection, and at the same time directs its operations. The Queen —or rather the whole royal family—Lafayette, and the Mayor of Paris,[1] are the objects of its perpetual pursuit. The former is compelled to the utmost circumspection. The other must give incessant and dangerous attention to the sanguinary and indigent rabble, who, always ripe for mischief, are frequently in a disposition to dispute the civil and military force of the metropolis. A strong party in the nation wishes for a republic. This idea is supported by a man who, having the ambition of Cromwell without his talents or his virtues, dares not openly avow or attempt what he is known secretly to covet. His influence, and that of his party, at the Jacobins is great. To oppose this influence another club has been established under the denomination of 'Les Amis de la Constitution monarchique' by men who, although they had an active share in the Revolution, are anxious to invest the sovereign with more power than he possesses, and to destroy the Jacobins, whose authority is certainly enormous. This new club, however, little attentive to the means by which its members are to accomplish their end, has made two vigorous efforts to captivate the multitude—the one by distributing bread at an inferior price to upwards of 30,000 indigent vagabonds, and the other by exciting a clamour against

[1] Monsieur Bailly.

the importation of British manufactures. Handbills for this purpose were distributed and stuck up in the Faubourg St. Antoine with a view to engage the workmen to pillage all shops which had English goods, and to exact from the National Assembly a promise to break the treaty of commerce with Great Britain.[1] The priests and *noblesse* at the bottom of this contrivance, and aware of the dilemma into which such a demand would throw the Legislature, did not neglect any means in their power to animate the mob last Monday. The National Guards could with difficulty and by the greatest precautions, taken in time, prevent the tumult. The same day a riot happened near Paris, in which ten people were killed and several wounded. A man was assassinated the Friday before at five in the afternoon near the Palais Royal. On Thursday the mob seized upon a man suspected to be a spy, and, in order to prevent the approach of the cavalry as well as infantry, collected a number of carts and waggons and barricaded the streets in St. Antoine. The military dare not fire, nor even assemble to disperse a mob, without orders from the first magistrate, and the magistrate dares not proceed to violence. The first shot he would order would produce

---

[1] 'Lille, which is surrounded by more windmills for expressing the oil of cole-seed than are to be seen anywhere else, I suppose, in the world. The cry here for war with England amazed me. Every one I talked with said it was beyond doubt that the English had called the Prussian army into Holland, and that the motives in France for a war were numerous and manifest. It is easy enough to discover that the origin of all this violence is the Commercial Treaty, which is execrated here as the most fatal stroke to their manufactures they ever experienced. These people have the true monopolising ideas; they would involve 24,000,000 people in the certain miseries of a war rather than see the interest of those who consume fabrics preferred to the interest of those who make them. The advantages reaped by four and twenty millions of consumers are lighter than a feather compared with the inconveniences sustained by half a million of manufacturers.'—*Arthur Young's Travels*, 1787, p. 73.

a carnage which I tremble to think on. You may judge of the weakness of the Government that dares not punish licence and revolt, and of the poverty of the Legislature that is reduced to the humiliating necessity of demanding the protection of the Jacobins against the enemies of the Revolution. Every event that happens is accurately traced to the Palace, as is believed, and logically proved to proceed from the Queen. The Jacobins by a circular letter have apprised all the provinces that the kingdom is menaced with a counter-revolution. In short, Paris is in a vortex of alarm and perplexity difficult to describe —not easy to dissipate—because it is the interest of some individuals to preserve the ferment until more blood has flowed. The club above mentioned has resolved to assemble every day. The frontiers are ordered to be immediately reinforced and put in a state capable of resisting any attempts of the Emperor or the German Princes. The Colonies are in revolt, nor can the Minister despatch a force to subjugate them. The officer named for the command refused to go unless they gave him half National Guards and half regular troops, because he was suspected of being an aristocrat, and, as such, he would be impeached if he went with all regular troops and the expedition failed. Such is the condition of this kingdom—and from this account, which you may be assured is just, you will perceive how far, how very far it is from the restoration of order.[1]

[1] 'The Duc d'Aumont was boasting one day at Monsieur de Lafayette's that in six months the new constitution would be finished and public order restored. I sat next to him, and inquiring "In what time?" he replied, "In six months." "Say rather, sir," I answered, "in six years, and you will be nearer the truth." This was in January 1791.'— *Conduct of France towards Great Britain Examined*, by Mr. Miles, 1793.

The assignats pay a discount of from 5½ to 6 per cent., and this will prove to you that the nation itself has but little confidence in its present Government. In one word, France has fallen, and appears as if she cannot get up again. You will believe me when I say that my heart is in England.

Mr. Miles to Lord Buckingham

Paris: February 3, 1791

I have this instant seen a letter from Berlin, which announces that war is declared against Russia; also another, dated Cologne the 28th of last month, from which the following is an extract:—'La Cour de Vienne travaille à force de faire renoncer le Baron de Dalberg à la coadjutorerie de Mayence en faveur d'un fils de Léopold.' This has already been hinted to me by a person of distinction from Germany, and should the intelligence be true I conceive it to be a matter of too much importance to be concealed from our Court. The distance of the two Ministers, Messrs. Heathcote and Walpole, from that Electorate, supposing them to possess the greatest vigilance and assiduity, renders it almost impossible that they should be early informed of the intrigues of the intermediate Courts; and, if your Lordship will condescend to look on the chart of the empire, you will confess that so great a tract of country as that which lies between Bonn and Munich, abounding with a number of independent petty sovereigns, perpetually intriguing and caballing, well deserves the attention of the British Government; and especially as the pretensions of the former in Alsace and Lorraine create a well-founded alarm in this kingdom of an attempt to recover what they have lost by the Revolution.

MR. MILES TO SIR EDWARD NEWENHAM

Paris: February 16, 1791

Although a warm friend to liberty, and perfectly convinced of the legality and justice of the Revolution in this country, I am very far from approving *in toto* of the conduct of the National Assembly. Anarchy is no less my aversion than despotism; and, as France has unhappily fallen into the former, and as that evil may eventually conduct her to the latter, I have but little pleasure in beholding her in a state so degraded—so fatal to that spirit of freedom, which, when the Bastille fell, I fondly expected would make the tour of Europe or rather of the world. You have desired me to send you an account of the police of Paris for the purpose of introducing it into Dublin. If you love order and security, if you are a friend to public tranquillity and to the happiness of your fellow-countrymen, if you have any regard for your character, whether as a citizen, a legislator, or a man of sense, never think of following the example of France in any one instance that has yet occurred. The police of Paris! Good Heavens! There is no such thing. The unfortunate object whom they have decorated with the title of *Maire*, and placed at the head of the magistracy, is without credit, authority, or respect. Tumults happen daily; the metropolis abounds with libels of the most diabolical tendency; whoever happens to fall under suspicion of the mob is menaced with death; and handbills are publicly distributed inviting the rabble to pillage and disorder. The civil power calls in the aid of the military; and Monsieur de Lafayette and his aide-de-camp are kept trotting about like so many penny-postmen. Battalions, horse and foot, are called out for the purpose of dispersing the people, but, not daring to fire, they are reduced to the humiliating necessity of becoming passive spectators of licence and injustice.

The municipality of Paris, without power to suppress a riot and submissive to the dictates of the mob, refused a passport to the aunts of the King, and his Majesty was addressed to persuade them not to leave the kingdom, although a decree of the National Assembly expressly establishes perfect liberty in this respect. A club named 'Les Amis de la Constitution monarchique' is vexed and pursued by every section in Paris without its being convicted of any offence against the State, or without any proof of any mischievous design, merely because it is called 'monarchique,' and because some of its members are hostile to the sanguinary and ambitious views of the Republican party. This is all the guilt that has been imputed to it. The Mayor and municipality, convinced of the innocency of this club, dare not protect it. I have heard them arraigned as traitors to the public interest because they declared, in their official capacity, that after the most minute investigation they could not discover any matter that could justify alarm or deserve accusation. A member of this club, who is also a member of the National Assembly, was insulted some days past as he stepped into a hackney coach by a man who, secure of the protection of the crowd, opened the carriage door, and vented a volley of oaths, whilst the mob joined in the abuse and vociferously exclaimed: 'A la lanterne!' The expedition of the coachman saved the life of the legislator. This, you may say, proves nothing more than that mobs are mobs everywhere; but, as these Parisian rioters assemble daily, in readiness for mischief, it proves that the Government is debilitated, and that there is no police. But what will you think when I tell you that the cowardly and sanguinary scoundrel who thus attempted to consign his fellow-creature to the fury of a senseless rabble had the audacity to mount the tribune the same night at the Jacobin Club, composed of 1,500 members when all assembled, and there boasted of his infamy? What will you think of the principles of the 1,500 when I tell you that his information was received with loud and repeated acclamations of joy and approbation? Have not these people whom you admire so much mistaken *licence* for freedom and overshot the mark? In the provinces much-ill humour prevails; taxes are refused, and although there is no danger of a counter-revolution, it will be at least twenty-five years, if not fifty, before this country becomes perfectly settled, happy, and respectable. Wait the conclusion of the Revolution in France before you think of introducing any of its regulations into Ireland, and, even then, examine them well, and see that they are adapted to your habits, your maxims of government, and your prejudices.

The frankness with which I am apt to deliver my sentiments renders it imprudent in me to write by the post. Few of my letters have reached you, and I know not where they are. I wrote to you last by the messenger; this letter will be delivered to you by the Baron de Roebeck, a Swedish gentleman, married to an English lady. His knowledge of this country and his love of liberty will recommend him strongly to your friendship, and, as he means to visit Dublin in the spring, I avail myself the more readily of his polite offer to charge himself with a letter to my friend. He is certainly capable of giving you a full account of public affairs in this country. We do not, I believe, perfectly agree on the subject. He beholds the disorders under a more favourable point of view than I do; he is more sanguine of a happy issue than I am; and he does not prognosticate a distant period for the re-establishment of order in this distracted land. I have no objection to his being the better prophet, for no man more ardently wishes than I do that the various nations of the earth should enjoy peace, freedom, and security; and it is with inexpressible concern that I behold this kingdom fallen into a state of anarchy which not only retards the completion of the Revolution, but serves the cause of despotism by intimidating other people from emancipating themselves from the fetters of tyranny. I am positive that, if all the necessary changes in government had been happily finished as soon as the great work was accomplished, and if all ranks of the people had joined in the glorious enterprise with the same ardour as they did to complete the Champ de Mars for the 14th of July, the example of France would have been embraced in all the little principalities in Germany, and the whole herd of contemptible despots would have been annihilated. I am vexed at the constant interruptions given to the great business of legislation in the National Assembly. M. de Lafayette I believe to be the only man engaged in the Revolution that is disinterested.

Adieu, and God bless you and yours.

[1] 'Quinze mille ouvriers travaillaient au Champ de Mars. . . . Le bruit se répand qu'ils ne peuvent assez hâter les travaux. . . . Accourt aussitôt une fourmilière de 150 mille travailleurs, et le champ est transformé en un atelier de 80 mille toises. C'est l'atelier de Paris, de Paris tout entier; toutes les familles, toutes les corporations, tous les districts y affluent. . . . Tous se tiennent trois à trois, portant la pioche ou la pelle sur l'épaule, chantant à la fois le refrain si connu d'une chanson nouvelle : *Ça ira, ça ira !* Oui, ça ira, répètent ceux qui les entendent.'— *Hist. Parl.* vi. 397.

Mr. Miles to Lord Buckingham

Paris: February 18, 1791

The enclosed is one of the numerous gazettes with which this distracted country is inundated. Its object is not so much to justify the principles of the Revolution as to encourage that spirit of licentiousness so favourable to the criminal designs of profligate adventurers, who live but in a tempest, and to whom a state of anarchy is a state of glory and prosperity. Attempts are daily made to persuade those whom it is their interest to deceive that even England—hitherto renowned for freedom—has been enlightened by France, whose example she is preparing to follow. I hear this language impudently asserted every Friday to an assembly consisting of from 800 to 1,000 people of both sexes, all composed of the middle and lower class, who alone influence and govern the nation. They are assured that clubs and associations are forming throughout Europe, and a number of letters—the pretended correspondence from the friends of liberty in foreign countries—are read with an affected pomposity to an infatuated multitude in love with ruin. Your Lordship will judge of the impatience of the 'Social Circle,' as it is called, to impose upon the public judgment, and thereby preserve the ferment that exists, by referring to the accompanying publication. It is by such inflammatory means that the people are unfortunately kept in a constant state of delusion and madness. I see no prospect of happier times but by an explosion that can at once prescribe bounds to despotism and preserve mankind from the mischiefs of tyranny and anarchy. I have made a collection of pamphlets, 1,500 in number, which, as a member of all the great patriotic clubs, have been presented to me *gratis*. They will throw an abundance of light half a century hence on the public affairs of this country, and, as such, they will be a valuable acquisition to your Lordship's library. It is for this purpose I have selected and preserved them, and I shall either forward them to London or take them to you myself.

MR. MILES TO MR. T. SOMERS COCKS

Paris: February 23, 1791

Your long wished for letter, my dear friend, arrived last night at the very instant I entered from being a reluctant spectator of a tumult which threatened in the beginning to produce the *dénouement* of the tedious and eventful tragedy that has been so long performing in this wretched metropolis. The drum beat to arms last night throughout Paris, and, from the incendiary harangues of the Lameths and Barnave for this month past to a senseless rabble in love with blood, there was every reason to suppose that the miseries and existence of the hapless family on the throne would have had one common grave. Reports of a counter-revolution, equally void of humanity and truth, have been in constant circulation since the commencement of the year; no arts have been left unattempted to give these reports a degree of authenticity. Every trifling dispute between even the lowest vagabonds in the filthiest cabarets has been magnified into a serious attempt to destroy the infant liberties of France, and notice has been instantly transmitted by circular letters to the distant provinces by order of the Jacobins, who have established a daily correspondence with every town in France. Fictions the most improbable, as well as the most pernicious in their tendency, have been invented and sent from the

capital to the Pyrenees and to the Rhine, with all the
malice and insolence which security and impunity inspire.
Their object is to preserve the people in a state of frenzy
in order to intimidate those whose love of equity might
stimulate them to insist upon moderate measures.
Harassed and alarmed by these reports and menaces,
a number of families have quitted Paris, and, though
this is precisely what the popular leaders wish, the
departure of the fugitives has been made an argument
of the truth of the rumours which have driven them
from their homes! The King's aunts, apprehensive of
danger, and aware that their very birth would be an
argument of guilt, announced their intention to go to
Rome. This was instantly advanced as proof positive
of a design to subvert the present Government; and the
municipality, whose duty it is to secure the citizens in
the enjoyment of their rights, and watch over the
faithful execution of the laws, waited on the King to
request he would violate the law of the country in the
persons of his dearest relatives. If anything can add
to the indecency and irregularity of this proceeding, it
is the abject meanness of offering this insult to fallen
majesty, in contradiction to their better judgment, and
in compliance with the insolent demands of a tumultuous
assembly. The King was firm: his answer was a momentary display of that regal dignity which faction
has obscured, and which awed even those who would
annihilate, if they could, the very idea of royalty.
Recourse was had to the *poissardes*, and this ferocious
troop of *infernales* assembled to pay the Princesses a
visit; the night being chosen in order, no doubt, to give
the greater energy to their mission. The King apprised
his aunts of the intended visit, and accordingly they
came to town, disguised as servants, in a wicker-coach,

or rather waggon. Resolved on their journey, the necessary preparations were continued, notwithstanding the clamour of the mob, now incensed on finding so little respect paid to their commands; and sensible that there were no means of preventing the departure of the Princesses, except by violence, the rabble proceeded last Saturday[1] night to Bellevue to seize the victims and conduct them as prisoners to Paris. Happily, notice was given in time. The ladies were at supper when they received the intelligence, and, as you will suppose, they did not stay to finish, but instantly got into their carriage, and had set off about ten minutes before the party arrived. Vexed at the disappointment, they vented the most furious invectives against the King, and particularly against Monsieur, whom they accused of a design to quit the country. He was denounced at the Jacobins, and a *motion* was made to prohibit the royal family from quitting the kingdom, which ' motion ' will certainly pass into a law, and the King will be compelled to sign his own commitment, as also that of his brother, his wife and children, to a perpetual prison. It is with difficulty I can withhold my indignation at the horrors to which I am an unwilling witness.

These wretched, despicable legislators exclaim against the mischiefs and misery they themselves occasion, and make the idleness and crimes they encourage a subject of complaint against those whom they would exterminate. It was not sufficient to impute to the brother of their sovereign an intention to abandon his country. The mere assertion without corroborative circumstances would not operate in the manner they wished. It was therefore reported yesterday afternoon that Monsieur

[1] February 19.

meant to set off that very night; that the King and Dauphin, with the Queen, were to follow; that 37,000 assassins, distributed throughout Paris, and armed with stilettoes imported from Turin, some of which have been shown to me, were to massacre the patriots in the metropolis; while the Emperor was to invade France on the side of Brabant with a powerful army, and the aristocrats were to rise in the provinces. The Luxembourg was invested by the mob before eight o'clock, and Monsieur, who resided there, was conducted to the château of his hapless brother, followed by the rabble, who, but for the firmness of M. de Lafayette, would have ascended the staircase and have penetrated into the interior apartments of the King and Queen. In that case I am satisfied neither of them would have beheld the 'morrow's dawn.' It was with difficulty the people could be restrained; cannon were placed before the entrance of the Tuileries; and men with lighted matches in hand were ready to fire on the first alarm. I was in the midst of this uproar on my return home, and was close to the Maire, M. Bailly, when he descended from the King. The women surrounded him, and insisted on knowing if the sovereign meant to depart. His assurances to the contrary neither silenced nor satisfied them; many were for extirpating every vestige of royalty, and all were for compelling the National Assembly to pass a law to keep him here, at all events, and all belonging to him.

The sword of civil war is drawn in Brittany, also at Uzès, near Nismes. Toulouse and all the south of France are ripe for revolt, and, though the calm is said to be restored in Alsace, I doubt it. Béthune, in Flanders, has solicited military assistance. No specie is in circulation except what must be bought at $5\frac{1}{2}$ or 6 per cent. discount against their assignats; and even this paper money pays a discount if for fifty livres. Perregaux[1] charged me 2½ per cent. for some assignats of fifty livres, and to convert them into cash I was forced to lose 30 sols on each. Yet the lands of the clergy sell well and rapidly. Their property sold at Gonesse, which is a short distance from Paris, produced between the 20th of December and the 17th of this month eight millions, which is the third of a million sterling, and yet France, with all this robbery and sacrilege, is poorer than ever. Many a scoundrel will feather his nest by this Revolution, and what ought to have been productive of general and substantial good will reflect eternal dishonour on the whole country, and may prove its ruin.

My feeble voice has been exerted in the great political clubs in favour of the rights of humanity, which have been more impudently violated since the 'Declaration of the Rights of Man' than ever they were under the iron hand of regal despotism. When the fears excited in the King's aunts were ridiculed, I desired the members of these clubs to recollect the height from which these insulted women had fallen, and to remember that they were not yet at the bottom of the precipice. Suspended as they were midway, and hanging by a thread, it was a cruel mockery of their distress to sport with their feelings and laugh at their well-founded apprehensions. It would be a flagrant injustice to prevent their departure, and the clamour made on the occasion and the fears expressed of its being the *avant-coureur* of a counter-revolution ill corresponded, as I observed to them, with the resolution taken to assist Spain against Great Britain and Holland, or with that extreme power they pretend to have acquired by the demolition of the Bastille, or with the parade they make

---

[1] Perregaux, Laflitte, and Co., bankers, Paris.

of four millions of freemen armed and resolved *à vivre libres ou mourir*. I further remarked that they must be conscious of weakness, and have an ill opinion of their Revolution, legislature, finances, and themselves, if two old women going to mass at St. Peter's in Rome can give them such uneasiness! I have both laughed and reasoned with them, a freedom I would not have presumed to take if my character as a passionate friend of liberty had been less known in this city. But I am no less violent for justice and decency; and, great as my aversion is to tyranny, my hatred of anarchy is still greater. Such is the language I have held at the Jacobins and the Club of 1789—in public, and in private, and, conscious of its truth, I will hold it though they should menace to suspend me from every lantern in Paris.

It is decided that the King, Dauphin, and Monsieur cannot quit the kingdom without forfeiting their right to the throne. On Friday it will be decreed. The Princesses were stopped at Moret, four leagues from Fontainebleau, by the magistracy, but 100 Chasseurs of Lorraine appearing at the instant, and insisting on the passage being free, the ladies proceeded on their journey, and in many towns were well received. This has been the subject of a serious complaint made to-day in the National Assembly, and the Minister, as usual, is already prejudged and found culpable. February 24.— It was the *poissardes* that went to the Luxembourg last night and insisted upon seeing Monsieur. He received a deputation of them, assured them that he never had a thought to separate himself from his country and his brother, and he gave his word of honour that he never would forsake the King. One of the women demanded 'Mais, si le Roi s'en va?' to which Monsieur answered,

'Qui est-ce qui est si indigne de me faire une pareille question?' They then insisted upon seeing his wife. He said she was at her *toilette*. No matter—they would see her, and finally Madame appeared.

A well-dressed man went to the Tuileries and demanded to speak to M. de Lafayette. He was told he was with the King. He must see him. Lafayette came with two officers of the municipality. The man desired to speak to him alone. Lafayette answered that he had no secrets from those gentlemen whose duty it was to be present. The man then reported that 'Monsieur' was to set off that night escorted by 1,500 cavaliers who were at the Luxembourg. The answer of Lafayette does him honour: 'Je vous donne ma parole d'honneur que si Monsieur part je l'arrêterai, et puisque les nouvelles que vous venez de me donner sont très importantes je vous arrête jusqu'à ce que vous ayez vérifié les faits.' I really trembled for Lafayette when he pronounced the order for seizing this man. I was at his elbow, and expected to see the informer changed into an assassin. The Lameths wish to supplant him, and they are leagued with those who wish the extinction of the royal family. There is a club underneath the Jacobin where women are admitted, and as they often mount the tribune I leave you to judge of the society, and of its principles and capacity. Its inclinations cannot be mistaken. Our public prints will have informed you that all the interior barriers will be destroyed on the first of next May, and no duties will be paid but at the frontiers. You will be surprised when I tell you that the Custom House officers have a right to visit all baggage and travellers eleven times between Paris and Calais.

The fugitive Bishop of Liège is returned in triumph

to his palace, and has resumed his insolence and oppression.[1] The Liégeois have been most shamefully plundered and deceived by Prussia. The Minister of the latter country received 100,000 florins, and each florin is worth fourteen pence, for his good offices at Berlin; the Comtesse d'Orion, a niece of the late Prince, had 20,000 for her good offices with the Minister, M. Döhm; and no doubt M. Hertzberg's favourable representations to his royal master and General Schlieffen's moderation were also properly acknowledged, whilst half the money expended on these despicable subalterns would have purchased the whole Imperial Chamber at Wetzlar. The patriots at Liège are insulted and enslaved. The Prince-Bishop has addressed a violent and curious letter to the Rev. M. Philibert at Sedan, of which the following is an extract:—'Notre surprise a presque égalé notre douleur en apprenant que non-seulement les Electeurs indiqués par la seule autorité de la soi-disante Assemblée Nationale de France ont procédé à l'élection d'un nouvel Évêque qu'elle prétend établir dans le canton circonscrit par elle sous le nom de Département des Ardennes, où se trouve une partie notable de notre diocèse.' After exhorting him to abandon the mitre, the Bishop begs him to observe 'que cette pension est hypothéquée et prélevée sur le prix de spoliation de tous les biens du clergé de France, et vous ne pouvez vous approprier cet accroissement de revenu sans vous rendre complice de cette spoliation et sujet aux peines

---

[1] 'La principauté ecclésiastique de Liège avait fait, en 1789, sa révolution particulière. Après diverses péripéties, cette révolution démocratique, miniature assez ressemblante de la nôtre, avait été comprimée, de même que le soulèvement aristocratique et clérical des provinces belges, par une *exécution* autrichienne, qui avait rétabli sans conditions l'autorité du Prince-Évêque, Janvier 1791.'—*Maret, Duc de Bassano*, par Baron Ernouf, p. 40.

de cette complicité.' After all, the clergy in France have been treated with wanton cruelty and insult.

There is an institution for the purpose of exciting a revolt in all foreign nations. Geneva is perhaps a scene of blood at this instant; some lives have already been lost, and the insurgents within had invited the peasants to scale the town. The Emperor has 50,000 men in the Low Countries, but not a man too much.

Minute.—It is matter of deep regret and afflicts me most sensibly to behold this imprudent Prince-Bishop restored, but I trust that his sceptre and the sceptres of all ecclesiastical princes will be broken. How it vexes me to see injustice triumphant! If the British Cabinet had valued the liberties of other nations, they would have protected the oppressed, and enabled the Liégeois, the Flemings, and Brabançons to emancipate themselves from their respective tyrants; but my suggestions to the Duke of Leeds and the offers I brought over from Liège and Brussels in January 1790 were rejected. My unavailing efforts in favour of oppressed humanity, my fruitless anxiety for the freedom and felicity of mankind, and the little attention paid to my hitherto verified predictions, incline me to believe that the amelioration of the hard condition of the great mass of the people forms no part of the duty of kings and ministers! It is this fatal delusion being acted upon as a principle that engenders revolutions, and hence the oceans of blood that are now flowing and will continue to flow for many years to come.

W. A. MILES.

M. DE CHARTRES TO MR. MILES

Paris: le 25 Février, 1791.

M. de Chartres désireroit parler à Monsieur Miles d'une affaire de la plus grande importance pour lui; il voudroit savoir à quelle heure il le trouvera chez lui demain.

Minute.—This note was brought to me at midnight, when all the family were in bed. The contents surprised me very much, as I have never had any communication with either the Duke de Chartres or with his father, the Duke d'Orléans. The former is a member of the Jacobins, where, being seated together once, mutual civilities passed between us. What he can have to relate important to myself puzzles me much, for, though Paris is in a manner without government, and I have expressed the horror I feel at the daily excesses committed by the populace at the instigation of some unprincipled and desperate leaders, I have not entered into any relation or correspondence whatever with any of the aristocratic party, or with any one who would wish to augment the troubles of this distracted country, and consequently I have no reason to apprehend any legal violence. Yet this note alarms me, and I am impatient to know its issue.

It is now noon. I have seen M. de Chartres. His servant made a mistake; he said it was for a M. Milin, who is, I believe, an abbé, a friend of Madame la Duchesse de Richelieu, part of whose house I rent, and this person has the apartments over the gateway. He is a sensible man, but violent against the Revolution.

W. A. MILES.

MR. MILES TO MR. SOMERS COCKS

Paris: February 25, 1791

I wrote to you yesterday by the post. This goes by the messenger, and will be forwarded to you from the Foreign Office. When I wrote all was quiet—no appearance of a tempest, and I had persuaded myself that the assurances given by the King's brother had effectually silenced all pretence for cavil and uproar on that subject; but my letter had not been in the Post Office half an hour when M. de Narbonne arrived in town with an express that the Princesses were stopped at a small town near Dijon. The municipality having refused to let them proceed without directions from the National Assembly, an application was instantly made for the required permission, but the Legislature, happy in an occasion to insult the royal travellers, but not daring publicly to support the magistrates in their detention, resolved that it did not concern them, and that the matter should be referred to the executive power! To have justified the arrest would have been contrary not only to the ancient laws of the kingdom, but to one of their own decrees, as well as to every principle of natural right. They found themselves in one of those dilemmas from which chicane alone could extricate them. They rejoiced in the event that had happened, and wished to see the King's aunts brought back captives to the metropolis; and in a Legislature so infamously composed, in which the very dregs of the law, men versed in all its dishonest practices and resources, have so much to say, in which men of the most dissolute manners and profligate morals have the greatest influence, expedients in abundance would be found to favour their iniquitous designs without exposing themselves to the reproach of inconsistency. They did not dare to decide against the law, nor had they the virtue and courage to decide against the rabble. They dexterously evaded the question in a manner which could not fail to answer their purpose, and they had also the malignant satisfaction of giving a fresh insult, and perhaps a fatal wound, to the sovereign, whom they have stripped, plundered, and bound hand and foot. At all events, they were certain it would augment his embarrassment and chagrin, and place him in a painful situation between the people and his aunts. To add to his distress, and to enjoy the greater pleasure in the accumulated miseries of the King, some of the deputies had the unexampled brutality and indecency to send a troop of prostitutes, gathered from the Palais Royal and its environs, to demand an audience of their sovereign, and to insist on his despatching an order to his aunts to return. These women, dressed for the occasion, were escorted by all that is vile and infamous in Paris. This was arranged with so much secrecy and expedition that the guards at the château had only time to shut the great iron gates. Five minutes later, and the royal apartments would have been invaded by a legion of assassins, and no doubt can be entertained but that the Queen, and perhaps the King, would have been sacrificed. Vagabonds to the number of 40,000 had besieged the *Palais* at seven o'clock last night. The Maire was sent for, and, more dead than alive, when he came into the royal presence, inquired *what was the matter*. Thus the man whose duty it is to be informed of everything, to foresee everything, and to preserve the public tranquillity, instructed indeed in the science of medals and ancient literature, knows but imperfectly the duties of his arduous office. His moral character, I am told, is excellent; but he is timid where he ought to be resolute, and he hesitates where he ought to be peremptory. His natural timidity is increased by age, perhaps by the continual tumults and horrors already committed, and, though conscious that firmness and decided severity can alone impose upon the populace, he is afraid to give directions to the military to fire. Paris was again under arms all night. Faction dividing itself into groups all over the town insisted on the necessity of having the princesses, at all events, brought back; and, exclaiming against the ingratitude of their spending the ample incomes allowed them in a foreign country, protested that their object in going to Rome was to solicit the foreign powers to invade France, giving force to these assertions by assuring the people that an army was in Luxembourg ready to desolate the country. It was then proposed to hang M. Montmorin, Minister for Foreign Affairs and War Minister.[1] M. de Lafayette was declared a traitor, and his life was menaced. At this time the main body of the factious crowd threatened the guards at the Tuileries to force the gates if the King did not receive the *ladies* or give a positive answer, *Yes* or *No*, to their patriotic demand. His Majesty sent word he would receive a *deputation* of six this day at eleven o'clock. Good Heavens! to what a melancholy and abject condition is the sovereign reduced! If he had opposed reform in the constitution, if he had shown a disposition to be hostile to the national movement, or to excite a civil war among his subjects, some excuse might be offered for the insulting manner in which they treat him. But the King has met them half way in all the necessary corrections in a Government which had degraded humanity to a mere

---

[1] M. Montmorin perished among those who were massacred in September 1792.

animal existence, and, instead of giving the law, he submits to receive it from the people. His pliancy has proved the ruin of himself and his family. The Queen is much to be pitied, if I may use the term without insult to her misfortunes. In the midst of the hurricane that menaces her life she preserves the dignity inherent to a noble mind. I see her superior to her destiny in the midst of danger. Monarchy in France, with all its valuable supports and appendages, the Church and the nobility, is destroyed, and, whilst the whole is one melancholy heap of ruins, she in the midst of it preserves her native majesty. Her courage is wonderful. It is superior to all the violence and change of fortune. The hand of the assassin can alone extinguish it by destroying her existence. Would to Heaven I could rescue her and her innocent and hapless children from these scenes of horror that almost daily interrupt their domestic felicity!

In the mob last night I perceived some of the members of the National Assembly abetting the tumult without revealing themselves. I entered into conversation with one of them without letting him perceive that I knew who he was, and, drawing him imperceptibly from the crowd, I asked him if he could in his conscience approve of those atrocious and incendiary discourses spoken to a dissolute rabble capable of committing every crime that shocks and dishonours manhood. I represented to him the meanness as well as cruelty of daily insulting the sovereign who had granted them everything, and whose abject and perilous state, compared with the ancient splendour and security of the Crown, was more than sufficient to excite compassion and regard, unless every generous and humane sentiment was extinguished in the country. If tyranny was detestable, I remarked, anarchy—both frightful and horrible—allowed security to none; and, since the people had renounced servitude before they were qualified for freedom, the disorders that reigned would inevitably soon lead to the worst species of *despotism* unless speedy and vigorous measures were adopted to suppress them. The insults perpetually offered to the King were a reproach to the nation, and I was sorry to find a people hitherto renowned for their gallantry and social manners giving way to all the excesses of brutal ferocity. Such conduct must not only degrade them in the opinion of Europe, but would arm all mankind, and form a crusade against them—a confederacy which they seem to provoke by the pains taken to excite other nations to riot and revolt in sending forth apostles of sedition to preach a dissolution of all those sacred and inestimable bonds that hold society together. It is known that clubs are established for this horrible purpose, as if it was their wish to involve the whole moral world in one dreadful chaos. He professed the same sentiments, and lamented that the laws were without force. Whereupon I observed that it will ever be so when the *legislators* are without credit, without talents, and without morals. On this we parted. Strong detachments by this time had got into the Tuileries, and, dividing into two columns, separated the rabble and forced them out, strict orders being then given not to admit anyone. Thence the mob adjourned to the Palais Royal and renewed their harangues. The club of *Quatre-vingt-neuf* is there. On quitting the Tuileries I went to this club, of which I am a member, and expressed my indignation at these tumults with as much warmth as I had just shown to the member of the National Assembly, and, lamenting the deplorable anarchy into which the country had fallen, I exhorted every gentleman present to join heart and hand in support of the civil power, and to stand between their sovereign and a ferocious populace. It was a duty, I said, they owed to themselves, that without some vigorous and decisive measures the people would become fortified in their insolence and licentiousness by the impunity they enjoyed; and France, under such a government, would be infinitely more terrible than ever Rome was under the most depraved and most cruel of her tyrants. If I had held this discourse at the Jacobins, I should have been expelled, or perhaps trampled under foot. There were, however, several of the Jacobins present, as many are members of both clubs.

On traversing the Palais Royal as I returned home I found the crowd so great that it was difficult to pass. The most sanguinary threats were made, accompanied with the most dreadful imprecations. A woman decently dressed, but who appeared to be too old and too plain to live by the casual bounty of momentary lovers, declared in an audible voice *qu'il y avait encore bien des aristocrates à Paris, et que le seul moyen pour s'en défaire fût de les lier tous ensemble, et de les tuer par un coup de canon chargé de mitrailles*; that, for her part, if she could once behold her countrymen resolve upon this patriotic execution, she would set the example by stabbing as many of the aristocrats as she could to the heart with a poniard. The rabble shouted applause, and the wretch went to another group to announce the same principles. Her language appeared to be addressed to me, as I happened to be the only decent-looking person near her. You will suppose I did not enter into any controversy with the lady.

In the midst of all these horrors, at the very

moment that these vermin are deploring the fate of their country, declaring it to be in danger, and vowing vengeance against thousands of their fellow-citizens, the people indulge in an obscene pleasantry, and break off in the middle of a serious harangue to chaunt a couplet or cut a caper. This shows at once the profligacy and frivolity of the nation.

There is a club of *female* Jacobins here—men are also admitted—and, as I have a right to enter, I was tempted by curiosity to go in last Sunday night, when M. Barnave was deputed to them. I accompanied him from the Jacobin Club above to the one below, in which latter, composed of both sexes, the women could be elected secretaries or beadles to preserve silence and had the right of speaking, but they could not take the chair. I was one of the deputation to this odd mixture. Barnave is a member of the National Assembly—one of the leading men in it—very popular, and of course very violent. It is owing to his incendiary harangues that Paris has been under arms these two days. In the most abject manner he concluded a fulsome address to this rabble, the *refuse* even of all that is infamous, in which he flattered their power and complimented their civic virtues. 'Votre volonté est notre devoir,' he observed; 'nous n'en avons pas d'autre; de vous plaire, de vous obéir, seront toujours notre gloire, et vos applaudissements seront les meilleurs bienfaits que nous désirons recueillir de nos travaux pour votre salut, pour votre bonheur.' I pronounced his fate when I heard his discourse.[1] What a pity it is that the people should be so bewildered, misled, and that their representation should be so burlesqued by this National Assembly!

[1] Barnave was guillotined in November 1793. On the scaffold he exclaimed, 'This, then, is my reward!'

The situation of M. de Lafayette, with whom I dine to-day, is hazardous. A powerful party, with the Duc d'Orléans at their head, are hostile to him; and if he should fall in the opinion of the National Guards he is lost beyond redemption. There is more intrigue than ever and more circumvention.

The deputation of prostitutes did not present themselves this morning, and all is quiet; four men were sent to prison two days since for inflammatory 'motions' in the Tuileries. It was demanded that they should be given up, but the magistrates have refused, and I trust this firmness will be continued.

I shall be happy to return to dear England, when I may arrange the papers and observations I have collected in the course of a life which, though not marked by an excessive number of years, has been passed in the study of men and manners. My reflections may be of use to posterity. As a member of the clubs, I have been presented with pamphlets sufficient to stock all Paternoster Row. I have preserved the best of them, and this selection will throw great light on the Revolution, when the actors are no longer in the world to relate the share they had in it. This pacquet travels free of postage, and I send you, therefore, one of the million of the gazettes with which my ears are daily stunned, and which are impudently sold under the royal apartments. As my letter travels free and uninterrupted, I have delivered my sentiments without reserve—a liberty, however, that I often take without this precaution. My love of truth is apt to run away with me in contempt of all the sober admonitions of prudence; and unless I pitch my tent in England soon it is probable that I may have reason to lament my indiscretion.

MR. MILES TO MR. T. SOMERS COCKS

Paris: Monday, February 28, 1791

I wrote to you on Thursday by the post, on Friday by the messenger, and this travels under the auspices of Government to Lombard Street, whence I trust it will be forwarded to you as soon as it arrives. My last two letters apprised you of the insurrection of the people at the instigation of a few factious individuals who wish to give every possible pain to the King and Queen, and who, envious of the popularity of Monsieur de Lafayette, leave no means unattempted to destroy him in public opinion and to precipitate him into an act of severity that may endanger his existence. Menaced and insulted as the royal family are, the military, subordinate to the civil power, do not dare use the least violence until the magistrate gives the order to fire, and hence the troops must remain passive spectators of every species of licentiousness. This restraint is certainly well founded. It is an idea adopted from us; but, whilst in France the presence and the orders of the magistrate are alone required before violence is used, the *Riot Act* must be read with us—a proclamation which proves the aversion of our Government to shed blood except in cases of extreme necessity. The timidity, however, of the Parisian magistracy supplies the defect of the law. Monsieur Bailly, the Maire, on the first alarm and before he had recovered his senses, recommended the King to admit the profligate women into his presence, and, on his Majesty expressing his impatience and dissatisfaction at these perpetual tumults, the Mayor observed *qu'il faut de la douceur*. 'Oui,' replied the King; 'mais pas de la foiblesse, monsieur.' The Queen, collected and tranquil —at least in appearance—continued her party at cards without once discovering the least uneasiness or alarm, and without seeming to hear the tumult, conversing with those about her on the game as if the most perfect calm prevailed. Whatever may have been her past conduct, her present behaviour under such trying circumstances atones for all her possible irregularities, and, were she even criminal, she has been punished more severely than she could have deserved. The French hitherto have been considered a gallant people; but the scandalous outrages offered to the Queen by one party, the infamous desertion of her by others, and the no less unpardonable indifference of the whole kingdom to the injuries she has received, are a sufficient proof that the present generation at least do not deserve the reputation they possess. Read their poets and prose writers, and you will suppose that the French are the most generous nation on earth, full of sensibility and virtue, and as zealous knights-errant for the whole female community as ever Don Quixote was for Dulcinea del Toboso; but their virtue, like their knowledge, is superficial—*le sentiment dans la bouche et le crime dans le cœur*. Their attentions, frivolous and unmeaning—a salutation the merit of which belongs more to the dancing-master than to themselves—and common-place conversation collected from authors who, with few exceptions, are manufacturers of phrases rather than men of reading, genius, or observation, compose the whole of a Frenchman's obligation to the sex destined by heaven to solace us in this world of trouble. It is equally impossible for the lacquey as for his master to take a pinch of snuff without discovering that both have been fashioned in the same manner and by the same agency. That France possesses men worthy of regard I do not deny. But, with respect to the bulk of the nation, the morals and manners of all ranks of persons are exactly the reverse of what they ought to be; and this will ever be the case in a country where they contradict the laws, and where truth and all the virtues of the heart and mind are sacrificed to a gaudy and deceitful exterior. I have not conversed with a Frenchman to whom I have not maintained this opinion, and assured him that a revolution in the Government will be of little benefit to the cause of liberty without a revolution in their manners. Their education must be totally changed: their children may possibly see their country free and happy; the present generation cannot. Even vice, frightful as it is, is disfigured here. The assassin indulges in a joke at the instant he gives the fatal wound, and the victim expires amidst the pleasantry of those who surround him. The despotism of their former Government concealed their character by the severity it exercised. The instant the restraint was removed, it displayed itself to the whole world, and we know more of France within the last eighteen months than ever we knew before.

The party hostile to the Revolution have assumed the name of *Royalists* in Languedoc. Their army amounts to 15,000 men, but, as the troops have been ordered to march and the adjacent districts have collected a force to oppose the insurgents, it is probable that the affair of Uzès, like that of Nismes last June, will soon be terminated, unless indeed Brittany, Alsace, and Flanders should declare. I have just seen a person from Metz, who informs me that *seven-eighths* of the town, containing 36,000 inhabitants, are for a counter-revolution. Troops are marching to the southward; Marseilles has offered 20,000 men; fresh troubles at Bruxelles; the inhabitants are under arms at Geneva. M. Necker, it is said, is going to England. Paris is quiet for the moment, but a patriotic member of the National

Assembly said to me, 'Dieu sait où nous irons,' and, for my part, I augur much ill from the ignorance and brutal ferocity of an inflamed populace set free from all restraint—from the selfish views of ambitious or mercenary men in the National Assembly, and from the cabals of the Royalists, whether they have fled or remain in the country. These three descriptions of people draw different ways, but their conduct tends to one deplorable end—the ruin of their own country and the desolation of all Europe. In a word, the people are cruelly duped, and, when they discover it, woe be to those who have thus sported with their patience and credulity.

It will be argued this day, but not decreed, that the King, the Dauphin, and Monsieur shall be prohibited from leaving France, and even the Queen until the Dauphin be of age. The emigrants will be punished by confiscation, and none of the blood royal can hold offices civil or military.

Minute.—The police had totally lost its vigour and activity, and neither M. Bailly nor M. de Lafayette possessed that commanding courage and presence of mind which at once imposes on the multitude and secures its confidence. The former of these was totally without credit or respect, for mobs know nothing of Academicians, nor is it indeed usual for Academicians to be at the head of revolutions. Bailly was, besides, naturally mild and timid. I was at the château in the Tuileries in February 1791 when one part of the rabble, on a report that Monsieur was going to leave Paris, proceeded to the Hôtel de Luxembourg, while another, conducted by Mademoiselle Théroigne, assailed the Tuileries. It was the most violent commotion that had occurred since the month of October 1789, and the people had nearly forced their way into the royal apartments. It was some time before M. Bailly arrived. He came in pale and trembling. The King, with a firmness and tone of voice he had never used before, inquired the cause of his being exposed to these perpetual insults and the city to these false alarms, and insisted on these tumults being suppressed. It was the firm manner in which Lafayette acted that imposed on the multitude and protected the lives of the King and Queen, who, you may be assured, will certainly perish in some of these tumults. I was present at this distressing scene, and was astonished to find the King more collected and less alarmed than the Mayor. I descended from the royal apartments, and, mixing with the mob, perceived several faces which I remember to have seen on better occasions and in better places.[1]

W. A. M.

MR. MILES TO LORD RODNEY

Paris: Tuesday, March 1, 1791

My friend Lafayette has had a most fortunate escape. I have just returned from him. The cannon were drawn out yesterday and marched to Vincennes, in the castle of which preparations are making to receive prisoners, and the populace believe they are to inhabit the dungeon. I went there some days since with M. Latude,[2] and saw many rooms being fitted up like soldiers' guard-rooms, and some with beds like those in an infirmary. Any trifling event is now of importance, and such is the heated state of the public mind that it is soon thrown into fusion.

[1] See *Vindication of M. de Lafayette from the Aspersions of Mr. Burke*, London 1796, p. 14, by Mr. Miles; also *Conduct of France towards Great Britain*, &c., p. 221.

[2] See Letter, March 13.

The Orleans faction has besides an interest in worrying Lafayette and the National Guards. If the General is remiss, or rather temperate, there is a cry of 'treason' against him. He must always be on the alert. Yesterday threatened much bloodshed. No man could be more quick, more gallant, more prudent, or more collected than was Lafayette. In the Faubourg St. Antoine a fellow swore he would have his head on a pike. 'Ce ne sera pas aujourd'hui, mon ami,' was his only answer, and in this undaunted manner he proceeded on his grey horse, a conspicuous figure, through the crowd. One of his aides-de-camp was shot at on the road to Vincennes. Indeed, I tremble for Lafayette. His enemies will leave no stone unturned to accomplish his ruin, and yet in his downfall they must also expect destruction. All here is confusion. Every swindler banished from the country has come back ripe for any mischief. They drive straightforward to anarchy. Madame de Lafayette leads a wretched life. She is one of the best wives and best mothers in the world. Her alarm for her husband, who never appears at table until the second course is served, is sometimes so visible that I could not help sympathising with her. She would then recover, and seem shocked at her fears being discovered. Yesterday, at dinner, when I was lamenting the horrible excesses of the people, she remarked that I could not go to England without crossing the Channel, that the Channel could not be crossed without the risk of meeting storms, and that, in like manner, the storms attendant on all revolutions would soon subside, and therefore she had no fears. Yet fear alone possessed her. Would to Heaven that she had no need![1]

[1] 'Mon père avait table ouverte. Elle faisait les honneurs de chez elle de manière à charmer ses nombreux convives ; mais ce qu'elle

But the people who cabal for places are too corrupt. Mirabeau beyond all doubt is sold to the Court. His prophecy to M. Kelly, the French Minister at Mayence, is become true. He told it to me himself. On the Envoy lamenting that the good offices of the Queen had not been accepted by him a short time back, Mirabeau answered, 'Bah! Elle aura plus besoin de moi dans peu que moi d'elle.' He is terribly venal and extravagant. The aristocrats, with whom he has made peace, consider him at present as their friend and as being entirely bought over. The fact is, he touches money from everybody, and will be well paid for everything he does. What a lamentable thing it is that his great talents should be so abused! I forgot to tell you that Santerre has been acquitted by the court-martial that sat on him, and that he has again denounced Lafayette and Mirabeau in the Jacobins. This man aspires to succeed to the command of the National Guards—aye, and he will have it, for a blind security conceals from Lafayette the ruin that will certainly befall him. The triumph of Santerre is a death wound to the popularity of Lafayette, and gives to the Duke of Orleans a power which, though temporary, will last long enough to destroy my friend.

Pray let me hear from you, my dear Lord Rodney.

---

souffrait au fond de son cœur ne peut-être jugé que par ceux qui l'en ont entendue parler. Elle voyait mon père à la tête d'une révolution dont il était impossible de prévoir le terme. Chaque malheur, chaque désordre était jugé par elle avec un manque complet d'illusion dans sa propre cause. Elle était pourtant toujours soutenue par les principes de mon père, et si convaincue du bien qu'il pouvait faire, du mal qu'il pouvait empêcher, qu'elle supportait avec une force incroyable les dangers continuels auxquels il était exposé. Jamais, nous a-t-elle dit, elle ne l'a vu sortir durant ce temps, sans avoir la pensée qu'elle lui disait *adieu* pour la dernière fois. Personne n'était plus qu'elle terrifié par les périls de ceux qu'elle aimait ; mais dans ce temps elle était au-dessus d'elle-même, dévouée, avec mon père, à l'espoir d'empêcher des crimes.'—*Vie de Madame Lafayette*. par Madame de Lasteyrie, Paris 1868, p. 215.

Mr. Miles to Mr. H. J. Pye

Paris: March 1, 1791

Incessant rain and incessant tumults have rendered this winter the most gloomy and uncomfortable of any that I have ever experienced. If the bad weather has given me low spirits, the riots with which this metropolis has been alarmed and dishonoured have given me the spleen, *et voilà plus qu'il faut pour accabler Hercule lui-même.* Sterne saw everything *en beau* when he travelled *post* through this country, and perhaps for *that* reason (for if he had stopped he would have had time to observe better), *moi, je vois presque tout en noir*, and, without being partial to my opinion or afflicted, like Smelfungus,[1] with the jaundice, I believe that I approach nearer to the truth than our English Yorick, whose memory notwithstanding will be ever dear to me. What a charming world would this be if every man possessed the benign and generous disposition of the 'sentimental' traveller! Would to Heaven that this life did not contradict the pleasing fiction, or that its painful conditions did not awaken us every instant to sorrow or misfortune! I have had frequent occasions to repent of a frankness which, however consistent with the precepts we receive in our youth, is directly contrary to what is practised in maturer age ; *mais, pour bien vivre ici-bas, il faut savoir bien dissimuler, et comme je me trouve dans l'impossibilité de m'y conformer, je songe à me retirer du monde,* that I may enjoy the ease, or rather the superiority, which the love of letters gives us over the bulk of mankind.

If the commencement of my letter savours of gloom and melancholy, do not expect that it will assume a cheerful aspect as you approach the conclusion.

[1] Dr. Tobias Smollett. See Sterne's *Sentimental Journey.*

Politics, at the best, are a dismal subject, and I know no nation on earth whose history is not a register of crimes and misfortunes. The affairs of France still continue perplexed. A conciliatory spirit would restore order and confidence; but this would be contrary to the views, though not to the interest, of the men who wish to govern the kingdom, and whose influence, notwithstanding their incapacity and *méchanceté*, is sufficient to exclude all idea of an accommodation with those who feel injured by the Revolution. It seems to be the object of a decided majority in the National Assembly to drive the aristocratic party to despair by every insult and vexation that unlimited power, influenced by hatred and revenge, can imagine; and, the better to execute their purpose, reports are daily circulated that the constitution is in danger, and that the abettors of despotism have resolved on a general massacre of the popular party. These rumours operate on an ignorant and ferocious rabble like strong doses of double-proof rum, and 6,000 men under arms, besides cavalry, have with difficulty prevented the mob from penetrating into the royal apartments of their hapless and degraded sovereign, and accomplishing the object that was attempted on October 5 and 6, 1789.

I cannot recount within the limits of a letter shorter than that of Mr. Burke [1] all the horrors and indecencies committed since I last wrote to you. The people are kept in a constant state of intoxication. They are not allowed a sufficient interval for reflection, and, as no absurdity is too gross for vulgar credulity and no atrocity beyond their capacity, the most factious have it in their power to excite at any moment an insurrection. The Club Monarchique, instituted for the

[1] *Reflections on the Revolution in France &c., in a Letter by the Right Honourable Edmund Burke*, London, 1790.

purpose of destroying the credit of the Jacobins, and perhaps of the Legislature, occasioned almost all the forty-eight sections of Paris to denounce its members to the municipality. The club was instantly declared anti-revolutionary, and whatever disturbance happened, either in the metropolis or in its environs, or even in the provinces the most distant, was said to proceed from its intrigues, and every man among the lower class of tradesmen became a spy and informer. They saw what never existed, and heard things that were never uttered. Those who mounted guard at the Palace read the countenance of every gentleman whom duty, respect, or curiosity led to the royal presence, and construed each look according to their ignorance, fears, or malevolence. It is impossible but the Queen must share the odium of the obnoxious club, and to render her still more hateful to the people pretended letters from the frontiers were published announcing an immediate invasion on the side of the Austrian Netherlands. This produced resolutions to march *au devant pour recevoir les troupes impériales et, par conséquence, de les égorger toutes sans miséricorde.* These voluntary offers of military service became general, and Gallic vanity insolently boasted of having an army of four millions of freemen resolved *de vivre libres ou mourir.* At no period of French history was gasconade more in vogue than at present, and yet, notwithstanding this force, every effort was exerted to prevent the departure of the King's aunts, under an idea that they were going to cabal against the State, and that their departure would be followed by a counter-revolution. The Maire, feeble and irresolute, was prevailed upon to solicit the King to prohibit the Princesses from going. The irregularity and indecency of urging the sovereign to violate the laws of the country in the person of his dearest relatives did not occur to them, or, if it did, it did not prevent the municipality from complying with the insolent demands of a populace set on to insult the royal family by those who wish its destruction. The King, however, was firm, and the Princesses were resolved. Recourse was then had to the *poissardes*, and an expedition to Bellevue was prepared. Notice was sent in time to apprise the ladies of the intended visit, and they came to town in disguise and in a wicker waggon. Their journey, however, was not put off, the hour of departure approached, and they returned to their house. It was then resolved to bring them to town by violence, and for this purpose the *poissardes* proceeded again to Bellevue on the Saturday preceding the 21st ult., on which day the Princesses were to set off. They were again apprised of the visit whilst they were at supper. They instantly got into their carriage and drove off ten minutes before the mob reached the château. At Moret, near Fontainebleau, they were stopped, but the Chasseurs de Lorraine compelled the municipality to respect the principles of justice and right, and the journey met with no interruption until they reached Arnay-le-Duc, near Dijon, where they were detained until an answer to an express arrived from Paris. The application was to the National Assembly, who declared there was no law to prevent their departure. The members, desirous to preserve the popular fermentation, and to destroy M. de Lafayette and the Maire, did not blush to exclaim against the ingratitude of those who were fed by national bounty living out of the country, that the nation could ill afford the exportation of so much ready money, and humanely hinted that the pensions of these two old women should be suppressed if they did not return. This not meeting with the desired success, M. Barnave, who is the parasite and creature of the Lameths, asserted as a rumour that Monsieur was preparing to depart. This was sufficient to set all Paris in an uproar, and the next day the *poissardes*, who never go on such expeditions unaccompanied, stormed the Luxembourg, and received an assurance from Monsieur that he would never quit his brother or the kingdom. The tumult was sufficiently great to alarm the police, and the troops were under arms. Monsieur was conducted to the Tuileries, and the populace made a vigorous effort to mount the grand staircase and penetrate into the royal apartments. The activity and firmness of M. de Lafayette prevented it. The next day the news arrived of the detention of the King's aunts, and the party, finding that the National Assembly would not second their infamous views, stimulated the prostitutes of the Palais Royal and its environs to go to the Tuileries and insist on the King's sending orders to the Princesses to return. Paris was again under arms, and the night threatened much mischief. The guards had just time to shut the great iron gates of the château before the rabble arrived, and, like a torrent, inundated the Tuileries. The Maire, more dead than alive, was for admitting a deputation. The King was warm, and displayed the dignity of his character. M. Bailly recommended *douceur*. 'Oui,' replied his Majesty, 'mais pas de foiblesse.' M. de Lafayette behaved wonderfully well. His wife has been menaced; and he is yet daily threatened by the crowd of itinerant politicians, who infest the streets and are subalterns to the Jacobins. I called on him next day to convey my impression that if he did not act with firmness he, and perhaps his country, would be lost. My intimacy with him justifies this freedom.

In Languedoc the Royalists, as they call themselves,

are in force. They have an army of from 10,000 to 15,000 men, but, as the troops and National Guards are marching against them, it is most probable this insurrection, excited by the priests, will soon be suppressed. The sword of civil war has been drawn and sheathed again in Brittany. Blois is menaced with a revolt, as also Béthune, and all the province of Artois. Metz contains 36,000 inhabitants, of which 30,000 are aristocrats. Thionville also possesses more anti-revolutionists than patriots, and these places are both strong fortifications. Alsace can with difficulty be kept quiet; and, if a formidable insurrection breaks out in any of the provinces and meets with any success in its commencement, the whole kingdom will be in a flame. The National Assembly have been occupied in arranging a law to secure the throne and public tranquillity, for which purpose it was proposed that neither the King, the Dauphin, Monsieur, or the Queen, can quit the country without leave of the Legislature or forfeiting the crown. It is a terrible chaos, without the least prospect of its subsiding until *crime* and *folly* have had their full career. I have offered to conduct the Queen to England; I would almost hazard to do as much for the King, from the conviction I feel that the Revolution would go on better without his being present, provided his residence abroad did not become a focus for the partisans of tyranny and fanaticism. His Majesty is beset by sharpers of all ranks, all jealous and envious of each other, all whispering in turn in his too credulous ears assurances of being reinstated on the throne, more firmly than ever, if he will surrender himself entirely to their guidance. He listens, poor man, to each artful tale, and changes his Ministers without advancing a step to the promised good or bettering his bankrupt for-times! These impostors—for what are they else?—are the champions of despotism in the Palace and of freedom out of it. They all intrigue and cabal to the full extent of their credit and genius; they are spies upon each other, and are fast betraying their hapless, weak, and ruined sovereign to his enemies.

The man held of the least account in the National Assembly by Mirabeau, by Lafayette, and even by the Lameths and all the Orleans faction, will soon be of the first consideration. He is cool, measured, and resolved. He is *in his heart* Republican, honestly so, not to pay court to the multitude, but from an opinion that it is the very best, if not the only, form of government which men ought to admit. Upon this principle he acts, and the public voice is decidedly in favour of this system. He is a stern man, rigid in his principles, plain, unaffected in his manners, no foppery in his dress, certainly above corruption, despising wealth, and with nothing of the volatility of a Frenchman in his character. I do not enter into the question of the forms of government, but I say that Robespierre is *bonâ fide* a Republican, and that nothing which the King could bestow on him, were his Majesty in a situation to bestow anything, could warp this man from his purpose. In this sense of the word, that is, *in his heart meaning well*, as to the destruction of the monarchy, he is an honest man. I watch him very closely every night. I read his countenance with eyes steadily fixed on him. He is really a character to be contemplated; he is growing every hour into consequence, and, strange to relate, the whole National Assembly hold him cheap, consider him as insignificant, and, when I mentioned to some of them my suspicions and said he would be the man of sway in a short time, and govern the million, I was laughed at.

An infatuation marks the Court. The Queen looks to Sardinia and Austria. So strong is the delusion of the royal family, that the wench or valet who sweeps their apartments is listened to with affection when they talk of counter-revolution, and are caressed if they say it will infallibly take place. The National Assembly is also cursed by an infatuation of a different kind. The two great factions in it work for their own purposes. The welfare of the country is out of the question. The Tuileries is said to have purchased Mirabeau. I would rather buy Robespierre, if Robespierre could be bought, or even that vile incendiary, Marat. Mirabeau has no longer any credit with the people; with the nobility and clergy he never had any. The Bishop of Autun and he cling together.[1] Clubs abound in every street, and almost in every hovel in Paris. The women assemble and discuss political questions. All is uproar and confusion; and, during the illusory pursuits of the red-hot Royalists, and the interested cabals of the Limited Monarchy party, the Republicans, under the cautious and wily guidance of Robespierre, are silently and rapidly marching to the great object they have in view.

MR. MILES TO MR. T. SOMERS COCKS

Paris: Friday, March 4, 1791

It is whimsical enough that, after the departure of the post on each of the three days on which I have

---

[1] 'I sat by Talleyrand at dinner the day before yesterday, who told me a good deal about Mirabeau, but, as he had a bad cold, in addition to his usual mode of pumping up his words from the bottomest pit of his stomach, it was next to impossible to understand him. He said Mirabeau was really intimate with three people only—himself, Narbonne, and Lauzun; that Auguste d'Aremberg was the negotiator of the Court and medium of its communications with Mirabeau; that he had found (during the Provisional Government) a receipt of Mirabeau's for a million, which he had given to Louis XVIII.'—*The Greville Memoirs*, ii. 384.

lately written to you, tumults should have happened of sufficient importance to justify another letter, or rather a postscript to the one then despatched. Monday last was the day appointed by folly and knavery to deluge this country in blood—such, at least, is the general opinion of the hour; and, although opinions are as variable here as elsewhere, and slander has its vogue and fashion as well as dress or any other article of luxury, I am disposed to give some credit to it on this occasion, not on account of its having maintained its ground three whole days, and yet reigns, but because, when all the circumstances are considered, it has the appearance of being founded in truth, and all my combinations cannot discredit the hypothesis. Take the particulars, the facts, and decide for yourself. On Monday[1] last the Faubourg St. Antoine, which has been kept quiet these eight months by the bounty of the Court, was in motion; the object, or rather the pretext, being to destroy the château and dungeon of Vincennes, situated nearly two French leagues from Paris, and which was formerly and is again a prison. An enterprise of this importance required much force, and mobs, you know, like snowballs, increase. To prevent the mischief without effusion of blood, a considerable body of troops was necessary, and so 11,000 men, with artillery, and M. de Lafayette at their head, arrived early enough to interrupt the business. At the time that public curiosity was directed towards Vincennes, and whilst the metropolis was in a manner abandoned by the rabble and regular troops, a movement was observed in the Tuileries, where a man was seized in the apartment of the Dauphin with a poniard and pistols concealed: he is a native of St. Domingo, a Chevalier of the Order of St. Louis, and very

[1] February 28.

well known in Paris. The alarm occasioned may be easily conceived. There was little doubt but the odium of an attempt to assassinate the King would fall on the most violent of the democratic party, and such a rumour was instantly spread. Towards dusk the royal apartments filled in a most astonishing manner, and a number of faces appeared, which, though familiar to the officers and servants of the Court, could not be recognised on account of the disguise of shabby clothing. The crowd became so great towards ten o'clock as to give much uneasiness to the officer on guard, and this anxiety was augmented by the whisperings, insinuations, and assurance of the group assembled. The pockets of these extraordinary visitors were remarked to be overcharged, and one of the guards, touching the vestments of a suspected individual, felt a pair of pistols, which proved to be twenty inches long in the barrel. This led to a general search and, of course, to much uproar and indecency and rough usage. It is worthy of observation that these adventurous knights were boasting the moment before of their gallantry and resolution to die in defence of their sovereign. Both their language and looks changed instantly on their persons being examined, and it was discovered that many members of the National Assembly, a Maréchal de France, and cordons-bleu, were among the number searched. The first of these insisted on an exemption from the ceremony and disgrace on the plea that their persons were sacred; but an affected disbelief of their assertions, accompanied with much sarcasm and assurances that it was impossible that the representatives of the nation could degrade their character so much as to appear in the royal apartments as assassins, was followed by slow blows and kicks, of which the effects will remain for some time.

They were narrowly searched, and eighty-two pairs of pistols and a number of Italian stilettoes, some of which had three blades, were thereupon seized. While this operation was performing on some of the party, others attempted to conceal their weapons in the room in which the King was seated, but, this manœuvre being discovered by the guards, an application was made to his Majesty, and they were given up. A violent opposition was made by some five or six individuals, and these, all men of distinction, were conducted to prison. The garden of the Tuileries had also its chevaliers, to the number of from 600 to 800, all armed and in readiness for the project, whatever it was, but, perceiving what was transacting above in the château, they made their escape. About fifty of the insurgents at Vincennes were taken, and thus ended at midnight an adventure that threatened much mischief at least to the capital. It is asserted that the Chevalier de St. Louis, who opened the ball and was arrested, began too early; that the project was to carry off the King, Queen, Dauphin, and indeed all the family, from the Tuileries, for which purpose a diversion was made to Vincennes so as to be more at liberty to act in Paris, and that a greater number *des cartes d'entrée aux Tuileries* were issued on that day than usual. The royal apartments were crowded with new faces—men in frocks, and old faces in old clothing. The instant the alarm was given of the seizure of the pretended assassin, all the conspirators flew down to the Palace armed with concealed pistols and poniards. Movements of a suspicious nature were observed before the guard was relieved, and a member of the Garde du Corps of the King recommended great vigilance to the officer in command, as *ce seroit un jour de crise pour le château.*

The people who excited the tumult in the Faubourg St. Antoine were those who had occasionally distributed money and bread to the poor to keep them quiet. On being relieved at the Tuileries, the guard, instead of retiring, remained as a reinforcement, and consequently was double. Those who were taken, and all those who were searched at the Palace, were the most furious of the aristocrats. Their object certainly was not to assassinate the King; the man whom they sent *en avant*, and who was the marplot of this tragicomedy, was reclaimed by the president and secretary of the Club Monarchique, which is known to be hostile to the Revolution. From all these circumstances it is evident that there was a design of some sort, but what that design was I cannot take upon me to assert. If, as they say, it was to carry off the King, it was poorly conceived and worse attempted, besides which, its execution is impracticable. They could not have gone ten leagues from Paris without being stopped. The whole country is in a state of alarm. The Jacobins have established a correspondence from the Pyrenees to the Rhine; and 287 different clubs of the same kind, and for the same purpose, in different parts of the kingdom are associated with them and are in daily communication. The interchange of thought is so immediate and universal that the whole country resembles the whispering gallery of St. Paul's Cathedral —all is known in almost the same breath and the same instant that it is uttered.

The aristocrats, no less cowardly than stupid, take measures so ill conceived, combine so poorly, and act so ineffectively, that it is impossible they can succeed: *pour chaque pas qu'ils s'avancent ils en reculent dix.* They have neither talents, virtue, nor courage; nor is there about the person of the hapless monarch an individual who would not desert him if he could thereby acquire the popularity of Mirabeau or De Lafayette. The spirit of low and profligate intrigue, in which parentage, friendship, truth, and honour are sold, bartered, or sacrificed to personal interest or favour, reigns as much as ever; all is as much as ever *espionnage et trahison*. The nation is too corrupt, too abandoned, to possess a sense of true honour; and it is melancholy, though severe truth, that no Frenchman hardly ever approached the Court of Versailles without becoming a complete scoundrel. There was not a man in the reign of Louis XV. who would not have prostituted his wife, or mother, or sister, or daughter, to their fanatic and libertine Prince. All who raised themselves into favour did it by administering to his pleasures. Pimps and parasites by inclination and profession, what else can be expected from the despicable *noblesse* of France but the conduct which they have pursued? Abject and fawning to their sovereign or the people, as either of them happen to be uppermost, they will remain slaves under any form of government; and, unless a revolution takes place in the morals as well as in the state, this country will continue for years in a condition of anarchy and degradation.

It was proposed to confiscate the property of the emigrants. The instant I heard it, I declaimed against the injustice and barbarity of the measure; and I asserted that it was tyrannical in principle, difficult in application, and impracticable in execution. Mirabeau was of the same opinion, and he prevented the absurd and iniquitous question from being debated by moving for the order of the day. The same night—Monday last—Mirabeau himself was denounced as a traitor to his country by the two Lameths and Duport at the

Jacobins. I sat next to Charles Lameth and opposite to Mirabeau. We were at least 1,600 in all. Never did a man defend a good cause so ill. Mirabeau is no orator, and yet he has the impudence to compare himself to Mr. Fox. The denunciation lasted full two hours. I saw him ascend the tribune dismayed and terrified. I never heard a man speak so badly in my life. In vice he is eloquent; in the cause of virtue and of justice he was abashed, because he was not at home. We move awkwardly out of our sphere. He spoke only ten minutes, and half the time was consumed in fulsome and dishonourable panegyric on the zeal and patriotism of his accusers. He never once entered into the question, although it was one of great extent and importance, involving the consideration of all the various links by which men are held together in society. It was a question in which reason and declamation might have displayed their whole force, and never could truth and genius have had a better occasion to show themselves. He contented himself with barely asserting that such a law would be barbarous and impracticable. Yet for the most meritorious, perhaps the only meritorious, action of his life he was condemned. What a fund of learning and eloquence Mr. Pitt or Mr. Fox would have displayed on such an occasion! They would have thundered conviction on those who heard them. This letter goes by the messenger to the Foreign Office. Adieu, and God bless you.

MADAME DE LAFAYETTE TO MR. MILES

Paris: ce 10 Mars, 1791

Madame de Lafayette a reçu avec bien de la reconnaissance le livre que M. Miles a bien voulu lui envoyer. Elle s'est occupée avec bien de l'empressement de chercher les moyens d'avoir des billets pour Mademoiselle Miles et pour lui, mais ses recherches ont malheureusement été infructueuses. Le Président avoit disposé de sa loge depuis une semaine, et du petit nombre de billets qu'il a eu sa disposition depuis plusieurs jours. Ce qui console un peu Madame de Lafayette c'est que la séance de demain sera peut-être fort peu intéressante ; la question des émigrants n'y sera pas traitée. Elle supplie instamment Mademoiselle Miles de vouloir bien lui offrir un moyen de réparer ses malheurs dans cette circonstance, en lui indiquant un autre jour où elle puisse être plus heureuse en lui procurant des billets pour une autre séance. Elle a l'honneur de lui offrir mille compliments et de lui renouveler l'assurance de ses regrets.

MR. MILES TO LORD RODNEY

Paris: March 12, 1791

It would be difficult to give you, my dear Lord Rodney, an exact picture of Paris at this moment. No pen, no pencil can describe it. Bedlam broken loose, and its wild and melancholy inhabitants giving full career to lunacy in Moorfields, would fall far short of what this distracted metropolis exhibits ; and to aggravate the horrors of this place, every maniac almost is an assassin either in thought or deed. There are as many political sects here as there are religious ones in the Christian system—all violent, all zealously pursuing their respective views by the foulest means; an unprincipled nobility and a clergy without piety or morality are endeavouring by intrigue to reinstate their phantom of a sovereign in all his pomp and authority. To this miserable junto a herd of despicable adventurers resort with offers of service, some of whom are well disposed to lift fallen greatness into the easy chair of state, whilst others desire merely to gain a knowledge of the royal plans in order to reveal them. Some of the German Courts have emissaries here—all apostles of liberty—preaching equal rights, and assuring the giddy multitude that their example will be followed by the whole world! Prussia for intrigue takes the lead. She pays court to each party as appearances may seem to favour. The Tuileries she disregards. All her agents vociferate against the House of Austria as plotting with the Queen for the purpose of destroying the Revolution. The King of Sardinia is also involved in this accusation; and, while the Emperor is said to have an army in the Netherlands, ready to enter France by Lille and Valenciennes, the Court of Turin is reported to have ordered several thousand poniards to be manufactured in Piedmont for the French emigrants on the banks of the Rhine, under the Cardinal de Rohan, the younger Mirabeau and others, and for the aristocrats at Paris in league with them. All these tales, absurd as some of the fabrications are, pass for authentic, and serve no less to bewilder than to inflame the public mind. That the Revolution will have its course, that it cannot be interrupted but must proceed, is a fact as clear as noonday. It is obvious to every man of discernment. But the King from imbecility, and the Queen, blinded by her wishes and her hopes, believe in a counter-revolution, and listen to every designing knave that chaunts the same tune. Mirabeau, too versatile to be steady to any one object, is already less ardent in the cause of liberty; and yet the Tuileries vainly imagine that, if they can get this man over to their interest, the counter-revolution would be instantly effected. I wrote to you that he had received from the

Spanish Minister a thousand louis-d'or for the vote he obtained in August from the National Assembly for forty-five sail of the line to aid Spain should the war have taken place between us. Most of the deputies from Brittany are in the pay of the King. M. Talon[1] is the confidential man of this hapless monarch, and has largely distributed money to several members of the National Assembly, reserving no doubt a much larger portion for himself—at least it is so said; and one of the deputies has cited himself as a proof of the dishonesty of Talon by declaring he had not received a sol, and that the other had kept what he ought to have given to the friends of his Majesty. It is distressing, specially to those who, like myself, are anxious for the establishment of rational liberty throughout this vast kingdom, to see how shamefully so good a cause is conducted. Freedom should go hand in hand with order. But all is tumult, and suspicion, and alarm. The National Assembly is not equal to the task of completing what it has begun. Many of its members are hostile to the very name of liberty, and these execrate us as the authors in some sort of their disgrace, as they call it, by our preaching in favour of freedom; while others are playing a double game—bellowing for liberty in public, and bargaining in private for the restoration of despotism. Prussia cabals in favour of the new order of things, and offers to recognise the present Government in France on condition that she will break with Vienna. As kings have no temptation to be dishonest from poverty, as they are supported in splendour at the expense of the million, who are forced to toil from sunrise to sunset to obtain bread to eat, every act of

---

[1] See Minute, December 18, 1792, on a proposal that M. Talon should endeavour to rescue Louis XVI.

knavery from a throne has a deeper stain of crime than when perpetrated by common men; but of all the sceptred miscreants who have dishonoured royalty since you and I have perambulated this earth, I know of none so base, so mean, so infamous as the present King of Prussia. He has authorised his agents throughout Europe to commit a kind of general pillage —to cajole and rob all nations. Liège has been cozened, beggared, and betrayed! After having been most impudently duped and plundered—abandoned to the fury of a rancorous and unforgiving priesthood, her old task-masters—attempts were made by the Court of Berlin to reap a harvest in Brabant by offers of support to resist the return of the Austrian authority. But the Flemings have had more discretion than to confide in any of the emissaries from the Court of Berlin. France offers a great game to the Prussian King and his Ministers, whose agents are indefatigable. I have again made through the Princesse de Tarente an offer to the Queen to convey her to England; but her Majesty is inflexible in her resolution to abide by and share the fate of her husband. I am convinced that they will both perish in this most terrible tempest.

Mr. Miles to Monsieur Latude

Paris: March 13, 1791

The paper which I have given to you is an order on M. Perregaux, the banker, for 120 livres. Do me the kindness to accept them. Your age and your misfortunes give you a claim on all feeling hearts. I know not by what fatality the Legislature in France, whose duty it is without doubt to destroy utterly the very least vestige of despotism, has been able to refuse succour to one of the greatest victims of tyranny. It is for the nation to protect you. It owes it to you, it owes it equally to justice and humanity, and I hope that, realising the inexpressible horrors which you have endured in the dungeons, it will render the end of your days as easy and tranquil as their commencement was persecuted and unfortunate.

Minute.—In the autumn of 1790, La Fleur, immortalised by Sterne in Yorick's 'Sentimental Journey,' waited on me at Paris, and his wife washed for me.

On the evening of March 13, 1791, the hapless object to whom the above letter is addressed mounted the tribune in the Jacobin Club at Paris, and solicited its recommendation of his claim to the National Assembly for a provision. His well-known story authorised the appeal. He had been for thirty-five years condemned, unheard, and without having in fact been accused of any crime, in the different jails of the Bastille, Bicêtre, and Vincennes. He was at this period (1791), at the age of seventy years and more, without money, relations, or protection. The mistress of that scoundrel King, Louis XV., was the cause of Latude being arrested and immured in dungeons, where rats disputed with him the miserable portion allotted to keep life and body together. He escaped from the lofty battlements of the Bastille at the hazard of his neck, and such was the inexorable fury of Madame de Pompadour, that orders were sent to all the foreign Courts in alliance with France to have him seized. He was taken at Bruxelles and brought back. His misfortunes inspired me with an interest in his happiness. I supported his 'motion' in the Jacobin Club, and was opposed by a man who has since perished in the Revolution. Not content with this, I declared that, if this fair demand was rejected by the National Assembly, I would open a subscription for him in England, and would myself subscribe annually the sum of five louis-d'or, and, asking Robespierre, who was opposite to the tribune, to give me some paper, I handed the old man a draft upon Perregaux for that amount.[1] W. A. MILES.

MR. MILES TO SIR EDWARD NEWENHAM

Paris: March 18, 1791

Believe me, dear Newenham, I am not an enemy to the Revolution in this country. It was an event that I wished would happen long before the attempt was made, a doctrine which I preached to Frenchmen whenever I met them, and whilst as yet the Bastille awed them into submission and held them in a mean and dishonourable bondage. My love of liberty is too well known, too

[1] 'Mazers de Latude, enregistré à la Bastille sous le nom de Danry, entra dans cette forteresse en 1749. Il avait écrit à Madame de Pompadour pour la prévenir de l'envoi d'une boîte remplie de poison. La boîte arriva; mais elle ne contenait point de substance dangereuse; et Latude lui-même fut convaincu de l'avoir envoyée. Il voulait exciter, par ce prétendu service, la reconnaissance de Madame de Pompadour. A force de patience, de hardiesse et d'industrie, il parvint à s'échapper de la Bastille avec un de ses compagnons d'infortune, et publia depuis, sur sa détention et sa fuite, des Mémoires où des faits exacts et des détails intéressans se trouvent mêlés aux aventures les plus romanesques. L'évasion de ces deux prisonniers est racontée de la manière suivante dans les pièces même trouvées à la Bastille : 'Ils firent une échelle de corde très-bien tissue et très solide, et employèrent près de deux ans à la faire. Au bout de ce temps, qui était au mois de Février 1756, ils grimpèrent au haut de leur cheminée, trouvèrent le moyen de défaire les barres de fer qui la traversaient, et gagnèrent la plate-forme du haut des tours; et ayant tiré à eux leur échelle, ils en attachèrent le bout à un canon, se laissèrent couler dans le fossé, percèrent un mur, et se sauvèrent.'—*Mémoire Hist. sur la Bastille*, tome ii. p. 282.

'Il paraît qu'après le 14 Juillet (1789) l'échelle de corde, qui avait cent quatre-vingts pieds de longueur, fut retrouvée dans les archives de la Bastille, et déposée au comité des électeurs, qui la firent remettre à Latude.' —*Mémoires de Linguet, &c. sur la Bastille*, p. 4.

Latude evidently deceived Mr. Miles by *personating* La Fleur. It was in 1762 that La Fleur was engaged by Sterne, at Montreuil, to attend

strongly woven into my very frame, for me to apprehend the reproach of aristocracy. But, attached as I am to freedom, I am not to be seduced into a wild and indiscriminate approbation of all the licentiousness which an abuse of freedom unhappily produces. If you attribute the Revolution to a virtuous sentiment, or to a courageous effort in favour of liberty, you are mistaken. Do not let us give credit to the nation, no less enslaved by vice than by despotism, for an event which I firmly believe in my conscience would not have happened but for the imbecility of its Government. Vergennes died in a lucky moment, or the rascal would have perished like Foulon.[1] He deceived and abandoned the Dutch. He thought he had outwitted us in the Commercial Treaty.

him on his tour in France and Italy. Latude, subsequent to his perilous escape, was confined within the Bastille from June 15, 1756, to September 18, 1765, when he was transferred to Vincennes.—See *The Bastille*, by Captain the Hon. D. Bingham, ii. 110-132.

Probably Latude is the author of the supposititious notes of La Fleur published in Davis's *Olio*. The question, which is not without interest, has been submitted by the Editor of these volumes to the consideration of Mr. Percy Fitzgerald, who, having weighed the arguments, accepts the hypothesis as being the most obvious, or the least difficult, solution of the problem. He says: 'I am quite come round to your view that this spurious account was written by Latude.'

See an interesting article on Latude in the *Revue des Deux Mondes*, October 1, 1889. See also the *Life of Laurence Sterne*, by Percy Fitzgerald, London, 1864, ii. 301, &c.

[1] 'After dinner, walk a little under the arcade of the Palais Royal, waiting for my carriage. In this period the head and body of M. Foulon are introduced in triumph—the head on a pike, the body dragged naked on the earth. Afterwards, this horrible exhibition is carried through the different streets. His crime is to have accepted a place in the Ministry. This mutilated form of an old man of seventy-five is shown to his son-in-law, Berthier, the Intendant of Paris, and, afterwards, he also is put to death and cut to pieces—the populace carrying about the mangled fragments with a savage joy. Gracious God, what a people!'—*Life of Gouverneur Morris, Minister from the United States to the Court of France*, i. 322. See also *Dr. Rigby's Letters*, edited by Lady Eastlake, London, 1880.

He was a successful quack, who quitted the political booth before his impostures were discovered. M. de Brienne was another mountebank, equally incapable, but more unfortunate because he had not the public opinion in his favour. I do not mention M. Calonne, whose profusion accelerated the Revolution. And the stupidity and vanity of his successor produced an explosion destructive to society. If you imagine that the Revolution would not have taken place if M. de Broglio[1] had been permitted to act with vigour according to the proposal made, you are again much mistaken. The States-General, now called the National Assembly, would perhaps have been dismissed, but, for all that, France would not have remained in fetters. You must not, however, suppose that the Gallic Revolution in 1789, though to the full as necessary as that in England in 1688, was produced by the virtue and courage of the people. No such thing. They found themselves on a sudden masters of the kingdom, without a struggle, without an effort, for the taking of the Bastille cannot be called a struggle. De Launay, the Governor, lost his head long before the rabble separated it from his shoulders. He had neither ammunition, nor provisions, nor troops, nor had he capacity to defend it. He could make no resistance; and, a panic having seized the Government, the King found himself abandoned and alone.

Compare the two Revolutions of England and France. The former proceeded from a determined spirit of liberty, which had disputed the ground for centuries, inch by inch, with despotism, and, having carried on a

---

[1] 'Victor François, Duc de Broglie, né en 1718, mort en 1804. En 1789 Louis XVI. lui confia le ministère de la guerre ; mais il fut bientôt forcé de se démettre et d'émigrer.'— Bouillet, *Dict.*

regular siege against tyranny, destroyed all its outworks and stormed its very citadel. There was everything that dignified our Revolution, not only in the heat and violence of the contest, but in the moment of victory, when obstinate resistance would have justified resentment and have excused severity. Our forefathers contended for liberty and won the prize; but France remained in slavery, and submitted to every injustice and ignominy which overgrown power could impose, without one effort to throw off the yoke.

Her tyrants, when confronted with the present difficulties, abandoned their post. The nation found herself unexpectedly free, and, when released from restraint and abjectness, flew into the extreme of insolence, ruin, and disorder. In England and Ireland we had the Catholics to subdue; we had Scotland to reduce; we had Louis XIV. to combat; besides the various factions who in the very heart of the kingdom favoured the banished family. France, on the other hand, encounters no power to dispute the freedom which has rather been given to her than acquired by her, and yet, at the expiration of almost two years, she is as far from a settled Government as she was at the commencement. All is bustle and confusion here—faction and intrigue, weakness and violence, economy and profusion. The assignats paid 5 per cent. discount in August last; at present I cannot convert them into cash under $6\frac{1}{4}$; and judge what a loss this must be on the annual or even daily expense of the whole kingdom! It is even impossible to have the small assignats of fifty livres without paying $2\frac{1}{2}$ per cent. discount, and yet, if you believe the French, they are in a flourishing condition. They pretend that the lands of the clergy sell at treble their valuation. In Alsace they do not sell at all. I suppose it is the same in other provinces. And as a proof that the sale is not so rapid or so beneficial as is reported, the paper money is more and more discredited, and specie becomes every day more rare. The State, relieved, as it is pretended, from much debt by this paper money and by the sale of the church lands, does not rise. The vessel does not lighten notwithstanding the lumber that has been thrown overboard. Yet the French people and the nations of Europe have been assured that this sale will produce six milliards, a sum equal to our national debt. Much rancour and jealousy are excited here against Great Britain; and too much vice and profligacy exist in her rulers for the present generation ever to see freedom and happiness. Factions retard the great work, and will retard it for years, because they are the factions of popular men ambitious of power.

I am much afraid that our friend the Marquis will fall a victim to his rivals, the Lameths. Traps are laid for him daily; his life is publicly menaced, and he has been denounced as a traitor to his country at the Jacobins. I have a high opinion of the sincerity of his patriotism, but there is no executive power to support him, and he does not act with sufficient vigour on his own responsibility. I wish he had talents equal to the perilous situation in which he is unhappily placed. He will fall a victim, cool and determined as he is. It is impossible that the enemies of the Revolution can ever restore the ancient Government; but the minds of Frenchmen are not yet sufficiently enlightened to derive immediate benefit from a change so great in their political position. Louis XI., who consolidated this vast monarchy into one compact mass, established his dominion by fraud and violence; dissimulation and injustice have supported the Gallic throne; and the Court of Versailles, from that period to July 14, 1789, has invariably exhibited one uninterrupted scene of all that is the most vile and infamous. These vices, although they mark particularly the higher circles, infected the whole nation, for, wherever despotism reigns, there vice and falsehood triumph. Sentiment abounds in all the French authors, a false and dangerous politeness has marked even the lowest ranks, but they were for the most part strangers to that blunt simplicity which always announces a fund of virtue in a people. How, then, is it possible that the community should become all on a sudden honest and disinterested? It is not in human nature. And I tell you, in all the pride of truth, that at least twenty-five years must elapse before France acquires a degree of stability and authority equal to what she possessed under her monarchs, and, moreover, that period must be a period of peace. The rising generation will receive an education different to that of their fathers. Their minds will then become vigorous and enlightened. They will lose their servility with their fears and ignorance, and they will yet become a great people. At present all is cabal and intrigue among the upper and middle classes, and anarchy and confusion pervade the lowest orders. The Government will inevitably remain crippled and imperfect until some transcendent genius arises in whom great talents and great probity are united; but this will not happen until the measure of Gallic misery is full—that is, until some great disaster takes place, or the public patience, exhausted, calls loudly for a stable and intelligent Government as the only basis of security.

March 27.—Be assured there was no design to carry the King off on the 28th of last month. The affair of Vincennes has been exaggerated, although Lafayette nearly lost his life on that occasion. The aristocrats who went to the royal apartments armed secretly with pistols and poniards acted from paltry and cowardly zeal which has rendered them the ridicule of all Paris, exposed them to much ill-treatment, and has injured the cause they meant to serve.

The Prince de Condé menaces the frontiers, which are ill-furnished with troops, ammunition, and artillery. He is at Worms. Orders were given to assemble an army of 20,000 men to oppose him, but they are unable to accomplish it for want of military stores, and this you may rely upon as a fact, as I had it from a member of the Comité Militaire, Felix Wimpffen. The German Princes would certainly do something if they could, and an army of 40,000 or 50,000 men, invading Alsace at this moment, would ravage the kingdom and threaten all France with ruin, because the clergy, the *noblesse*, the lawyers, and other Royalists would join them, and these amount to some 300,000. Never was France so nearly being inevitably ruined as at this instant. If she escapes, she will owe much to the folly or the generosity of Europe. I see with my own eyes, hear with my own ears, and judge for myself. I am no stranger to what is going on. No honest and sensible man can tell you that France is in a flourishing state. Nor does she deserve to prosper so long as the spirit of intrigue, which has always marked and dishonoured her politics, continues to prevail. Instead of uniting heart and hand in the great and glorious work set before them, a part of their attention is devoted to sow discord in neighbouring nations, for the purpose of throwing all into confusion, and by that means preventing their King and *noblesse* from receiving foreign succour. You may judge of their own opinion of the Revolution in having recourse to such despicable means. I know that you have French emissaries in Ireland to stimulate you against your Government and force you into rebellion. Do not be the dupes of Parisian artifice. I write to you as a friend. Be on your guard, for if you should unhappily fall into the snare Ireland will exhibit a scene similar to that of Brabant, and finish as Brabant has done. I cannot say more at this distance.

It remains for me to thank you for supporting Administration on the subject of the Convention, or rather for the deference you paid to my opinion in complying with my request. The clause to which I alluded is novel, and, although common-sense long since pointed it out as necessary, Mr. Pitt is the first minister that introduced it in treaty, and he alone has the merit of putting it out of the power of subalterns in distant regions to involve their respective countries in a war. You can inform Mr. Pitt how warmly I pressed you to support his convention with Spain. On Friday week I shall set off for London. You know my address. At this moment we are quiet. Adieu, my dear Newenham. Do not press your countrymen to follow the example of France, for nothing beneficial to man can yet be said to have issued from her National Assembly; they are, with few exceptions, involved and lost in cabals. Ever yours.

Observations on Reading the 'Reflections on the French Revolution by Mr. Burke'

Paris: March, 1791

Two consequences are to be apprehended from the Revolution in France of greater magnitude than is generally imagined. The first relates to the effect its example may have in our country, and the more so as it has been held in all the extravagance of praise for imitation as alone capable of correcting the defects in a constitution hitherto deemed the perfection of human wisdom. Mr. Paine comes forward with a pamphlet of considerable ingenuity, containing a string of self-evident propositions, abstractedly taken, which are well calculated to act on vulgar minds. If the understandings of men were on a level—that is, if all men were good and wise—the *theory* so forcibly urged by that writer could be carried into practice with great facility; but the striking inequalities in the capacities and dispositions of mankind make the system he recommends impossible, and, as long as these disproportions exist, so long must the different gradations established in society be maintained. Mr. Paine, reasoning always from the *abstract* 'Rights of Man,' asserts the contrary; and, since the art and simplicity with which he declaims against these gradations are well adapted to make an impression on the class the most easy to be seduced and the most capable to disturb the public peace, much mischief may result from his publication. But this pamphlet would never have had an existence except for the ill-judged and ill-timed rhapsody of Mr. Burke. The sermon of Dr. Price, against whom this rhapsody is partly levelled, would have been forgotten had it not been for the forward zeal of his officious adversary. It was scarcely known beyond the limited circle who professed the same principles, and, consequently, it could do little harm; but controversy gave it a more extended publicity, and unhappily diffused the poison throughout the kingdom. By controverting its arguments in print, an appeal was made, as it were, to the nation. The people were called upon to judge between the parties, and thereby the cause of faction was more completely served by the means taken to counteract it than it would have been by fifty discourses from the pulpit of the dissenting minister. Disputes on forms of government, like contests for modes of faith, may be carried on to eternity. That the motive of Mr. Burke was to support good government cannot well be doubted, but, by a strange fatality in the character and conduct of that gentleman, he has treated the subject in a manner imprudent and unlike a writer of candour and information. The discourse of Dr. Price did not deserve notice; it was sinking fast into oblivion, and would soon have shared the common fate of most sermons. It was still more impolitic to make a violent and public attack on the Democratic party in France. The outrage committed by Mr. Burke was instantly placed to the account of the British Government. Mr. Pitt was declared to be an enemy to freedom, and Mr. Burke was considered as a mercenary bravo hired by despotism to assassinate civil and religious liberty. Such was the effect produced on the Continent by his pamphlet, and hence the idea of our country being hostile to the Revolution in France is confirmed. How it has operated in England I know not, except that it has given birth to the very artful and dangerous publication of Mr. Paine, from which much serious mischief may arise. The ground for Mr. Burke to have taken, if he took up the matter at all, ought to have been that of establishing first the general satisfaction of the English people with their own constitution and Government, and, second, the impertinence of attempting to disturb the public tranquillity by recommending a total change in their political constitution. The question of *Cui bono?* could never have been applied with greater force and propriety; for, if a nation is happy under its form of government, let that form be what it may, why hazard its felicity by a change?

This was not the case in France. The people here were insulted, oppressed, and plundered. They had Bastilles to demolish and tyranny to resist; nor had they the means of restoring themselves to the indubitable 'Rights of Men' living in society except by the dreadful expedient of a revolution.[1] That they have fallen into a state of anarchy, infinitely worse than the regal or ministerial despotism by which they have been long enslaved, will be readily acknowledged by every candid and intelligent observer of their conduct. The bulk of mankind, however, seldom reason or reflect, and hence the danger to be apprehended from the example of successful revolt, and from the various publications destined to persuade the unthinking multitude that the different gradations of rank are usurpations which reason requires should be abolished.

The second consequence to be anticipated from the Revolution, should we happily escape the contagion of revolt, is the power which France will derive from a free Government and from a knowledge of her immense resources. It may not be improper to observe that, however much we may owe to our zeal, courage, and industry, we owe perhaps still more to the weakness, indolence, and ignorance of our neighbours. If France should preserve the unity of her empire, it cannot be

---

[1] 'Pass the Bastille—another pleasant object to make agreeable emotions vibrate in a man's bosom. I search for good farmers, and run my head at every turn against monks and state-prisons. . . . The gross infamy that attended *lettres de cachet* and the Bastille during the reign of Louis XV., carried to an excess hardly credible, to the length of being sold with blanks to be filled up with names at the pleasure of the purchaser, who was thus able in the gratification of private revenge to tear a man from the bosom of his family and bury him in a dungeon to die unknown!'. *Arthur Young*, pp. 63, 532.

doubted but in the course of less than fifty years she will become a formidable nation; and hence arises the question, how far it is the interest of Europe to suffer her to consolidate her revolution. She has indeed formally renounced every idea of conquest; but, giving her credit for the sincerity of her present declaration, what certainty can be given that she will adhere to it when her strength and resources enable her to violate the faith of treaties with impunity? This is a question difficult to be solved. But, even if it could be solved in her favour, we are not to trust what she will now do, but to look to what she may do hereafter; and it is more incumbent than ever on those who are entrusted with the administration of affairs in England to look forward to a distant period, and legislate for the future security and prosperity of the kingdom. The lure held out to the indigent and enterprising by the National Assembly in France—declaring every man a citizen and eligible to all places of trust and emolument—may occasion very numerous emigrations from Great Britain and her dependencies. No man is fit to be Minister whose mind is not extensive enough to secure, as far as human wisdom and the means he possesses enable him to secure, the prosperity and safety of his country to the remotest period. A British Minister, while he attends to the exigencies of the moment, should look forward. The occurrences of the day need not be overlooked when providing for distant events; but, unfortunately, the preservation of patronage which power confers, together with the emoluments of office, are too often the principal objects of ministerial solicitude, and hence the general interests of the Empire are sacrificed to the despicable vanity or avarice of individuals. Hence also we seldom see anything grand and magnificent in our foreign politics, or permanent and provident in our domestic concerns; and so, temporising perpetually abroad and at home, the whole system of government has often exhibited a miserable piece of patchwork, in which neither skill, industry, nor convenience are to be discovered.[1]

W. A. M.

Mr. Miles to Lord Rodney

Paris : 5 o'clock p.m., April 1, 1791

My letter was sealed and the pacquet despatched to be forwarded by the usual channel, when I received information that Mirabeau was dead. This event may possibly occasion some confusion in the National Assembly, and a momentary surprise to the nation, but the surprise will only be momentary, for the natural vivacity of the French people will prevent its being of longer duration. If Mirabeau had been an honest man, or if he had possessed either virtuous pride or noble sentiments, he might, by his talents and acquired knowledge, have rendered his country most essential service; but he was mercenary, though extravagant, and vain, vulgar, and mean—ready to sell himself to any party who thought him worth buying. I knew him personally. You may form some idea of him when I inform you that he was an object of dread and contempt to all parties. The confidence which his countrymen had in his capacity and superior attainments obtained him a degree of influence in the National Assembly; this influence he preserved to the last; and it would be an injustice to his memory to deny that the Revolution owed much to his collected firmness. You will not suspect me of partiality towards him when I inform you that he decided that important event by his courage and presence of

[1] On Dr. Price's Sermon, see Lecky's *History*, v. 448–450.

mind in a moment of alarm and consternation, and when his colleagues, intimidated by an order from the Court to separate, and by the appearance of a military force, were on the point of abandoning their mission. It was then that Mirabeau stood forth the champion of their honour and the vindicator of the nation's freedom. It was a moment worth ages. It has immortalised his name; and, if his subsequent conduct had been as glorious and consistent, it would have atoned for all the vices and irregularities of his former life.[1] There is no doubt but the whole family of the Lameths will rejoice in his death. They expect to succeed to his popularity and influence, both which they lately attempted to destroy in the Jacobins, denouncing him as a traitor to his country on account of his opposing in the National Assembly a decree of confiscation of the property of emigrants. I was present at this extraordinary denunciation. The conduct of Mirabeau, whatever might have seduced him into the path of rectitude at the time, was highly meritorious; and yet, virtuous and laudable as it was, the consciousness of the act could not sustain him under the pressure of the attack. I sat next to Charles Lameth, who, while Mirabeau, trembling and pale, was defending himself in the Tribune, frequently exclaimed, 'O, le scélérat! O, le gueux!' and while the Marquis de St. Huruge, with his usual vulgarity

[1] After a pause, the Marquis de Dreux-Brézé, Master of the Ceremonies, said, 'Messieurs, vous connoissez les intentions du Roi.' Mirabeau replied, 'Oui, monsieur, nous avons entendu les intentions qu'on a suggérées au Roi, et vous qui ne sauriez être son organe auprès des États-Généraux, vous qui n'avez ici ni place, ni droit de parler, vous n'êtes pas fait pour nous rappeler son discours. Cependant, pour éviter toute équivoque et tout délai, je déclare que, si l'on vous a chargé de nous faire sortir d'ici, vous devez demander des ordres pour employer la force, car nous ne quitterons nos places que par la puissance des baïonnettes.'—*Hist. Parl.* ii. 22.

and violence, vociferated, 'Ah, le coquin, vous l'avez déterré. Il faut le pendre!' You would have been astonished at the miserable answer which Mirabeau made to an accusation in which justice, humanity, and policy must have furnished him with abundant matter for defence. Instead of availing himself of any of the arguments to be drawn from these considerations, he appealed to the generosity and candour of the club, requested the members to recollect that he renounced the society of 1789 for that of the Friends of the Constitution—the Jacobins, from whom death alone would separate him. This assurance, and the gratification felt at his defection from the club in the Palais Royal, procured him a pardon, and, amidst plaudits, he descended from the same tribune which, amidst groans, reproaches, and hisses, he had mounted in a panic, and in which he was some time before he could obtain a hearing.

General Wimpffen has this instant called on me by appointment, and I must leave you abruptly. He has just received from Germany a letter, which mentions that 14,000 Austrians are on their march to Fribourg. Shame on the intrigues at the Tuileries and of the emigrants! They lead to war! Adieu, my dear Lord.

MR. MILES TO MR. T. SOMERS COCKS

Paris: April 4, 1791

Mirabeau is no more. He died on Saturday last, between ten and eleven in the forenoon. He has left his sister sole executrix. His secretary, in a fit of grief and despair, attempted to destroy himself; his wounds were not mortal, and he was conducted to the Abbaye de St. Germain to be kept in confinement. The public places of amusement were shut by violence on the night of Mirabeau's death. The company were assembled, the actors were ready to begin, when the police—that is to say, the rabble (for there is no other police force here)—compelled everybody to turn out 'by order,' as they said, of the nation! The Jacobins have resolved to mourn for him eight days, and to devote the anniversary of his death to sackcloth and ashes. A mausoleum is to be erected to his memory, and busts without end are to be stuck up in every hole and corner. No plays last night, and none this evening; to-morrow they will re-open, and Mirabeau, his services, and his very name will cease to be regarded. The frivolous, inconstant character of the people around me prevents them from feeling real grief: all is caprice for the moment, ostentation and dissimulation. Slander says he was poisoned. The account of his surgeon and physician was read to me last night, whence it appears that his head, heart, stomach, and intestines have been examined, and they all prove that his death was natural. The Lameths are accused, and credit is given to the accusation. All is faction, falsehood, and intrigue here. The death of Mirabeau has rendered the National Assembly blind of an eye, but on my saying this to a lady she replied, 'Vous vous trompez, monsieur; elle est devenue aveugle.' Thus has ended the life of a man who was at once the pride and infamy of his country, and on whom her hopes of resurrection finally rested. In England his abilities would not have advanced him to a place of trust. Few men but what have virtues that atone for their vices— I speak of men in exalted situations; he had none. Scenes of low debauchery marked his career through life, and, with petty larceny among his vices, he would have been excluded from good society. Talents he unquestionably possessed: and his answer to the officer when the assembly of the States-General at Versailles was surrounded by guards, and the deputies were ordered to disperse, makes me regret that his character was so degraded. That answer, which deserves to be recorded in letters of gold, will alone rescue his memory from oblivion.[1]

An express arrived from Strasbourg reports that the Cardinal de Rohan has assembled troops, that the French fugitives resort to him, that the Prince de Condé has had frequent conferences with the Cardinal, and that great apprehensions are entertained of an attack on Strasbourg. Nearly the whole of Alsace is hostile to the Revolution. They have not 12,000 men to keep it in subjection, and even these are not all well-affected or well-disciplined. The assignats fall daily; they are now from $6\frac{1}{4}$ to 7 per cent. below par. The alarm is so great that this very day the National Assembly will decree, or at least receive a decree for adoption, that the Cardinal de Rohan should be impeached of high treason.

Every action proves great fear, and, in case of an invasion, it will be found that this country is so fallen that it is not likely to rise again soon. Nor is it the interest of England that France should rise, unless, indeed, the two countries could become friends and allies,

---

[1] '*April* 4.—The funeral of Mirabeau, attended, it is said, by more than 100,000 persons in solemn silence, has been an imposing spectacle. It is a vast tribute paid to superior talents, but no great incitement to virtuous deeds. Vices, both degrading and detestable, marked this extraordinary being. Completely prostitute, he sacrificed everything to the whim of the moment—*Cupidus alieni, prodigus sui.* Venal, shameless, and yet greatly virtuous when pushed by a prevailing impulse, but never truly virtuous because never under the steady control of reason nor the firm authority of principle, I have seen this man, in the short space of two years, hissed, honoured, hated, and mourned. Enthusiasm has just now presented him gigantic. Time and reflection will shrink that stature.'—*The Life of Gouverneur Morris*, i. 355. See *Life of Hugh Elliot*, by Lady Minto, p. 285, 'On Mirabeau.'

which I much wish; but, whether she continues friendly or becomes hostile, I shall wish her to preserve the freedom which she has acquired.

April 7.—France yet intrigues in the Low Countries; nor does she think her revolution secure from counter-revolution so long as the House of Austria holds any dominion in the Netherlands. Paris is the centre of every kind of intrigue; and, while the French are endeavouring to detach the Flemings from the Emperor, the King of Prussia is no less anxious and indefatigable in his endeavours to dissolve the alliance between the Emperor and the French. The Court of Berlin has already offered money and men to the French if they will annul the treaty with Vienna of 1756.

The priests are hard at work in the Venaissin, and Comtat, and Avignon, to excite a religious war. They publicly declare that the Revolution has been accomplished by the Protestants, several of whom have in consequence been murdered. At Nîmes the commotions have been sanguinary, and since November 1789 the priests have employed money, threats, and promises to incite the Catholics to take arms against the Protestants. The following extract taken from an advertisement of the deputies from the Department of the Gard confirms this statement: 'Il est prouvé par la procédure que des hypocrites jouant le zèle ont égaré une partie du peuple catholique et l'ont engagé à s'armer contre les Protestants; elle dit que les Protestants ont formé et exécuté le projet de massacrer les Catholiques.—(Signé) JEAN PAUL RABAUT[1] et ETIENNE MEGNIER, Citoyens de Nîmes.'

[1] Jean Paul Rabaut-St. Etienne, son of Paul Rabaut, pastor at Nîmes, known as 'Pastor of the Desert,' was elected a member of the Constituent Assembly. In the Convention he voted for the reprieve of Louis XVI., and, as a member of the Girondins commission, he was proscribed and guillotined in 1793.

I see Lafayette daily; he is a perfectly honest man, attached to his country and desirous of nothing more than to see a free government established in France. For himself he covets nothing. But I have repeatedly remarked to him that, unless he destroys the spirit of cabal and intrigue which reigns in Paris, the business he has in hand will not be speedily accomplished. A revolution in the Government will be of no avail to liberty so long as the people remain morally degraded. Truth compels me to repeat that I know of no place so corrupt as Paris in every sense of the word. I tremble for Madame de Lafayette; her sufferings are extreme. I generally sit next to her at dinner, and observe her inquietude.[1] She lives in a constant state of alarm, and no wonder, for the Duke of Orleans is exerting all his efforts to crush her husband. Lafayette is attacked every night in the Jacobin Club by Santerre, a b.ewer in the Faubourg St. Antoine, whose beer is excellent, but whose politics are detestable. He is a great orator, so also is the Marquis de St. Huruge. I have often wondered that Lafayette never had friends in the club to defend him. In order to obtain him some support, for I am weary of hearing him constantly abused, I have had General Wimpffen proposed, and, with much

[1] 'Les Jacobins excitèrent, le 17 Juillet, 1791, une émeute considérable. Les brigands commencèrent par massacrer deux hommes. La loi martiale fut proclamée. Il est difficile de se faire une idée de l'état d'angoisse de ma mère, pendant que mon père était au Champ de Mars, en butte à la rage d'une multitude furieuse qui se dispersa en criant *qu'il fallait assassiner ma mère et porter sa tête au-devant de lui*. Je me rappelle les cris affreux que nous entendîmes, l'effroi de chacun dans la maison, et par-dessus tout la vive joie de ma mère en songeant que les brigands qui arrivaient n'étaient plus au Champ de Mars ... On avait doublé la garde, qui se mit en bataille devant la maison; mais les brigands furent au moment d'entrer chez ma mère par le jardin qui donnait sur la place du Palais-Bourbon et dont ils escaladaient le petit mur, lorsqu'un corps de cavalerie, qui passait sur la place, les dispersa.'—*Vie de Madame de Lafayette.* p. 225

difficulty, elected a member of the Jacobin Club. Of all men in the world, who should be proposed at the same time but Le Brun,[1] whom I relieved in 1787, and who has fled from Liège and Brabant! He is in treaty, I hear, with the Emperor to return to Bruxelles in support of the Court of Vienna; but the Court of Vienna is parsimonious, whilst he is avaricious as well as indigent. Everything goes ill here, matters get worse every day, and several members of the National Assembly have assured me that assignats will be at 20 per cent. discount before winter. There is certainly some grand project in contemplation by the aristocratical party, and I have reason to suspect it is meant to carry the King off. Some of the Royalists are even indiscreet enough to propose taking him away by force. The priests aim at a civil war on account of religion. The nobles, who do not care a straw for religion, now court the clergy and stimulate the incendiaries to fire the nation. The struggle of contending factions inspires these priests and *noblesse* with hopes; and I see no calm likely to succeed the terrible tempest that shakes this country in all directions. Compliments to Mrs. Cocks and the family. Sincerely yours.

Miss Miles to her Father

Paris: April 15, 1791

Almost a week has elapsed since your departure, and, after all, I know no news, for we have seen nobody since except the Maréchale[2] once, and then she was not alone, and I could hear nothing. Your two friends have sent no letters yet, but as it is early we may perhaps

---

[1] Le Brun became Minister of Foreign Affairs in Paris after the affair of August 10, 1792.

[2] The Duchesse de Richelieu.

receive some in time enough to inclose. How much, my dearest father, do I envy your being in dear, delightful England, and yet, notwithstanding a superiority over every other country, you give your preference to France! I must accuse you of want of judgment, and I tremble lest you should settle on the Continent, for then I shall lose all hopes of seeing my native home for at least some years. I am all impatience to hear if you had a good passage. From the letter the courier brought last Monday you seemed to fear the contrary—certainly to be *eleven hours* crossing from *Calais* to *Dover* is a long time.

They talk of an insurrection in Spain, but I doubt the truth of it; if such an event was to take place in that country, it would be more surprising than the Revolution in France. It is true, perhaps, that the Government is more despotic there, but at the same time the people are bigoted, and I believe a bigoted people care little or nothing about liberty. Madame de Beaufort and her husband were here last night, and assured us that the reports about Spain were entirely without foundation, and that it was only intended to *soulever le peuple*. Her brother, who is only three leagues from Spain, and from whom she received a letter the day before yesterday, assures her that everything is very quiet in that country, and that they have no idea of a revolution. Madame de B. told us that there had been some troubles in Malta, but that there were hopes of affairs being settled, as they had made an example of the principal conspirators. She said, however, that she could not answer for the truth of this report, for so many falsehoods are told at present that it is impossible to say whether that was not one also. Scarce a day passes but some twenty, thirty, or forty thieves are taken up. Last Wednesday near forty passed our door at different times, half of whom were women; they have taken up their quarters at the Faubourg du Roule. I hope they will be routed. It is said that there are upwards of 30,000 in town. The Maréchale is very poorly; she intends going into the country after Easter, and staying there till Pentecôte, when she will return with her daughter, the *chanoinesse*. The Miss Balmers dined with us last Wednesday. They are well, and send you their compliments. When we fetched them out, the nuns of their convent were taking their oaths, and I saw the old prioress very busy signing; but they greatly suspect some will get whipped, as they vow they will neither take the oath nor confess themselves to a priest who has taken it.[1]

I enclose you one of the many papers printed relative to Spain. The man who sold it assured Joseph that there was not a word of truth in it, and that those who printed such wicked things—for it was to *soulever* the people—ought to be made an example of. Mirabeau's praises are chaunted in all the streets, but in M. Gobel's supposed *mandement*, which I also enclose, he is finely cut up. It will make you laugh, as will the letter of the Abbé Arthur Dillon. Last Saturday we had a violent thunderstorm here; the thunderbolt fell opposite our garden by the fourth tree in the Champs-Elysées. I wish Master Jupiter would send his bolts elsewhere than in our neighbourhood.

---

[1] 'The nuns de la Charité des Hospitalières were flogged and beaten by people sent for that purpose in presence of the National Guard because they desired to hear mass from a non-juring priest.'—*Annual Register*, 1792: *Chronicle*, p. 89.

'Sisters of Charity, engaged in tending the sick in the hospitals, have been dragged into the streets and scourged for no other crime than that of receiving the Sacraments from a priest who had not submitted to the revolutionary test.'—Lecky, v. 514.

Mr. Miles to Sir Edward Newenham

Westminster: April 16, 1791

I seize the first leisure moment to inform you of my arrival in London, and that I left M. de Lafayette in perfect health and spirits on Friday last. He desired his compliments to you, and begged me to remind you of the dog of the wolf breed which you promised him. Your son Robert had not arrived in Paris when I left. I postponed my journey ten days on purpose to see him; and then, taking it for granted that I must meet him on the road, I stopped every carriage travelling *en poste*, and nearly got into several scrapes, the French *voyageurs* being specially displeased at being interrupted, and still more so at being taken for Englishmen. My family are in Paris, consequently I shall not continue long absent from what I call my home, and shall hope to hear from you as soon as you can write.

As a friend to your country and my own, as a friend to the civil and religious liberties of mankind, I cannot but lament that M. de Lafayette should have so little confidence in the pacific disposition of the British Government, which, he imagines, is hostile to Gallic freedom. With difficulty I convinced him that the armaments last year were not destined against France, and that Spain sought the quarrel with us. He entertains the same suspicion relative to the conduct which the King seems disposed to observe towards Russia, although our interference in wishing to prescribe bounds to that profligate, ambitious, and abandoned woman,[1] must eventually promote the interests of France, and, indeed, secure the dignity, existence, and independence of maritime Europe. If ever that woman should drive the Turk into Asia, adieu to every other navy and to all

---

[1] Catherine II., Empress of Russia.

commerce in the Mediterranean, except to vessels permitted by the Russian Empire. You have only to open the chart, and behold the wonderful power the acquisition of Constantinople will give to the Muscovite nation. The Russians will be able to embrace the whole Continent, and, in possession of the Black Sea, with of course an open navigation, they will become formidable to all Europe. I could enlarge upon this subject much more, but I have said sufficient to convince you of the propriety of forcing the Empress to peace, and, if this matter should be brought before your Parliament, I trust you will support the Administration. You have confidence in my opinion, and I trust upon this occasion I shall not be refused. I wish you would write to M. de Lafayette, and say how much France has to dread if Russia should establish herself on the Black Sea and get the Dardanelles. I wrote to him a very long letter last night on the subject. I have a high idea of his integrity, his love of truth and of liberty, but he appears to want political information. The ambition of Russia is to become a *maritime* Power. The possession of the Black Sea can alone ensure success to her favourite object, and, if she gets Constantinople, depend upon it she will dictate the law to Europe. You do not know, perhaps, that this was the idea of the Empress, and of the late Emperor Joseph II.[1] That wicked blockhead was flattered with the idea of sharing with Catherine the dominion of the world. It is the wisdom of this Government, or ought to be, to confine the Great Bear to the Zodiac, or else the universe will be deranged. Mr. Fox had it in his power to have prevented all this discussion when the Russians seized the Crimea. M. de Vergennes and the Spanish

[1] Emperor of Austria.

Court both applied to Mr. Fox, then Secretary of State, for leave to stop the progress of the Russian arms; they only desired us to remain neutral, not to arm or say a word. This was peremptorily refused, and the answer given was that Russia should be protected in her usurpation by Great Britain. This I pledge myself to be a fact; yet, if he had done his duty, all this long and bloody war would have been avoided, many lives saved, and the present disputes would not have been called into existence.[1]

April 27.—The last accounts from France will confirm the melancholy conjectures I have already sent to you, and prove that, although the Revolution is accomplished, neither peace nor freedom is established. M. de Lafayette insisted on resigning. He will remember, I am certain, my advice to him on the 28th of February and 1st of last March—viz. that he was *undone* if he did not act with vigour, and awe the factions into submission and respect. I trembled then for his safety. I was on the spot, and saw perhaps better than he did. My fears are in part realised: he is no longer commandant. The troops refused obedience, and, if he holds the employment, he has certainly lost the authority. The Court of Versailles exists no more; but its infamy, falsehood, and duplicity are disseminated throughout the country, and which joined to the excessive mass of ignorance in matters of legislation and government will retard the re-establishment of order. Corrupted as they are, *jusqu'au fond du cœur*, it must be their children who will complete the work

---

[1] In 1791 Mr. Miles published *The Expediency and the Justice of Prescribing Bounds to the Russian Empire*, a work which is preserved in the Imperial Library at St. Petersburg. On Russia extending her power, and on the action of Pitt and Fox in this matter, see *Authentic Correspondence with M. Lebrun, &c.*, pp. 124-130, published by Mr. Miles in 1796.

they have begun. This I have told them repeatedly, both in the Jacobins and the club of '89, for, having no object more at heart than the advantage of truth, I refuse to flatter vice or folly. My love of liberty cannot be doubted, and no consideration on earth would induce me to support despotism, but anarchy is no less abhorrent to my mind. Many years must elapse before France becomes settled or acquires a permanent Government. Recollect the hazardous situation at this instant of our friend Lafayette, of whose integrity and love of liberty no doubt can be entertained. It is not by the aristocrats that he is menaced, but by the very people who enabled him to subvert the ancient Government, and who now revel in the ruins they have created. He has more to apprehend from the rabble—whose condition he is labouring to ameliorate, but who seem disposed to wrest the whole conduct of the Revolution, in future, from the hands of those who are certainly better qualified to manage it—than he has from a court humiliated to the meanness of intriguing with the very lowest orders of the people for the power which it has lost. I told M. de Lafayette repeatedly that he would either be assassinated or ignominiously driven into exile. The French know nothing of the business of revolution. They resemble a parcel of monkeys playing at legislation. The times are perilous and awful, but they are more so for the future than for the present moment. It is a great and wonderful convulsion. If properly treated by us, it may be a very advantageous event; if not, a ruinous one. We must be the friends of France under her present circumstances; if not, our doom is sealed, and the doom is destruction.[1] Adieu, and God bless you.

[1] 'It was easy to foresee that the effects of the French Revolution

Miss Miles to her Father

Paris: Friday, April 22, 1791

Yours by the messenger is this moment come to hand inclosing one for M. de Lafayette. On Monday, the 18th, there was terrible uproar at the Tuileries. The King wished to go to St. Cloud: he was scarce in his carriage when the mob assembled, and stopped him. M. de Lafayette told the populace that his Majesty was only going to St. Cloud, and that he would answer for his going no further. They replied that this would not satisfy them, that *his* head was not that of the King, and that out of Paris he should not stir till the constitution was *achevé*. The King called to the General, and very peremptorily said: 'Faites place, monsieur; je veux partir; je n'entends pas cette insolence d'oser m'arrêter et m'empêcher d'aller à Saint-Cloud.' The General answered that it was absolutely impossible—that the mob was enraged, and he finished by intreating the King to give him his dismission. Upon this, the *poissardes* forced their way to the carriage, and with knives in their hands said to the King, 'Non, *tu* ne partiras pas; non, sacré-dieu, tu ne partiras pas, et, si on ose faire avancer les chevaux, les guides payeront cher leur audace.' Then, turning to M. de Lafayette, who was as pale as death, they said: 'Quant à toi, n'espère pas que tu auras ta démission; non, nous aurons plutôt la tête du Roi, et, s'il nous échappe malgré tous nos soins, nous aurons la

would speedily pass the boundaries of the French territory, and extend beyond the details of domestic government. Its operation was instantly felt in the most powerful of the ecclesiastical electorates, where, at Franckfort. I happened to be at the time, and from which place I compared it, in a letter to an English Peer (Lord Lansdowne), *to a violent earthquake that would extend to and shake each extremity of the globe.* How far my prediction, in September 1789, has been verified is within every man's knowledge.'—*Authentic Correspondence with M. Lebrun, &c.*, p. 131.

tienne et celle du Maire.' They complain of his having favoured the priests who have not taken the oaths.[1] Among those in whom the King places the greatest confidence are the Cardinal de Montmorenci and the Evêque de Senlis. The Cardinal de la Rochefoucault was in a carriage to accompany the King to St. Cloud; the mob stopped him, and were in the act of throwing him into the river, when, fortunately for the *red-hatted* gentleman, somebody knew him to be a member of the National Assembly, and then they very respectfully conducted him back to his coach. The King has since dismissed both the Cardinal de Montmorenci and the Evêque de Senlis. He afterwards went to the National Assembly and offered to renew his oaths. He said that it was his wish, as well as his intention, to maintain the constitution as far as was in his power; but he insisted upon going to St. Cloud, and observed to the Assembly how important it was for *Liberty* not to put any obstacle to his departure. The President answered that his Majesty had never ceased being beloved by his subjects, and that, if they had been more violent than they should have been, it was owing to his favouring the clergy, who were enemies to the Revolution, and that, if he had placed his confidence in the *ecclésiastiques assermentés*, the people, who had opposed his departure, would have regarded him as their *Dieu tutélaire*. After having heard

[1] 'Vous avez lu dans l'histoire de la Révolution qu'il y eut une émeute considérable le Lundi Saint—18 Avril 1791 – afin d'empêcher le Roi d'aller à Saint-Cloud, où il voulait faire ses Pâques par les soins de prêtres non-assermentés. Il ne put partir malgré les efforts de mon père, qui le conjura de persister dans un projet qu'il répondait de faire exécuter. Le Roi refusa. Mon père, mécontent de la Garde Nationale qui l'avait mal secondé devant l'émeute, de la faiblesse du Roi qui rendait impossible de réparer les torts de cette journée, crut devoir donner sa démission de commandant de la Garde Nationale de Paris.'—*Vie de Madame de Lafayette*, p. 221.

the President, the King retired, and the National Assembly resounded with 'Vive le Roi!'

On Monday night there was to have been a concert in the Faubourg St. Honoré: the carriages were waiting at the door, but as there had been so much bustle all the day, it was imagined that they were meditating a counter-revolution, and consequently a mob was shortly assembled, and the coaches were ordered by the people to drive to the Porte St. Honoré. After this, they forced their way into the room, and, pretending that no music had been heard, nor any preparations for a concert visible, the company were forced out, and obliged to walk almost down the Rue du Faubourg St. Honoré *au milieu des huées du peuple.* The company was composed of two hundred people, among whom were the former Minister, M. Guignard de St. Priest; M. F. de Beauharnais, Member of the National Assembly, and M. de Vaudreuil, also of the National Assembly, and who had the good fortune to escape by the Champs-Elysées, and avoided being laughed at. Among other ladies present, they particularly mention a Madame de Bonneuil. I know not whether she has done anything remarkable to be specially noticed. This is all I know, but probably before the post goes out I may hear something more. They say the King is determined to go to St. Cloud. Mr. Newenham arrived yesterday very much fatigued. He had inquired at Messrs. Biddulph & Cocks' after you.

I have just this moment heard that M. de Lafayette had sent to the district to obtain his dismission, but they have so earnestly entreated him not to abandon them that he has consented to continue his charge. The King may go if he chooses, but I am persuaded that if he attempts it the people will be outrageous. If what they say is true, the King has acted an impolitic part. He had a confessor who had taken the oath, and to whom he had been accustomed for some years, an honest man; but, when he confessed for this Easter he changed for a priest who was not *assermenté*; and, besides this, he has given pensions and apartments at St. Cloud to seventeen of the most rebellious towards the Revolution. How true this is I cannot tell; I doubt it, because I think his Gallic Majesty has not courage to act so very directly in opposition! Joseph went out for a commission the other day, and, seeing a great crowd at the house of a Hebrew female convert, he asked a woman what was the matter. She pointed to a large rod stuck up at the door, and said: 'C'est pour voir le châtiment qu'on prépare aux bigotes. Ainsi, monsieur, si vous êtes bigot, ça ne doit pas vous faire plaisir.' The Maréchale is frightened out of her wits; she proposed going the latter end of next week, instead of which she will set off tomorrow. They much fear a counter-revolution. Madame Mourgue [1] called the day before yesterday and has pressed us very much to go to St. Denis; we shall accept her invitation, and dine one day next week with her. Adieu, my dearest father. Pray write to us. Mamma sends her affectionate love to you. The 'bow-wows' are well.

Lord Fortescue to Mr. Miles

April 26, 1791

Many thanks for the letters you have been so good as to send me, which I now return enclosed. By them it appears that the present crisis at Paris is very alarming and eventful. If the King had shown as much courage at an earlier period of the business, it might

---

[1] M. Mourgue was Minister of the Interior when Dumouriez came into power in 1792.

have availed him better than I fear it will now. I hope at least that your next accounts from Mrs. Miles will show that her alarms for her own safety will have been without ground. I have heard nothing further yet of our ministerial arrangements.

Miss Miles to her Father

Paris: April 29, 1791

Your letters by the safe conveyance and one by the post we received last Tuesday just as we were on the point of going to dine at Madame Mourgue's in the country. On last Tuesday I heard a speech that has turned me against a so-called patriot. In the course of conversation a dog was mentioned that will never suffer a beggar or a poorly dressed person to stop at his door without flying at and biting him, and, in answer to an observation of mine, he replied that so far from correcting the dog he should always encourage him, for *poverty* in every rank engendered *vice*. Yet this is one who approves of arms, titles, &c., being abolished, who wishes to be thought equal to the first in the kingdom, but who spurns the beggar and the poor. This is a *democrat*, one of the many who have or wish to have a share in the government of his country and to make everyone, as they term it, *equal*, free, and happy, but who will suffer no beggar to come to his door without setting on his dog and abusing him, as if it was not as easy to send people away with a civil word as to make them feel their wretchedness the more! This speech did him no honour, and I am persuaded that, if he had heard that the *Queen* had said it, the worst word in his mouth would have been too good for her, for never was any person detested so much as the unfortunate Marie Antoinette is by all his family. In short, what you told me of the Duke d'A. may justly be said of him—that to his superiors he is a democrat and to his inferiors he is an aristocrat.

M. Lafayette only resumed his place last Sunday night. The people said next morning that he had only given his *démission pour se faire désirer*. Had this rumour unfortunately gained ground, I should have been in pain for the General. In the tumults the other day a fusilier attempted to stab Lafayette with his bayonet; he missed his aim, and only wounded the horse. They did not know which of the men it was, but orders were given to break the company, and next morning the General despatched some of his aides-de-camp to endeavour to discover who it was, but they returned for answer, 'Nous sommes tous coupables ou tous innocens, voilà notre réponse.' They were resolute, and a report is gone about that M. de Lafayette will not break the regiment. A decree is passed at the National Assembly that every master workman must send each of his shopmen and apprentices for two hours every day to learn the exercise; this will appear very hard, and makes me think that something is in agitation. Drums are beating and troops are marching the whole day long. Yesterday there was a tumult at Versailles, the particulars of which I do not know, but no doubt your correspondents will inform you of them. The change of assignats for money is at present at 7 per cent. and money exceedingly scarce. The 1st of May is approaching, and we shall see if things will be cheaper.

Miss Miles to her Father
Paris: Thursday, May 6, 1791

The distant hope you give of our visiting England affords us some consolation: nothing would or could make me so happy.

You require me to send you news. The Pope[1] was burnt in effigy last Tuesday in the Palais Royal. In the 'Journal de la Révolution,' which I inclose, you will read the full account. M. Clermont-Tonnerre narrowly escaped being *à la lanterne*, and having his house burnt last Wednesday. At the National Assembly he loudly accused M. Mouchard of having sent incendiary letters and money to Avignon to promote a tumult, and said that he had proofs which no one could contradict. What he had said in the Assembly was, I suppose, misrepresented, and on his return home the mob flew to his hotel in a rage, called him an aristocrat, and had actually lowered the lanthorn before his door. His wife, who is a beautiful young woman, threw herself upon her knees, said a short prayer, and then, returning to her husband, said, 'If you die I will die; the wretches who demand your life shall have mine, for I cannot, will not, survive you.' Luckily for them the National Guard arrived, and dispersed the mob with great difficulty, but not until they had broken every window. This is the boasted liberty of France; none but the populace enjoy it, and they, on the other hand, commit the greatest excesses. In Martelle's paper of yesterday mention is made that Avignon remains to the Pope. 'O honte! O infamie! le vœu des Avignonais est repoussé! Le Club de '89 et les aristocrates ont remporté la victoire! Avignon est conservé au Pape! La guerre civile va embrasser nos provinces méridionales. Lâches! Députés patriotes! Comment vous laver jamais de cet opprobre!'

The preceding account of M. Clermont's escape I had from Madame de Beaufort. It is related in a different manner in Martelle's paper; I know not which

[1] Pius VI.

is the authentic one, but I will send you both: 'Clermont-Tonnerre, triomphant du décret qui assure Avignon au Pape, s'est permis en sortant de l'Assemblée Nationale de narguer le peuple. Il a été bientôt environné d'une foule immense et menaçante; douze Gardes Nationales ont protégé sa marche, sans quoi la fatale lanterne! Le peuple s'est porté à sa maison pour la brûler, la cavalerie est accourue et l'a préservée des flammes.'

There are services and processions for Mirabeau every day: sometimes it is a coffin they carry about, at other times it is a crown of laurel. In going last Wednesday to the Convent for the Balmers, we met above 5,000 workmen in procession, above half of them drunk, swearing most shockingly against the aristocrats and praising Mirabeau, and that merely because they could now drink wine at eight sols a bottle, and before they were obliged to pay twelve. The consequence is that they get drunk every day, no work is done, and it will not be astonishing if great mischief is committed by them. Refuse a beggar charity, and you will be called a '—— aristocrate.' This happened to me the other day. We were sitting on the bench at the bottom of the garden, when a beggar woman came and attacked us. There are such numbers in the Champs-Elysées that if you give to one the rest will also expect, and you will be persecuted out of your life. I said civilly to her, 'Je n'ai rien, ma bonne—une autre fois.' She immediately answered, 'Comment osez-vous dire que vous n'avez rien? Je vois par là que vous êtes une aristocrate, et c'est vous, —— aristocrates, qui êtes causes de nos misères. Sors un peu de ton jardin, si tu en as le courage, et je te tordrais le nez comme je te tordrais le cou, si je pouvais en faire à ma guise.' A woman, standing next to her with a child in her arms, asked if she did not blush to hold such language, and whether the ladies were not at full liberty to dispose of their money to those they thought deserving. She added that she also was as poor as she could be, but when she got anything she was thankful. This reasonable beggar obtained some partisans, and the other was obliged to quit the walk. A party of workmen, to the number of eighty or ninety, went yesterday afternoon to the Maison de Ville to insist upon having each ten sols a day more, not being contented with the thirty that they have for doing nothing the whole day. I know not whether it was granted—I imagine it was, since it will be imprudent to refuse them, as they are, and will be, masters. M. de Bonne-Carrère, Secretary to the Jacobins, called here, and desired to be remembered to you. He was named six weeks since to be Envoy to Liège, but the Prince-Bishop refused to receive him, and objected to his coming.

MR. MILES TO SIR EDWARD NEWENHAM

London: May 11, 1791

You are mistaken if you suppose that any conduct on the part of Ministers could diminish that zeal and affection for my country which have marked almost every action of my life. There is political as well as moral honesty; and, antique and unfashionable as the plain garb of truth may appear, I will persist in wearing it until death terminates this strange, eventful history. It is not to any man or set of men that I am attached—my attachment is to our country, and into whatever hands the administration of its government may fall, I will support the constitution to the last moment of my existence. With respect to Mr. Pitt, I own that I gave him credit in advance for great talents and great rectitude; of the former there is but one opinion, and I forbear pronouncing on the latter until my information is complete and I can express my opinion of the Minister without being accused or suspected of paying court to his patronage. I will candidly confess that I went upon presumption, but I knew that the public interests could not be in worse hands than in those from which they were wrested; I say wrested, for it was absolutely a contest for dominion between the sovereign and the nation on one side and a faction on the other. The event has proved how much we have to apprehend if the party should unhappily come into office again. I will not comment on the indecency, not to say infamy, of those principles which Mr. Fox avowed in a recent debate in Parliament. He has not blushed to triumph in the misfortunes of his country, nor has he hesitated to approve of the anarchy and disorder that prevail in France, and, what is still more extraordinary, he has had the effrontery to recommend them to us for adoption. Imagine your acres torn from you by the rude hand of ruffian violence, your person and your very name proscribed, your habitation destroyed, and your wife and children reduced to beggary. Such, my dear Newenham, is the dreadful example before you. Approve it if you can, follow it if you dare. Do you think the picture overcharged? No such thing. Recollect, I beseech you, the hazardous situation of our friend Lafayette at this instant—the man who has had the most considerable share in the Revolution, and whose integrity and love of liberty no one can impeach. If the life of Lafayette is insecure, who can be safe? It is not the aristocrats who insult and menace him, but the very people who enabled him to subvert the ancient Government, and who in riotous excess revel in the ruins they have produced. He has more to apprehend from the rabble, whose condition he is labouring to ameliorate, and who seem disposed to wrest the whole conduct of the Revolution from the hands of those who are certainly better qualified to manage it, than he has from a Court humiliated to the meanness of caballing and intriguing for the power it has lost with the very lowest orders of the people. I told him repeatedly that he would either be assassinated or ignominiously driven into exile. Mark my words, the French know nothing of the business of revolution. I have been a spectator of scenes that would harrow your very soul, and I will defy any intelligent and candid mind acquainted with all the circumstances of the Revolution in France not to condemn the mode of conducting it and the anarchy it has occasioned.

The uniformity of my principles gives me a claim to your confidence, and that claim is strengthened by the intimacy that has subsisted between us for very many years. Be assured that I do not wish to pay my court to Ministers by flattering despotism or to promote my own interest by apostacy. I mean merely to forewarn you, as a citizen, of the mischief you will prepare for Ireland, and consequently for your family, if you recommend what I am sure on nearer inspection you would behold with horror and indignation. You must not follow the lead of France. I count much upon your confidence in my judgment, but much more do I depend on your patriotism and love of humanity. Thus assured, I hope to hear soon from you that my account, drawn from observation and experience on the spot, has had the desired effect. The times are perilous

and awful, but they are more so for the future than for
the present moment. It is a great and wonderful convulsion. If properly treated by us it may be an
advantageous event, if not, a ruinous one. Under
present circumstances we must be the friends of
France, for, if not, our doom is sealed and will entail
the most lamentable consequences.

I declare upon my honour that our friend Lafayette
is very suspicious of us; that he believed our armament last year was destined to effect a counter-revolution, and that Spain was only the pretext. The event
alone could convince him of his error. My arguments
were thrown away. Mirabeau favoured that belief
among the vulgar. Lafayette is of the same opinion
relative to the Russian controversy. You may do a
service to him and to his country as well as to our
own by assuring him that his fears are ill founded.
Write to him without delay on the subject; for I assure
you he is of opinion that our fleet is meant to attack
France at home or abroad. Adieu, and God bless you.

Miss Miles to her Father

Paris: May 20, 1791

Your welcome letter was brought to us last Monday
night, to our utter astonishment, as we never have
received them sooner than Tuesday at twelve o'clock.
I am very happy that you are pleased with my letters
and the information they contain. You may rely on my
communicating to you all I know, which is not much,
as we seldom see anybody, and it is better not to send
anything unless it is authentic. As to whether the old
regiments are recruited, and if recruits are readily
obtained, I cannot tell. But as to the National Guards
being well disciplined and often exercised, it is neither

one nor the other. It was on account of not being obeyed that M. Lafayette gave in his resignation. In the time of riot they are forbidden to fire, and, although he demanded permission of the municipality, it was refused. They have not exercised them since you have been away. This morning a general review was to take place to see if more had deserted. They greatly fear a counter-revolution, and the surgeon, the last time he was here, said that an idea prevailed that England was arming against France, instead of against Russia, but I told him I was sure it was not so, and, even if it was true, France had no right to complain if she recollected the part she took in favour of the Americans. Money is at 15 per cent.; last Saturday morning it was at 8, and before night it rose to 12. On Tuesday a gentleman bought money and paid 15 per cent., and half the cash he received was counterfeit. On hearing this the people became outrageous and declared that no more money should be sold; but their passion soon subsided, and yesterday the money-vendors were more numerous than ever. It is said that Navarre would not pay the taxes, and that the clergy refused absolution to those who bought their lands in the province of Languedoc.

I send you a few extracts from the 'Orateur du Peuple:'—

'Strasbourg est presque dégarni de troupes, et cette ville est journellement menacée d'une invasion, qui n'est dangereuse qu'autant qu'elle causeroit un soulèvement dans l'Alsace. Il y a sûrement beaucoup de bons patriotes, mais les prêtres réfractaires y ont bien des amis. Il y a peut-être deux à trois cents villages qui n'attendent qu'un signal pour se soulever; leurs efforts seront vains, mais si on n'est pas en force pour leur résister, il peut en résulter beaucoup de mal. Deux régiments encore, et les ennemis perdront toute espérance.'

'L'argent n'est si rare et si cher que par les nombreuses émigrations, qui se multiplient plus que jamais, et le bruit, fondé ou non, d'une contre-révolution prochaine engage ceux qui restent dans la capitale à entasser le numéraire dans leurs coffres. Je ne sais quelle sera l'issue de toutes ces convulsions politiques, ni pourquoi tous les aristocrates, mâles et femelles, quittent Paris en toute diligence; mais ce qu'il y a de constant c'est que la municipalité a donné depuis trois semaines plus de soixante-six mille passe-ports.'

You perceive by this last extract that everybody gets off as fast as they can. I must own I am afraid. You know the effect that the firing of cannon has upon me; and to have shot flying about my head like hailstones is what I have no ambition for. The cellar will be my refuge, as in the time of thunder and lightning. Your little Tot has not much courage to boast of, and, should the counter-revolution take place, I do not answer for my existence. God send us well out of this plantation of Liberty, and into a land of safety and comfort. Democrats and aristocrats equally believe in the counter-revolution, and that it will shortly take place. I tremble at the thought, and the more so when I reflect that the greater number dislike the English. You will receive some papers. The Pope has taken a longer journey than ever you took—he has been to heaven! The account of his voyage *à l'enfer* is being cried about in the streets.[1] I do not suppose his Holiness is much pleased with the conduct of the French; they never possessed much religion, but now they have broken

---

[1] This allusion to the Pope refers to the burning of the *effigy* of Pius VI. in the Palais Royal on May 4.

through all bounds, and I imagine in a few years the Catholic religion will not exist in this country. No regiments old or new are recruited, and the National Guard of Paris is not at all well-disciplined. The frontiers of France are well guarded; but they expect to be speedily attacked on all sides. The King has reformed his household.

We have had dreadful weather here; the peasants are ruined; it has frozen these few nights; the most tempestuous winds, and the leaves fall as in the month of October. For my part, I prefer this weather to the very intense heat we had in March—it agrees better with me; but I must then renounce the fruit and every other *agrément* of summer. Mamma does nothing but grumble, as we have been obliged to commence fires again, it is so terribly cold; the chimneys were cleaned and everything arranged for the summer months. The expense of buying wood is no small one in Paris. The 1st of May, so much boasted of, has brought no great change in the price of things. The merchants, who formerly said that they could not sell reasonably on account of the high duties they were obliged to pay, now change their tone, and pretend that the duties were so trifling that they were not worth mentioning, and hardly anything but liquors are abated.

MR. MILES TO MR. PITT

May 31, 1791

In consequence of a conversation with the Marquis of Buckingham this morning, I take the liberty to inform you that I shall feel myself honoured by your commands, and shall wait with great pleasure until the recess of Parliament will allow you leisure to receive me. It is also his Lordship's particular wish that I should enclose for your perusal a letter from General de Wimpffen, at Paris, and I do it the more readily as I am well acquainted with the talents of that intelligent officer, and know that he could be rendered useful to this country if he should be rejected by his own. I have given Lord Buckingham the memorial which the General presented in 1788 to M. Necker, in which it is proposed to make the Rhine the boundary of France, and which also contains a plan for re-modelling the French army. Both these projects will be executed, unless prevented by the success of the very desperate attempts which I am grieved to see are making to accomplish a counter-revolution. That an explosion of some sort will happen and interrupt the march of the French people to liberty is most woefully evident. I cannot but dread such an event, from the certainty I feel of the pernicious consequences that would result to this country, whose true interest it is that France should become free, and consolidate her freedom, as the friend, and, if possible, the ally of Great Britain. If the explosion in France should take place, I am sure that Wimpffen will declare, not for the Republican party, but for the King and the Constitution. I know his sentiments well, and, from his connections in Alsace, which is his native country, he would be enabled to collect a very formidable force against the Cardinal de Rohan and the Prince de Condé.[1]

GENERAL WIMPFFEN TO MR. MILES

Paris: June 17, 1791

I will not speak of the decrees which have been issued for some days past, since the public papers will have acquainted you with them. These decrees prove

[1] 'The letter of General Wimpffen, with several other communications from Paris, which I sent to Mr. Pitt for perusal, were never returned to me: their contents are interesting.'—W. A. M.

conclusively that there is much uneasiness as to the movements and re-assembling of troops on the frontiers of the kingdom; but, unfortunately, the precautions taken are very insufficient An army of the Line is required, and none exists; that which is so called must be counted for nothing, since it is without discipline. The insurrections are more frequent than ever; even the artillery, the first in Europe, has just driven away its officers. Who would wish to command such troops? A week ago to-day, when a French grenadier mounted the tribune to maintain that severe discipline was not at all necessary to make the arms of France victorious, he was applauded with the utmost enthusiasm, and the printing of his speech was demanded by acclamation.

With respect to the Jacobins, you know that the generalissimo is at law with the Commandant Santerre; that this lawsuit, which has made much noise, is remitted for judgment to a court-martial. I am still in uncertainty as to my destination. The intrigues and jealousies commenced under the old *régime* are maintained under the present.

Bonne-Carrère will be no longer Minister at Liège; the Prince-Bishop has refused him. He has left for Bordeaux—a very different direction.

I rather believe in a general war than in a general insurrection, either in favour of monarchy or of democracy, and that the war will begin either with you or with Austria. More than ten general officers have refused to serve. This will enable me to penetrate a little into futurity, but the spirit of intrigue, which is as great as under the ancient Government, will counteract the means I have taken to put forward my pretensions. I have nothing to expect from favour or protection. It is possible that my enemies may be buried under the same ruins with myself. Your friend Wittgenstein fares better here than I have done.

Madame de Staël, the daughter of M. Necker, and wife of the Swedish Envoy at Paris, is hard at work for her friend Narbonne, who reckons much upon the friendship of Lafayette, Lückner, and Rochambeau.[1]

MISS MILES TO HER FATHER

Paris: Sunday, June 26, 1791

What will you think of our silence, or, more properly speaking, what have you already thought? for, long before this reaches you, you will be able to account for not having heard from us as usual. A short letter was prepared, and I sent to General Wimpffen to know if he had anything for you. He was obliging enough to come and inform us that neither post nor express would be permitted to depart from hence before the King's return. Notwithstanding this intelligence, I sent our packet as usual, but was told that no messenger would depart that day. After dinner we went to ask when we could write, and received for answer that it was uncertain. Mamma wrote to Lord Gower, desiring permission to send a letter by the first express. He politely answered her note, but told her he could not say when he should have an opportunity.

---

[1] 'Count Wittgenstein, whose offer to raise a regiment for the ex-Princes had been accepted, and almost completed, when it was discovered that he was in correspondence with the Jacobin Club at Paris, and had engaged to desert with his whole regiment to their service. This negotiation was detected while he was at Franckfort at the time when the Electors were assembled—July 1792—to elect an Emperor. He gave his honour not to quit the town. The Ambassador from the Elector Palatine also pledged his honour that the Count should not quit Franckfort until his innocence was proved. He, however, decamped privately. His papers were seized his guilt discovered, and many other important secrets were brought to light of the blackest treason. He was appointed as a general to a command in the South of France, afterwards recalled, and he was one of the hapless victims that perished on the 2nd of September following. His uncle was massacred at Orleans.'—MS. note by Mr. Miles.

The King, Queen, and royal family arrived in town yesterday, escorted by 150,000 men. The crowd assembled to see them enter was astonishing. The interment of Mirabeau did not produce such a number. The King, Queen, Dauphin—whom they call her *loureteau*—Madame Royale, and Madame Elisabeth, are in separate apartments, with separate guards. The Dauphin is to have a governor named by the nation; the King is no longer regarded as such. The National Assembly is to finish the constitution; and when it is settled a deputation is to be sent to Louis XVI. to know whether the mode of government that is adopted suits him: if it does he is to be their sovereign, if it does not a Regent is to be chosen until the Dauphin is of an age to be crowned. The King and Queen are to be conducted to the National Assembly to answer the questions that will be asked them. A report goes about the town that the enemy has entered France, and it is advised, if that is the case, to chop off the King's head, and to tie the Queen to the tail of a horse and drag her through Paris till she dies.[1] If you did but know what we risk and suffer, you would repent having left us here. I forbear all comments on what has passed, judging it imprudent to trust my sentiments in a letter. I sincerely hope that you will join us soon. It is impossible to tell you the fright we have undergone. The dread we had of yesterday is not to be described, but, thank God, everything passed off astonishingly quiet. The King and Queen were suffered to enter Paris without receiving the least insult; this I did not expect, because I think the former acted a cowardly part in sneaking off, after appearing to be so well satisfied with the present constitution. He has cer-

---

[1] Similar was the fate of Brunehaut, Queen of Austrasia, in 613.

tainly perjured himself, and given his enemies an opportunity of triumphing over him.

M. de Montmorin is acquitted by the National Assembly, but still remains guilty in the eyes of the people.[1] It was in consequence of the passport given to the King and Queen that he was arrested. Madame de Kortz had applied to him for a passport, including two children, a *femme de chambre*, and a valet, and she sent it to the Queen. The King passed for her *valet de chambre*. But all their precautions proved useless; they were discovered at Sainte-Menehould, and arrested at Varennes. It is said that M. de Bouillé is arrested, but, for certain, M. de Choiseul is in prison. It is also rumoured that Monsieur will return to Paris of his own accord; he has sworn never to abandon his brother, and, as the latter is arrested, he will come back and share his fate.

A thousand thanks for your having subscribed to the great edition of Shakespeare; it will certainly afford me much pleasure, but I hope there will be no necessity for bringing it over, as I would prefer reading it in England—particularly at this moment. We have undone the packet. Lord Gower sent off an express this morning at six o'clock, and, as he could not let us know, we must send this off by the post. I cannot say more at present.

MISS MILES TO HER FATHER

Paris: June 27, 1791

It is imagined that the King will be deposed, that his son will be crowned, and that during his minority a Regent will be chosen. The people wish for a Republic; in short, it is impossible to say what will be

---

[1] Montmorin perished in the September massacres. He had been Minister of Foreign Affairs, &c.

the result. We are much alarmed, and know not what to do. I wrote a few lines to you this morning by the post, but did not dare say a word about affairs, since all the letters are now opened. This goes to Lord Gower, to be ready when another express is sent off. No one is suffered to go in or out of the Château des Tuileries, and the Queen is to be removed to the Abbaye de Val-de-Grâce, Faubourg Saint Jacques. All the signs, where 'Parfumeur du Roi,' or 'de la Reine,' or 'Loterie royale,' &c., was written up, are knocked down, and perhaps in a short time their names will not even be mentioned. The Queen fainted several times on her return to Paris, and, when she was taken, she entreated them to kill her, saying she could not support being separated from her children. She has scarce any hair left; in her despair she tore it off. They cut her meat and bread as if for a child, for they fear she would stab herself were they not to take that precaution. She is separated from her husband and children, and will in a short time be removed. The three young men who were their couriers were brought back to Paris chained upon the coach-box. It is reported they will lose their lives, and there is no probability of their escaping. Had the King not stopped to eat cutlets, he would have escaped. He was within six hours of the Austrian territory. It was by an assignat that he was found out. A peasant passing by said, 'That face resembles an assignat,' and, as the King kept looking out at the coach window, others had time to observe the same resemblance. The postilion was secretly ordered to drive to the District at Varennes, another man was sent on before, and, when they arrived, the coach was surrounded by Guards, and a man coming up to the door said to the King, 'Je crois que c'est à Louis Seize, Roi des François, que j'ai l'honneur de parler.' He answered, 'Oui, monsieur; mais je vous assure que ce n'étoit jamais mon intention de quitter les limites du royaume. Je n'allois qu'à Malmédy. Ne me faites pas du mal, ni à ma femme, ni à mes enfans, et je me rendrai tout de suite aux ordres de l'Assemblée Nationale.' I think this answer little became a king! I suppose the assignats will be altered, and the King's name and face be left out. God knows when this will reach you. It goes to-night to Lord Gower to be ready to be sent off. We are thankful that you were out of the bustle. Mama sends her affectionate love.

A Member of the National Assembly to Mr. Miles

Paris: June 30, 1791

The flight of the King was injudicious, to say no more of it, and ill conducted by those who managed it here, and who were in the secret at Varennes. It is very true that the Dauphin said to his father, 'On nous mène mal, papa,' and no less so that the post-boy answered, 'Je vous mène bien, et où vous devez aller.' The Queen has never been allowed to be alone since her return, and your friend M. de La Colombe has been asked to take charge of the Dauphin, which he has prudently declined in obedience to the advice of his relative, Lafayette, who was as ignorant of the departure of the royal family at the time as you were. This matter has given fresh courage to his enemies, notwithstanding his innocence. Santerre already plans his destruction, and, if Mirabeau was alive, his ruin would be assured.

The Duc d'Aiguillon cannot succeed in obtaining a pension for your friend, Madame la Duchesse de Richelieu, nor can your *protégé*, Latude, obtain one from the National Assembly. Your bounty to that man was misapplied; he is an *escroc*, and always was.[1] The assignats will soon be at 60 and even 80 per cent. discount. The Count de Maulde, whom you remember at Liège, is intriguing for employment.

On the Flight of Louis XVI

Subsequent events have convinced me that those who denounced the King and his brother in the Jacobin Club were well informed of the intrigues going on at the Tuileries. I therefore acknowledge my error in the letter which I wrote on the 23rd February and own that the departure of the King's aunts appears to me to have been part of the project formed by the royal family to quit the country contrary to their repeated declarations, their duty, and their oath. The flight of the King to Varennes was surely connected with the departure of his aunts for Rome; and it is probable that, if the populace had allowed his Majesty to go to St. Cloud, everything was arranged for his going much further. I shall only observe that France would have acted with superlative dignity if on apprehending Louis XVI. she had ordered him to be conducted to her frontiers and forbidden to return under pain of death. It would have been the proper mode of punishing his flight. Having destroyed the monarchy, the monarch, degraded to the rank of a mere individual in the State, could not have been mischievous. I was in private conference with Mr. Pitt on the very day that the news of the king's escape from Paris arrived. It was from Mr. Pitt I received the first intelligence, and, on my doubting its truth, he assured me that it came from our Ambassador. I then said, 'If so, his Majesty has taken

---

[1] 'Latude is, as usual, incorrigible, and plays the devil.'—*The Bastille*, by the Hon. D. Bingham, ii. 123. See Letter, March 13, 1791.

either the road to Metz or to Mons,' and I asserted this from having been assured when in Paris that the garrison and inhabitants of the former town were favourable to his cause. My conjecture was well founded. His Majesty took that route, and his brother went by the other.

Mr. Burke has accused M. de Lafayette of having connived at the escape of the royal family, and allowed them to proceed to Varennes, that he might enjoy the malignant triumph of bringing back the sovereign as a degraded prisoner to the metropolis.[1] The improbability of the story is itself a proof of its falsehood. It cannot be credited that Lafayette, if he had been privy to the departure of the King, for the purpose so inhumanly attributed to him, would have allowed his Majesty to travel within fifteen miles of the frontier before he had him stopped, especially as Varennes was the last town through which the hapless monarch had to pass with any apprehension of danger. If Lafayette had played so foul a part, one of his aides-de-camp, not the postmaster, Drouet, who alone derived *éclat* from the arrest, would have stopped the royal travellers. His claims to innocence are established on the declaration of the Queen alone, whose evidence under the distressing and awful circumstances in which she found herself commands respect and confidence. She declared that 'Monsieur de Lafayette was ignorant of her departure.' Her account of the manner in which she left Paris corroborates her assertion. The Marquis de Bouillé, with whom I was intimately acquainted, assured me that Lafayette is innocent of the charge brought against him. He was in the secret of that ill-managed flight of an ill-advised sovereign,

[1] See Burke's Speech in the House of Commons, March 17, 1794.

and has since publicly vindicated in his printed memoirs the character of Lafayette from the unmanly aspersion, an aspersion the more atrocious for having been thrown on him whilst immured in a dungeon and without the means of refuting it.[1]—W. A. M.

MR. MILES TO MR. PITT

July 1, 1791

From the confidence that M. de Lafayette has in Sir Edward Newenham and the influence which an inti-

[1] An interesting narrative—*Relation du Voyage de la Famille Royale à Varennes*—is supplied by Mr. Oscar Browning in an Appendix to the Despatches of Lord Gower, as received from an eye-witness, pp. 372-376. The tragic end of Count Axel Fersen, who acted as coachman to Louis XVI. on the night of the escape, Monday, June 20, and whom Lord Gower characterises as 'the principal contriver of this scheme,' may be briefly related here:—

'Fersen, malgré le danger, rentra dans Paris en Février 1792 à la faveur d'un déguisement pour s'efforcer de s'entendre avec la famille royale et travailler encore à son salut. En même temps, il travaillait avec Gustave III. à toutes les démarches extérieures qui pouvaient contribuer à la contre-révolution. L'assassinat du Roi de Suède, pendant la nuit du 16 Mars, 1792, interrompit à peine ces entreprises, qu'excitèrent à nouveau les nouvelles qu'on recevait de la France, la mort du Roi et de la Reine, et la guerre déclarée.'

The Revolution of March 13, 1809, which dethroned Gustavus IV., proclaimed Charles XIII. King of Sweden on June 6. The Prince Royal suddenly died. The brothers Fersen and their sister, the Countess Piper, were suspected of conspiring in favour of Prince Vasa, son of Gustavus IV. Axel Fersen was falsely suspected of having poisoned the Prince Royal. On the day of the funeral, June 20, 1810, the excitement in Stockholm was formidable. Axel Fersen, regardless of friendly warning, attended in full state at the obsequies, but he was compelled to fly for refuge from popular vengeance, his asylum was discovered by the mob, and, realising his position, he fell on his knees and prayed: '*Mon Dieu! dit-il, devant qui je vais dans un instant comparaitre, je pardonne à mes bourreaux et je vous prie pour eux.* A peine avait-il dit qu'un de ces bourreaux, non pas un homme du peuple, mais un officier, décoré de la médaille de la bravoure et chevalier de l'ordre de l'Epée, déguisé cette fois en matelot, un nommé Tandefelt, s'élança le premier dans le corps de garde, renversa Fersen, et lui sauta des deux pieds si violemment sur la poitrine, qu'il la lui brisa. Ainsi mourut celui qui avait représenté jadis avec tant d'éclat à Versailles le caractère chevaleresque de son pays.'—*Revue d'Histoire Diplomatique*, deuxième année, No. I. p. 90.

macy of many years generally gives, I have since my arrival in England pressed the latter to write to the General and dissipate his fears relative to the destination of the British armament, and to assure him that France has nothing to apprehend from this country. A conference of near two hours with M. de Lafayette the night previous to my departure from Paris made me extremely anxious to do away the ill impressions he had conceived against your administration, and I knew no way so effectual as to engage his intimate friend to convince him of his mistake. It is with pleasure I inform you that Sir Edward has complied with my request.

Lord Fortescue to Mr. Miles

July 5, 1791

I am not the less obliged to you for the French intelligence, although it made such a circuit as to lose the character of news before it reached me. I am now, however, on my journey for Castle Hill, and shall not fail to receive very thankfully any further accounts that you may think worth communicating to me. As to the *dénouement* of this strange state of things, nothing short of prophecy can reach it. Chance, to which they all fear to trust, must gradually unravel it into something different from the present anarchy; for it is impossible that twenty millions of people should exist in society without being governed at all! I tremble for the fate of the last remains of the gallant *gardes du corps* who were brought back upon the coach-box. I am afraid they are fallen into savage hands. As to the persons of the King and Queen, I reckon them pretty safe, and that the National Assembly, having carried their point, will take the credit of moderation in forbearing from any violence against them. Perhaps their natural thirst for blood may satisfy itself upon a wretched *femme de chambre* or two. I have read your pamphlet with very great pleasure, and am much obliged to you for it. It puts the question just in that point of light in which I have always wished that the public might view it. It gives me very sincere pleasure to hear of your having at last in some degree succeeded in your applications to Government.

MR. MILES TO MR. JOSEPH SMITH[1]

July 6, 1791

When you recollect how painful a state of suspense is, and, above all, the awkward situation of my family at Paris, you will pardon my reminding you to mention to Mr. Pitt on his coming to town this day that it is very material for me to know whether I am to continue in England or return to the Continent, and this very necessary and important information, I trust, it will be in your power to give me when I call in Downing Street at three o'clock. In the meantime, believe me to be, with unaffected sincerity and esteem, yours, &c.

LORD GOWER TO MR. MILES

Paris: July 8, 1791

Lord Gower presents his compliments to Mr. Miles, and is very much obliged to him for his kind attention in sending him the useful pamphlets he has published since his journey to England. As Lord Gower is persuaded that the public will read them with the same pleasure as himself, he hopes that every intention of the author will succeed according to his wishes.

---

[1] Private Secretary to Mr. Pitt.

LORD RODNEY TO MR. MILES.

Old Alresford: July 14, 1791

I am much obliged to you, dear Miles, for the favour of your pamphlets. I have read them and am pleased with their contents. I am sure they will do good, as they will open the eyes of people in general, and make them love and respect the constitution of Great Britain, and not be led astray by the disgraceful conduct of that infamous Assembly at Paris, or by that fellow Paine. That the constitution of England may last to the end of time is the most sincere wish of him who is with truth yours sincerely.

MR. MILES TO SIR EDWARD NEWENHAM

London: July 14, 1791

My last authentic intelligence from France announces much ill-humour on the part of Russia towards the National Assembly. Three deputies waited on M. Simolin on the subject of the passport he obtained for the hapless monarch and his family. The Russian envoy enquired in what character they came to him. They answered that they were deputed by the National Assembly. 'Then, gentlemen,' he replied, 'I have express orders from my sovereign not to treat with you.' He then retired. M. de Condé's letter to the National Assembly in the 'Oracle' of this date is well written. An explosion will certainly happen. All Bouillé's officers have sworn to effect the King's restoration. The foreign ministers expect to be recalled. Confusion augments in that distracted country. What else can be expected from ignorant and bad men invested with power? The individuals who have usurped the government and direct the vast machine at present are short-sighted politicians, abounding in much low and ungenerous cunning, whilst they are shamefully deficient in sound sense, useful information, and high estimates of honour. Mrs. and Miss Miles leave Paris for London this day.

Mr. Miles to Sir Edward Newenham

Dover: July 16, 1791

Here am I, my dear Newenham, waiting on the briny margin of this happy and glorious island to receive my family, who were to leave Paris last Wednesday. Seaport towns are my aversion, and last night began to wear heavy upon me, when the pacquet from Calais arrived, and brought to the City of London Inn a very intelligent English merchant just come from Bordeaux and Paris. His principles were rather democratic until ameliorated by the danger to which he and all the British subjects were exposed through the ignorance of the magistrates at Bordeaux, who, on the first alarm that a British squadron was on the coast, had printed papers stuck up that Mr. Pitt was hostile to liberty and resolved to attempt a counter-revolution! The nearer approach of these vessels proved them to be French ships from St. Domingo; but this discovery, although it contradicted the calumny of the municipality, could not influence the gentlemen to have the justice or the candour to acknowledge their error. Assignats, he assured me, were from 15 to 16 per cent. discount, whilst he received thirty-one livres for a pound sterling. The Tuileries are shut, and sentinels on the top of the Palace, and even at the apartments of the King and Queen, whose conversation can be no longer in secret. The vast number of enormous abuses in France certainly required reform. All sensible and good men must acknowledge this truth. But the abuses that have been committed since seem to have become a part of the present system. Two thousand vagabonds assembling every day in the Palais Royal to debate political subjects relative to foreign and domestic policy —and these vagabonds varying from day to day, both as to numbers and persons, as well as on the points they discuss—give no pleasing prospect of tranquillity; and it is this deplorable anarchy into which France has fallen that distresses me. I ever was, and will remain, a firm friend to the civil and religious rights of mankind, to the constitution of my country, and to the wise and equitable Government which provides for the security of the peasant as effectually as it does for the prince. Last Wednesday they were deciding the fate of the King and Queen in the National Assembly. I have not yet heard the result. The Prince de Condé, it is said, has 20,000 men at the Abbey d'Orval, and the foreign ministers expect to be recalled. Enclose your letters under cover to Evan Nepean, Esq. (an old acquaintance of mine), Secretary of State's Office, Whitehall. I have rented a furnished house, No. 7 Cleveland Row, St. James's. Adieu. I am going to see the pacquets arrive.

MR. HUSKISSON TO MR. MILES

Paris: August 12, 1791

I received the obliging favour of your letter of the 5th with the 'Morning Chronicle,' for which I return you many thanks. I have executed, I believe, all your commissions, except that on which you seem to lay the most stress—reminding General Wimpffen of his promise. I have not been very well this week and seen very few people, so that I have not hitherto met with any person that could inform me where the general was to be found.

I have read 'Brutus's Letters'[1] with pleasure, more particularly the first to Sheridan and to Burke, with whose character he seems well acquainted. The situation of this country is alarming. The Assembly and the people are so much divided; the want of discipline in the army is so irremediable, as long as it is fomented by incendiary publications, clubs, &c., that it is impossible to indulge any flattering hopes of order, peace, and prosperity being soon restored. The Assembly is debating the *acte constitutionnel*, of which they have adopted one half without any great alteration. I am persuaded that the King will accept, but I am equally persuaded they cannot set him at liberty, so that his signature will be considered by his party as a mere mockery, and possibly treated, too, as such in a very short time. The general peace, which is very near taking place in Europe, adds to the critical situation of France; but, as it is never so difficult to prognosticate upon the event of a disease as during a violent crisis, I shall entirely suspend my opinion. I think, however, we shall very soon be able to examine more closely the state of affairs so falsely presented to the public by our intriguing and factious leaders.

MR. HUSKISSON TO MR. MILES

Paris: September 15, 1791

Having found upon enquiry that no paper was so much esteemed as the 'Gazette Universelle' for the news of the Low Countries, and in general for all foreign intelligence, I have subscribed to it for three months; but these things are carried on in this country in a manner so ridiculous that I shall not receive it till the first of next month. The 'Gazette de la Cour' was so stupid that

---

[1] Written by Mr. Miles.

I have not kept the numbers of this week, which really were not worth sending to you. After a good deal of trouble, I found Wimpffen's brother last night. He told me the general was employed, and at this moment at Colmar. This scrawl points out the reason which must make you excuse the shortness of this letter.[1]

A Member of the National Assembly to Mr. Miles

Paris, le 4 Octobre, 1791

Tout ce que je vous ai dit, mon cher Miles, relativement aux menées du Roi de Prusse était bien vrai ; il a un agent secret ici actuellement. L'objet de la Cour de Berlin est de nous détacher de la maison d'Autriche. Montmorin et Lessart s'y opposent. Une personne de confiance a été envoyée au Roi de Prusse de la part de l'Assemblée Nationale, et on est très bien disposé à rompre toute liaison avec la Cour de Vienne, dont on n'est pas trop content ; mais la Reine, qui se mêle de tout, s'y oppose, ainsi que Montmorin et Lessart, et il y a lieu de croire qu'il y a sur le tapis quelque chose qui doit changer la face politique de toute l'Europe. Au reste, les aristocrates sont fiers depuis peu, et nous font croire qu'il y aura une crise. Adieu !

Lord Fortescue to Mr. Miles

Castle Hill : October 5, 1791

I am much obliged to you for all the communications you have been so good as to give me ; at the same time I think it but fair to add that Lord Buckingham having by this time finished his rambles, and being

---

[1] 'The Wimpffen whom Mr. Huskisson saw at my desire was then a member of the National Assembly, and afterwards he defended Thionville and saved France. The brother, François, was a general in the French army, and the man whom I introduced into the Jacobin Club for the purpose of defending Lafayette from the Orleans fury.'—W. A. M.

returned to Stowe, the first claim to the fruits of your correspondence will naturally revert to him. He spent about a week here, and then pursued his route home by Weymouth. I cannot but agree with your correspondent on the subject of the 'Journal de la Cour,' which, though it may have a good effect by its circulation in France, does not seem to convey much interesting intelligence beyond it. I am at a loss to foresee any *dénouement* to this strange business, and yet, like all other wonders, it must cease, and it seems already to have outlasted their usual term. I return you the letters which I received inclosed in yours to-day. The state of things has since taken another appearance by the King's acceptance of the constitution.[1] In all events I can see nothing as yet that is to warrant our revolutionists in congratulating mankind upon their attainments.

Mr. Miles to Lord Fortescue

December 28, 1791

The French papers arrived so late yesterday that I had not time to peruse them before they were despatched to Lord Buckingham. The assignats have fallen to above 40 per cent. discount, and the explosion, temporary bankruptcy, and all the evils attendant on the guilt and folly of these sorry legislators in Paris cannot long be deferred. Yet, mark my words, France will recover from her present delirium; the fulness of her crimes will be the measure of her debility and misfortune, and, acquiring a wise and free Government, she will overawe the imperial eagle and threaten the liberties of Europe.

My letters from Ireland also announce serious mis-

---

[1] The constitution was accepted by the King on September 14, 1791.

chief, so much so that I have forwarded to Stowe my information received from Sir Edward Newenham. I am grieved at heart to find disaffection associating itself with the spirit of reform, so as to subvert with greater facility the laws and the constitution of this country.

Mr. Miles to Lord Buckingham

December 28, 1791

The knowledge which your Lordship has of the country to which the inclosed papers relate, and the very great interest you have in the preservation of order and good government in Ireland, will, I hope, justify the freedom of trespassing again so soon upon your time. The papers were sent to me by Sir Edward Newenham. I must beg leave to inform you that I have not the smallest wish to go to Ireland, but, on the contrary, a very sincere desire to keep out of it. The warmth of my temper would expose me to much risk among a people too obstinate to reason with, too violent to listen to the dictates of moderation and equity, and with whom the strong hand of coercion is more likely to succeed than the mild language of advice. I feel much pain in making these communications, but you ought to be apprised of every circumstance likely to draw your rank and fortune into hazard.

Maréchal Lückner to the War Minister

General Quarters, Menin: June 29, 1792 [1]

The despatches which I have sent by M. Beauharnois, Adjutant-General, must have given you full information respecting my political situation, and the arguments which they must have furnished can have left no doubts in your mind with respect to my subsequent conduct.

---

[1] The correspondence for the previous six months cannot be found.

The *éclaircissements* which I may have omitted in my letter M. Beauharnois has orders from me to communicate verbally.

I will again enter into some details which, although they be known to you, will serve to justify my conduct, which has been solely guided by long experience, by principles of delicacy, and by my inviolable attachment to the welfare of France.

After the adoption of certain measures by the late Ministry, and a full reliance on an insurrection in Brabant, the King was led by them to declare an offensive war. I consequently adopted proper plans for penetrating with my army into the enemy's country. M. de Lafayette marched towards Maubenge with a view to awe the troops encamped near Mons; I placed a body of 5,000 men at Maulde, to check the troops who had taken post at Tournay. I have marched into the enemy's country by way of Menin and Courtray, where I collected together 4,000 men. I am posted at Menin; my advanced guard is at Courtray. The whole country between Lannoy, Bruges, and Brussels is covered by my army, and is entirely destitute of hostile troops; notwithstanding all this, there is not the least appearance of an insurrection among the Belgians. I do not even entertain the smallest hopes that this insurrection, so confidently announced, is likely to take place, and, though I were master of Ghent and Brussels, I am almost certain that the people would never come over to us, say what those few persons will who care nothing for the safety of France, provided they gratify their ambition and avarice.

Lisle and the Canton of Rouloy have forbidden that forage be sent to my army. The peasants in the environs of Menin have repeatedly fired upon French patrols. My advanced guard and my reserve at Courtray are perpetually harassed by the enemy, who daily receive reinforcements near Tournay, between Ghent and Courtray. Thus situated with 20,000 men, which form the whole of my army, all I can do is to keep the enemy at bay, and not leave Lisle exposed. My retreat will run risk of being cut off by the enemy, and the only step which I could then take would be to file off towards Nieuport, Furnes, and Dunkirk. Judge of the inconveniences attending such a movement. I have at this moment no more than from 500 to 600 Belgians with me—you see how I am situated; but an object of the last importance demands the particular attention of the King's Council. The strongest motive which impels me to retreat is the situation of our frontiers; between the Rhine and the sea, between the Sambre and the Rhine, there are now no troops. The head of the enemy's columns is advancing into the Electorate of Trèves, and not into the Low Countries. M. de Lafayette cannot quit his station without leaving me exposed to forces twice superior to mine. Then Valenciennes and Lisle will be totally defenceless. This requires the attention of the King's Council. As to what concerns me, my whole thoughts and the whole of my experience are employed in devising means of defence between Dunkirk and Saar-Louis; since I have found that the Belgians are not well affected to us, I think of nothing but this night and day. One single measure remained for me to adopt, with a view to avert from France a very great calamity, and that measure is to retreat with my army to Valenciennes; every moment presses my departure. I have thought it proper not to wait for your answer relative to the situation of my army, and therefore I shall march to-morrow, the 30th, for Lisle, the 1st of July for Chilly, the 2nd for St. Amand, and the 3rd for Valenciennes. I despatch at the same time with this a courier to M. de Lafayette to inform him of my movements, and to say that I have given orders to M. Lanoue, Lieutenant-General and Commandant of the Camp of ——, to march with his 5,000 men for Maubeuge. In consequence of this information, Lafayette's army may take the necessary steps, and retreat wherever it shall be thought convenient. I foresee that the measures which I have adopted will set a swarm of malcontents against me, who will calumniate my principles and intentions; I have nothing but the public good in view, and I should think myself a traitor to the country if, in the present circumstances, I had adopted any other mode of conduct.

I request, Sir, that you will lay before the King and Council a detail of my proceedings, that they may be appreciated. Without this, as I have already had the honour to observe to you, I cannot retain the command of the army.

(Signed)   Le Maréchal de France,
Général d'Armée, LÜCKNER.

MR. AUST[1] *TO MR. MILES*

Foreign Office: July 4, 1792

I shall with pleasure comply with your wishes in forwarding your French weekly packet to Lord Buckingham at once. I hope to treat you with another Gazette to-morrow, with an account of the glorious Indian peace. *Courage, mon ami!* Let the prosperity of England dispel all lesser feelings. Let your heart say 'Vincit amor patriæ!' The Duke of Leeds comes to town Friday next to dine, and returns to Mimms in the evening.

[1] Under-Secretary of State for Foreign Affairs.

M. Mourgue[1] to Mr. Miles

Paris: July 6, 1792

I received, my dear Sir, with the greatest pleasure your letter full of the kindest interest. Our hearts have been deeply touched by your kind offers for my dear Eglée. Your reflections on girls' schools in general are very just. The one in which I have placed my daughter deserves to be excepted on account of the intelligence and tone which reign there. At her age she will acquire that reserve and modesty which I admire so much in the education of Englishwomen. A short stay in London on her return, and the tone she will soon acquire in Paris, will produce a combination which will be beneficial to her for the rest of her life. It is my intention not to leave her too long separated from us or from the charm and ease which the habits of society confer.

Be assured, my dear Sir, that the kind feeling expressed in your letters has been appreciated. The critical and unfortunate position under which we are groaning, makes me congratulate myself that my dear children are far from danger, while at the same time their education will make progress. My young sons are well placed as regards their morals and the acquisition of the English language and literature. I have also the happiness of knowing that my eldest son is out of danger. He has always desired the diplomatic career, and I have just obtained for him from the Minister of Foreign Affairs the post of Secretary attached to the Legation at the Court of London.[2] It is a happy intro-

---

[1] Late Minister of the Interior.

[2] Scipion Mourgue, who, as will appear further on, was associated with M. Maret as an agent from the National Convention, under Le Brun, Minister of Foreign Affairs.

duction to a career for which I have reason to think he unites the germs of several qualifications. He will have the honour of seeing you as soon as he knows you are in London.

My elevation and my descent from the Ministry have followed quickly on each other. I entered it full of hope. I would have held it firmly, but our unhappy country is so agitated that, having seen I should be more exposed to the disagreement of parties than useful in the administration of affairs, it became my duty to abandon a post which in calmer times I should have had the courage to occupy. I received very flattering expression of general esteem even from parties the most opposed.

What shall I say to you, my dear Sir, of our political condition? I am broken-hearted. I told you long ago that the bulk of our nation was not ripe for so philosophic a revolution. Alas! The people are much more divided than you imagine. This miserable Religion, which has kept them in ignorance, is still the cause of our misfortunes; add to that cause the desire for Republicanism, fomented by the remnant of Jacobins, who have revived since we left that society. On the 22nd of June, 1791, we came out nearly 1,800 at once, and I may say they were all chosen men on account of their morals, and talents, and property. The present association consists only of people gathered from the *pavé*, people without morals, without property, whom disorder alone calls forth from nothing, from which they should never have emerged! It is this circumstance that makes the anarchy under which we live horrible. Our National Assembly is of a detestable composition. There are 400 or 500 members who ought not to be in it. Do not think, however, that it is for want of finding better men, or for lack of good and worthy representatives. For our honour, I must explain the causes of this disastrous choice. The flight of the King on the 21st of June¹ last year put all intelligences in motion. Wise people said that it was a thoughtless act—a misfortune that must be repaired; and that, as royalty is a necessary lever to the government of a great nation, we must keep the King, but mark the true limits of his regal power. Such was the spirit that equally animated people of good sense throughout the kingdom, and the 'committee of the constitution' of the Constituent Assembly. The giddy, the turbulent—those whom the Revolution had called forth out of nothing, who had everything to hope from anarchy—cried out that the King must be punished, that he was a traitor, and they spoke of nothing less than following your fatal example in the case of Charles I. This is the spirit of the Jacobins; it is this which caused us to withdraw; they propagated it among the people. Royalty had become degraded in their estimation; hence the project of signing on the 17th of July, 1791, in the Champ de Mars, a petition by thousands of individuals for the punishment, they said, of the King, and for the abolition of royalty altogether. You know the indignation of honest and good Frenchmen against this project, which was no less perfidious than senseless; you will remember that we were obliged to disperse this *canaille* with shot. The actual chiefs of the Jacobins could not pardon the action of M. Bailly nor of M. de Lafayette on that day, and that is the cause of their being hated and persecuted. The electors were appointed to nominate the members of the new Legislature. This election took place soon after.² People were really indignant at this

¹ During the night of June 20-21.
² The Constituent Assembly was dissolved on September 30, 1791,

flight of the King. It happened that almost throughout France the spirit of the Jacobins communicated itself as by an electric spark, and hence it resulted that, men of sound principle being in the minority amongst the electors, the choice fell, not on the worthiest, but on those who cried and clamoured the most. I was an elector in Paris. I saw the infernal intrigues; but good patriotic men form scarcely a third of our number, and hence the selections which we dared not acknowledge. Of twenty-four deputies for Paris, there were not more than seven or eight whom we were able to nominate, and these only because they were not generally known. See, my dear Sir, the cause of the bad composition of the National Assembly—the cause of the misfortunes under which we groan. Shall I speak to you of the effects? Kindly excuse me. Tears come to my eyes. I will talk to you about it another day. It would be even so much the better if we were in a real crisis; every day sees bloodshed; and perhaps tomorrow we shall be no more. I will hope, however, to write to you next Friday.[1] Be assured of the tender sentiments with which you have inspired me.

I profit by your kindness to beg you to forward the inclosed. If you will accompany these letters with a few words to my dear Eglée and to my dear Eugène, they will be much appreciated, for they were disappointed at not having found you in London. I embrace you most cordially.[2]

and was immediately replaced by the Legislative Assembly, *i.e.* after the King had accepted the constitution.

[1] On every Friday Lord Gower sent a messenger from Paris with despatches for the Foreign Office.

[2] 'M. Mourgue was a Protestant. He had the direction of the works at Cherbourg, under Dumouriez, before the Revolution. He was Secretary of State for the Interior on the ever-memorable 20th June, 1792, when a lawless, senseless rabble forced their hapless and degraded

M. Mourgue to Mr. Miles

Paris: July 13, 1792

Our situation has not improved, my dear Sir, since I had the pleasure of writing to you last week. The German armies are reinforced on our frontiers, and the majority of the National Assembly only sees and occupies itself with its intestine divisions. It has declared the country in danger; but, in accordance with the views of all good Frenchmen, it should rather have avowed that it is the National Assembly itself which has placed and still places the country in that terrible position. You will have seen with pleasure the momentary reunion which took place the same day that I wrote to you. The scene was noble and affecting, but it was *un feu de paille*. The characters were not changed; the bitterness was not softened. The suspension of the Mayor, Pétion, by the Department soon became a subject of discord; in any well-ordered State he would have merited a much more serious punishment. The dominant party in the Assembly, who wish to humiliate the King and royalty, support this Mayor Pétion; hence all that has been said and done on that subject. The King confirmed the suspension of the Mayor yesterday; we expect to see the Assembly disapprove this decision and quash the Department which conducts itself under all circumstances with the greatest wisdom.[1]

sovereign to put on a red cap. He soon resigned office. He afterwards applied for the appointment of Minister Plenipotentiary, which, however, Bonnecarrère had the dexterity to obtain, although he was displaced before he proceeded to his post by another faction coming into power.'—W. A. M.

[1] 'With a like issue works our Department-Directory here at Paris; who, on the 6th of July, take upon them to suspend Mayor Pétion and Procureur Manuel from all civic functions, for their conduct, replete, as is alleged, with omissions and commissions, on that delicate Twentieth of June.

These unexpected incidents are very *mal à propos* on account of the crowds which assembled under pretext of federation. Mayor Pétion presented himself yesterday at the bar of the Assembly and made the most extraordinary statements. 'I will regard,' said he, 'the confirmation of the suspension by the King as the most honourable mark of esteem.' All was in the same tone; he spoke only of the people, and through the people, among whom, he said, he included those who have not sufficient property to be active citizens—that is, what *you* call the *Mob*. That factious Mayor has got such a *posse* in the Assembly that we fear many troubles on his account. You will have learnt that the Ministers, harassed, fatigued, insulted, by an Assembly which has no idea of dignity and propriety, have all tendered their resignation. They are obliged to continue in office until the King has named others—it will not be easy to find them; and, in truth, it is very unfortunate that we are reduced to this strait, for, in spite of the German coalition, I can assure you that we have every resource, and that a well-selected Ministry, with an Assembly who would support it, would soon restore France to the point of consideration which her soil, industry, and position naturally assign to her.

I am not pleased with any of your English papers on our affairs in France; they all talk unreasonably, and publish falsehoods in a manner quite inconceivable. They are more exact on the affairs of China than on

---

Virtuous Pétion sees himself a kind of martyr, or pseudo-martyr, threatened with several things; drawls out due heroical lamentation; to which Patriot Paris and Patriot Legislative duly respond. King Louis and Mayor Pétion have already had an interview on that business of the Twentieth; an interview and dialogue, distinguished by frankness on both sides; ending on King Louis's side with the words, *Taisez-vous*, Hold your peace.'—Carlyle.

those of France. Since you have the advantage of a
free post once a week, I am surprised that you have not
some of our best papers, especially the 'Moniteur,' which
reports what is actually said at the Assembly without
adding any remarks, and which appears daily in the
same form as your newspapers. The German Confederacy against us is contrary to all policy, and proves
how unreasonable men are when influenced only by
vanity. There is not one of these German Princes, from
the least to the greatest, who would not sacrifice half
the men in the world rather than allow the idea to be
propagated that *they* are merely human, and of the same
nature as other people! The astonishment inspired by
this pride is further aggravated by the wickedness of
attacking people who, far from having done anything
to them, are only unfortunate for upholding the imprescriptible rights of men. *O mens insana!* You have
always seen that men have rushed to sacrifice their lives
in the wars of despotism; you scarcely ever see them
rush to uphold the cause of liberty!

My son leaves on Tuesday for his post in London.
I commend him to your friendship, to surround him
with good companions in a country where youth encounters so many snares. He has been brought up in
good society. The sentiments he has expressed towards
you show that he considers you as his support in London.
I believe that he will reside at the Embassy.[1]

If our affairs continue to grow worse, so that we
should have neither safety nor tranquillity, I shall seek
a refuge in some retired corner of your country, for my
dilapidated fortune would not admit of our living in
London or its neighbourhood. I avail myself of your

---

[1] In Portman Square, the residence of M. Chauvelin, the French Ambassador.

kindness to beg you will forward the inclosed to my dear children. It will be a great comfort to my wife.

M. Scipion Mourgue to Mr. Miles

Portman Square : 7 Août, 1792

Nous sommes perdus, mon cher monsieur ! Je ne vois plus de ressource pour la malheureuse France ! Je suis au désespoir. Imaginez-vous que l'infâme Pétion a demandé au nom des 48 sections de Paris la déchéance du Roi. Mon Dieu ! Que veulent ces gens-là ! Si je vous eusse vu en ville, je vous serois bien venu voir, car j'ai besoin de soutien et de conseil. Je viendrai vous voir demain ; nous causerons de tout cela. Croiriez-vous que Bonne-Carrère est nommé Ministre plénipotentiaire à Philadelphie à la place de M. de Jernan ? Bon jour.

M. Scipion Mourgue to Mr. Miles

Portman Square : 17e Août, 1792

Ah, monsieur ! Oh, mon ami ! Je ne puis suffire à vous tracer les scènes d'horreurs qui déchirent l'âme de votre malheureux jeune ami ! Ah ! que devient mon père ? Est-il en vie ? Je ne puis vous dire autre chose si non qu'on compte que 2,700 hommes ont perdu la vie. Le sang inonde mon pays. Le sang de l'honnête homme est proscrit. Je n'ai pas la force de vous donner les détails, mais-jugez les. Hérault de Saint-Jean-d'Angély, and the brave loyal old D'Affry,[1] Colonel General of the

---

[1] 'On fait lecture d'une lettre du juge de paix de la section des Quinze-Vingts ainsi conçue : "Monsieur le Président,—Le peuple s'est porté en foule à la maison de M. d'Affry, qui demeure dans ma section. Des soldats citoyens se sont empressés de le protéger. Je l'ai fait transférer dans les prisons de l'Abbaye, pour le mettre à l'abri des violences."'— *Histoire Parlementaire*, vii. 16. See *Despatches of Earl Gower*, August 23, 1792.

Swiss, Clermont-Tonnerre, &c., are dead, massacred—
the Prince de Poix too! And Le Brun is Minister of
Foreign Affairs.[1] Roland, Clavière, Servan, are come in
again, and some other men of the same sort. Adieu!
Oh, good Sir, where is my unhappy father?[2]

Mr. Aust to Mr. Miles
August 18, 1792

I am sorry that an engagement to dine a little way
out of town will prevent my having the pleasure of
meeting M. Mourgue next Wednesday. I sent your
history of Le Brun to Lord Grenville by a messenger
to-day, and in an hour after it was gone I was surprised
by his Lordship's sudden return to town.

Mr. Huskisson to Mr. Miles
Paris: August 18, 1792

The Thuilleries was forced on Friday morning, the
10th instant, by the mob, after a brave resistance from
the Swiss Guard, who were most of them killed at their
posts. The King, Queen, and royal family escaped at
the beginning of the tumult to the National Assembly,
across the garden, and were still in a room adjoining
on Sunday when the messenger set out. The Assembly
decreed that the executive power was no longer with the
King, nor with his Ministers, but invested in Ministers
of their naming till the final decision of a National Convention to be summoned for the 20th September. Many
persons of distinction are killed, particularly M. Clermont-Tonnerre. The mob have destroyed all the

---

[1] 'M. Le Brun, nouvellement nommé au ministère des affaires
étrangères, se présente à l'Assemblée, et prête le serment de maintenir la
liberté et l'égalité, ou de mourir à son poste.'—*Hist. Parl.* xvii. 43.

[2] The sudden transition from French to English was not uncommon
in the letters from Scipion Mourgue to Mr. Miles.

furniture of the Palace, and burnt the barracks and the outbuildings adjoining, and, it is feared, massacred all they found within.

M. Mourgue to Mr. Miles

Paris: August 30, 1792

It is long, my dear Sir, since I had the pleasure of writing to you. First, I had not the courage to speak of the horrors of the 10th. My ideas and sentiments on the French Revolution are known to you, and are in accordance with your own. This tissue of errors and clumsy legislation has conducted France to the miserable point at which she finds herself, and we see that she profits little from the lessons of history, for, instead of giving herself up to discover and practise whatever would be beneficial, each party thinks only of revenging itself on the opposite party and of gratifying its passions. The King and his Council might have done much for the restoration of order immediately after the constitution was accepted, but, not liking the new order of things, they have done nothing towards the execution of the laws, which limit their power too much, and have even impeded them by an inactivity that has brought the royal family into their present state. This Legislative Assembly is composed, in great part, of members who are more interested in discovering and exposing the faults of the constitution than in calmly taking practical measures for their gradual correction. The result has been a feeling of hatred towards the members of the constituent body equal only to that against royalty, and see to what this has brought us! It is a state of things that finds no parallel in history. I will not permit myself to say more. It will be a matter for consideration as to how far it may become the neighbouring Powers, and specially Spain and England, to allow France to be crushed by the sword of Germany. But I must not enter on a political dissertation that cannot be fully treated by correspondence; it will be the subject of our conversation if I am able some day to breathe the air of liberty which is secured by obedience to the laws which reign in your happy country.

I appreciate from the bottom of my heart the anxiety you have manifested at seeing me still here with my wife. But it is impossible for us to leave— even to go twenty miles from Paris. I assure you I shall not stay in this country longer than is necessary. We must see what all this will come to, and, at the first moment of liberty, dispose of our persons and estates. If I cannot live near London, I will choose some rural part where it is less expensive. I will advise you of our wishes and ask your good counsel. I still commend to you my dear son. His position is cruel; he needs the support of friendship and experience, and under this twofold aspect I cannot do better than commend him to you. Whatever turn affairs may take, I do not wish him to return to France.

The present state of things here gives little hope or courage to enter the Administration. It will become much worse if our enemies accomplish their designs. You see, my dear Sir, there is no reason for moderate men to cherish hope for a long time to come. I am vexed, for I have seen, as through a gap, how much good might be done both at home and abroad. My wife thinks, not without pain, of the necessity of expatriation. She salutes you cordially. If we can still write to you under cover to your Foreign Office, let me know. *Je vous embrasse de bon cœur.*

Mr. Aust to Mr. Miles

Whitehall: August 30, 1792

Many thanks for your obliging intelligence received to-day. We have letters from Lord Gower dated Paris, the 27th, who only waited for his final municipality passport to set out.[1] Lord Grenville is to pass the greatest part of next month in Cornwall.

Mr. Lodge to Mr. Miles

Hastings: September 19, 1792

Scarcely a day has passed since my coming here without the arrival of one cargo at least of the unfortunate French clergy. Multitudes have been sent in carts to London, and yet more have gone from hence to Dover, in order to cross to Ostend. Many have taken their residence here, and are determined to continue during the winter. It is distressing to see these poor people wandering about in little groups, silent, dejected, and wrapped in odd disguises, the dresses in which they escaped, and the only ones they now have to cover them. I see several subscriptions advertised in the London papers for their relief; but I perceive also that even the hand of charity must be guided by party spirit, as shown in an appeal, evidently on behalf of the first revolutionists—disciples of Barnave and the Lameths —who have been driven in their turn from the horrors of anarchy. I hope the good sense and virtue of this country will distinguish the mild and inoffensive suf-

---

[1] 'After having gone through a number of forms, perhaps necessary in the present circumstances, I am in hourly expectation of receiving my final passport from the municipality, and I hope in a few days to be able to pay my respects to your Lordship in London.'—*Lord Gower to Lord Grenville, Despatches,* August 27, 1792.

'His Excellency Earl Gower set out on Tuesday morning with part of his family on his return to England.'—*Mr. W. Lindsay to Lord Grenville, Despatches,* Paris, August 29, 1792.

ferers from those ruffians. It is highly necessary that the conductors of the subscription for the clergy should have the assistance of some persons of rank in that order; and perhaps none is fitter than the Bishop of Avranches, who landed at this place last week, and is now in London.[1] I thank you for your intelligence of the Vicomte de Noailles and M. de Grave (who lately dined with you in Cleveland Row), for your judgment of the French clergy, and for your news of the *renommé* M. Egalité.

MR. MILES TO MR. LONG [2]

London: September 24, 1792

I do not know that the inclosed will be printed in either of the two papers to which I have addressed it, as I have observed that by a kind of etiquette established between the conductors of our public prints they are never to arraign each other's conduct; so that these gentry, who claim and exercise the right of attacking all mankind, are by this cartel secured from all attack and rendered invulnerable. But I have had several hints at different times from Frenchmen in constant relation and intimacy with M. de Chauvelin and his family, that the editors of the 'Morning Chronicle' and of the 'Argus' have received considerable sums of money, and that they have each of them a large monthly allowance. I have no doubt of the fact, and wish it could be proved in Westminster Hall, and the purpose for which the money is paid. This I know, that the personal attendance of the parties in Portman

---

[1] 'The total number of French refugees landed at all the ports in this kingdom between the 30th August and the 1st October is 3,772. The subscriptions received by the committees for the relief of the suffering clergy of France amount to upwards of 15,000*l.*'—*Annual Register*, 1792: *Chronicle*, p. 39.

[2] Mr. Charles Long, Joint-Secretary to the Treasury.

Square[1] is constant. All this perfidy and meanness in men who might serve the cause of liberty and of letters disgust me more and more with political literature, and make me anxiously wish to get out of a kind of bustle and warfare for which my dejected spirits but ill qualify me.

Lord Fortescue to Mr. Miles

Castle Hill: September 26, 1792

I have been prevented acknowledging the favour of your letter sooner. Tom Paine is just where he ought to be—a member of the Convention of Cannibals! One would have thought it impossible that any society upon the face of the globe should have been fit for the reception of such a being until the late deeds of this National Convention have shown them to be most fully qualified. His vocation will not be complete, nor theirs either, till his head finds its way to the top of a pike, which will probably not be long first. The *export* trade would not hurt us if it was to extend to a few more of our active citizens, whom we could spare; but I dread the consequence of the numberless *importations* from that abandoned country. How we are to feed and provide for them I don't know, and the bulk of them are probably of very little better description than those who remain behind. Heaven preserve us from the last scourings of that sink of all crimes! The meeting of the Convention last Thursday must be eventful. I shall be curious to hear the result of it. If you should have any intelligence beyond what the newspapers contain, and should have leisure to communicate it, I shall receive it with thanks.[2]

---

[1] The French Embassy.

[2] 'I was told by Colonel Bosville, a declared friend of Thomas Paine, that his manners and conversation were so coarse that a stranger would

Mr. Aust to Mr. Miles

Foreign Office, — October 1792.

Many thanks for 'The Cave of Neptune.'[1] We have a clear confirmation of Dumouriez being surrounded by the Duke of Brunswick from the 24th to the 28th, in which interval there was a negotiation, which, it is supposed, was broken off when the messenger who brought the news to Brussels left the camp.

Minute.—Lord Elgin, who was Minister at Brussels, sent a messenger announcing the complete defeat of the French Army by the Duke of Brunswick at the very instant that the latter retreated, and, by so doing, ensured to France all the greatness she afterwards acquired. The despatches of Lord Elgin at this momentous period were frequently followed by others for the purpose of correcting errors in his information. I had this fact from the Under-Secretary of State.—W. A. M.

Sir Edward Newenham to Mr. Miles

Dublin: October 13, 1792.

I cannot divine how the King of Prussia could hope to make his entry into France without being certain of supplies of men and provisions; and to retreat without

feel disposed to order a servant to open the door and dismiss him, and that he also loved the brandy bottle. How humiliating that genius and profligacy should be united! Men of talent should feel the value of character, and make themselves respected by the rectitude of their conduct. They would then be a check on all bad Governments, and a benefit as well as a credit to mankind. If this man had felt the value of his talents; if, proud of character, he had properly estimated the force and profundity of his deep and inquisitive mind, he would have been a most formidable antagonist to sceptred tyrants; but his manners were vulgar, and his want of pride destroyed the force of his talents.'—MS. note, W. A. M. See *Conduct of France towards Great Britain Examined,* p. 246, &c.

[1] A poem published by Mr. Miles in 1784, and reviewed in *The Critical Review* for August in that year. It celebrates the victory of Lord Rodney.

any decisive action is unaccountable—the city of Spires taken, and the Austrians defeated. That is an unfortunate free city; it was three times sacked in the Marlborough war. The French will now have time to settle some general plan of confederacy, and gain strength every day, and arm 200,000 additional men. The Prussians and Austrians ought to have waited until the Russians and Spaniards were ready to enter France on different sides. The last accounts of the retreat of the combined forces pass all my political understanding. What brought Brunswick into France unless he was certain of recruits for his army, money, and provisions? The excessive watchfulness and the terrors of assassination must prevent any French loyalists from joining him unless he gained some important victory. Should he retreat, the Democrats will have an army of 400,000 men in the field next spring, well disciplined and well armed, and the interior Government of the country will be fully organised, although I think it impossible, even if left to themselves, that the whole of France can remain a republic. The South would never submit to the Paris Democrats. Lyons and Marseilles united are equal in strength, and five times as rich as the people of that unfortunate capital. England ought now to take a part. An English fleet, with a few regiments on board, ought to threaten St. Malo and Brest in order to draw part of the forces to those places. The last mail has just arrived. The French generals in pursuit of the Prussians and Austrians! Good God! How has this reverse happened? We ought to have 10,000 good troops to keep Ireland quiet. A French emigrant of considerable property, who escaped two months ago, has been at my house ever since without one penny of money.

Mr. Miles to Sir Edward Newenham

London: October 19, 1792

I avail myself, dear Newenham, of the departure of a messenger to Dublin with despatches to say that you are wrong in your politics. The King of Prussia is playing an artful game. He is as false as dicer's oaths, and on no account to be trusted. As to our taking part in the war, may Heaven bestow more wisdom on our Ministry than to adopt so fatal a measure! It is our interest to avoid hostilities. If the French *force* us into the business, we cannot avoid it. Adieu! Excuse haste.

M. —— to Mr. Miles

Paris: October 20, 1792

What a pity it is, my dear Miles, that the Queen did not accept the kind and heroic offer you made her through Madame de Tarente! Her dangers become greater and more evident every day—I may say every hour—so true has been your saying that she holds her life at the mercy of the mob! Her days are menaced at every instant. Everything announces a terrible crisis: one half of us are pale through fear, while the other half have fury in their countenance, and will make torrents of blood flow through all the streets of Paris, and become our assassins. Lusignan was wrong, or did not know what he said, when he told you, in answer to your observation of Robespierre being a man to be dreaded, that he was of no account—without credit or influence, and would never be anything. I do assure you he is to be dreaded. He has the people with him, and will be the leading man in the Convention. All your old friends have disappeared. The fatal 10th of August and the horrible 2nd of September have driven all the moderate men away, and Paris is become a den of tigers.[1] I live retired, leading a miserable life, distrusting everybody, and almost avoiding everybody. I will write to you when an opportunity serves, but God knows when that will be. Do not upon any account write to me; and, if you do not hear from me, conclude that I have followed the fate of others, and perished in the tempest.

Mr. Miles to Mr. T. Somers Cocks

7 Cleveland Row: October 29, 1792

My silence proceeds from indisposition, which incapacitates me for writing, and also from chagrin at the gloomy prospect opening to this country and to the rest of Europe! The conduct of Prussia amounts to a proof—or, at least, it illustrates one of the favourite positions of Parisian legislators, that 'Courts are fraudulent;' that of Berlin is, at this instant, playing an artful double game. My last packet to you contained a private letter from Sir Edward Newenham full of Irish politics, and some Irish papers that did not exhilarate my spirits. Much industry is employed to excite a rebellion in Ireland, and it is *there* that the infamous banditti in France expect the explosion will happen. You have already heard of the total evacuation of France by the Prussian troops, and I was this day informed, and by an authority that I respect, that the Duke of Brunswick had it in his power to destroy the entire army of his adversaries by the sacrifice of some 2,000 men. The Austrians and emigrants were all under arms, full of

---

[1] 'Voltaire says *que les Français sont ou singes ou tigres*; and, if he says true, I may venture to assert, from the samples we have of them in England—*les émigrés*—that the *tigers* have kept possession of their country and made us a present of the *monkeys*.'—W. A. M. *Conduct of France towards Great Britain*, p. 173.

ardour, and impatient for the signal to attack the enemy, when, after waiting some time, news arrived that a suspension had taken place, whereupon their hearts fell into their shoes. It is generally believed that the negotiation with Dumouriez related to the preservation of the royal family; there is, however, much mystery in the business, and perhaps much duplicity. I can aver for a fact, that the best disposed and best informed party at Paris are anxious to save the King and Queen, that they evade the trial, and, should it finally be forced upon them, it will be rendered as long as possible. This is a point that I have laboured at for these two months past with the confidential French emissary in this country, and he has assured me that these representations of mine have been transmitted to my friend Le Brun, Minister for Foreign Affairs. The retreat of the Duke of Brunswick has had the effect of a defeat, and, if the French do not quarrel among themselves, their Revolution is established and other revolutions will follow. It is this that I dread, and it is from this dread that my spirits are so much below proof, for, if France becomes hostile to us and is not enfeebled, we may be crushed. The atrocities committed in that distracted nation chill my hottest blood, and, when I behold those enormities not only escape justice, but meet with triumph and reward, I am almost led to doubt the existence of a divinity.

You have had the gout, and I have had the spleen, so you see we have all our complaints, and some malignant spirit or another haunts us through life. You will suppose from these grave reflections that I am in a philosophic mood worthy of the season; no such thing, I have a tolerable flow of spirits, but the misfortune is, I do not look forward, and the *retrospective* view is apt to fill the mind with gloom. Boys may look backward, but not men; for what can the former behold but the orchard that they have robbed, or the old woman whose pippins they have kicked into the kennel? But man, arrived at your age or mine, turns round and beholds a vast cemetery—a sepulchre of friends and relations, with the melancholy certainty of soon adding one to the bills of mortality! This world, after all, is a poor business, for, with all our omnipotence, all our boasted reason and affinity to heaven, we are miserable atoms, vibrating, like the pendulum of a clock, for one short, painful, sorry moment, between two eternities.[1]

Minute.—The reasons for the retreat of the Prussian army are described by Dumouriez himself. When he had collected his troops and was joined by Kellerman, the troops of the Duke of Brunswick were three leagues nearer to Rheims than were those of the French, and it was proposed that the Duke should instantly march to Paris. He agreed at first, but, revolving in his mind all the circumstances, he stated to the King of Prussia that, in the event of his meeting any check, however trifling, at Rheims, it would give time to Dumouriez to come up with him; that if he passed that city and advanced on his road to Paris there was no doubt he would be able to repel any force that might oppose him, but it must be recollected that these different bodies, falling back on each other as he advanced, would finally form a terrible mass of men by the time he reached Paris; and, although he would be able to make a stand, an army coming to their assistance in the rear of the Prussians, he, the Duke of Brunswick, would find himself between two

---

[1] 'A little section cut out of eternity and given us to do our work in: an Eternity before, an Eternity behind; and the small stream between floating swiftly from the one into the vast bosom of the other.'—*Robertson's Sermons.*

fires and be infallibly compelled to yield at discretion. It was then resolved to retreat, and the only condition required by the King of Prussia was that the Convention should grant to Louis XVI. a position, no matter what, in the State. When Dumouriez joined the army to take command, he found it in a terrible state of insubordination, in a state of mutiny. The men in the ranks as he passed along the line exclaimed, 'Voilà le petit —— qui nous a amené la guerre!' Of these he took no notice, but he seized an officer by the collar on hearing him use insulting language, and made an example of him.

W. A. M.

Mr. Miles to Mr. T. Somers Cocks

November 5, 1792

Prythee scold the lazy or ignorant blockhead of a postmaster at Hereford that the voluminous packet inclosed in an official cover from the Under-Secretary of State did not reach you in time. Town is so sterile in news, and conjecture is so busy—and, as usual, so erroneous—in accounting for the mysterious conduct of the Duke of Brunswick, that I have felt little inclination to add to the impertinences which you must have read in all the papers and have heard from all you met and conversed with. The most plausible reason alleged for the retreat of the Prussians is, that the lives of the King and Queen have been secured by a negotiation, which the world knows little about, even if it credits it; yet, however extraordinary the conduct of the Court of Berlin may appear, the rapid success of the French in various directions is not less so, and the temerity of their passing the Rhine puzzles my faith to believe, and my comprehension to account for, especially when I recollect that a military despot—the Landgrave of Hesse—exists within four leagues of their present post, Franckfort, and that his Serene Highness must advance and give them battle, or else risk a revolution in his dominions. Avaricious, brutal, and detested as he is, I shall not be surprised if a revolt has taken place among his subjects, and that the strong fortress of Hanau has declared for the French. That town contains some hundreds of French manufacturers, whom the Landgrave and his father had seduced to settle there, and whom a Government ignorant and tyrannic had neglected to encourage. In 1789 they had shown a spirit of disaffection. The contribution levied at Franckfort is absolutely a robbery, which these *freebooters* would commit here, if they could get over, and to a much larger extent than what they have done in Germany. The King of Sardinia is reduced to Piedmont, and his title to Nice, Savoy, and Sardinia are, or will be, gone, as well as the oath of the French that they would not make conquests nor be the first to wage offensive war. Geneva and the Thirteen Cantons are awed, and Brabant and Liège are menaced. The whole of them will become French. Perhaps these latter are already invaded, and the standard of revolt again hoisted in both countries. It is said that a cessation of hostilities has taken place. If so, the triumph of the French is complete, but if not, the confusion will become more serious and extensive, for the mischief most to be apprehended from the inroads of these *boutefeux* is, that their principles will be the easier disseminated through Italy and the empire, and the people throughout Europe may be seduced into a state of insurrection. If Dumouriez enters Brabant, he will find the *bons bourgeois* disposed to serve him. Liège will join in the revolt, and the fire will extend to all the ecclesiastical electorates on the Rhine, and destroy their episcopal Highnesses. I know too much of the profligacy, the insolence and tyranny of these little German Courts to wish well to the despots who inhabit them, but, as the Power that seeks to destroy them seems to have no bounds, and since freedom as well as tyranny is menaced by these Gallic legislators, I feel interested in the preservation of Mayence, Trèves, and Cologne, notwithstanding my aversion to priestly Governments. A friend of mine, General François de Wimpffen in the French service, proposed soon after the peace of 1762 to make the Rhine the frontier of France. He proposed it repeatedly afterwards; it is possible his idea will be realised. His brother commands at Thionville; he is a very gallant and gentlemanlike officer. I know him a little. His sentiments are changed, for in 1790 and 1791 he was a staunch Royalist and aristocrat. So much for foreign politics, which exhibit no pleasing aspect; and domestic politics will be to the full as unpleasant if parties do not unite for their common defence. The seditious, whose object is mischief, mean that the mine should be first sprung in Ireland, and emissaries go from shop to shop, introduce politics, and exclaim at the extravagance of allowing an individual a million per annum. The sum strikes the vulgar and the uninformed, while the comments made upon it add to their surprise and excite their indignation against the Civil List; no mention, however, is made that the judges, foreign ministers, and many pensions, are paid out of it, for this would reduce the mountain to a molehill. These are a few of the arts employed to raise discontents, and the success of the French rabble gives to faction and sedition a boldness that is no less offensive to decency than it is dangerous to good government. God grant that these 'levellers' may be scourged into moderation, and that fear may have the effect of virtue, and compel them to respect the rights of nations in their great zeal for establishing what they call the rights of men!

MR. MILES TO MR. LONG.

November 12, 1792.

I hear that Vandernoot and four deputies from Brussels are in town, and that Mr. Pitt, after having agreed to see them, has declined. I assure you that Vandernoot is not qualified to direct a revolution, though his coarse oratory may contribute to accomplish one; besides, his credit is almost extinguished in Brabant. He lost himself and his country when he fell into the pocket of that contemptible bigot, Van Eupen. Vonck, a barrister of more knowledge and better character, succeeded him in popularity, and established a party that adopted his name. The wonderful events that are taking place with a rapidity that bids defiance to all calculation may render this trifling information useful, and with that view it is given. Almost every Government on the Continent appears to have had a stroke of the palsy, and this third stroke, lately inflicted on the Austrian Netherlands, will prove mortal. Liège is again in commotion, and the bishop a fugitive. Heaven keep the distemper from this country, although, from all that I can learn, and from all that I see and hear, the Ministry will have much to do to keep everything quiet; and, as to Ireland, I expect that the sword of civil war will be drawn before the return of summer unless the demands of the Catholics are complied with. My labours in the midst of this shock of opinions and of universal bustle have been in all necessary directions. I have endeavoured to counteract both in England and in Ireland the venom of sedition; but stronger antidotes than what an individual can furnish must be administered, or the poison will spread like a leprosy, and infect the three kingdoms. Government must not at this moment strain its authority, or the string will snap. Neither must it show itself paralytic. Never was the maxim *suaviter in modo* more necessary than at this moment; but to observe it without relinquishing the *fortiter in re* demands much judgment and address. I do not perceive the great revolutions preparing in men's minds with indifference; on the contrary, I behold them with much pain and apprehension, and certainly I will oppose the whole force of my efforts—feeble, God knows, at the best—with unremitting zeal to this torrent of opinion that threatens to subvert every state in Europe. I must confess that I have very little hope of success. I have no confidence in any Government being bolstered up by newspaper articles, and the period is approaching very fast when such means will be of no avail.[1] The success of the French will have a very bad effect in this country; it will inspire the seditious with boldness and decide the wavering. Custine and Dumouriez, at the head of troops that know the value of victory, seem to be inflamed with a kind of zeal like that of Omar, and hitherto they have preached this new species of Mahometanism with a degree of success equal to that of the Arabian. If the fury of these modern Caliphs is not successfully and speedily checked, every sceptre in Europe will be broken before the close of the present century, and the Jacobins be everywhere triumphant. I am much afraid the storm will increase and extend to these happy shores. Our best resource, perhaps, would be an alliance with a people now be-

---

[1] At this date, the Ministerial papers contained letters, or articles, written by Mr. Miles, with various signatures, almost daily.

come formidable by being united, and whose union has been occasioned by the imbecility and wickedness of the nations that surround them.

What is your idea of a union of parties? I am not sufficiently versed in the intrigues of this country to know how the leading men in Administration feel, or rather how Mr. Pitt is disposed on this subject, but such a measure appears to me to be one of the means of salvation for the empire, and I have some reason to believe that the measure is as practicable as it is necessary. One thing is certain, that the reign of delusion is at an end, and that no Opposition whatever can any longer make a stalking horse of patriotism to ride into power. The understanding of the people has been too often insulted, and their confidence too often abused by this species of swindling, for such means to serve any *ex-party* in future, and the very best thing that Opposition can do is to join with Ministers, or they will endanger the whole.[1]

Mr. Miles to Lord Fortescue

November 12, 1792

The political atmosphere in this country is becoming very gloomy, and I am much afraid that the storm will

[1] 'The French Embassy had some hope that a Coalition Ministry would be formed, which would be more favourable to their cause. The summer of 1792 was occupied by correspondence, interviews, and conversations, all bearing on the possibility of including Pitt and Fox in the same Cabinet, and providing the country with a Ministry resting on a broad foundation. The true history of these intrigues has yet to be written. The account generally given of them is that Pitt was not unwilling to receive some of the Whig party, but that the scheme shattered upon the obstinacy and impracticability of Fox. . . . It is certain that the idea of a coalition was mentioned to Pitt and the King in June, but the Duke of Leeds' diary shows that neither of them seriously entertained the idea, and that Fox was perfectly justified in believing it to be impossible.'— *The Fortnightly Review*, February 1883, p. 260, article by Mr. Oscar Browning.

not subside on the Continent without making us feel most lamentably its sad effects. I do not know how Ministers feel under all these alarms, but the successes of the French seem to have occasioned an entire revolution in the minds of men, and you will find that the thrones on the Continent will be levelled to the ground, the sceptres of kings broken, and monarchy abolished before the close perhaps of the present century. A universal change is preparing in the opinions, manners, and customs of men; whether for the better or the worse, time must decide. It is an experiment which I shall regret to see tried, for I am an advocate for peace. It will give me infinite pleasure to find that your Lordship approves of my humble efforts to preserve this country from the calamities of war, and especially at a moment like the present, when the general fermentation would render such a measure extremely hazardous, if not eventually fatal, to monarchy in England.

Minute: November 13, 1792.—This morning Scipion Mourgue called and informed me that a Minister would soon be named to this Court by the Executive Council at Paris; that, if he was received, an alliance would be proposed; but that, if rejected, ill consequences would result, and war would be declared against England. I inquired whether he was authorised to make this statement. He replied, 'Not absolutely, but that he would be soon.' I asked whether he knew for a certainty that it was the wish of France to be united to this country. He answered that, if he had no other assurances, the debates in the Committee of Ministers proved it, and, moreover, he knew from his correspondence with the Executive that it was their wish and intention to put the good or bad dispositions of England very speedily to the test. I mentioned the possibility of being deceived by France, and expressed the fear that the distrust prevailing in this country might operate against any treaty of alliance with his nation. His reply was that the actual Government could be better depended upon than that of Versailles. My next question, as to whether the French Government would pledge itself not to attempt any revolution in England by intrigue and cabal, received an answer in the affirmative—that France felt herself so powerful, as also so well-disposed towards England, that she would make the offer of friendship for the purpose of securing the peace of the world; but, on the other hand, she as little dreaded England as she did the Republic of Ragusa.

Mourgue acknowledged that the *intention* of England would be demanded under the impression that it had already been resolved to take part against France in the spring. I gathered from the drift of his conversation that the Council at Paris was much alarmed; that people had been employed to start questions in the debating societies in London with the view of inflaming the populace against a *neutrality* considered dangerous and suspicious. He further gave me to understand that the present moment was favourable for a union with France; that, as it was known on the Continent that I was a friend to liberty, Le Brun now made the offer to me to pave the way for this desirable alliance, and that, if I would undertake it, I should receive every confidential communication that I could desire relative to the views of France as to the basis on which it was proposed to form a treaty. My questions are to be transmitted to Paris by the messenger this evening.[1]

[1] 'This is the origin of the interview which M. Maret afterwards had with Mr. Pitt, and it deserves attention, not only from its matter, but from its date, for it was at the period when the storm which has

In September I received a first visit from the Abbé Noël; he called on the part of Le Brun with the object of my obtaining for him an interview with Mr. Pitt. The abbé, I believe, had been at the same college with Le Brun. But I declined to interfere until I was authorised by the Executive Council to make the application. Since that date Mourgue and Noël have frequently called and have shown anxiety in favour of peace. Mr. Pitt received much about the same time similar information from a gentleman worthy of credit, and who had been a member of one of the ephemeral Administrations in France (I certainly do not mean M. Bertrand), but due credit was not given to the accuracy of his statement. Mr. Pitt would have done well to have attended to it. Unhappily, a faithful representation of the actual state of the public mind in France is attributed, not to truth or patriotism, but to Jacobinical principles or prejudices.[1]—W. A. M.

since fatally burst upon both countries assumed a very ill-foreboding aspect. It is also worthy of observation that the Executive Council had made up their minds at this time on the part they had resolved to take.'—*Authentic Correspondence with Le Brun, &c.*, p. 87; Append. p. 57.

[1] 'Au moment le plus critique de l'invasion prussienne, Le Brun fit partir pour Londres un de ses chefs de divisions chargé d'une mission secrète. Cet agent était Noël. A l'époque de son départ (30 Août) les événements prenaient une allure telle que l'intervention officieuse de l'Angleterre semblait notre dernière planche de salut. Noël devait s'aboucher avec un Anglais nommé Miles, ancienne connaissance de Le Brun. Cette homme, désintéressé ou non, a mérité de la France un souvenir. Il fit, jusqu'à la dernière heure, d'intelligents efforts pour combiner des démarches utiles au maintien de la paix. Il ne cessait de répéter que Chauvelin compromettait tout : pressait Le Brun d'envoyer quelqu'autre agent, dont les antécédents et le caractère n'inspireraient pas la même répulsion, et promettait de le mettre en relation directe avec William Pitt lui-même, qui était loin, suivant Miles, de partager l'aversion irréconciliable de ses collègues pour les derniers changements politiques survenus en France. Dans les premiers jours de Septembre, notre situation intérieure imposait les plus larges concessions pour obtenir l'appui du cabinet anglais. . . . Noël ne peut arriver jusqu'au premier ministre ; nous ne savons s'il faut attribuer cette exclusion seulement à

Mr. Miles to Mr. Aust

November 15, 1792

When I perceived a reluctance to acknowledge the French Republic, I declared that the Republic of France was fixed beyond the power of Europe, combined as it was against her, to prevent it; that the existence of the monarch, or of the monarchy, was not an object for which the prosperity of this nation ought to be sacrificed; and that it would be better to do with a good grace in the first instance what we should hereafter be compelled to do with a bad one. This, I found, was very unpalatable; but, convinced of its justice, I insisted upon it, and, when lately quitting Mr. Long in Alice's Coffee-House,[1] I could not help peevishly exclaiming to him, How long is this country to be misgoverned in its foreign policy? I repeat to you that history does not afford an instance of perfect co-operation, or of any good resulting from the confederacy of many Powers; that the present coalition will make France, and, perhaps, unmake England, or, at all events—and mark my words—no good will result from it either to ourselves or to the rest of Europe.[2]

Mr. Aust to Mr. Miles

Foreign Office: November 16, 1792

I know that Mr. Pitt has been extremely engaged these three days. If you have no objection to write

l'impression d'horreur produite par les massacres de Septembre, ou bien aussi aux antécédents personnels de cet agent, ex-abbé, de mœurs fort relâchées, et ci-devant journaliste révolutionnaire.—*Maret, Duc de Bassano*, par Baron Ernouf, Paris, 1884, pp. 79, 80.

[1] 'Alice's, at the Parliament House.'—*Social Life in the Reign of Queen Anne*, by Ashton, vol. ii.

[2] 'October 1796.—England, which had commenced the war with so many confederates, saw herself not only deprived of all her maritime allies, but the whole coasts of Europe, from the Texel to Gibraltar, arrayed in fierce hostility against her.'—*Alison's History of Europe*, v. 306.

your intelligence to me, as it concerns Lord Grenville's department, you may be assured of my immediately laying it before his Lordship. I shall be in Duke Street this evening from seven to eight o'clock, if you should have leisure to look in upon me.

Mr. Miles to Mr. Aust
November 16, 1792

In the course of a week or ten days I may have occasion to request Mr. Pitt to admit me to an interview. As to Lord Grenville, there is a reserve about him that looks like distrust or pride, or perhaps it is the offensive offspring of both; this occasions much dislike, and is not calculated to facilitate the public service. Yet, as I consider his Lordship the same as Mr. Pitt, I have no objection to impart my foreign intelligence to him. I must observe that, without great judgment and address, the Government of this country will have a tempest to encounter that may end in the wreck of the constitution. I tell you that a fierce and tremendous storm is brewing, the effects of which it will require much wisdom to avert. I will call on you this evening.

Mr. Miles to Mr. Aust
November 17, 1792

I send for your perusal a copy of my letter to Mr. Long written on the 12th instant. The more I reflect upon the actual state of public affairs, the more I am convinced of the necessity for that union of parties which you pointed out last night; so much so, that it appears to me the only expedient to save, I will not say the country—for *that*, thank Heaven, is beyond the reach of either faction—but the monarchy. In my opinion, then, all contention for power must cease: every man must join heart and hand, and put his shoulder to the wheel, or the cart will remain in the slough. An entire change in the political system of Europe is about to take place, and the impulse that produces this change cannot but materially affect the *internal* and *external* administration of affairs in this country. I do not despond, because I know there is a force in England equal to any contingency that can happen, but that force should be concentrated and properly directed. For myself, so far from wishing to engage in any of the wild and visionary schemes of our modern reformers, I repeat to you what I said to the Duke of Leeds, that while my mind retains its health and my arm its vigour I will write or fight for the constitution, as occasion may require, to the last moment of my existence.

MR. AUST TO MR. MILES

November 17, 1792.

Lord Grenville arrived at the office just as I was reading your letter to Mr. Long. I am curious to know whether he and Mr. Pitt encourage, or discourage, the idea of a *union* of parties. I have delivered your message to his Lordship, who says he must decline receiving the communication you offer; but, from his manner, I think it right to say that the refusal did not seem personal to you, but to *anything* from the French Executive Council. I had given your Irish packet to the porter before I met your servant.

Minute: November 18, *Sunday.*—Mr. Long called upon me. We had a lengthened conversation on the affairs of Ireland, France, and England. I found from him that Ministry were disposed to grant the elective franchise to the Catholics in Ireland. On the subject of French affairs, I assured him that the Republic was fixed beyond the forces combined against it. He acknowledged that the Powers on the Continent could do nothing against France, and that the life of Louis XVI. was not to be put in competition with the interests of this kingdom; but he seemed unwilling to acknowledge the new Government. As to this country, he said, the Ministry were resolved to act with vigour against those who should attempt to disturb the public peace or inflame the public mind; that Grey, Lambton, and Whitbread went one way, but that the Duke of Portland and his friends would be with Government on all great questions, and that there would be *no union* of parties—that is, no coalition. I mentioned my apprehensions of a tumult in England from the entire revolution that had taken place in men's minds, but he seemed perfectly assured that all would be well.

I wish to stop the effusion of blood, and to see this country relieved from a state of anxiety and imminent danger. France is disposed to an alliance with England; but she will soon put our good or bad disposition to the proof by demanding an acknowledgment of the Republic; and a refusal will produce war—a war more sanguinary and furious than ever yet distinguished the contests of the two nations since the days of Edward III. Ministry in this country affect to treat the Executive Council with contempt—so they did the Congress in America; but the Congress triumphed, and Lord Grenville, with all his *hauteur*, will be compelled to treat with statesmen who, whatever may have been their origin or former social position, have already proved, by turning the tables against those who would have crushed them, that they possess no mean knowledge of the art of government.—W. A. M.

Mr. Miles to Mr. Long

November 19, 1792

I lament that I missed seeing you when I called this morning in Hill Street. The matter I wished to communicate was that Spain is veering fast round to the French interests. I have strong reasons to believe that her acknowledgment of the new Republic will not be long delayed—at all events, the French have a powerful interest in the Spanish Council—and, if this should be the fact, you will find the *Family Compact* converted into a *National Compact*. In all probability I shall be better informed before Saturday, and, *in the interim*, I wish to know whether any communications from the Executive Council in France will be acceptable to Mr. Pitt. Should the French be able to establish their present Government, I will not conceal from you my wish that this country may acknowledge the Republic, as England ought to do, not only from motives of justice and from the respect due from one nation to another, but even from the convictions of sound policy. I hear you are going out of town. Let me see you on your return.

Mr. Miles to Mr. Pitt

November 26, 1792

You may rest in full confidence on the authenticity of the following information, which is too important at this awful crisis to be withheld from you a moment. I have it from a source in Paris that is unquestionable, and I pledge my credit with you for the veracity of the intelligence:—' L'Espagne n'en est pas si éloignée qu'on le pense. The Count d'Aranda tells everything to M. Bourgoing, our Minister at Madrid. Yet we would prefer the neutrality of England to an alliance with Spain, and, if England agrees to it, measures will be taken to open the Spanish markets in South America to her manufactures. D'Aranda told M. Bourgoing what was lately communicated to him from your Minister at Madrid, and we can count upon D'Aranda.'

Mr. Miles to Mr. Aust

November 26, 1792.

The decree that arrived yesterday from Paris is written in blood and denounces war against all the world! An attempt will be made, I believe, to have it repealed, as the general opinion is that the Convention was *surprised* into the measure. The more I reflect on it, the more I am struck with horror at the unexampled infamy of a 'declaration' formidable at this moment, extravagant as it is, and which is meant to cut the sinews or rather to hamstring all existing Governments. One of the ideas of the French Executive is to form an alliance with Holland, which, they say, is ripe for revolt, and also with Flanders and Brabant. I am told that the object of the mission, which Lord Grenville has promised to receive, is to know the intentions of France relative to the Seven United Provinces, which, by the by, is tolerably well explained by the decree of the 19th instant.

M. Sémonville is at Corsica, whence he will soon depart for Constantinople with M. Truguet and ten sail of the line. The French Admiral is in pursuit of some Russian vessels in the Gulf of Genoa; he means to capture them. It is meant to excite the Turk to declare war against Russia. Count d'Aranda at Madrid has no secrets from Bourgoing, the French Minister Plenipotentiary. France will force the Spanish markets in the South Seas to be opened to us if we will only pledge ourselves to be *neutral*; whilst, in the event of our refusing, the French will offer to insure Gibraltar to Spain, on condition that *neutrality* shall be observed by *her*.

I am promised on Thursday, or sooner, some very important intelligence. In the interim I beg the favour of you to lay this letter before Lord Grenville for his perusal, with my best respects to his Lordship, and a humble offer of my services to go to Paris in case it should be necessary to send anyone, as I have reason to believe that I should be well received and be enabled to serve our country.[1]

Mr. Miles to M. Scipion Mourgue

November 28, 1792

I did not delay a moment after your departure yesterday to communicate to Mr. Pitt, according to your desire, that, on the part of the Executive Power, you wished to have the honour of a private interview with him, or with the Minister for Foreign Affairs. Mr. Pitt has asked for your name. You have failed to inform me whether you are fully authorised by the Executive Power to treat with the Court of London. I shall wait for your reply before giving an answer to

---

[1] Déclaration pour accorder fraternité et secours à tous les peuples qui voudront recouvrer leur liberté : —

'Du 19 Novembre, 1792 = 23 du même mois

'La Convention nationale déclare, au nom de la nation française, qu'elle accordera fraternité et secours à tous les peuples qui voudront recouvrer leur liberté, et charge le pouvoir exécutif de donner aux généraux les ordres nécessaires pour porter secours à ces peuples, et défendre les citoyens qui auraient été vexés, ou qui pourraient l'être pour la cause de la liberté.

'La Convention nationale décrète que le pouvoir exécutif donnera des ordres aux généraux de la république pour faire imprimer et proclamer en toutes les langues, dans toutes les contrées qu'ils parcourront avec leurs armées, le décret rendu.'—*Collection du Louvre*, xii. 213.

the Minister. If you have any propositions to make to the English Minister on the part of the Executive Power, do not close your despatch to Dumouriez until you see me. It is absolutely necessary that I should speak to you. *Bon soir*.[1]

Minute: November 29.—Long called upon me; he wished to know the particulars of Mourgue's mission, he being authorised by Mr. Pitt. I learned from him that if France would enter into a negotiation with the Court of Vienna and surrender at least a portion of its conquests, and consent to a general pacification, the Republic would be acknowledged—the not insisting on the opening of the Scheldt to be always understood. Soon after his departure I received from him the following note: 'Will you introduce me to M. Mourgue this forenoon? If you can do so, I will call upon you for that purpose, provided you think he will make his communication to *me*. It seems the best channel, for you must see how impossible it is for Mr. Pitt or Lord Grenville to admit him to an interview as things stand.' Another note was almost immediately afterwards handed to me by a King's messenger from Mr. Long as follows: 'Pray let me know whether you have heard from M. Mourgue, and whether he has made any appointment for us to meet this evening.'

[1] 'Mr. Miles, who during the time that he was intrusted with a mission to the Prince-Bishop of Liège had contracted an intimacy with Le Brun, afterwards French Minister for Foreign Affairs, who continued his correspondence with Le Brun and other men of consequence in France, till the National Convention thought proper to break with England, who had frequent intercourse in the latter part of the year 1792 with French agents in London, and even acted as mediator between them and the British Ministry, who may be supposed therefore to have been well acquainted with the views of the French Government.'—Herbert Marsh, i. 141.

The messenger informed me that the Minister and Mr. Long were alone, and were waiting for my answer. This extreme impatience is a proof that Mr. Pitt desires to preserve peace.—W. A. M.

Mr. Miles to Mr. Long

November 29, 1792

I have reflected much on the business in question, and, as the result of the different conversations which I have had with M. Mourgue and the Abbé Noël, I am convinced that a general pacification is practicable, provided Mr. Pitt will make it the *sine quâ non* to acknowledge the Republic. The spirit of loyalty lately manifested in the provinces, in our theatres, and in the Association at the Crown and Anchor Tavern, have very much alarmed all the French emissaries in England; and I am certain that, if it could be intimated to the Executive Power that the British Cabinet would recognise its authority on condition that it recalled its troops within its own frontier and entered into a negotiation with Vienna, the whole affair would be instantly concluded. I feel so assured of Le Brun's sentiments on this subject— and he has certainly the most weight in the Council— that I am satisfied he would come into that idea immediately; indeed, I may almost venture, from the knowledge in my possession, to affirm it. Acquainted as I am with Le Brun, and having rendered him an important service in a moment of very great distress, standing as I do high in his opinion, I will make, if Mr. Pitt approves, an excursion to Paris, and sound him on this question, *sans le nommer Monsieur Pitt, sans le compromettre*. I can set off at five minutes' notice and would not be absent more than six days. I am positive that peace can be obtained; and, as I told you this morning, Mr. Pitt can *will* it. Your letter has this instant arrived. I have had no answer from Mourgue. I am all impatience to know Mr. Pitt's determination.

MR. MILES TO MR. PITT

November 29, 1792.

I have the honour to inclose copies of the letters which I wrote to M. Mourgue yesterday, together with his answer. On his leaving me yesterday afternoon I pressed him repeatedly not to deceive me with respect to his position. I said to him: 'Ne me trompez pas, monsieur; ne m'ienduisez pas en erreur. Etes-vous vraiment autorisé par le pouvoir exécutif d'entrer en négotiation avec la Cour de Londres?' His answer was: 'Oui, monsieur, je le suis.' He added: 'Qu'il rendroit l'âme à Monsieur Pitt, et dès qu'il l'a vu il feroit partir une dépêche à Monsieur Dumouriez pour suspendre des opérations contre les Hollandois.' He assured me that the decree of the 19th instant will be amended in such a manner as will do away all cause of offence to nations not actually at war with the Republic, and that orders have been despatched to Dumouriez to retard his designs against Holland by not opening the Scheldt. You will, perhaps, be surprised when you are informed that it was one of the extravagant projects of that madman, Dumouriez, to march direct into Holland and countenance the revolt of the party disaffected to the Prince of Orange. I have given M. Mourgue to understand that an attempt to open the Scheldt would not only be a breach of faith on the part of his country, but, by attacking our ally, be tantamount to a declaration of war against England. The decree offering succour to those who revolt against their respective Governments is to be amended by the addition of the words: '*The oppressed people of those nations at war with the Republic.*'

I will only trespass further to assure you that, in the several conversations I have had with M. Scipion Mourgue, as also in my letters to the Minister of Foreign Affairs in France, I have endeavoured to convince them of the iniquity and madness of wantonly disturbing the repose of this country. The father of M. Mourgue is a confidential friend of Dumouriez, and was Minister of the Interior on the disgraceful 20th of June.

Mr. Miles to Mr. Pitt

November 30, 1792

Forgive me if I again repeat my firm belief that by an immediate interference you have it in your power to restore peace to Europe. I am not apprised of what M. Mourgue has to propose, or whether he wishes only to know the intentions of the British Court respecting the French Republic.

Allow me to express my conviction that Le Brun would open himself to me without reserve, and that all operations against Holland and the Scheldt would be renounced *in toto* if only the Executive Council were assured that, by such a renunciation, and by agreeing to enter into a negotiation for peace with the Courts of Vienna and Berlin, this country would acknowledge the Republic. It is the great point they aim at; and, as the Convention has not yet decreed what the Council has recommended, I wish you would permit me to set off instantly to Paris, and prevent, if possible, a blunder and an extravagance that would extend and prolong the flames of war. The experiment is worth trying. I desire no recompense but the continuance of your good opinion, no expenses paid except my post-horses, and

I will be in Paris on Monday early enough to breakfast with Le Brun, and before this day week you shall know his intentions fully.

I am told that the emigrants bring their arms, and that they arrive daily in numbers in the character of deserters from the Republican army. These arms may be turned against us, and the fable of the Trojan horse realised. I beg, therefore, to submit to your judgment and reflection the propriety of compelling all foreigners arriving with arms in any part of his Majesty's dominions to deposit them at the Custom Houses of the respective ports where they land, giving to the collector or mayor their names, situation in life, and the object of their coming to England.[1]

MR. MILES TO MR. LONG

November 30, 1792

I have this instant received the enclosed note, from which you will perceive that M. Mourgue has no objection to meet *you* to-morrow morning at ten o'clock. I am really of opinion that, if you obtain nothing material or satisfactory from him, Mr. Pitt would do well to let me run to Paris and back. I am acquainted with Carré and Grouvelle. Mourgue's father is also at Paris, and I know he will aid my efforts most forcibly. I have taken the liberty to repeat this offer to Mr. Pitt since I saw you, but in my zeal to serve him I travelled too fast, for I offered to be at Paris on Monday *morning*. Monday *night* I might be there, and will be, if only the wind permits, and I set off before nine o'clock this evening. I told Mr. Pitt that I require no recompense. I *know* that by an immediate interference war may be prevented. If Mr. Pitt approves of my

[1] This letter was the origin of the Alien Bill. See *Minute*, December 8, 1792.

idea he may, perhaps, think that I should stay some days in Paris, in which case a messenger might accompany me and bring back my despatches.

Minute: November 30.—At nine o'clock this evening Long called and stayed until ten. We talked on various public questions. I found him candid, unreserved, and communicative. He stated that, if the French would desist from opening the Scheldt, the Republic would be acknowledged and peace restored. I wrote to Mourgue to be with me at ten o'clock to-morrow. I am certain peace may be made if my advice is attended to—but Brabant, Flanders, and Liège must be free. Long vowed to me that not one member of either House of Parliament received a farthing for their vote.—W. A. M.

Minute: December 1.—At half-past nine Mourgue came. I found him elated with the expected interview, and as much a *garçon* as ever boasted in the reign of Louis XIV. He talked of the glorious principles of equity, of the imprescriptible rights of men, and the determination of France to open the Scheldt. 'If England,' he continued, 'opposed the measure, *tant pis*—so much the worse for her—the arms of France would vindicate her just pretensions in favour of the Anversois, and it was impossible that France could recede.' In that case, I replied, war is inevitable, for England was bound by treaty to defend her ally if attacked. Mourgue exhibits in his conduct a proof of the difficulty there is in some minds to bear with prosperity. A few months since he was in extreme despondency, and on the affair of the 10th of August he resigned his political employment. He was violent against the Republican party; and both he and his father have frequently declared to me in their conversation and letters an attachment to monarchy, that no other forms of government would suit their country, and that Pétion and Manuel were two villains. Scipion has changed his sentiments and principles, and now talks of the virtue, the pride, and the courage of a Republican.

At half-past ten Mr. Long came, agreeable to the appointment. I introduced them to each other, and, having already apprised Mourgue that Mr. Pitt had commissioned Mr. Long to hear what he had to say on the part of the Executive Council, I left them together for an hour and a half. Long afterwards informed me that nothing could be done with Mourgue, who, it appears, had insisted on the rights of the Republic, and on 'the immutable laws of nature,' much in the same strain as that with which he had previously occupied me. I expressed the wish that I could go to Paris and try my personal influence with Le Brun. War is a hazardous measure at this time; the French know it, and count upon it. Mourgue has this very day told me, and I cannot deny it, that there is much discontent in this country and that the people are ripe for revolt.[1]

---

[1] 'Trois jours après [November 19] la Convention lui créait un nouvel embarras [a new embarrassment for Le Brun] en déclarant " qu'elle accorderait protection et secours à tous les peuples qui voudraient conserver leur liberté." Elle paraissait ainsi prendre sous son patronage toutes les insurrections qui pourraient se produire en Hollande, en Irlande, jusque dans l'intérieur de l'Angleterre ! Cette provocation semblait concorder avec la conduite de Chauvelin, qui entretenait des rapports secrets, ou qu'il croyait tels, avec des clubs dont il s'exagérait l'importance. Il assurait que le gouvernement anglais n'oserait pas nous faire la guerre, ou que, s'il l'osait, il en serait châtié par une révolution semblable à celle du 10 Août. Le Brun n'avait pu dissimuler à ses collègues et au comité diplomatique ces appréciations, conformes aux passions du temps. Elles déterminèrent les ovations qu'on fit aux députés de ces Jacobins de Londres, de Manchester, de Norwich : manifestations insensées, qui ne firent qu'irriter non seulement le ministère, mais le vrai peuple anglais.'
—Ernouf, p. 83. See *Conduct of France towards Great Britain*, pp. 230-235.

M. Bourgoing, Minister from the Republic at Madrid, has written to the French Consuls at the different ports in Spain to send away all the French vessels. France, by relinquishing a project which does not concern either her foreign interests or her internal government, has it in her power to avoid involving herself in a contest in which she must *eventually* fall the sacrifice, but she seems bent on mischief to others and to herself. It is now a fortnight since Mourgue came to me with the assurance that he was authorised by the Executive Council to request an interview with our Minister. —W. A. M.

Mr. Long to Mr. Miles

December 1, 1792

The 'Sun' has established its reputation in the circles in which I live for good writing, to which I know you have contributed much, and I have traced you through several of the different signatures. I send you a copy of the 'Protest' against Paine's 'Rights of Man' doubled down in that part which relates to the Civil List, and which answers the question you put to me. The 'Protest' contains excellent matter and good reasoning. I wish the style was as forcible as it would have been from your pen. It is, however, clearly the best answer to Paine that has appeared, except a book written by the American, Adams, which is admirable, proving that the American Government is not founded upon the absurd doctrine of the pretended rights of man, and that, if it had been, it could not have stood for a week.

Minute: Sunday, December 2.—Received a note from Mourgue informing me that he is going to Paris. He tells me that Mr. Pitt, who had promised to see M. Maret at eight o'clock last evening, made excuses on his arrival, and did not receive him until eleven o'clock this morning. I called upon Mourgue. He read to me Maret's despatch to the Executive Council, from which it appears that he and the Minister were pleased with each other, and that the latter had agreed to treat with Maret as agent from the Council. Mourgue gave me some particulars of the interview between Lord Grenville and M. Chauvelin—it was a private interview on Thursday last. He inquired whether I thought the Minister would send an agent to Paris. I drove at once to Long's house and asked him the question. He replied that he knew nothing of the intentions of Mr. Pitt on that subject. To my remark that the Minister lost many friends and gave offence by his reserve and coldness, Long admitted that it would be better if Mr. Pitt had lived more in the world and had travelled more; that he had a distrust as to the sincerity of every one that approached him with whom he was not intimate; and that, if he acknowledged the letters he received, he would conciliate many friendships. We then conversed on the probable consequences of the Revolution in France as respects England. I insisted on an alliance as the only means of preserving peace; and, in reply to an observation made by Long, I remarked that Ministers too often look only to the moment, content to live by shifts, from hand to month, instead of providing for the future by measures calculated to insure the public weal. He inquired about the character of the Abbé Noël. I returned to Mourgue. He starts to-morrow morning at three o'clock for Paris, taking with him the despatch from Maret and a letter from me to Le Brun.[1]

[1] A translation of this despatch from Maret to Le Brun will be found in the *Annual Register*, 1792, *State Papers*, p. 190. It gives an account of the interview with Pitt.—See *Archives, Quai d'Orsay*, Paris, vol. 584, p. 19, for the original.

Mr. Miles to M. Le Brun

London: December 2, 1792 [1]

I write a single word by my friend Scipion Mourgue, who leaves early to-morrow morning for Paris. His talents, his zeal, and above all his *civisme*, are already known to you. Attached to his country and to the rights of humanity, he has not ceased since his arrival in England to labour for the prosperity of the one and in favour of the other. Interested as I am in the welfare of the two nations, I have always desired to see them united by the most sincere alliance. In conformity with this idea, and full of ardour for its accomplishment, I have long sought to bring our respective countries together; and if you feel the same desire to spare human blood and to assure peace to the world, my exertions will not be without fruit.

I recall with infinite pleasure the time that we were at Liège, and, though I owe you a grudge for not having replied to my reiterated inquiries through M. Noël for news of our mutual friend, the Burgomaster Fabry, I cannot deny myself the pleasure of meeting you again. I have many things to say to you; but M. Mourgue is in haste, and he is master of my opinions. I refer you to him to explain the sentiments of esteem with which I am, &c. &c.

Mr. Miles to M. Maret

December 3, 1792

The circumstance which affords me the long-desired pleasure of making your acquaintance is infinitely

---

[1] Received in Paris, December 6. *Archives, Quai d'Orsay*, vol. 584, p. 12.

agreeable, since it enables me to obtain, notwithstanding obstacles and intrigues, the faint hope of a speedy alliance between our two countries. For more than ten years I have used all the means in my power to effect this great object; but if there is to be success, it is essential that prejudices which have so long blinded the two nations should be uprooted and effaced. Happily, both for France and England, and, indeed, for the whole world, the moment appears, as I think, to have arrived when Reason, the elder daughter of Truth, in reclaiming her rights, will no longer permit herself to be deceived or enchained. These sentiments, Sir, proceed from my heart. But I will not conceal from you my well-grounded fear that, if the Executive Power in Paris thinks of meddling with our internal affairs, or seeks by direct or indirect means to sow dissension in England, this alliance, so much desired by all sensible people, will never be realised.

I shall have the honour of waiting on you without fail at eleven o'clock this morning and of presenting a letter from our mutual friend, Scipion Mourgue. In the mean time, I beg you to believe me, &c. &c.[1]

[1] 'A l'époque de la bataille de Jemmapes [Nov. 6, 1792], les vues des hommes qui exerçaient la principale influence sur les actes du pouvoir exécutif n'allaient que jusqu'à l'établissement d'un État belge indépendant. C'était encore sur cette base que Lebrun voulait préparer un arrangement, quand il adjoignit à Noël un autre agent, le jeune Mourgue, dont le père avait tenu le portefeuille de l'intérieur dans le ministère Girondin de Louis XVI, et ne s'était retiré qu'avec Dumouriez. Mourgue père était connu par des travaux sérieux, notamment par un ouvrage estimé en Angleterre, sur le traité de commerce de 1786. La première pensée du ministre avait été d'adjoindre Mourgue fils à Chauvelin, avec le titre de secrétaire de légation, et ce fut pour prendre possession de ce poste qu'il fut envoyé à Londres au mois d'Octobre. L'amour-propre de Chauvelin vit dans cet arrangement une tentative maladroitement déguisée pour le remettre en tutelle. Il refusa d'y accéder, sous prétexte qu'il n'avait pas été consulté. Mourgue resta alors comme agent secret, et fit preuve d'intelligence et de zèle. Il n'existait

Minute: December 3.—I had the pleasure this day of making the acquaintance of M. Maret, whom I found extremely affable, frank, and communicative. He told me he had been well received by Mr. Pitt, who appeared to be equally well pleased with him; the conversation had been very long, and he had assured Mr. Pitt that instructions were transmitted to Dumouriez to be circumspect in his conduct towards the Dutch, and to make no attack either on the sovereignty, or privileges, or independence of that people. Maret came by Flanders and saw Dumouriez at the battle of Jemmapes, November 6. Dumouriez had resolved to besiege the Austrians in their intrenchments, as if they had been in a citadel, and to take them by storm, if they had not fought. A schism having broken out among the patriots at Liège, Maret had reconciled their differences, and they had entered that city as friends. Fabry had been at Bouillon. Chauvelin, informed of the uneasiness of Ministers as to Holland, had written to Lord Grenville desiring an interview merely to apprise him of the determination of the Executive Council not to invade Holland. Lord Grenville answered the note

contre lui aucun motif de répulsion personnelle : aussi Miles laissa bientôt espérer qu'une rencontre de ce nouvel agent avec Pitt ne serait pas impossible. . . .

'Le but réel de son voyage (Maret) était de prendre la place de Mourgue dans la conférence secrète qu'on espérait obtenir prochainement avec Pitt, grâce aux démarches de l'agent anglais Miles. Cette substitution, combinée entre les ministres Lebrun et Garat, et plusieurs membres du comité diplomatique, semblait commandée par de graves considérations. Le républicanisme de Mourgue était suspect aux exaltés de Paris. De plus, il avait eu à se plaindre de Chauvelin, et, comme on savait d'avance qu'il serait question de celui-ci d'une manière peu favorable dans ces communications secrètes, le rapport de l'homme dont il avait dédaigneusement repoussé le concours aurait paru entaché de partialité. L'exagération patriotique, qui rendait le jeune ambassadeur si nuisible à Londres, faisait malheureusement sa force à Paris.'—Ernouf, pp. 82, 86.

in a cold, equivocal manner, and declined to see him on the ground of etiquette. The communication from Chauvelin was made privately, not officially, he having no authority. The next day the correspondence of Lord Auckland with the States-General appeared in the public prints.[1] Lord Grenville then relaxed his *hauteur*, and appointed a meeting with Chauvelin on the usual day for receiving foreign ministers. His Lordship, as usual, was cold and reserved. Chauvelin was of course equally so. And thus they parted.

Noël is gone hence to Bruxelles with despatches for Dumouriez urging him to be cautious. Pitt assured Maret that he hoped he would be appointed by the Executive Council to treat with him. Chauvelin intrigues to circumvent our efforts to obtain peace. The French are taught to believe that this country is ripe for revolt. Mourgue told me that we did not dare trust the Militia. Four days later the Militia was called out, and, as I believe, in consequence of what fell from Mourgue in his conference with Long.[2]—W. A. M.

[1] See *Parliamentary History*, xxx. 341, November 16, 1792.

[2] 'A l'époque de l'entrée des Français à Bruxelles, Chauvelin reçut donc l'ordre de demander au secrétaire des affaires étrangères un entretien particulier, pour lui donner l'assurance des dispositions pacifiques de la France à l'égard des Provinces-Unies. Les succès de Dumouriez produisaient une telle impression que le ministre anglais, qui avait d'abord éludé cette demande, se ravisa quelques jours après. L'entrevue eut lieu le 28 Novembre : l'ambassadeur s'y montra hautain, provoquant de langage et d'attitude, et fit allusion plusieurs fois aux espérances qu'il fondait, en cas de rupture, sur les révolutionnaires anglais. "Il semble, dit-il, que plus les individus des deux nations se rapprochent, plus le Roi d'Angleterre s'éloigne de nous. . . . La mésintelligence *entre les deux peuples* n'existe pas : jamais elle n'a moins existé." Lord Grenville s'efforça en vain d'obtenir de lui quelques renseignements positifs sur les intentions ultérieures du conseil exécutif français. Chauvelin n'en savait pas plus, à cet égard, que le ministre anglais : mais pour se donner de l'importance, il s'avisa de répondre que les événements avaient marché en Belgique pendant qu'on hésitait à lui donner audience à Londres, et que le lan-

Mr. Miles to Lord Buckingham

December 4, 1792

If I have refrained for some months past to write to your Lordship, it was from the consideration that I had nothing of importance to communicate; and if I now trespass on your time by asking you to second the request I have made to be sent to Paris as a person *non accrédité*, it is from a full conviction that it is in my power to render the most essential service to my country. Your Lordship will have heard of the part I have had in facilitating an interview between Mr. Pitt and M. Maret, who is here from the Executive Council, and who, pleased with the reception he has had, will exert all his credit to engage France to suspend her project relative to the Scheldt. The degree of estimation in which I stand with the leading man in the Council, M. Le Brun, to whom I rendered a kindness some years past, gives me every reason to believe *que je pourrois aplanir toutes les difficultés qui se sont élevées entre les deux pays au sujet de l'Escaut.* I know to a certainty that my presence would be very acceptable, and that any person sent from this country to Paris would occasion a sensation in France highly advantageous to the British Government. I have made an offer of my services to Mr. Pitt with the assurance that no emolument as a recompense is desired. I am given

gage pacifique qu'il était autorisé à tenir huit ou dix jours auparavant pouvait bien n'être plus à la hauteur des circonstances.'

'En entrant dans le cabinet du ministre anglais, il s'était plongé dans un vaste fauteuil, écartant avec dédain une humble chaise avancée auprès du feu, dans l'intention, selon lui manifeste, d'humilier la République en sa personne.'—Ernouf, pp. 84, 88.

On this interview of M. Chauvelin with Lord Grenville, see Letter of Maret to Le Brun, November 29. Also Chauvelin's Letter to Le Brun, December 3, *Archives, Quai d'Orsay*, vol. 583, p. 346; vol. 584, p. 32.

to understand that the proposal should be made by Lord Grenville, but, as I am apprehensive from the cold and distant manner which his Lordship has observed towards me that I do not stand so well in his opinion as I feel conscious of deserving, I decline to address myself to him. If I thought that Lord Grenville would accept of my services, I certainly would have taken the liberty to write to him, especially as I have every reason to believe that the Executive Council will request the Ministry to send an agent over to Paris on their sending one to London, and in which case, as I am informed, my name will be mentioned as being acceptable to the Council.

It will give me infinite pleasure to find that your Lordship approves of my endeavours to prevent this country from feeling the calamities of war, and especially in a moment like the present, when the general fermentation in the minds of the people would render such a measure extremely hazardous, if not eventually fatal to the monarchy.

Minute: December 4.—M. Maret has just left me. He comes again in a few days. He informed me that the French fleet was as forward for sea as ours, that war is almost inevitable, not so much to open the Scheldt as *de s'en défaire de* 300,000 *brigands armés, qui ne devraient pas rentrer dans la France.*[1] He assured me that he would not see Lord Lansdowne

---

[1] 'The French, after the affair of the 10th of August, and in hostility with Austria and Prussia, had no resource but in war, and the answer that Roland gave to a friend of mine, at that time in credit and power in France, deserves notice: "*Peace is out of the question. We have* 300,000 *men in arms. We must make them march as far as their legs will carry them, or they will return and cut our throats.*"'—W. A. Miles. See *Authentic Correspondence*, &c., p. 144.

nor anyone who is in opposition to Government. His Lordship has endeavoured to see Maret, and desired that a friend would bring him to-morrow at one o'clock. He has met Sheridan at Chauvelin's and been invited to his house at Isleworth. Madame de Flahaut[1] has seen Mr. Fox, and, on being asked her opinion of him, replied: 'Il est vaste, il est grand, il est sale, et sans ornement comme l'Eglise de St. Paul.' Chauvelin is very angry that Maret has seen Pitt.

Lafayette, on the affair of the 20th June, proposed to Lückner to march with the two armies on Paris and rescue the King. The troops, at that time under the command of Lafayette, were disposed to obey him. Lückner gave notice of this proposal to the Executive Council, and assured them that, if Lafayette moved, he would follow with his army, defeat him, and bring him a prisoner to Paris.—W. A. M.

MR. AUST TO MR. MILES

Whitehall: December 6, 1792

Many thanks for your Irish news. The prospect there is lowering. I am sorry to acquaint you that Lord Grenville declines your offer of going to Paris, but with thanks.

MR. MILES TO M. SCIPION MOURGUE

December 6, 1792

As to the object of your mission, I have a thousand disquietudes. Would to God that they may have suffi-

---

[1] Madame de Flahaut, whose husband, Comte de Flahaut, was guillotined at Arras in 1793, remarried, and, as Madame de Souza, became well known as a clever novel-writer. Her son, Comte de Flahaut de la Billarderie, rose to high rank in the French service as a soldier, and, from 1860 to 1862, was Ambassador at the Court of St. James. The Duc de Morny, son of Queen Hortense by the Comte de Flahaut, the father of the Ambassador, was brought up by Madame de Souza.

cient wisdom in Paris to put off as long as possible every pretext for war! I have reason to believe that the Court of St. James desires nothing better than to avoid hostilities, but at the same time you will admit that it cannot balance between war and solemn engagements made with its allies. If France makes any attempt on the independence or on the privileges of the Dutch, it will be imperative on England to fly to their assistance, or she would risk being any longer considered as a nation; but I hope that the Executive Power, enlightened by the information which you are able to impart to it, and assured of the earnestness with which the Court of London desires to avoid every subject which might separate the two peoples, will find means to preserve peace, and establish at the same time the basis of a perpetual alliance between the two nations. I desire it all the more because the public mind is excited, and you would see in the event of war that it will be rather a war of the English people than of the Minister. Those who tell you the contrary, and who seek to make you believe that England is ripe for a revolution against its Government, seek only to mislead and deceive you. Adieu, my dear friend! I am wearying to see you return with an olive branch. A thousand kind wishes to M. Le Brun and to all my acquaintances in Paris. Write to me in detail, inform me of everything that passes, and let us labour in concert for the welfare of the human race. Adieu! I embrace you with all my heart.

Minute: December 7.—Saw M. Maret at my house. He related the occasion of his journey to Bruxelles in April last, his successful interview with the members of the *État ecclésiastique*, and with the nobles on the night of his arrival, and his having engaged them to refuse the subsidy to the Emperor, and to send a deputation to Paris soliciting an alliance and assistance to throw off the Austrian yoke. M. de Gravier, the Minister at Bruxelles, is a favourite of the Archduchess, who used to *thee* and *thou* him familiarly, and his secretary was devoted to the Executive Power. M. Maret had the recall of M. de Gravier in his pocket. On his arrival at Paris he went in pursuit of Dumouriez to give him an account of his embassy, and found he was gone down to the National Convention to declare war against the King of Hungary. He then returned to the Low Countries and formed the Belgic Legion. The declaration of war at that time was the salvation of France; for the army was reputed to be well provided with everything, whereas it was found to be the contrary. This called forth the exertions of the country, discovered the disaffected, and secured the independence of the Republic, for, if the enemy had then advanced in force, France would have been lost past redemption, having but few troops, no magazines of any kind having been formed, and the few soldiers she had were ill appointed.—W. A. M.

LORD BUCKINGHAM TO MR. MILES

Stowe: December 7, 1792

I am favoured with your letter of the 4th, but, having been in a constant state of hurry with my Militia, it has been impossible for me to acknowledge it sooner. My high opinion and good wishes towards you are the same, but, as I have had no communications whatever with Mr. Pitt or Lord Grenville upon the details of their official business ever since it has taken the serious aspect which it now bears, or indeed for the last three months, and as I have the most decided reasons for not conversing with them upon matters of the nature which you have opened to me, I fear that it is impossible for me to comply with your request, unless they should converse with me upon the subject. I can assure you that I do not believe Lord Grenville's mind is prejudiced against you, or insensible to your abilities and services.

Mr. Miles to Lord Buckingham

December 8, 1792

I steal a moment from some confidential business [1] entrusted to me to acknowledge the honour of your letter of yesterday's date. If I am anxious to have peace established, it is from a conviction that war would be a very hazardous measure; and, from the result of the recent conference of M. Maret with Mr. Pitt, I am inclined to hope that an event so auspicious is within the power of the latter to obtain. Although I am fully master of the intentions of the Executive Council, and saw the despatches which left Portman Square [2] last Monday morning at five o'clock, I cannot by letter reveal them. I could give your Lordship much important information were you in town.

I have borrowed the inclosed pamphlets on purpose that you may peruse them, after which I shall entreat the favour of their being returned. The proposal which I made to the Duke of Leeds, in January 1790, was, that the union of Liège with the Austrian Netherlands, and the independence of both, should be facilitated and acknowledged by this country. The advantages resulting from this measure would have been commercial as well as political, *toutes les entraves que la tête mal organisée de Joseph II. avait fait mettre sur le commerce seroient*

[1] The translation of the Defence of Louis XVI.
[2] The French Embassy.

levées, and Holland would have had a broad and impenetrable barrier on the side of France. Happy to have been emancipated from the odious perfidy and tyranny of the House of Austria, the Flemings would have ratified the different treaties which condemn the Scheldt to roll its slumbering waters disgracefully and unprofitably to the sea. The French would have had no pretext for entering into Brabant. The result of my conference with his Grace convinced me more than ever that the ideas of magnitude and futurity, as well as of right and expediency, are necessary furniture for every man's mind to whom the interests of a nation are in any degree confided. What I proposed in 1790, and for which the people, whose cause I pleaded, would have been obliged to this country, is now accomplished without any merit to us, and, indeed, against the wish of Government, with this advantage to them, that what they have acquired cannot be taken away, for, whatever may be the event of the war, I will venture to predict that the dominion of Austria in the Netherlands is extinguished for ever. The Duke of Leeds said to me it was going great lengths, but it was easy to foresee at the time, without the gift of prescience, that the moment was not very distant when France would go *far greater* lengths.

Mr. Long to Mr. Miles

December 9, 1792

I return the pamphlets. I have read them with some interest, though I think them mischievous in the extreme. The production of Condorcet is artful and insidious. How easily these fellows talk of plunging a whole nation into the horrors of a civil war!

As to my going to Paris, you may set that down

among other false reports, such as that of an impending coalition, &c., in which Walter[1] indulges. I do not suppose Mr. Pitt ever had the idea of sending any one to Paris. I should think it extremely improbable.[2]

What think you of the defence of Louis XVI.? I have not yet read it. How do you like the 'Word in Season'? The 'Protest' against Paine's 'Rights of Man,' published by Nichol, is worth your reading.

Mr. Miles to Mr. Long

December 9, 1792.

I did not believe that you were going to Paris, although the 'Times' said you were already gone, nor do I suppose that you would wish to go. I cannot but hope that, whenever such a measure becomes necessary, Mr. Pitt will accept my offer for many reasons too obvious to repeat, and which, were he to decline, I confess would afflict me much, because I dread war, and foresee the consequences of it. I have had ' Avis aux Bataves,' by Condorcet, which I did not judge prudent to show you at the moment lest it should indispose the mind of Mr. Pitt towards a negotiation. It is grossly personal to the King, insidious to the Dutch, and artful in the extreme. Another reason for not showing it was that I had taken measures to put a stop to these publications, and I can assure you for certain that strong remon-

---

[1] Proprietor of the *Times*.

[2] 'There exists in the English Record Office proof that the English Government was sincere in desiring the resumption of friendly relations with France, and that in spite of Burke and the *émigrés* they now contemplated sending a Minister to Paris. At the end of the volume of French papers for December 1792 are the imperfect drafts of two despatches intended for some one proceeding as envoy to France. It does not appear for whom they were intended, and they have no date. But from internal evidence they may be referred to December 1792.'—*Fortnightly Review*, February 1883, p. 268.

strances are gone to Le Brun both from M. Maret and myself to check the licentiousness of Condorcet's pen. I admire many parts of the 'Defence,' which, I trust, will lose nothing by being translated. I fag at it *sans relâche.* I suppose it comes from Lally-Tollendal, Calonne, or Bertrand de Molleville. There is much good argument, and the author is occasionally eloquent. But of what avail, just Heavens! is truth, or argument, or eloquence, against prejudice, and, above all, the prejudice of a barbarous and unenlightened multitude? This I can assure you, that the ruling party wish to preserve the life of Louis XVI. and his family.[1]

Mr. Miles to M. Fabry

December 9, 1792

I do not despair of peace, my dear Fabry, neither do I despair of the enfranchisement of the Austrian Netherlands and of Liège, but all depends on the wisdom of Le Brun and of his colleagues in Paris. If Le Brun, elated by his situation, exacts the opening of the Scheldt, all is lost, war will follow, and the whole world will experience the most terrible of plagues. All my labours as well as all my hopes will end in nothing. It is a great misfortune for the human race when men without acquirements or without principles are found

---

[1] Lord Stormont, in the House of Lords [December 13, 1792], quoted the following passage from the *Address to the Dutch* written by Condorcet: 'Such union between free states is their primary want, their dearest interest, so long as the earth is stained by the existence of a king, and by the absurdity of hereditary government, so long as this shameful production of ignorance and folly remains unproscribed by the universal consent of mankind. . . . George III. sees with anxious surprise that throne totter under him which is founded on sophistry, and which republican truths have sapped to its very foundation.'—*Parliamentary History,* 1792, xxix. 1572. See *Annual Register,* 1793: *History of Europe,* p. 17.

at the helm of affairs. Ignorance very often causes as much mischief as an exorbitant ambition. Le Brun is not deficient in attainments, but, dazzled perhaps by his ephemeral elevation, he may be led astray, and, as he has already shown a very misplaced haughtiness, I frankly confess that I fear for the future. I am ignorant of the degree of credit which he has in France; but, if he possesses a decided influence in the Council proportioned to his talents, and if his talents are guided by circumstances and prudence, I will answer for peace. The English Cabinet, though urged on by some evil-intentioned persons, is notwithstanding pacific; but these people will have a good chance if France does not observe a wiser and more moderate course than she has hitherto done. I know that the Abbé Sieyès is for war, and I believe he has too much to say at this moment in Paris not to be listened to. I know his sentiments thoroughly in regard to England, and, as he is of opinion that she is not in a position to measure herself with France, and that war is necessary to the latter in order to strengthen the Revolution, his political labours will assuredly have no other end. It remains to be seen whether his compatriots, who, thinking differently, believe with me that an alliance between these two nations is preferable to a war, will allow themselves to be led by a priest who has never taken the Gospel for his guide.

I long to see you, my dear Fabry, and to talk over the past and the future, but I am tied here by circumstances. I cannot conceal from you my uneasiness as to the fate not only of my country, but of all Europe, probably about to become the theatre of frightful carnage. Although I have not the honour to be in the counsel of my sovereign, nor to play any *rôle* which would give me the right to meddle in public affairs, I cannot refrain from using my credit with Le Brun to avert a misfortune; and all the more since I have reason to believe that Mr. Pitt, to whom I am still much attached, is decidedly in favour of peace. The greatest service I can render to him, as well as to my country, is to counteract the atrocious efforts of the emigrants, both clergy and *noblesse*, who, in order to regain a credit and influence too long abused, would set fire to the four corners of the world. Whilst I am now writing to you, these infatuated people make a fierce and misguided populace believe that the English only want the favourable moment to attack France. The Prussian emissaries, who swarm in Paris, and almost all the Germans and Spaniards who are there, hold the same language.[1] You can understand that so many falsehoods cannot but operate against liberty and against peace—the two objects which I have most at heart, and for which I would make any sacrifice.

Bon soir, mon cher Fabry. Je suis à vous pour la vie.

P.S.—Allow me to congratulate you on your return to Liège. No person rejoices at it more than I do, and I flatter myself that your country will at last be free. I have inquired many times about you, but without success; nobody could give me any news of you, nor say where you were. It was only on the 4th instant that I heard of you from M. Maret. I am sorry that you did not follow the counsel which I gave you in 1790, to shake off the yoke of the empire; but it does

---

[1] 'The unfortunate emigrants speculate with complacency on the troubles extending themselves to England, though England is their only place of refuge; and the partisans of the allied Powers engaged in a disastrous war are impatient also to see us share their calamity.'—*Auckland Correspondence*, ii. 470.

not signify, all will go well. I labour vigorously, in concert with the Executive Power of Paris, to render the country of Liège and the Austrian Netherlands free for ever, that is to say, independent, and I hope that this much-desired project will soon be realised; but, in the name of God, never dream of uniting yourselves to France. I know that it has already been discussed. Kindly send me all your news.

Mr. Miles to Mr. Pitt

December 12, 1792

This is merely to inform you that M. Noël arrived this morning from Liège, and has been with me these two hours.[1] He assures me that M. Dumouriez is decidedly of opinion that the Executive Council was too precipitate in declaring the Scheldt free; and that this measure, so likely to involve France in a war with England, would not be accelerated by the forces under his command. The troops he detached under Captain Molson were to assist at the siege of Antwerp, and not to facilitate the opening of the Scheldt. M. Noël is of opinion with me that the Executive Council had no right to form any resolution on the above subject, and he assures me he will despatch messengers to-morrow express to Liège and to Paris, recommending that the execution of this decree of the Council should at least be deferred. I have also suggested that orders be sent

---

[1] 'Je suis revenu hier dans cette ville, d'un voyage très pénible et très contrarié, soit par les vents, soit par la nature des chemins. . . . Le matin, Maret, de la meilleure grâce du monde, me mit au courant de ce qui s'était passé. En ouvrant mes lettres, je trouvai un billet de Miles qui me priait de passer chez lui aussitôt après mon retour. Quoique brisé de mon voyage, je me rendis sur le champ chez lui. Il me fit part de toutes les démarches qu'il avait faites.'—*Noël to Le Brun*, December 13, 1792; *Archives*, vol. 584, p. 135.

to countermand the vessels destined to mount the river to Antwerp. It is with pleasure I inform you of the sincere disposition which Dumouriez announces to preserve peace with England, and to this effect, I am persuaded, both M. Maret and M. Noël will co-operate. If you should wish any matter to be suggested, as from myself, either to Le Brun or to Dumouriez, and will do me the honour to confide it to me, I will execute your commands with all possible promptitude and fidelity. This day the Liégeois meet to give themselves a free government.

If M. Mourgue, who was despatched to France on the 3rd inst., and whose return is expected every moment, should bring an unfavourable answer from the Executive Council, and render war a measure of necessity, I take the liberty to suggest the expediency of great precautions in the event of letters of marque. Private commissions should be issued that the vessels so armed do not pass over to the enemy, as I have *strong reasons* to suspect that some mercantile men have it in contemplation to fit out privateers under the national flag of France, and that such speculations will be warmly encouraged by the French should a rupture take place. I cannot explain myself further on paper.[1]

MR. MILES TO MR. LONG

December 13, 1792

Noël has just returned from Liége, and came to me the instant of his arrival. I have sent a line to Mr. Pitt in consequence. Dumouriez is decidedly against the opening of the Scheldt, at least by the Executive

[1] See remarks on this subject by Baron Ernouf, quoted further on, February 8, 1793.

Council, nor will he invade the Dutch territory unless the Austrians should enter it, and then he will certainly pursue them. The Liégeois assemble again this day to emancipate themselves at once from ecclesiastical tyranny, and from that of the empire, which was my advice to them in 1787–89; and, if the Duke of Leeds had not been frightened at the propositions I made to him at Whitehall in January 1790, our present armaments would not have been necessary; we should have no cause of alarm for Holland, the Scheldt would have rolled its drowsy waters to the sea in indolence, and the Dutch would have had a glorious rampart between them and the French. But the boldness of my project alarmed his Grace. He said it was going great lengths. Yet, if those lengths had been accomplished by our interference, and we had become guarantees for the independence of Liège and the Low Countries, the Scheldt would not have compelled us to arm or have threatened Europe with a general war. Mr. Pitt is highly esteemed in France, and considered as an able, frank, and honest Minister. But Lord Hawkesbury is suspected, and more than suspected—he is detested—and considered as hostile to the cause of freedom in all nations, and that he has more to say behind the curtain than he ought.

If I have shown a strong desire to preserve peace, it has been from a natural horror that I have to war, and a sincere wish to see averted so direful a calamity from this country, and, if possible, from the world. I am sorry that I did not go to Paris, unknown to you and to Mr. Pitt, two months or even six weeks ago. The Scheldt, in that case, I am assured, would never have engaged the attention of the Executive Council. Noël allows *que ce fut très maladroit* in the Council.

Dumouriez is of the same opinion, and, if Le Brun and his colleagues attend to the advice given to them by Dumouriez, Maret, Noël, and myself, this business will yet be suffered to die away. This advice has been repeated this very night in a despatch transmitted to Paris, with strong recommendations to countermand those vessels sent to force a passage to Antwerp. I have laboured to engage the Executive Council to this renunciation for some time past; but I am afraid that its members are too much under the influence, or rather the dread and control, of the mob to dare to follow any opinion except that of the rabble; and success has made that rabble insolent—so true is it that few minds are proof against prosperity. If war, however, should be the alternative through their fault and obstinacy, my part is already taken. I shall renounce all commerce and correspondence with the French, and take an open and decided part against them. I will refute the libels of Condorcet, and state to my countrymen the tricks and turpitude of that unprincipled meddling writer and his associates.

You see it is the idea of Mr. Fox that Government should have somebody at Paris.[1] It is expedient for many reasons. And, if no other good was to result, it would be desirable to destroy ill-founded reports that may affect the peace of both countries, and to explain difficulties and misunderstandings. For example, an idea prevailed that, with plenty of corn in this country, we laid an embargo on purpose to starve the French. I have done away that impression, which had rendered the people furious.

Noël and Maret dine with me this day. Mourgue is

[1] See *Annual Register*, 1793; *History of Europe*, p. 23; also *Parliamentary History*, 1792, xxx. 66, 80.

hourly expected. I am more than half asleep. It is past midnight, but do not suppose that I dream; these solemn thoughts of mine are no reveries.

A Member of the Convention to Mr. Miles

Paris: December 9, 1792.[1]

Maret will certainly be recalled; but orders to that effect have not yet been transmitted to him. He has a warm and inflexible friend in Garat.[2] His enemies are indefatigable, and, as he was not charged with any mission to London on public affairs, jealousy has seized hold of the circumstance of his having had an interview with Mr. Pitt. Chauvelin's interest, believe me, is too well supported in Paris to authorise any hope of his speedy recall in order to make room for Maret or any other person. Great expectations are formed here of a change in your Administration, and it is this expectation that acts so powerfully in favour of Chauvelin, and gives additional force to the arguments of his friends for his remaining in England. M. Truguet has twelve sail of the line with him, with which he is to force the Turks to receive Sémonville, retake the Crimea for them, and compel them to declare war against Russia. Our fleet is in as forward a state as yours, great exertions are making in all our ports, and the conflict between our two countries, whenever it happens, will be dreadful. War to a certain extent is inevitable, not so much for the purpose of opening the Scheldt, for that is rather a pretext in order to animate the people and preserve their enthusiasm, but to get rid of 300,000 armed vagabonds, who can never be allowed to return without evident risk to the Convention and

---

[1] Received December 14. [2] Minister of Justice.

Executive Council. These men must be expended; and the ardour which generally prevails for military fame must be diminished or subdued before my country can hope to enjoy peace. You are too sanguine when you assert that a rupture between our two nations will not take place. I tell you again that it is unavoidable, and that, if we had no cause of complaint against the Cabinet of St. James, it would be necessary from policy and for our internal security to break with the Court of London rather than consent to a general peace, which, I conceive, is the principal object of your Minister. I am not insensible to the difficulties and dangers of a general war, and that, whenever England declares against us, we shall have to contend with all Europe; but you seem to have a very imperfect idea of our resources, and of the wonderful enthusiasm that prevails throughout France. Believe me, we are not intimidated by the force that will be brought against us. In case of defeat, we shall rally at the word *Liberty*; and despondency in the cause of freedom is an infamy which those who, sincerely embarked in it, will never deserve. Our sugar colonies will fall into your hands. What then? You will restore order and good government in all of them; you will keep them in a high state of cultivation, and at the end of the contest you will return them to us in much better condition than you found them. It cannot be otherwise. And, with such a prospect before us, what have we to fear from a war? Clavière is of your opinion, and dreads a contest from which, he says, ruin to both nations must ensue; but this is not so much the effect of reasoning as of fear. He is in Council the most timid of men, and has frequently interrupted us in the midst of debate by beseeching us to recollect that walls may have ears. Man is certainly a very contradictory animal, and differs more from himself at times than he does from the rest of the creation. Fearful and irresolute as Clavière naturally is known to be, yet I have seen him extremely collected, and exhibit great courage and great presence of mind in moments of very imminent danger. Roland is firm and decided, in which he is confirmed by the undaunted and unsubdued spirit of his wife, whose talent for business and skill in political intrigue surpass everything that your imagination can suggest. Madame Roland is the very soul of the party, and devotes her whole time and attention to public affairs. It is her opinion, as well as mine, that we cannot make peace with the Emperor without danger to the Republic, and that it would be hazardous to recall an army, flushed with victory and impatient to gather fresh laurels, into the heart of a country whose commerce and manufactures have lost their activity, and which would leave the disbanded multitude without resources or employment. Reflect well upon our situation, within and without, and you will allow that the prosecution of the war to a certain extent can alone save us and the glorious cause for which we contend. The messenger waits, and I can only say that I am yours for ever.

M. SCIPION MOURGUE TO MR. MILES

Paris: December 9,[1] 1792

I have been so occupied that I could not find a moment to write, nor can I yet command time to write to you at length. I had a very good voyage, and I gave your letter on the day of my arrival to the Minister, who received it with great pleasure. *I fear much that our efforts will be in vain unless your Government renounces*

[1] Received December 14.

the Scheldt. This state of affairs makes me miserable. The situation in Paris is critical. I am assured that the King will be condemned and executed before the end of next week: that will bring about many events. Neither you nor I, my dear friend, have had any idea of the situation of this country, and I shall have a great deal to say to you on this subject, but I dare not write about it. You know the tender and inviolable attachment I have vowed towards you. Adieu!

Minute: December 14.—Despatches arrived to-day from the Executive Council. M. Maret came to Cleveland Row at half-past one, and showed me his instructions from Le Brun in full. Remarks on our calling out the Militia, and on our arming the country, occupy a part of this despatch, with some gasconade as to the French not being alarmed; also insinuations about the progress of public opinion in England in favour of liberty and equality, and the fear of our Government for its own safety. A recognition of the Republic, and an absolute refusal on the part of the Executive Council to treat by means of any person *non-accrédité*, form the basis on which alone they would agree to enter upon negotiations. M. Maret then mentioned M. Chauvelin, who has also received by this day's courier from Le Brun full instructions authorising him to give to our Ministers every proper explanation relative to the Scheldt and to the decree of November 19 'offering assistance to all the people who would revolt.' I desired Maret to demand an immediate interview with Mr. Pitt. He wrote the note at my house, and my servant took it. The Minister replied at once and appointed eight o'clock for the interview. As the communication was not much, the audience soon terminated; Mr. Pitt declining, very improperly, I think, to give any answer as to whether he would see M. Chauvelin or enter into the subject-matter. Thus have Ministers and the Executive Council by their folly and insolence lost all the fruits of the labour hitherto expended on behalf of peace!—W. A. M.

Mr. Miles to Mr. Pitt

December 14, 1792

The inclosed is from M. Maret, who has just received a despatch from Paris. I have read it. Forgive me if I again make an offer of my service to go to Paris, as I cannot but entertain great hopes that, on a personal explanation with Le Brun, in conjunction with M. Maret, the calamities of war may be avoided.

Mr. Miles to M. Le Brun [1]

London: December 14, 1792

I am distressed at the lamentable turn which the negotiation I had opened with Mr. Pitt for a *rapprochement* of the two countries has taken. Not having the honour of knowing M. de Chauvelin, and having for a long time known M. Mourgue, I have concerted with the latter the means for removing all subjects of discord between France and England. You are not ignorant of my efforts on this matter, nor of my zeal and frankness. Show on your part as lively a desire to preserve peace, and I will hold myself responsible for success. I have but a moment to write. If you should still decide on not sending M. Maret to this country, I pray you to recollect how essential it will be that public affairs should be treated by some one who has already appeared on the scene, who is known to Mr. Pitt, and who would

---

[1] *Archives, Foreign Office, Paris*, vol. 584, p. 147.

not be unacceptable to him. For the rest, M. Maret will tell you how much I have desired to see the two nations united, and how distressed I am by the slight hope held out by his last interview with Mr. Pitt this evening.

I shall be delighted to receive your news. I repeat to you once more that you cannot do better than authorise M. Maret to enter on the subject with our Government.

Minute: December 15.—Saw Lord Buckingham. He expressed himself pleased at my zeal on behalf of Government, but declared that, although he loved his brother [1] and Mr. Pitt, he did not approve of their conduct towards France; he did not wish, however, to enter into or to know anything about the negotiations I had opened. He thought that, from the spirit shown in the Houses of Parliament, it was not likely the Ministers would offer to treat at present with Paris.

Long mentioned to me to-day his desire to obtain a copy of 'Brissot's Journal' on account of an article relative to the intentions of the Opposition. I applied to Noël for it. He sent the 'Journal' at once, with a note, in which he says: 'J'espère encore sur l'arrivée de Maret à Paris. J'attendrai ici sa première lettre, et ne me retirerai qu'en désespoir de cause.' When I told Noël on the 13th instant that Pitt certainly would not abandon the Dutch, *coûte que coûte*, he replied 'que la guerre était inévitable, et que les Français porteront la perte avec eux partout; qu'ils s'enrichiront de nos richesses, et qu'il y a beaucoup de personnes ici prêtes à faire des armements sous le pavillon françois pour nous enlever nos bâtiments marchands et détruire notre commerce.' I sent notice of this to Mr. Pitt. Sheridan

[1] Lord Grenville.

in the House of Commons threw out this menace in the very words of Noël as spoken to me—*this proves correspondence*. Fox also stated on the opening of the session, word for word, what I read in a private despatch from Le Brun that arrived the day following.

December 16.—Received a note from Long sent from the House of Commons, where he and Mr. Pitt were anxiously waiting for my reply. He says: ' What I mentioned to you is not in the journal you forwarded. We had mistaken the date. I understand it is the " Patriote " of the 9th of this month. Will you endeavour to see it? and, if there is anything relative to Fox's motion, you would do us a great service in sending it.'—W. A. M.

Mr. Miles to M. Noël

December 16, 1792

A thousand thanks, my dear Sir, for your kindness in sending me the 'Journal of Brissot.' Show me your further friendship by forwarding the journal of the 9th of this month, and, if you can supply me with it regularly, you will give a real pleasure.

A thousand thanks also for the hope with which you inspire me that the journey of our friend Maret will bring about a change in the system which they have unhappily adopted in Paris, a system that can produce only evil. I shall be verily in despair if our efforts to give peace to Europe and to reunite the two nations should be in vain. I have succeeded in removing, after much labour, some of the difficulties which seemed to prevent a *rapprochement* of the two countries; and to see all these attempts fail at the very moment when I expected they would triumph will occasion pain to me beyond your conception. Do not forget that, when you have a spare moment, I shall be enchanted to exchange thoughts in conversation with you. Adieu![1]

Mr. Miles to Mr. Pitt

December 16, 1792

It is with some degree of pleasure I announce that it will be proposed to the States of Brabant to petition the Executive Council at Paris to suspend the execution of their *arrêté* relative to the Scheldt, as its prosecution, by involving the country in a war with Holland, will produce greater evils than those from which they have been released by the Revolution. This expedient is proposed to save the honour of the Executive Power, and, if it succeeds, it is probable that war will be avoided. I am this day assured that there is no Batavian Legion formed, nor Liégeois Legion; that the report of Dumouriez having attacked, or even encouraged any attack, on Maestricht is void of every foundation, 'qu'il n'est pas sur le terrain de la Hollande, et qu'il se portera plutôt vers Aix-la-Chapelle, qu'il y a de petites contestations dans l'armée, et qu'on écrira à Monsieur Dumouriez pour qu'il ne fasse aucune démarche contre les Hollandais.'

On reading the despatch to the Executive Council, and finding so perfect a disposition to avoid hostility, I could not help observing *que les Français avaient été induits en erreur par quelques mal-intentionnés ici.* It was at once allowed by the French agent that there had been personal intercourse with Lord Lansdowne, but not with Mr. Fox, that it was the opinion at Paris that the Opposition must come into power, and that the

---

[1] 'The *Journal* was obtained, and there was found asserted the part which Mr. Fox would take, and the language he would hold, on the night in question.'—W. A. M.

French were resolved to insist on having the Republic acknowledged. I did not fail to ask whether they would have proceeded as far as they have done in Paris if the Executive Council had not been promised support in this country. It was confessed that they had been led into an error, and that the 'associations' and the majority in Parliament sufficiently proved the little credit due to the assurances held out by the Opposition. I am certain that strong language will be used to persuade the Executive Council to give up the Scheldt, and I do hope that before you treat with them the decree of the 19th of November, as also that which annexes Savoy to France, will be abolished, for both these articles will be much insisted upon in the despatch that Maret takes with him to Paris. In the 'Journal' of Brissot of the 9th inst., which I procured for Mr. Long this day, are contained the intended operations of the Opposition, and in a manner so accurately stated, that no doubt can exist but that the party is in correspondence and accord with the French.

MR. MILES TO M. LE BRUN[1]

London: December 18, 1792

I am in despair, Sir, at seeing all my efforts to preserve peace and draw together the two nations ready to collapse through the unfounded prejudices, misunderstandings, and, it may be, the underhand and dangerous intrigues so contrary to the veritable interests of the two countries.

If Scipion Mourgue has given a faithful and detailed account of all that has passed between him and me relative to the great objects which interest not only

---

[1] *Archives, Foreign Office, Paris*, vol. 584, p. 190.

France and England but the whole world, you cannot be ignorant of the loyalty and frankness of my proceedings. My frankness and loyalty, however, are not the points in question. My political principles, from which I shall never swerve, are well known to you, as well as the personal esteem with which your talents and misfortunes have inspired me. I will only say that, having no other aim than the happiness of the human race, and no other guides than common sense and integrity, I by no means fear to expose my principles and conduct to the full light of day. Permit me, then, to fulfil a duty by making clear to you some very important matters, concerning which it appears to me you entertain very incorrect ideas.

I undertake this task so much the more willingly as I know you to be a man too just not to listen to reason and truth. During my sojourn in Paris in 1790–1791, I observed with much regret the very ill-founded suspicions in regard to the intentions of the Court of London towards France, and to which the events that have since happened have given a denial. These suspicions were very strongly supported by the intrigues of the aristocrats, who thought they saw in a war between France and England the re-establishment of the ancient Government. Animated by a hope more than criminal, they have laboured, with a cowardice worthy of their continued infamous conduct, to impose upon a people always easy to deceive by their credulity that our armaments against Spain were destined to wrest from France her Windward Islands, and to bring about a counter-revolution. It was not surprising, my dear Sir, that a people released from their fetters and still surrounded by their former tyrants, the *noblesse* and the clergy, who labour incessantly to plunge them again under despotism, should give credit to falsehoods invented by evil-intentioned persons, and supported, so to say, by fear. But that people well informed should be dupes, that these enlightened people should be credulous enough to believe the thousand and one tales propagated against the British Government, astonishes and afflicts me.

The report, equally devoid of all foundation, that Mr. Pitt was the sworn enemy of the new French Constitution, was received with that blind confidence which always gives to falsehood a victory over truth. I dare to assure you that the English Minister, since the commencement of the Revolution of 1789, has made it a duty never to meddle with the internal affairs of your country. He has rejected with firmness all the proposals made to him to attack France; he has never entered into any project in favour of a counter-revolution, but, on the contrary, he has carefully preserved a neutrality the most decided. If, then, he has made it a duty not to disturb France, he will make it his glory, and you should be grateful for it, to hold himself firm to principles so wise and so equitable.

Not content with having reproached him for wishing to declare war against France, not content with having accused him of being the sworn enemy of the Revolution, they have pushed the calumnious falsehoods so far as to say that he has sent money into France to excite and keep up the disturbances. The impossibility of the thing is a sufficient answer to an accusation as ridiculous as it is atrocious. No English Minister can squander in this way the public treasure. He is obliged to render an account, even to the last farthing, of all that he expends on secret service; and when I solemnly declare to you on the faith of an honourable man that the secret expenditure of the Foreign Office has not exceeded the sum of 4,000*l.* sterling yearly during many years, I leave you to judge whether it is possible, with such small means, to proceed far in exciting discord. Remember also the system of economy which Mr. Pitt has adopted, and the savings which he has made, and you will agree with me that he could not have lavished the money in the way they affirm.

Moreover, I beg you to consider well the state of your country and of ours, and, without consulting either justice or good policy, answer whether at this moment it would be expedient for you to add England to the number of your enemies.

When I saw M. Noël here for the first time, and he had told me the object of his journey, I promised to furnish him with the means of obtaining the interview he desired as soon as he had secured from the Executive Council its authority. The conduct which he has prescribed for himself has been very prudent and very wise, and, if he had been here a fortnight ago, he would probably have had the conference which M. Maret, through my mediation, has procured. I commend the conduct of both one and the other, honourable in respect to myself, and loyal towards their country, and, if you had permitted the latter to finish what he has so well commenced, I believe that you would have had reason to be well satisfied with him.

After having now explained myself, after assuring you that I have no personal interest in the negotiation which I had all but succeeded in opening, I hope that you will yield to wise and prudent counsels, and not lose the opportunity which presents itself of insuring the welfare of your country and the tranquillity of

Europe. Do not imagine that the English are disposed to revolt against their Government; do not imagine that they desire war. Not at all. We desire to live on good terms with France, and we will do so provided she does not attack our allies.

After the steps which I took to obtain for M. Maret a conference with Mr. Pitt I was much astonished that you should have referred the Minister to M. Chauvelin for explanations. I was also greatly surprised that you have not replied to any of my letters. But when it concerns the public weal I do not make any difficulty, nor do I regard forms or fastidious ceremonies. Beset with business, I forgive you an omission which proceeds perhaps more from circumstances than from anything else, and I flatter myself that I shall have news from you by the first courier.

M. Maret will explain to you many things which must not be said on paper.

Be assured that I will not lose sight during his absence of the great object which interests me.

Salut et amitié. Bon soir.

Minute: December 18.—Received a note from Aust, in which he says: 'Lord Grenville's motion is for a bill for disarming foreigners coming to England. It is the measure you advised.' This motion of Lord Grenville originated with me. In my letter to Mr. Pitt (November 30) I had recommended that orders should be sent to all the outports to seize the arms of foreigners, and there detain them until their owners left the country, for several disbanded officers and soldiers from the emigrant army had come over, and it was not unlikely but that the French might invade us in this fashion, since they firmly expected an insurrection in England.[1] A secret committee was held in France in 1788 at the house of the Duke of Rochefoucault, composed of the Duke d'Aiguillon, the Bishop of Autun, Talon, Sémonville, and others, the object being to destroy the *noblesse*. The above was assured to me this day by Noël. The cause of the Duke of Rochefoucault being murdered was his acting in concert with Lafayette, before and after the 20th of June, in favour of the King.

PROPOSAL TO RESCUE LOUIS XVI

December 18.—A confidential person[2] from the Executive Council came to me this evening at half-past nine. He declared himself a friend to humanity, and, although a Republican, he was perfectly persuaded that the death of the King would not be of any service to the new Government in France; that, having reduced Louis XVI. to the rank of a citizen, France had nothing more to fear from that dethroned monarch; that it was the destruction of royalty and not the execution of the man, that France required, and which former object had now been fully obtained. Having premised

---

[1] 'As the number of foreigners and aliens which were at this time in Great Britain was very considerable, and as many of them had conducted themselves in such a manner as to justify a suspicion of their evil intentions towards this nation, it was thought a necessary measure by his Majesty's Ministers to apply to Parliament to provide for the public tranquillity by subjecting the resort and residence of aliens to certain regulations. Accordingly, Lord Grenville, on December 19, brought a Bill into the House of Lords for that purpose.'—*Annual Register*, 1793, p. 35. See debate on this Alien Bill in *Parliamentary History*, 1792, xxx. 146-170.

The above note suggests the remark that, if the insular position of England was not considered a sufficient guarantee against invasion in 1792, the House of Commons decided wisely when it refused to allow the risk to be increased through the medium of a Channel Tunnel.

[2] The Abbé Noël. See Letter, February 21, 1794.

thus much, he said that, as he saw a disposition in the Executive Council to avoid shedding the blood of Louis XVI., and as he supposed that Mr. Pitt and the Government attached some importance to this merciful desire, he had come on purpose to communicate to me the only certain method by which the life of the King could be saved. He then told me that there was an individual in London who commanded the means, but that, being impeached, it was impossible he could see him on the subject. He dwelt upon the vigorous mind of this individual, said that his resources were immense, his knowledge extensive, and that, having had an active share in the Revolution, having kept on good terms with all parties, and being deeply and confidentially engaged in the King's affair, he alone could succeed in the enterprise. He then inquired if I would mention the matter to Mr. Pitt, but that he himself must not be revealed; that he had nothing more to say on the subject but to give me the name and the address of the party,[1] and I was then to act as I thought proper. I inquired in what manner Mr. Pitt could interfere. I was answered that it must be done secretly, and not openly. I asked him to explain himself. He said he could explain himself no further; that he mentioned the matter in confidence to me, and there the affair, so far as he was concerned, must rest. Suspecting that it might be a feint on the part of the Executive Council to discover if our Government interested itself to preserve the life of the King, and knowing that, if such an idea should be adopted, England would be accused of wishing to effect a counter-revolution, I thought it prudent to appear extremely indifferent as to the life or death of Louis XVI., and the more so as the gentle-

---

[1] M. Talon, 116 Sloane Street, Chelsea.

man who came to me had reason to complain of rudeness and ill-treatment formerly received from the King. I was also of opinion that it was prudent to enforce a belief at Paris that Mr. Pitt had prescribed to himself, as a duty, not to meddle with the interior government of France on any account, or under any pretext, either directly or indirectly. The observation was made that it was to be done secretly. I replied that I was too well acquainted with the world to believe that the proposed interference would remain a secret twenty-four hours, and that, as I knew Mr. Pitt to be averse to meddle with the internal affairs of France, and of course to be thought to intermeddle with the subject of the King's trial, I must decline the proposal, not only from a full conviction of its being useless, but also from delicacy towards Mr. Pitt himself. He desired that, since I would not mention it to Mr. Pitt, what he had said might be confidential—*entre quatre yeux*. Thus ended the conference. I perceived that he was much gratified at finding that the Minister was neutral. On going away he expressed the hope that the state of France might be an *example* to *England* and prevent us from destroying our *excellent* constitution.

Mr. Miles to M. Le Brun[1]

London: December 21, 1702

I have already written to you, my dear Sir, by M. Maret, who left the day before yesterday on his return to Paris. I write to you again confidentially; and it is M. Noël who will have the goodness to forward my letter.

I do not know in what manner Scipion Mourgue explained what has passed here, but it appears to me

---
[1] *Archives, Foreign Office, Paris*, vol. 584, p. 248.

that you are under an erroneous impression, which may lead you to act otherwise than as duty would indicate. You were induced to believe that Mr. Pitt had originated the conference with M. Maret; and it is probably in this belief that you assumed a tone scarcely suitable to present circumstances, and which may alienate, but cannot unite, the two nations. This conference was brought about by me: I proposed it to the Minister, and obtained it. Scipion Mourgue, for some months past, and from time to time, had allowed words to escape that led me to believe he held direct relations with the Executive Power in Paris, and was authorised to treat secretly with our Government. As I have always desired, and perhaps more than any one else, the union of the two countries—as I have always set great value on an alliance as being expedient both for France and England—I determined to put myself forward to realise an object very sincerely at heart ever since the year 1781, and which I communicated at the time to the Marquis de Bouillé and to the Vicomte de Damas. The resolution being formed, I asked Mourgue, when he first called upon me, '*if he was authorised to treat with the Minister.*' Do not find fault, Sir, if a zeal, very patriotic and praiseworthy, made him reply in the affirmative; he desiring, like myself, to preserve a good understanding between the two nations, and, not being ignorant of my connection with the Government, thought he saw the means, by my intervention, to avoid the scourge of war and give peace to Europe. I then took the measures necessary to obtain the conference as desired. After much difficulty and many *pourparlers*, I was asked the name of the person who had arrived on the part of the Executive Power. I declined to name him without his permission, and without the positive assurance that he would be received. It was agreed to receive him. But I leave you to judge of my surprise when I learned that it was M. Maret, and not M. Mourgue, who should see Mr. Pitt ; and, if astonished at what had happened, I could not but feel so much the more surprised when informed that M. Maret was not charged with any mission to our Government.

Such, then, is the brief history of this ridiculous adventure, which will deprive me, it may be for ever, of the means of opening a negotiation—unless, indeed, you authorise either M. Maret or M. Noël to give satisfactory explanations on the points which appear to cause, and justly so, disquietude to the British Government. You will see by this detail, as also from the letter herewith enclosed, with what delicacy and good faith and firmness I have conducted myself; and that it has not been Mr. Pitt, but really Mr. Miles, who *initiated* the interview which M. Maret had with the Minister.

I pray you to reflect well on the earnest entreaties which I still make to you not to lose a moment in repairing the error which a misunderstanding, as it appears to me, has produced. Doubtless M. Maret has already given explanations on many things which you could know only through him. I will restrict myself, then, to repeat the friendly assurances which I have always shown towards you ; and I pray you to believe that my personal esteem for you, as well as my philanthropic sentiments, make me desire very ardently that peace may be given to Europe, that you may enjoy the recompense due to a task so difficult, so prolonged, and that you may obtain the gratitude of your country and the admiration of the world.[1]

[1] ' Miles avait écrit plusieurs fois depuis le retour de Maret. Dans une lettre du 21 Décembre il rappelait tout ce qui s'était passé relativement

MR. MILES TO M. MARET

December 22, 1792

In the name of God, my dear Sir, do act in such a manner that the Executive Power may retrace its steps relative to the opening of the Scheldt, and that the Convention may renounce its error in wishing to support insurrections in foreign countries. It is the only means of avoiding war, and of extinguishing in our respective nations the firebrands who, labouring vigorously, intrigue and cabal, and make all possible efforts to produce the outbreak of a general explosion! I know your principles. I believe that you are sincere, and do not cease to employ means to preserve peace. But it is necessary to thwart the efforts of evil-disposed persons. I extend my views far beyond a peace which hitherto has been neither more nor less than a truce between the two peoples. I wish that peace should be established for ever, and that the great object of our alliance should be to secure concord throughout Europe, and thus contribute everywhere to the happiness of mankind. I am not authorised to say it to you, but you may rely upon what you now read as implicitly as if I had been instructed to make the communication: Renounce the opening of the Scheldt and the attempt to assist the insurgents in other countries—a project neither wise nor just—and we

à la précédente négociation, et se plaignait—*d'être discrédité, frappé d'impuissance par suite de cette ridicule aventure; de la substitution de Chauvelin, l'homme impossible entre tous, à Maret, dont la conduite avait été parfaite, &c. Il assurait que Maret était regretté, que ce qu'il y avait de mieux à faire c'était de le renvoyer à Londres. Cette lettre a dû exercer une certaine influence sur les résolutions concertées avec Dumouriez.*'—Ernouf, p. 113.

On the substitution of Maret for Mourgue, see *History of the Politics of Great Britain and France*, &c., by Marsh, ii. 6-17. See also *Authentic Correspondence*, &c., Appendix, p. 63.

shall not have war; all will then go well, and the foundation-stone of the alliance which I have so long desired will perhaps be laid.

I pray you to make Le Brun feel how much more glorious it would be for France, after having enfranchised the Austrian Netherlands and the country of Liège from the yoke of Germany, to give peace to Europe instead of plunging into hostilities, the termination and consequences of which no one can foresee, but which may easily put in danger not only the liberty recently acquired by the Liégeois and Belgians, but even the new order of things in France itself. The Executive Power would then enjoy the honour of having consolidated the French Revolution; it would command time to re-establish its dilapidated finances, restore the dislocated machinery of Government, and revive commerce, which is almost annihilated. Public tranquillity, as well as the prosperity and fortune of individuals hitherto debarred from success, would be thus assured by universal peace. Adieu!

Minute: December 23.—Received last night important intelligence from Paris in letters from Scipion Mourgue and General Dampierre, also a copy of the 'Decree of the National Convention' and an 'Extract from the Register of the Executive Council,' which latter is sent by M. Grouvelle at the express desire of Le Brun. Grouvelle is well known to me. He is a member of the Council.—W. A. M.

DECREE OF THE NATIONAL CONVENTION

'Décret qui détermine les règles à suivre par les généraux de la République dans les pays où ils ont porté et porteront ses armes, suivi d'une proclamation.

Du 15 Décembre 1792=17 du même mois :—

'La Convention nationale, après avoir entendu le rapport de ses comités des finances, de la guerre et diplomatique réunis, fidèle aux principes de la souveraineté du peuple, qui ne lui permet pas de reconnaître aucune des institutions qui y portent atteinte, et voulant fixer les règles à suivre par les généraux des armées de la République dans les pays où ils porteront les armes, décrète :—

'ART. I.—Dans les pays qui sont ou seront occupés par les armées de la République, les généraux proclameront sur le champ, au nom de la nation française, la souveraineté du peuple, la suppression de toutes les autorités établies, des impôts ou contributions existans, de la dime, de la féodalité, des droits seigneuriaux, tant féodaux que censuels, fixes ou casuels, des banalités, de la servitude réelle ou personnelle, des priviléges de chasse et de pêche, des corvées, de la noblesse, et généralement tous les priviléges.

'ART. II.—Ils annonceront au peuple qu'ils lui apportent paix, secours, fraternité, égalité et liberté, et ils le convoqueront de suite en assemblées primaires ou communales, pour créer et organiser une administration et une justice provisoire : ils veilleront à la sûreté des personnes et des propriétés ; ils feront imprimer en langue ou idiome du pays, afficher et exécuter sans délai, dans chaque commune, le présent décret et la proclamation y annexée.

'ART. III.—Tous les agens ou officiers civils ou militaires de l'ancien gouvernement, ainsi que les individus ci-devant réputés nobles ou membres de quelque corporation ci-devant privilégiée, seront, pour cette fois seulement, inadmissibles à voter dans les assemblées primaires ou communales, et ne pourront être élus aux places d'administration ou du pouvoir judiciaire provisoire.

'Art. IV.—Les généraux mettront de suite sous la sauvegarde et protection de la République française tous les biens meubles et immeubles appartenant au fisc, au prince, à ses fauteurs, adhérens et satellites volontaires, aux établissemens publics, aux corps et communautés laïques et ecclésiastiques ; ils en feront dresser, sans délai, un état détaillé, qu'ils enverront au conseil exécutif, et ils prendront toutes les mesures qui seront en leur pouvoir, afin que ces propriétés soient respectées.

'Art. V.—L'Administration provisoire, nommée par le peuple, sera chargée de la surveillance et régie des objets mis sous la sauvegarde et la protection de la République française ; elle veillera à la sûreté des personnes et des propriétés ; elle fera exécuter les lois en vigueur relatives aux jugemens des procès civils et criminels, à la police et à la sûreté publique ; elle sera chargée de régler et faire payer les dépenses locales, et celles qui seront nécessaires pour la défense commune ; elle pourra établir des contributions, pourvu toutefois qu'elles ne soient pas supportées par la partie indigente et laborieuse du peuple.

'Art. VI.—Dès que l'Administration provisoire sera organisée, la Convention nationale nommera des commissaires pris dans son sein pour aller fraterniser avec elle.

'Art. VII.—Le Conseil exécutif nommera aussi des commissaires nationaux, qui se rendront de suite sur les lieux, pour se concerter avec les généraux et l'Administration provisoire nommée par le peuple, sur les mesures à prendre pour la défense commune, et sur les moyens à employer pour se procurer les habillemens et subsistances nécessaires aux armées, et pour acquitter les dépenses qu'elles ont faites et feront pendant leur séjour sur son territoire.

'ART. VIII.—Les commissaires nationaux nommés par le Conseil exécutif lui rendront compte, tous les quinze jours, de leurs opérations. Le Conseil exécutif les approuvera, modifiera ou rejettera, et en rendra compte de suite à la Convention.

'ART. IX.—L'Administration provisoire nommée par le peuple, et les fonctions des commissaires nationaux, cesseront aussitôt que les habitans, après avoir déclaré la souveraineté et l'indépendance du peuple, la liberté et l'égalité, auront organisé une forme de gouvernement libre et populaire.

'ART. X.—Il sera fait état des dépenses que la République française aura faites pour la défense commune, et des sommes qu'elle pourra avoir reçues, et la nation française prendra, avec le gouvernement qui sera établi, des arrangemens pour ce qui pourra être dû ; et au cas que l'intérêt commun exigeât que les troupes de la République restassent encore à cette époque sur le territoire étranger, elle prendra les mesures convenables pour les faire subsister.

'ART. XI.—La nation française déclare qu'elle traitera comme ennemi le peuple qui, refusant la liberté et l'égalité, ou y renonçant, voudrait conserver, rappeler, ou traiter avec le prince et les castes privilégiées. Elle promet et s'engage de ne souscrire aucun traité, et de ne poser les armes qu'après l'affermissement de la souveraineté et de l'indépendance du peuple sur le territoire duquel les troupes de la République seront entrées, et qui aura adopté les principes de l'égalité, et établi un gouvernement libre et populaire.

'Art. XII.—Le Conseil exécutif enverra le présent décret, par des courriers extraordinaires, à tous les généraux, et prendra les mesures nécessaires pour en assurer l'exécution.

'Proclamation.

'Le Peuple français au Peuple ——

'Frères et amis,—Nous avons conquis la liberté et nous la maintiendrons. Nous offrons de vous faire jouir de ce bien inestimable qui vous a toujours appartenu, et que vos oppresseurs n'ont pu vous ravir sans crime.

'Nous avons chassé vos tyrans. Montrez-vous hommes libres, et nous vous garantirons de leur vengeance, de leurs projets et de leur retour. Dès ce moment, la nation française proclame la souveraineté du peuple, la suppression de toutes les autorités civiles et militaires qui vous ont gouvernés jusqu'à ce jour, et de tous les impôts que vous supportez, sous quelque forme qu'ils existent, l'abolition de la dîme, de la féodalité, des droits seigneuriaux, tant féodaux que censuels, fixes ou casuels, des banalités, de la servitude réelle et personnelle, des priviléges de chasse et de pêche, des corvées, de la gabelle, des péages, des octrois, et généralement de toute espèce de contribution dont vous avez été chargés par des usurpateurs : elle proclame aussi l'abolition parmi vous de toute corporation nobiliaire, sacerdotale et autres, de toutes les prérogatives et priviléges contraires à l'égalité. Vous êtes, dès ce moment, frères et amis, tous citoyens, tous égaux en droits, et tous appelés également à gouverner, à servir, et à défendre votre patrie.

'Formez-vous sur le champ en assemblées primaires ou de communes ; hâtez-vous d'établir vos administrations et justice provisoires, en vous conformant aux dispositions de l'Article III. du décret ci-dessus. Les agens de la République française se concerteront avec vous pour assurer votre bonheur et la fraternité qui doit exister désormais entre nous.'[1]

'Extrait du Registre des Délibérations du Conseil exécutif provisoire du 16 X^{bre} 1792, l'an 1er de la République :

'Le Conseil exécutif délibérant sur la conduite des armées françoises dans les pays qu'elles occupent, spécialement dans la Belgique, un de ses membres a observé—

'1. Que les gênes et entraves que jusqu'à présent la navigation et le commerce ont souffert, tant sur l'Escaut que sur la Meuse, sont directement contraires aux principes fondamentaux du droit naturel que tous les François ont juré de maintenir.

'2. Que le cours des fleuves est la propriété commune et inaliénable des habitans de toutes les contrées arrosées par leur cours ; qu'une nation ne peut sans injustice prétendre au droit d'occuper exclusivement le canal d'une rivière, et d'empêcher que les peuples voisins, qui bordent les rivages supérieurs, ne jouissent d'un même avantage ; qu'un tel droit est un reste des servitudes féodales, ou du moins un monopole odieux qui n'a pu être établi que par la force ni consenti que par l'impuissance, qu'il est conséquemment révocable dans tous les moments

[1] *Collection du Louvre*, V. xii. p. 380.

et malgré toutes les conventions, parce que la Nature ne reconnoit pas plus de peuples que d'individus privilégiés, et que les droits de l'homme sont à jamais imprescriptibles.

'3. Que la gloire de la République françaişe veut que partout où s'étend la protection de ses armes, la liberté soit rétablie et la tyrannie renversée.

'4. Que, lorsqu'aux avantages procurés au peuple Belge, par les armes françoises, se joindra la navigation libre des fleuves et l'affranchissement du commerce de ces provinces, ce peuple n'aura plus rien à craindre pour sa propre indépendance, ni à douter du désintéressement qui dirige la République ; de même que les nations de l'Europe ne pourront dès lors refuser de reconnoitre que la destruction de toutes les tyrannies et le triomphe des droits de l'homme sont la seule ambition du peuple françois. Le Conseil, frappé de ces puissantes considérations, arrête que le général commandant-en-chef les armées françoises dans l'expédition de la Belgique sera tenu de prendre les mesures les plus précises et d'employer tous les moyens qui sont à sa disposition pour assurer la liberté de la navigation et des transports dans tout le cours de l'Escaut.'

'Par ampliation conforme à l'original,

(Signé) 'GROUVELLE, Secrétaire du Conseil.'

M. SCIPION MOURGUE TO MR. MILES

Paris : December 15, 1792

I hope that when you receive this letter our friend Maret will have left you. I expect him with impatience. It is necessary that he should come soon. From the moment of his arrival we will strike together and crush quickly the scoundrels who wish to injure him. I see the Ministers every day. Le Brun is much pleased that you have not forgotten him. The Executive Council *est bon et pur*; but they have not here any correct idea of your country, nor of its internal affairs. Chauvelin has cruelly deceived us. There is great difficulty in destroying prejudices. I repeat to you that they hold firmly to the Scheldt. Tell me if your Ministry still contends for its closure. If your Government would be content with the assurance of peace towards Holland, we should soon be brothers. Tell me what they think on this point. You have seen my disposition and the temper in which I parted from you. I am still the same. The peace of Europe is still my object. But, my dear friend, what passions, what interests, both private and general, are encountered on the road! Men are always the same. The destiny of Europe hangs as by the thread of a spider; chance alone prevents it from breaking, and, if it breaks, we fall together into chaos—we shall devour one another, we shall tear one another to pieces, and some years hence, everything will finish in a frightful despotism. O Philosophy! behold thine own work! When I reflect upon it, I become misanthropic. I feel that we are but wretched animals, who have need, and for a long time will have need, of the curb of *religion*, or, it may be, of *superstition*, as the only power that can retain the *people* within the bounds wherein *thinking* men are retained by *wisdom*. I groan under the excesses, but I do not desire ever to desert the flag of liberty. Still once more, my friend, let us unite our efforts, and we shall succeed. As for me, I have courage to oppose myself to all excesses, and, strong in the armour which I expect from your counsels, I am quite ready to enter the lists against them. I know not why, but when I converse with you I cannot arrest my

pen. And yet I have not time even to write to my
parents. But ought you not also to keep me *au courant*
in respect to all that passes with you, with your Parliament and your King? Adieu![1]

General Dampierre to Mr. Miles

Paris: December 17, 1792

It is through the intrigues of Edward Walckiers, the Bruxelles banker, that our Executive Power will require, as a preliminary step to any explanation whatever, that the Republic should be acknowledged in the person of M. Chauvelin.[2] This gentleman was absolutely recalled on the return of Lord Gower. M. Noël was charged with the official letter to that purpose, and M. Reinhard was to have remained Chargé d'Affaires. M. Chauvelin, alarmed, entreated Noël not to deliver the letter of recall; he entreated him to consider the consequences that might attend his abrupt departure—'that the Court of London in that case would certainly demand an explanation, and a rupture between the two nations would ensue; that, though he was not on good terms with the English Minister, yet he was perfectly so with Mr. Fox and with some other members of Opposition, and would it be prudent in France to lose the fruit of all his labours with these gentlemen, and their subsequent

---

[1] *Conduct of France towards Great Britain*, page 144.

[2] 'Le citoien Maret est chargé par la dépêche que je lui adresse aujourd'hui de s'informer que la république a effectivement à faire sur ces trois points [1st, as to the decree of November 19; 2nd, the intentions of France in respect to Holland; and 3rd, on the opening of the Scheldt] des déclarations propres à calmer les inquiétudes du Ministère britannique et opérer le rapprochement des deux nations, *mais que vous seul êtes autorisé à les faire comme représentant avoué et connu de la république*. Le citoien Maret s'en tiendra là, et la difficulté se réduisant alors à une chose de pure forme, nous verrons si ce vain scrupule l'emportera chez M. Pitt sur le besoin qu'il doit avoir de connaître nos sentiments sur ces points.'—*Lebrun à Chauvelin, Paris*, 9 X^{bre}, 1792, *l'an 1er de la République*.

services, for a vain form of diplomatic etiquette?' These
and some other reasons alleged at the time induced M.
Noël to enter into the views of Chauvelin, and even to
enforce his arguments and recommend his remaining in
England. In return for this frankness, Chauvelin began
by endeavouring to fortify himself by his intrigues
among us. Walckiers is his relative by marriage; and,
as he has the ear of Le Brun, and has been all the time
at Paris, he has employed his own credit with the
Minister for Foreign Affairs, and every engine he could
put in motion, to have Chauvelin maintained in his
public character. Among other things, it was represented to Le Brun by M. Walckiers that it was incompatible with the dignity of the Republic to treat with
the British Minister in private, or by a secret agent—
that nothing less than a public acknowledgment of the
Republic should induce the French Executive Council to
enter into any explanation with the British Court, and
that it should be insisted upon that, as M. Chauvelin
was on the spot and had credentials, he should formally be invited by your Minister to appear at St.
James's in his public character. While this language
was insisted upon by the friends of Chauvelin here,
similar advice, I am told, was transmitted from your
country, and hence the reason that Maret is prevented
from acting, and that Le Brun forbids him to enter into
any detail with your Minister.[1] Noël, I am afraid, will
have cause to repent his candour to Chauvelin. There
is combustion in the hive. And Noël, who, I assure you,
is a perfectly honest man—very different to diplomatic
men in general—and very anxious to prevent the war,
has incurred much disgrace for endeavouring to undeceive Le Brun with respect to the strength of the Oppo-

[1] See Introduction, page 70.

sition and the internal state of your country, which latter was believed to be in a state of insurrection, until he wrote to the contrary; and on that account it is that the Executive Council has gone to such lengths, and may still go to greater. It is proposed to send Noël to the Hague as Minister, and, if this should take place, it is probable the storm raised against him may blow over. You may be assured he is very anxious for peace; so is Maret, and young Mourgue; and, rely upon it, they will exert all their influence and credit to preserve it as far as they can consistent with what they owe to their own country. This is all that at this distance, and by this conveyance, I can say to you at present, except that our politics are very dark and intricate, and, what is worse, they are variable. The most pacific councils of to-day may be overcast by some madman in the Jacobin Club to-morrow, and, much as peace is desired by the wise and honest, I doubt much whether fools and bad men will not carry the question of war in Paris.[1]

MR. MILES TO M. NOËL

December 23, 1792

I have just received a letter from Mourgue. I am sorry that they work underhand in Paris to injure Maret in the opinion of the Executive Council. I

---

[1] 'On the death of M. La Luzerne it was proposed to nominate a Jacobin to the British Embassy, but the late Bishop of Autun, from motives that will appear at some future period, pretended that the Court of London, holding itself very high, and still attached to ancient forms, would be offended at having a person of that description sent over, and that, rather than shock its prejudices, it would be advisable to name some one who was strongly attached to the Revolution, and yet eligible for presentation at St. James's. Hence the origin of M. Chauvelin's appointment. For the present I will only observe that, if ever his official correspondence with the Executive Council should be made public, it will

acquainted you yesterday with the sentiments held here, and that M. Chauvelin has no political character. I have no doubt whatever that, if France would renounce all projects of aggrandisement and consent to enter into a negotiation with the Court of Vienna for a general peace, all would go well. Surely France will be wrong to regard these mild propositions as severe! What satisfaction, what glory for France, if, after having freed herself from despotism, she obtains for the Belgians and the Liégeois liberty for ever! Behold, then, the reward of her labours! Could she, without failing in self-respect, aspire to a greater?

Inclosed you will receive the French gazettes which you lent me. I beg you to make me acquainted with your news from France as soon as you receive any, and do me the kindness to say when your courier leaves for Paris. I shall have a letter to send to Mourgue.

Adieu! *Je suis tout à vous. Bon jour.*

Mr. Miles to Lord Fortescue.

December 23, 1792.

I return the 'Alien Bill,' which you were so obliging as to lend me, and I append a note to the first enacting clause for your Lordship's consideration. If no penalty is decreed in cases of neglect or disobedience, I do not see that masters of vessels are bound to comply with the part of the bill that relates to them.[1] Government must not depend upon their patriotism. I take the liberty to make this suggestion all the more readily as I have been the primary author of the bill, and, ap-

---

appear how indecently he libelled this country and how egregiously he imposed upon his own.'—*The Conduct of France towards Great Britain Examined*, page 92. See Ernouf, p. 76.

[1] 'This hint was attended to, and a penalty enacted.'—W. A. M.

proving its principle as well as its justice and expediency, I could wish to see it perfect and rendered impossible to be evaded. It is a full month, if not more, since I urged upon Mr. Long to have orders sent to all the outports to seize the arms of foreigners as they arrive, and there keep them until their owners re-embark from this country. I gave him notice that foreigners came over with arms, and hinted that, although they pretended to be the disbanded emigrants, it was possible that the French, counting upon the information they received of the general disaffection of the country towards Government, might send over troops in that disguise, and, by the novelty and economy of such an invasion, carry their point. It would be an expedient more efficacious and ingenious than the Trojan horse, and what we might well expect from a people anxious to render anarchy universal. This communication, I am happy to find, has produced the bill which Lord Grenville has so ably brought forward, and, as it is partly my bantling, I wish well to it.

On my return from the theatre last night I found on my table a letter from Paris. I inclose an extract. It comes from a quarter well-informed, or rather from an immediate actor in the great scene now under representation. You may, if you please, transmit it to Lord Grenville. I have been asked what are the conditions this country exacts from France, and am assured that, if they are not too hard, they will be acceded to. If Ministers would explain themselves—for the French are ignorant of what is meant to be exacted of them—I am of opinion that a satisfactory *éclaircissement* would almost instantly ensue, and the peace of Europe be obtained and preserved. But if no hints are thrown out, no communications made, directly or indirectly, how

in the name of common sense are the differences to be
adjusted? I have no doubt in my own mind but that
France would come into the idea of a general pacification,
renounce the Scheldt, and all projects of aggrandisement,
upon the condition of being acknowledged, and
having Liège and the Pays-Bas Autrichiens declared a
free and independent republic. These countries are so
in fact; they ought long since to have been so; and if
the Duke of Leeds had adopted my plan in 1790 the
present armament would have been unnecessary. The
Dutch, secured by a broad and sufficient rampart, would
have had nothing to fear from France, whose troops
would not have been nearer to them than Lille or
Valenciennes; whereas they are now at their very
doors, and a disaffected party within are ready to open
them.

I own to your Lordship I am for peace; *et je crois
que mes conseils valent bien mieux dans cette occasion
que ceux de Mr. Burke,* who is almost always under
the dominion of passion,[1] and whose imagination seems
to have run away with him. If Ministers will only
suggest the concessions they expect from France, I will
contrive to have them transmitted *sans compromettre
personne*; and, as those with whom I am in correspondence
have credit, influence, and indeed authority, and
are as warmly disposed to peace as myself, I can count
upon their assistance. I tremble for the consequences
of a general war, and especially under the impressions
that have gone forth in the world. The strong spirit
of loyalty that happily manifests itself in this country,
which I will endeavour to keep alive and in vigour,[2]

---

[1] 'It is impossible to deny that they [*the writings of Burke*] are steeped in passion and exaggeration.'—Lecky, v. 521.

[2] By means of the public press.

preserves us for the moment from civil tumult; but the events of war are uncertain, and the interests of humanity totally out of the question. There are motives innumerable to engage us to peace, if peace can be preserved with honour and with safety. These are the two points that are to be considered; and the instant that it is known at Paris what it is that our *honour* and *safety* require, I have no doubt but that a person will be appointed to treat confidentially with Ministers. But it will not be Chauvelin; for, though he has lately received instructions to enter into explanations on these topics, he will be recalled—at least, I am labouring at this point, and shall, perhaps, accomplish it. In a word, if this country does not rise in her demands and exact severe conditions from France, she may give peace to Europe, and, by giving peace to Europe, obtain stability and security for the different governments that are in it.

Mr. Miles to M. Scipion Mourgue

December 24, 1792

If I have delayed writing to you, my dear Mourgue, it was because I expected you were on your return to England with the *olive branch* in your hand—with overtures for a future alliance between our respective countries. It is impossible to describe the agitation of my mind whilst waiting for an answer to the letter which you took to Paris; but this uneasiness was greatly enhanced when the despatch from Le Brun arrived on Friday, the 14th instant, in which our Minister was referred to Chauvelin for a full explanation of the grievances complained of, and which left to Maret no other mission than that of communicating to Mr. Pitt this unhappy determination on the part of the Executive Council.[1]

An expression contained in that despatch persuades me that your zeal to serve the two countries has led you into an error which, if not remedied, may prove fatal to both. You have asserted, unwittingly perhaps, that Mr. Pitt *initiated* the Conference with Maret. This statement gives a complexion to the business quite contrary to the fact, and which justifies in some degree the language used by Le Brun. The negotiation confided to you was so important, so delicate, that the utmost circumspection was necessary. And yet, as I fear, you have allowed it to be understood in Paris that England was alarmed; that we did not dare call out the Militia; and that, soliciting peace as a favour, she would accept any terms that your country might propose. You left London with the idea that our people were disaffected and ripe for revolt. I assured you to the contrary. This fact you should have stated to the Executive Council, and by so doing we should have travelled in a direct line to our great object—the peace of Europe. The despicable intrigues of Chauvelin would have had less force, less credit, and less success. But now it will require much address and patience, as well as zeal and perseverance, to recover what has been lost by indiscretion. I must, therefore, entreat you to lose no time in undeceiving Le Brun on this subject. Tell him frankly that it was Mr. Miles, and not Mr. Pitt, who *first broached* the idea of a private conference between our Minister and an agent accredited from Paris. The contrary opinion alters the whole face of the affair. It is, therefore, necessary that you correct this error, and relate without reserve the whole history of the trans-

[1] See Introduction, page 70.

action. I have never had but two guides through life—
common sense and common honesty; and those who
follow their directions will seldom lose their way.

The debates in Parliament will demonstrate to you
that I was not mistaken in what I said in November;
and that you have nothing to expect either from the
Dissenters, or from the partisans of Tooke and Paine,
or from the Opposition. The former, afraid of becoming
the victims of popular fury, are quiet. Tooke, Paine,
and their adherents who sought mischief, not reform, are
silenced, and can do no harm. And as to Opposition,
the whole party is dissolved—melted in the great mass
of the people; and, so far from being able to rally or make
a stand, its members have become political bankrupts,
and, finally, have acceded to the measures of Ministers.
Unanimity prevails within Parliament, and, what is its
best security, unanimity prevails among our people.
The whole nation has taken fire at the scandalous efforts
to disturb its peace and prosperity, and every parish
has entered into resolutions to defend the King, Lords,
and Commons. Our constitution, although it has some
blemishes, some defects, is substantially good, but,
since a party of political adventurers has shown a desire
to destroy it and throw everything into confusion, I
think the measures we have adopted are perfectly just,
and the most likely to counteract any attempt that may
be made to disturb our tranquillity. Believe me when
I assure you that the French Revolution has now very
few advocates here. And why? Because it has been
proved that *anarchy* produces *more mischief* than *despotism*, and finally ends in tyranny. Adieu!

P.S.—The public papers inform me that there is a
question of inculpating your father. I possess a letter
from him, dated in June, in which he tells me that 'he

tendered his resignation to the King because his Majesty would not follow his advice, which was, that he should sanction the decree against the ecclesiastics.' Both truth and friendship demand from me that they should neither be uninformed nor deceived as to the civism of your father.[1]

MR. MILES TO MR. AUST

December 26, 1792

I am told positively that Lord Lansdowne received a letter last Saturday from Lisbon assuring him that Spain has acknowledged the French Republic. The person who told me this had read the letter. This is in confidence, though I have no objection to your communicating it to Lord Grenville. If the intelligence is true, it will confirm what I told you two months since, and prove that my source of information was pure. I was also told that D'Aranda repeated to Bourgoing the subject-matter transmitted to him from his Majesty's Ministers, and I have reason to believe that I have not been misinformed.

Chauvelin dreads going back to Paris and is intriguing to remain here, for which purpose he urges the Executive Council to insist on his being received and acknowledged as Minister Plenipotentiary from the Republic. Noël goes as Chargé d'Affaires à la Haÿe, and sets off on Friday next *viâ* Liège. He offered me a place in his coach if I wished to visit my old friend Fabry, &c. And, if Lord Grenville should think that the real state of that country and of Flanders, also of

[1] 'The resignation of M. Dumouriez is to be attributed to his Most Christian Majesty's refusal to sanction the decree relative to the transportation of the clergy who refuse to take the oaths, &c., &c.'—*Despatches of Earl Gower*, p. 193. M. Mourgue was Minister of the Interior in the same Cabinet with Dumouriez.

the army of Dumouriez, is a matter of importance, I have no objection to quit my fireside for a fortnight and travel under the auspices of his passport. I throw out this hint merely as such, without the least desire of holding even an opinion on the subject.

Mr. Miles to Mr. Pitt

December 27, 1792

M. Noël has just left me in deep sorrow. He read to me the letter he received from Le Brun, who expresses much dissatisfaction with him for the arguments he employed to persuade the Executive Council to give up the Scheldt and avoid all possibility of conflict with England. M. Noël also read the report of Le Brun to the National Convention, dated the 19th instant. He pays a compliment to Mr. Fox *sans le nommer* in his speech. He insists that M. Chauvelin shall positively be received here, and has transmitted to him instructions to that purpose. He asserts that, in case of war, an appeal shall be made to the English *people* as against the Minister.[1] All this language arises from the

[1] 'Du reste, citoyen président, j'ai chargé en dernier lieu le Ministre de la République française à Londres de demander une nouvelle conférence à Lord Grenville, qui a dans le pays le département des affaires étrangères; et après lui avoir rappelé toute la futilité des griefs qu'on veut nous opposer, je l'ai autorisé à déclarer au nom de la République française que, si contre toute attente, l'intention du ministère de Saint-James était d'amener une rupture à tout prix—comme alors nous aurions épuisé toutes les explications propres à démontrer la pureté de nos vues et notre respect pour l'indépendance des autres puissances—comme il serait évident que cette guerre ne serait plus qu'une guerre du seul ministère britannique contre nous, nous ne manquerions pas de faire un appel solennel à la nation anglaise—(*On applaudit*)—que nous porterions au tribunal de sa justice et de sa générosité, l'examen d'une cause dans laquelle on verrait une grande nation soutenir les droits de la nature, de la justice, de la liberté, de l'égalité, contre un ministère qui n'aurait engagé cette querelle que par des motifs de pure convenance personnelle; qu'enfin nous établirions la nation anglaise juge entre nous et lui, et que l'examen

intrigues of Chauvelin at Paris. I would send the report to you, but you will probably see it in print tomorrow. The bulletin of the National Convention accompanies this letter, and, lest you should not be at home, I will proceed with it myself to the House of Commons. Le Brun will find that, if his ambition and the vanity of Chauvelin force you into hostilities, the nation will support you; and, in this case, we trust that the termination of the conflict will be as successful as was the war which your immortal father conducted.[1]

M. Scipion Mourgue to Mr. Miles

Paris: December 24,[2] 1792

Maret has arrived, my dear friend, and brings me no letters from you. Really it is too bad: since I have been here I have received only one letter from you, and that ten days after its date. Arouse yourself, then, *mon cher*, and let me hear from you often, for you know that, whilst nothing is more agreeable to me, your correspondence is most useful in the interests of peace between the two nations. I thank you much for the friendship which you have accorded to Maret. I do

---

de ce procès pourrait amener des suites qu'il n'aurait pas prévues.' (*On applaudit.*)—*Extrait de la Gazette Nationale ou le Moniteur Universel du Vendredi,* 21 *Décembre,* 1792.

[1] 'At the period to which I allude the French envoy in England showed his instructions to Mr. Sheridan, with whom I am well acquainted, and who is in the confidence of Mr. Fox; and these instructions positively stated that the Scheldt would not be given up, and that Le Brun was resolved to insist on the acknowledgment of the Republic in the person of M. Chauvelin *preliminary* to all explanation of the differences that had arisen. As to M. Chauvelin, he made no secret of declaring that, if he was not received at St. James's, the height of his ambition would be to leave this country with a declaration of war.'—W. A. M. *Authentic Correspondence,* &c., page 84.

[2] Received December 29.

not doubt that you will be pleased with him, for he is everything that is calculated to gratify a virtuous mind. He has come back in an excellent mood, and, like an intelligent man, has observed and judged your people without prejudice. I am persuaded that from his wise deportment, in conjunction with the purest principles of patriotism, the greatest benefits must accrue to our respective countries. I rejoice to think that your Ministry and ours will be wise enough to avoid the horrors of war. I love to believe that they will find the means of doing so; and that they will not be influenced by the passions of dangerous men by whom they may be surrounded. But I confess, it is not without indignation that I have read the ungenerous expressions of several of your Members of Parliament against the French. What! You complain that they speak sometimes in the noisy tribune of the Convention with little consideration for your Government, whilst in an assembly of intelligent men accustomed to political discussions they hear a Mr. Windham insult an entire nation by the extravagant assertion that *'before a Frenchman keeps his word his nature must be changed.'*[1] Certainly, my friend, never have even the Jacobins employed such an impertinent insinuation. You see how imprudent, how dangerous it is, for you know that a free people keenly resent injuries, and above all the French, who, as incipient pupils of liberty, have all the fire of youth. I pray daily that these personalities, these failures of decorum, may not further interrupt the harmony between France and England. You know the interest I take in the welfare of your country, and how faithful I am to my own nation and to liberty. I detest the crimes which

---

[1] Debate in the House of Commons, December 13. *Parliamentary History*, xxx. 40.

are committed in France. I abhor the cowardly agitators who cause our alarms. But, because these horrors exist under the pretence of defending liberty, ought we—we who are not influenced by passion, but seek only the happiness of mankind—to abandon a cause so noble and just? No, my friend! Let us rather work together, and be assured of the success of our united efforts.

Le Brun never speaks of you without expressions of friendship. He is most desirous that circumstances should place him in political relations with you.[1] Adieu, my dear friend! Be assured that no one is more tenderly attached to you, and that I shall always seek occasion to prove it. *Maret vous fait mille amitiés.* He is unable to write to you to-day, but he will do so before long. Adieu!

General Dampierre to Mr. Miles

Paris: December 24, 1792

Your *souvenir* has greatly touched me. I write to you at all hazards to say that I believe war to be inevitable, that there will be a general conflagration. Yes, without doubt, peace is always preferable to democracy—that is to say, we must not molest our neighbours on account of their opinions, but neither must we be content with repressing the enterprises of despotism: *il faut couper la tête à l'hydre, et pas se borner à lui mordre la queue.*

They tell me that you have written some articles in

---

[1] 'This night, December 24, 1792, Le Brun sent me a verbal message by a confidential person to the effect that Mr. Pitt could not send to Paris any one more capable than myself to preserve harmony between the two nations, or who would be more welcome, that my sentiments were known to be favourable to an alliance, and that France had it much at heart to be united by a treaty to England.'—W. A. M.

strong language against the French Revolution. They even say that you are no longer a friend to liberty. However, you cannot abandon its cause without renouncing your reason. I esteem you too sincerely to believe it, but, if it is so, I shall be much concerned, not only at having lost a friend, but because liberty will have lost one of its best defenders. I repeat to you that they breathe nothing here but war.[1]

GENERAL WIMPFFEN TO MR. MILES

Paris : December 28, 1792

The courier is on the point of starting. I have only a moment in which to write a word. You correctly divined the fate of the King and Queen : assuredly they will perish. See the infamous requisition of a man who thirsts only for blood. I was present at the Convention at the very moment when that villain Hébert, known under the name of Père Duchêne,[2] rose and said, 'Je

---

[1] 'This gallant and good man—General Dampierre—warm even to enthusiasm in the cause of liberty, was the son of a captain in the French navy, and was in the action of April 12, 1782. A stranger to intrigue, he detested parties and factions. He saw nothing but his country; and, be the cause of quarrel in itself just or unjust, he fell, according to his judgment, in her defence, at the head of an army, the command of which devolved on him on the base desertion, for it cannot be called repentance, of Dumouriez.'—W. A. M. See *Conduct of France towards Great Britain*, pp. 131, 154.

'By the activity of the Commissioners sent from Paris, the northern army was in some degree reorganised, and General Dampierre was appointed the provisional Commander-in-Chief; nor did he wait many days before he had an opportunity of displaying his military talents. He had reoccupied the camp of Famars, and on the 8th May made an attack on the Austrian and Prussian posts, which brought on a very serious engagement that ended in favour of the Allies. . . . In this battle Dampierre finished his short career. . . . He lost his thigh by a cannon-ball, and died of his wound the following day, leaving the command of the army to General La Marche.'—*Annual Register*, 1793 : *History of Europe*, p. 252.

[2] 'This man was the author of a vile inflammatory daily paper in the height of the Revolution, in 1790-1791, which was vociferously hawked

demande que les Commissaires du Temple fussent tenus de ne mêler à leurs rapports sur cette prison aucun détail capable d'apitoyer sur le sort des détenus.' Ah, my friend, will you believe that this atrocious measure was adopted by a legislative assembly still more atrocious than the man who proposed it? They do things quickly here. Read, my dear Miles, what I now send you in haste, and pity the fate of your friends in Paris. *A vous pour la vie.*

Extracts from the Papers forwarded by General Wimpffen

'*Paris Sections.*—The patriotic society of the Section of the Luxembourg orders that Louis shall perish, or that no Republican shall survive him. This order was accompanied by an oath in the following *formula*:—If the men whom we have charged with the execution of our vengeance are faithless to their promises, I swear that I will never inhabit the land soiled by traitors. It is further said in this order, addressed to the other forty-seven sections of Paris, that, in case it should be possible for the National Convention to fall into a snare, it would be necessary to name an officious defender of the Republic.

about the streets by that description of people, the great bulk of whom it was to put in motion. *Père Duchêne fâché contre l'Assemblée Nationale,* or, *Père Duchêne en grande colère,* was in great request by the rabble.'—W. A. M. Hébert was guillotined on March 24, 1794, and his widow on April 10 in the same year.
  '*Père Duchesne* of Hébert, brutallest newspaper yet published on earth.'—Carlyle.
  'He had formerly been ticket-collector at the theatre, and after the Revolution he edited the *Père Duchesne,* the foulest of all the democratic journals, in which with curses and obscene raillery he led on the proletaries and vagabonds of the capital to the destruction of existing society.'—Sybel, ii. 209.

'The section of the Théâtre Français declared itself in permanent insurrection, and ordered that the *tocsin* should sound in the hearing of the tyrant and of those who desired to prevent his capital punishment.

'The section of the Sans-Culottes declared that, since Pierre Manuel had demanded in the Convention that the "Defence of Louis" should be printed and circulated in the departments, and that the discussion should be adjourned for three days, he had forfeited its confidence, and it invited the other sections to supersede him.

'*Commune de Paris.*—A deputation from the section of the Panthéon Français came to denounce Charles Villette as likely to kindle the torches of civil war. "Behold *that* Villette," they exclaimed, "who has not denounced the Austrian Committee,[1] holding its sittings at the house of Tourzelle in the Faubourg Saint-Germain, who has not stirred up the people at this epoch to

---

[1] 'It was Carra who in 1790 accused in the Jacobin Club the hapless Queen with having an *Austrian Committee* in the Tuileries. I was present when she was first denounced, and, believing it to be slander invented for the horrible purpose of keeping the populace in constant ferment, I expressed my indignation at such base and unmanly arts. Carra, on descending from the tribune, approached me, and, seating himself by me, declared that he had positive information that Marshal Bender had directions from the Emperor to march into France immediately from Bruxelles with 50,000 men, the whole effective force at that time in the Austrian Netherlands! The next night a letter, pretended to have been written by the Field-Marshal, and addressed to the President of the Club, was read, containing this menace, but in language so coarse and extravagant that its forgery was evident. The next morning I read in several parts of the Tuileries printed bills addressed to the Queen as follows: "On dit que ton frère viendra avec 50,000 hommes. Qu'il vienne : nous irons au devant de lui avec 100,000, portant ta tête sur une pique." From that time the clamours against the Austrian Committee, universally propagated and believed, never ceased, and, gathering strength daily, finally accomplished the destruction of the monarchy and the monarch.'—W. A. M. *Conduct of France towards Great Britain,* page 88.

gratify their personal hatreds, who, whilst pity is felt
for the fate of the *ci-devant* King, which spreads like
gangrene over a large portion of the departments, establishes
himself as the trumpet which the aristocrats
place in advance to test public opinion!" The greater
part of the members decide that the Procureur of the
Commune should prosecute him. Hébert remarks that
the conduct of Villette did not astonish him; that, without
doubt, this individual regretted the *young ladies* and
the *red-heels* of the Faubourg Saint-Germain, but he could
wish that they would act much more severely against
Brissot and all the journalists hired by Roland. He
cited on this occasion the journal of Gorsas, of which, he
said, the Minister purchased every day 2,000 copies.
"*It is not surprising, then,*" he added, "*that we are depicted
as cannibals and murderers.*" "It is not our pens, but
our pikes, that we must sharpen," exclaimed Bernard.
"We are, so to say, in insurrection. Ah, well! since
the outburst of civil war is meditated, let us rise to the
grandeur of the tenth of August!" After some other
sallies not less violent, the speaker resumed by demanding
the previous question, on the motion of Hébert,
for the prosecution of Brissot[1] and the other
journalists, "for," said he, "the same arms which we employ
against them, the aristocrats would employ against
Marat, Robespierre, and all good patriots." The discussion
was prolonged. It was then ordered that the
Procureur of the Commune should prosecute Charles
Villette through the law, and, at the same time, he was
charged to prosecute a Vicar of the Church Notre Dame
for having refused to baptize an infant in the name of
Alexandre *Pontneuf.*'

[1] Brissot was proscribed with the Girondins, May 31, 1793, and perished on the scaffold in October.

Mr. Miles to M. Le Brun[1]

London: January 2, 1793

You still express, dear Sir, in your different reports to the Convention, and in the despatches which have fallen under my notice, the desire to preserve peace between England and France. But how can we rely on protestations of friendship contradicted by facts? How can we believe in your pacific intentions while your conduct is hostile? During four consecutive months your secret emissaries have made numerous attempts to obtain an interview with Mr. Pitt, whose compliance, when granted, has been attributed, not to sincerity, nor to the interest which he is considered to take in the prosperity of his country, nor to sound political principles founded on the basis of uprightness and humanity, but to weakness, or to a still less excusable motive, which could only be attributed to him by disingenuous men, who, being destitute of all feeling of honour, do not believe that such feeling can exist in others. According to them, it was to fear or treachery that M. Maret owed his interview with Mr. Pitt. Great God! what fear could he have had? And what had he to gain by treachery? Menaced by an army already on your frontiers—all the machinery of your Government as well as the minds of the people disorganised by your convulsions in the interior—fear has led you to hold language not only inaccurate, but which was soon changed into a tone you should not have permitted, and to which still less could we have listened.

[1] See *Authentic Correspondence with M. Le Brun*, &c., Appendix, p. 92. Herbert Marsh, ii. 52, &c., discusses at length the contents of this letter, which, however, is not to be found among the archives in Paris

The rapidity of your conquests in the Austrian Netherlands, as in Germany and Savoy, has made you lose sight of what you owe to yourselves and to others; and, because you succeeded by the boldness of your arms against some governments naturally weak and already infected with the contagious vices of the times, you believed yourself able to dictate the law to all Europe, and to force her to adopt the same principles of anarchy of which you have been the victims since the 14th of July, 1789. I am in despair at finding a resemblance so perfect between the conduct of liberated France and that of France in bondage, as if it was her sad destiny always to groan under a despotism more or less frightful.

I have traced the course which you ought to pursue, and if you follow my counsels the English Cabinet will never think of war. But you must act in good faith—*n'écoutez pas ces petits messieurs qui vous entourent et vous flattent, et qui aimeraient mieux jouer au plus fin que de marcher droit.* Recall to your memory that, by chance the most extraordinary and the most whimsical, you hold in your hands, so to say, the destiny of the whole of Europe, and that, in deviating from the principles traced in my former letter, and which Maret has certainly repeated according to my request, you will pronounce a decree of death against millions, perhaps, of your fellow-creatures! Can you—dare you think of it without shuddering? Peace, I repeat to you, may easily be preserved. The English are well disposed towards France, and, as the public voice counts for much in this country, the Government will never dare to proceed in a contrary direction. But, on your side, it is necessary that you should neither shock nor weary the people by decrying a constitution to which their attachment is inviolable. Here, however, is the rock on which, I fear, you will be stranded; and without discussing the impropriety of your wishing to interfere in the internal affairs of another nation, it must be acknowledged that so incautious a step would be not less improper than unjust and dangerous. The misfortune is that you seem to have the mania for universal interference. Remember, my friend, that by meddling with everything you may spoil everything.

Recall, then, all your emissaries—let the propaganda cease—and do not any longer seek to disturb public tranquillity in this country. Your decrees of the 19th of November and 15th of December are menaces which no Government could hear without taking immediate precautions for its own safety; and you must feel that, while such decrees exist, we cannot rely on your pacific assurances. Moreover, when you speak in a sense contrary to the explicit declarations of the Convention, you can only be regarded as a private individual. In the name of God, then, if you would avoid a universal conflagration, do not interfere with our Government. I dwell all the more on this subject because I am not ignorant of the ill-founded hopes which you have conceived of a general revolt; and while you encourage such projects it will be impossible for me to help you, or even to hold any correspondence either with you or with the Executive Council.

You ask me if Lord Hawkesbury and Mr. Dundas are not for war? I have not any acquaintance with these persons, and am absolutely ignorant of their opinions. I have never had any connection with them; but I frankly confess that their advice on the unfortunate American war, equally imprudent and ruinous, deprives me of all confidence in their wisdom and in their principles.¹

I conjure you to listen to me yet once more. Do not render hostile armaments a necessity for us, either as a measure of precaution or as being needful to repulse an aggression, and, in that case, there will be no war. You may rely upon what I say. I can even recognise the most favourable dispositions in the direction of peace. Do not, then, force Mr. Pitt by your imprudence to declare himself against you.²

It would be a wise course to restore liberty to the Belgians and Liégeois. The Emperor will have nothing more to say; and a loyal and brave people will be freed from a yoke which has too long oppressed them. England would not now be averse to an arrangement which imperative circumstances have dictated. I have proposed to Mr. Pitt this arrangement as the condition on which

---

¹ 'I do not know from what source M. Le Brun derived his information, but it was the opinion of others as well as his own that both Lord Hawkesbury and Mr. Dundas were eager for war. Whenever this language was held to me, my answer was: 'If so, why give them by your conduct an advantage over you and favour their views?'—W. A. M. *Authentic Correspondence*, Appendix, p. 103.

² 'Il n'est qu'un seul point cependant sur lequel le Roi et tous les siens, plus maîtres encore de l'opinion populaire que Pitt, qui a maintenant besoin d'eux pour se soutenir, ne paraissent pas encore parvenus tout à fait à leur but; ils ont fait haïr les français et leurs principes, ils les font persécuter en Angleterre, ils ne réussissent pas encore à faire désirer la guerre avec eux. Non, citoyen, quelque chose qu'on puisse vous dire là-dessus, la guerre avec la France n'est pas encore populaire ici, on n'y voit pas de cause, on n'en espère point de profit. L'effet qu'a produit votre rapport en est la preuve. Quelques expressions de ce rapport ont révolté la Cour, choqué les ministres, effarouché peut-être un peu le servile esprit national par ce mot d'appel au peuple qui a été ici mal entendu, et cependant depuis que les bassesses sont connues, les fonds ont déjà un peu remonté. On parle plus de paix, on se demande quelle serait la cause de la guerre, et quoique les intentions de la majorité du Conseil soyent probablement toujours les mêmes, il parait désirer d'attendre une meilleure occasion pour les faire connaître,' &c., &c.—*Extract from the Despatch of Chauvelin to Le Brun*, London, December 31, 1792.

you might consent to reopen the affair of the Scheldt and agree to peace with Prussia and Austria. It is for the Executive Power to decide. Consider, then, I pray you, that, if they refuse in Paris to comply with advice so reasonable, a frightful war will ensue: you would have to combat the whole of Europe, and the two peoples, the Belgians and the Liégeois, for whom I have so long laboured, will fall back into bondage. You are master of their destiny. You can assure to them liberty and independence. My proposal to the Duke of Leeds in January 1790, and which was rejected by him, has been pretty well accepted to-day. I will answer for the establishment of a new republic on the *débris* of despotism, *si vous ne gâtez pas la chose*. Adieu! I have written to you by Noël.

MR. MILES TO LORD FORTESCUE

January 2, 1793

I do yet entertain a hope that peace will be preserved, not only for the sake of humanity and for the interests of our country, but from my great and sincere personal regard for Mr. Pitt, whose popularity will suffer and be eventually destroyed by going to war with a people who are in fact contending for freedom, however unjustifiable some of their means may be to obtain it. Need I add that such a war will sound ungracious and offensive in the ears of every Englishman attached to the principles of our own Revolution which seated the present family on the British throne?

I have been told that Mr. Bland Burgess[1] has asserted that Maret meant nothing more by coming to England than to play with our funds, and that, if he corresponds upon public affairs with the Executive

---

[1] Under-Secretary of State for Foreign Affairs.

Council, *c'est seulement pour faire sa bourse*. I have no reason to believe that Maret has any connections with our brokers or commercial men; but I know to a certainty that no man can be more anxious than he is to prevent hostilities, or more desirous to see an alliance proposed and ratified between France and England. I also know that no man can reprobate in stronger language than he has done the horrible and atrocious cruelties of his countrymen. He had even the virtue to propose in council that the assassins—the guilty perpetrators of the massacres on the 2nd of September —should be brought to trial. On the very mention of punishment, Clavière was bereaved of his senses—expressing his astonishment that any man should make so daring a proposal; and, as if he had fancied himself assailed by the assassins, asked Maret if he was not afraid to make such a proposal, surrounded as they were by spies and murderers. 'Comment osez-vous la faire?' said Clavière in a faltering voice; 'ne savez-vous pas que les murailles ont des oreilles?'

Maret says that Danton, Robespierre, and Marat are proper objects to be employed in the commencement of a revolution; but in this I differ from him, because men of that description, and with such talents, are likely to have a great influence over the rabble, and to be looked up to by them. It is for this reason that these men, at least in my opinion, ought to be kept in the background. Maret is certainly a friend to the Revolution. Whether so violent a convulsion was necessary is a question on which the wisest and the best men seem to differ, while all agree that the abuses in the French Government were enormously great and stood in need of extensive reform. All men are in accord on this point, and only differ as to the means.

I am decidedly of opinion that nothing short of a revolution could have reformed the abuses in that country. The men who thought so, and who acted upon their convictions, could not have foreseen the excesses that have ensued; most probably they never meant that the changes should have been carried to such an extent; and I do not, therefore, think it candid, whilst I am sure it is not just, on the part of the French clergy and nobility to instruct their advocate, Mr. Burke, to charge all the atrocities committed by the rabble to the account of those who took the lead. The Revolution was sustained by the French with a view to have their nation better governed, and all descriptions of their countrymen brought under the dominion of known laws, and thereby emancipated from the caprice of kings and their ministers. All this, however, is matter of opinion, and as such only I hazard it. Whether Maret be right or wrong in thinking as he thinks upon the subject matters nothing. But he is certainly not a stock-jobber.[1]

I am interrupted by a letter from Paris. It assures me that the Executive Council approve very fully and warmly of my idea of an alliance between the two countries. If our Government would also approve it, I should be the happiest of mortals after the ratification of such a treaty, because I am convinced that it would not only be for our mutual benefit, but also for the good of humanity throughout the civilised world. Of this be assured, my dear Lord—and remember, I conjure you, the prediction—that this country will not be allowed to steer a middle course between enmity and friendship.[2] We are too near to France, and too formidable

---

[1] 'Mr. Bland Burgess seems to have cherished an unfriendly feeling towards M. Maret.' See *Auckland Correspondence*, ii. 493.

[2] See Letter of M. Chauvelin to Lord Grenville, *Annual Register*, 1793: *State Papers*, page 114.

for her in her present situation—assailed, as she is, by all the great Continental powers—not to insist on our declaring for or against her. It must necessarily come to this very soon, and France is prepared for either alternative. I doubt much whether there is an equal degree of preparation in this country; and, above all, I doubt whether Government has sufficiently calculated what the probable consequences of a rupture will be under the enthusiasm, or, if you will, the *delirium* by which our neighbour appears to be actuated at this moment. For my part I dare not contemplate the issue of a decision so grave, so rash, as a declaration of war, viewing the positive advantages—as I view them, and which stare us in the face—of our resolving, as her friends, to defend France against the whole herd of German despots, whether they are great or small.

Forgive this long letter; but as you have allowed me from our long acquaintance to hazard my opinions on public affairs—and we are now in a crisis—I have availed myself of the indulgence to deliver the thoughts as here expressed without reserve, and shall conclude by saying, God direct us for the best![1]

[1] 'Les documents publiés par M. Pallain font très bien connaître les phases de la négociation dirigée à Londres par Talleyrand, mais ils ne pouvaient pas dégager le principe même de cette négociation. Heureusement, l'un des derniers confidents de Talleyrand, un historien dont la réserve égale la sincérité, ce qui ajoute à la valeur de son témoignage, Mignet, dit formellement que Talleyrand allait à Londres pour tenter d'établir une *alliance nationale* en opposition à *l'alliance de famille*, que les agents de la Cour resserraient sur le continent avec les maisons d'Autriche et de Bourbon. . . . On comprend enfin pourquoi Talleyrand doit s'efforcer de faire ressortir la ressemblance entre la révolution qui vient de s'accomplir et la révolution de 1688, qui a consacré la liberté anglaise. C'est qu'il s'agit, comme Mignet nous l'apprend, de séduire l'Angleterre et de l'amener à contracter, non pas une alliance avec le Roi de France, mais une alliance avec la Révolution française. . . . Dans son introduction et dans de nombreuses notes, M. Pallain expose avec sa clarté habi-

Minute: January 3.—M. Reinhard, Secretary of Legation from France, called on me about noon and stayed with me more than two hours. We canvassed the different interests of our respective countries, and entered fully into the various subjects of mutual complaint which had unhappily arisen. It was impossible, I said, that England could view without alarm the rapid conquests of France, and the still more rapid progress of the principles which, with an assiduity as great as the motive and object were criminal, she avowed and promulgated wherever her armies penetrated or wherever her newspapers, which were in fact so many hostile manifestoes, could obtain admission. He enquired if there was the possibility of preserving peace; or if Mr. Pitt was resolved on war, observing at the same time that he thought Mr. Pitt too wise and too just to adopt so violent a measure, and concluded by wishing to know if I thought all passage to reconciliation was barred.

I asked what effect he imagined the despatch received by M. Chauvelin from Lord Grenville on Monday, the 31st of last month, would have in Paris. He answered, a very bad effect, and that perhaps it would occasion the immediate recall of Chauvelin, although he had in a few words at the end of the despatch earnestly recommended the Executive Council to allow him to remain in London. Reinhard added that it was his sincere wish to preserve peace; he would be happy to contribute to it; he lamented that Maret had by his intervention rendered it in a manner very difficult, if not

tuelle les vues de Talleyrand au sujet de l'alliance de la France et de l'Angleterre, il les explique, les commente, les justifie.'—*Revue d'Histoire Diplomatique*, troisième année, No. 4, page 593, &c. See *La Mission de Talleyrand à Londres en* 1792; *Correspondance diplomatique inédite de Talleyrand*, publiée, avec Introduction et Notes, par G. Pallain. Paris: Plon, Nourrit et Cie, 1889.

impracticable, and that the last interview with Mr. Pitt
had produced a bad effect both in London and in Paris.

The Alien Bill was the next topic of conversation.
Reinhard was extremely shocked on being informed
that Chauvelin and his family were within its power,
and that he enjoyed no diplomatic character or privilege
in this country. I assured him that it was a measure
of precaution demanded by the times; that the influx
of Frenchmen, many of whom were armed, had created
a general uneasiness; and that this alarm was fortified
and augmented by the proofs which Government had
received of the secret machinations of private emissaries
against the internal tranquillity of this country, and
specially by the far more flagitious and more public
appeal of the Convention to the labouring classes of all
nations to throw off their obedience to legal authority,
and to destroy all the distinctions of rank—adopting a
chimerical system of equality, a system which does not
exist in nature, and which men will not admit, either
in a savage state or when advanced to civilisation.
The more than criminal indecency of the Convention in
receiving addresses from any description of people, no
matter how profligate or how obscure, and especially
from men avowedly hostile to the laws and constitution
of their native country, were so many gross and palpable
wrongs that the servants of the Crown had been forced
to take strong and perhaps harsh measures as the only
means of averting much public calamity and preserving the country from the terrible predicament in which
France herself was involved, not by her desire for
liberal and necessary reform, but by the spirit of wanton
revolt and licentiousness which, at all times, tends more
to deface, subvert, and destroy than to ameliorate or
amend. The almost unpardonable imprudence of M.

Chauvelin in receiving at his table the editors of newspapers in opposition to Government, and in dining at their houses, had also aggravated affairs.

Reinhard acknowledged with an air of great candour that Chauvelin might certainly have acted with greater judgment, but, at the same time, he could not refuse seeing those who applied for an interview. I remarked that the complaisance for which he contended was a departure from long-established usages, and a palpable deviation from that dignified conduct which ought always to characterise the diplomacy of all nations; that it was unworthy of M. Chauvelin, and ill corresponded with his professions of respect for the Government to which he was accredited, to mix familiarly with those who wished to subvert it; that, if he was sincerely desirous of preserving peace between the two countries, he certainly would not have countenanced men known to be hostile to his Majesty's Ministers; that it was impossible he could have any business to transact with the editors of opposition journals, and that, invested as he claimed to be with a public character, the conduct which he had pursued was an affront to this Government. Reinhard inquired what I would have done in the situation of Chauvelin. I answered that, under the critical and delicate circumstances of the moment, I should have avoided as much as possible all intercourse even with men of rank who were in Opposition, although their being in Opposition would not in times less tempestuous have been a sufficient reason for depriving myself of their society. I inquired in my turn whether the National Assembly or Executive Council would have been pleased with Lord Gower while he was the British Minister at Paris if his Lordship had lived on terms of intimacy with the editors of public prints known to be hostile to the new order of things in France, such as the 'Journal de la Cour et de la Ville,' 'Les Actes des Apôtres,' 'L'Ami du Roi,' and 'Gazette de Paris.' Reinhard acknowledged that my conduct would have been dignified, but that, as to the Opposition, there was some excuse for Chauvelin, who finding himself ill received by the Ministry and their supporters, regarded as an object of suspicion and avoided, alone, and in a strange country, it was not to be supposed he could live insulated, and, as it were, proscribed; and that his associating with Lord Lansdowne, Mr. Fox, Mr. Sheridan, and other gentlemen of that party was a matter of necessity into which the million of slights, not to say affronts, which he had received at Court had forced him. I was too well acquainted with the cold, ungracious, and distant, or rather insolent carriage of Lord Grenville and the *hauteur* and reserve of Mr. Pitt not to feel in all its force and poignancy the justice of the remark, and inwardly to subscribe to a truth I could not deny. I found in their conduct a sufficient apology for the behaviour of M. Chauvelin, so far as it related to his intimacy with the Parliamentary Opposition in this country.

Reinhard then delivered to me Chauvelin's message, which was that he would be happy to make my acquaintance. I answered that it would give me pleasure to see M. Chauvelin in Cleveland Row, but, for reasons that must be obvious, it was impossible I could call on him. After many assurances of the pacific disposition of Chauvelin and his extreme desire to preserve peace, Reinhard wished to know if, in the event of France refusing to renounce her project of opening the Scheldt, giving up Savoy, and consenting to a general peace, war would still be inevitable. I answered that, not being sufficiently apprised of the intentions of his Majesty's Ministers on these points, I could not say anything to which the least consequence ought to be attached, and that I should be sorry to give his judgment a wrong bias by hazarding an answer to questions upon which I was not competent to decide. Being earnestly and repeatedly pressed to give my opinion—to say what I really thought ought to be done on such an occasion, *i.e.* if France peremptorily refused to abandon her project and her conquests—I frankly declared that, if I had the honour of having a share in his Majesty's councils, I should most certainly consider the obstinacy of France as extremely hostile to this country, and would recommend that every possible mode of amicable negotiation should be employed to engage her to accede to the only conditions which could prove that her desire to preserve peace was really sincere. Being further pressed as to what I thought was the opinion of Mr. Pitt in the event of a refusal on the part of the Executive Council to concede any of the above points, I again entreated him not to urge me to an answer that might be wrong by its being hazarded: all I could permit myself to say on the subject, and all that I begged he would expect me to say, amounted only to a very ardent hope that the Executive Council would not pertinaciously adhere to points which are totally unconnected with the re-establishment of the civil government and with the honour and interests of France, but which, by being persevered in, might widen the breach into a wild and ferocious war, the issue of which nothing short of prescience could foretell. The inference that Reinhard drew from these last remarks was that, since France would not give up

nor would England recede, war is inevitable. He took his leave of me apparently anxious and melancholy.[1]—
W. A. M.

MR. MILES TO MR. LONG

January 4, 1793

Do forgive an anxiety certainly in the extreme for the interests of our country, and exert all your credit and influence with Mr. Pitt to engage him—however opposed he may be by the *cabal* at Buckingham House—to preserve his pacific disposition at this momentous crisis. You cannot count upon any beneficial effects from a union with the Continental powers: remember, I tell you this; all history offers to your observation the little danger there is to the power assailed from confederate forces acting together. *Confederacy is not union*; and a confederacy of any kind against France will fortify and augment among her people that enthusiasm which seems already invincible.[2]

---

[1] 'Reinhard, précepteur à Bordeaux avant la Révolution, était entré dans la diplomatie sur la recommandation des députés de la Gironde, qui ont été rarement mieux inspirés. C'était un homme d'un esprit très-fin, très-français, malgré son origine allemande et l'accent dont il ne put jamais se défaire.'—Ernouf, p. 121. After the declaration of war Reinhard remained for some time attached to the Foreign Office in Paris. He was afterwards sent Minister Plenipotentiary to the Hanse Towns, and resided at Hamburg as his head-quarters. Local disputes caused his removal to Aix-la-Chapelle. He was subsequently sent by Bonaparte as Resident to the Hospodars of Wallachia and Dalmatia. In 1814 he reappears at the Foreign Office, whence, writing to Mr. Miles, August 6, he says: 'Soyez bien sûr que je n'ai jamais oublié l'obligeance que vous m'avez montrée à Londres, et les preuves que vous m'avez données de votre bienveillant souvenir ; et je m'estimerai vraiment heureux de trouver des occasions pour vous prouver ma reconnaissance et mon amitié.'

[2] 'L'expérience prouve que dans le nord les Puissances ont pris de mauvaises mesures, car depuis qu'elles ont adopté dans leurs succès toutes les formes de la conquête, les départements du nord, qui s'étaient montrés d'abord les plus éloignés de l'esprit républicain, sont aujourd'hui les plus dévoués à la Convention, et que le midi, qui était primitivement républicain

I own to you that I dread the consequences of a war, because I feel assured that it will have no resemblance either in its march or conclusion to former wars, and that we have everything to risk; that we stake the salvation of our constitution on its issue, and must be a loser at all events, even if nothing worse results to us from engaging in it. I have opened my heart to you on this momentous subject. I know that there are firebrands in this country, as well as in France, who breathe nothing but war and desolation; but I trust Mr. Pitt has more firmness—more wisdom he certainly has—than this cabal; and, if the former bears any proportion to the latter, he will resist their clamour and their efforts to involve this country in hostilities, and I am sure he will command the voice, and, if necessary, the arm of the nation to support him. I will merely add that, although I am not the friend of Mr. Fox, and although I think his conduct faulty on the regency business and in the cases of the Middlesex Election and London printers, yet on this occasion he is right. He is the temperate, judicious, prescient statesman, and not Mr. Burke, who appears to have whirled about since he so justly defended the Americans in their legitimate resistance to Parliamentary despotism, and to have hired himself to priests to assassinate freedom,

---

ardent, n'ayant point d'inquiétude de la part des étrangers, est disposé à revenir à la monarchie limitée. J'invoque la grâce de M. Pitt pour lui demander de se placer au milieu de la France pour bien juger les moyens de succès. Il y trouverait trois factions très inégales qui la partagent: les aristocrates, les constitutionnels et les républicains. Les constitutionnels et les républicains sont deux classes déterminées, elles ont un code écrit; les aristocrates forment une classe vague, subdivisée et sans accord, dont on ne connait que les haines et les intrigues, et dont personne ne connait ni le but ni les effets. M. Pitt! M. Pitt! ne croyez aucun des partis, ne croyez aucune des personnes qui vous parlent, mais regardez et faites!'—Lettres de M. de Talleyrand, Londres, 8 Octobre, 1793. *Revue d'Histoire diplomatique*, quatrième année, 1890, No. 1, p. 85.

reason, and philosophy.[1] I write to you in warmth, for all my feelings are awakened by my fears; and I should dread a conflict with France in her present situation, even were I not an advocate for an alliance with her. Adieu!

Minute: Friday, January 4.—M. Reinhard called on me again this morning and brought me letters from M. Maret and Scipion Mourgue dated the 31st of last month. His stay was rather longer than the day before. He complained of the Alien Bill, which, he said, was levelled directly against France, and stated that the exportation of foreign corn to France in particular had been excepted, and that the merchant who had shipped the corn had been offered an indemnity by Ministers. He went over the same ground of argument as before; and, towards the conclusion of the visit, he conjured me to endeavour to keep open, if possible, a channel of communication between Mr. Pitt and M. Chauvelin, who, for the sake of peace, was content to waive his diplomatic character and treat privately and confidentially with Ministers.

I asked whether he was authorised by M. Chauvelin to make that request. He said yes, and he was to add that it would give M. Chauvelin great pleasure to see me in Portman Square. I replied that, in the present crisis, it was impossible I could go to the Embassy, and that, although I should be happy to receive M. Chauvelin at my house, or to meet him at a third person's—if he considered that an interview

---

[1] 'Que signifient ces rodomontades de plusieurs membres de votre Parlement? Que signifient les insolentes épithètes que Burke distribue à toute la nation française? Croit-on ne pas aliéner les esprits par ces appellations, qui ne siéroient même pas dans la bouche d'un insensé!'—*Extract from Letter of Scipion Mourgue to Mr. Miles*, Paris, December 31, 1792.

would be beneficial—I thought it advisable to avoid all personal intercourse, but that he may rest assured that the whole of the very little credit I possessed with Mr. Pitt and with those in his confidence would be exerted to keep open the communication he desired. I told Reinhard that I was so anxious to preserve peace, and to see France and England united by a treaty of alliance, that I would consent to relinquish life on seeing so desirable an event accomplished; and I instructed him to say to M. Chauvelin that, if the Executive Council would follow the advice I had given to Le Brun, the Minister in this country, were he even disposed for war, which he is not, would not dare to embark on it. France had only to be temperate and just, and all would go well. Reinhard endeavoured to do away my objection to going to Portman Square; but, finding me resolved, he said the interview should be as I proposed.

I wrote to Mr. Long that I wished to see him. He requested in reply that I would go down to the House of Commons. He came to me, and we went to 'Alice's Coffee House.' I gave him Maret's letter to peruse, and lamented that Mr. Pitt should have interdicted all kind of communication with the Executive Council and with its agents. He answered that it was ridiculous to have any private negotiations at the very moment when the Government were denying them in the House; yet, if I had anything to communicate, or if he knew anything that would be of service, he would communicate it. I then delivered to him the message of M. Chauvelin, and on reading it he seemed at first struck with its importance, and would probably have said something on the subject if his attention had not been wholly absorbed by tossing up for the tavern-reckoning and disputing upon the doctrine of *chances* as to whether he or I should pay the bill! Of course the more important object of public welfare was lost in the nonsense of idle controversy; and, on desiring him to say *Yes* or *No*—would he, or would he not, deliver M. Chauvelin's message to Mr. Pitt, he refused. I asked how, in the name of God, if such conduct was to be persisted in, could any explanation ever take place between the two countries. He replied that no explanation could take place until France had retracted what she had said and what she had done—and that publicly, either by the National Convention or by the Executive Council. I desired him to make a distinction between the Government of France and the nation, for, if ever such a distinction was well founded and ought to be made, it was now; that France at this moment ought not to be considered in her sober senses, but, on the contrary, as in a state of intoxication, and that, as it was neither politic nor humane to resent the senseless insults of a man who, being placed in these circumstances, did not know what he was doing, so France must be treated as in a delirium, whilst her political guides are even more so than the people, but management and address may awaken these guides to better thoughts and proceedings.

I went home dejected at the sad prospect, wrote to Mr. Long stating the inevitable mischiefs that would ensue from a rupture with France, and conjured him again, if he really had the interests of his country and of humanity at heart, to engage Mr. Pitt to keep open an amicable intercourse with the French Government, and not to shut the door to all accommodation. I posted down to the House of Commons at a quarter past nine with this letter, and gave it to the door-keeper to pass up to him.

Mr. Miles to Mr. Long

January 4, 8 p.m.

I think the requisition made to me by M. de Chauvelin to be so reasonable and at the same time so important, that, from a sense of duty, I commit it to paper with an urgent request that you will lay it before Mr. Pitt without delay, and favour me with his answer. I do not presume to dictate to the confidential servants of the Crown; I know what is due to their characters and official situation, and I will not offend against decorum; but, if peace can be maintained on terms honourable to this country by preserving a channel of communication open between the two nations, I feel assured that Mr. Pitt would not wish to bar all passage to reconciliation. I do, therefore, entreat—nay, I conjure you to state to the First Lord of the Treasury that M. Chauvelin, who now shows anxiety to avert the calamities of war, is content to waive his public character, and begs to be permitted to treat privately and confidentially with Mr. Pitt on the different subjects that have given offence to the British Government.

M. Maret[1] to Mr. Miles

Paris: December 31, 1792

I received only yesterday, my dear Miles, your letter of the 22nd. I do not reply to it to-day in detail, but I am anxious to thank you for the friendly feeling which dictated it. The conduct of your Ministry is not in perfect accord with the pacific dispositions of which you speak. I would still wish to believe in the personal intentions of Mr. Pitt; but yet, how can we reconcile

---

[1] Chef du Département des Affaires Étrangères.

the friendly manner with which he treated me, what he said to me, the assurances which you have given to me and which you still transmit, with the violent, I will say even the hostile, proceedings of your Government? This evident contradiction is explained by the supposition of Mr. Pitt's diminished credit and influence in the Council; but this supposition would be absurd. Tell me, then, why, if they attach any importance to peace, if there is among you that respect for treaties of which they spoke to me incessantly in London, and of which they boast every day in your Parliament—tell me, then, why Lord Grenville proposes, and your Legislature adopts, a Bill which breaks the engagement reciprocally and solemnly contracted in Articles 4 and 5 of the Treaty of Commerce by a stipulation thus expressed: 'It shall be free to the subjects and inhabitants of the respective States to enter and to leave, without hindrance and in safety, without requiring permission or safe-conduct, general or special, whether by land or by sea, the kingdoms, states, provinces, &c.; to return to them, to sojourn therein, &c.; and they shall be reciprocally treated with every sort of goodwill and favour,' &c. Have we failed in this engagement? Have we not rather done honour to ourselves, even in the midst of our troubles, by a fraternal and religious respect for all individuals who adhere to the English nation? Everywhere your compatriots have been aided, succoured, and treated ' with every sort of goodwill and favour,' whatever were their opinions, their connection with the enemies of liberty, or their relations with men too evidently hired to keep up the agitation in our departments, which can alone place our liberty in peril. And it is as the reward for this generous conduct that the French find themselves included in an Act of Parliament which confers on the English Government a latitude of authority the most arbitrary towards foreigners, which compels them to ask for permission or safe-conduct in order to enter, or leave, or remain on British territory, which permits your Ministers to subject them to the most odious formalities, to fix for them such a district beyond the limits of which they cannot pass, even to reject them from your territory, if, in its caprice, your Government so wills it. No, my dear Miles, it is not thus that a loyal and generous nation, hitherto faithful to its engagements, ought to conduct itself towards a free people who have never been wanting in respect to their engagements to her. If some scoundrels disperse themselves through your country to agitate the people and lead them to revolt, they would cease to be Frenchmen. You have laws against this crime, and you would not see us advance a claim in favour of criminals. Your Ministers will regret to have been the first to strike a blow at stipulations which were all in your favour, and which were signed by the agents of the Government we have destroyed only by a cowardly surrender—only by a mercenary and venal betrayal of the real interests of my country. These stipulations were burdensome to France, they were a crime of despotism. Judge, then, whether we are scrupulous and faithful observers of treaties, since, notwithstanding their radical vice, we have maintained the stipulations. Perhaps there is still time for your Government to anticipate the results of our just discontent, and not to expose itself to the reproaches of all the English mercantile community, whose interests she has so thoughtlessly compromised.[1]

Adieu! *Je vous embrasse, mon cher Miles.*

[1] 'I heard it suggested, and plausibly supported, at Paris, that the

MR. MILES TO M. MARET[1]

January 4, 1793

I have but a moment to acknowledge the receipt of your letter. You must excuse my replying to it till I have more time. As to Lord Grenville's Bill, the intrigues of your countrymen here and in Ireland—and these intrigues supported, not to say authorised, by the decree of the Convention—appear to have provoked so severe, but necessary a measure. If you give attention to the Bill, you will see that merchants and traders are excepted. I am broken-hearted at seeing that all my efforts to ward off the war end in nothing; and this, on account of the obstinacy of Le Brun, who is certainly very ill informed as to the internal situation of this country. Indeed, I see no other means of avoiding war than by very precise declarations on the part of France

Court of Versailles, anxious to get rid of the Commercial Treaty, by way of doing a popular act, and desirous of diverting the minds of the people from the contemplation of their miseries, had engaged Spain to offer the insult at Nootka to the British flag with the view of engaging the two nations in war, and coming into it as an ally; that, having no just cause of quarrel with England, a breach could be effected no other way so well as to its appearances; and that such a measure would, perhaps, allay the spirit of liberty which was beginning to display itself so forcibly and universally in the kingdom, and calm, or at least suspend, the popular discontents. A reference was then made to dates, and some people were disposed to admit that Spain was merely the tool of the Court of Versailles, whilst others refused all credit to the ancient Government for such ingenious refinement in politics.'—W. A. M. See *Conduct of France towards Great Britain*, p. 217.

' M. Chauvelin received instructions from his Government to inquire of Lord Grenville if the subjects of France were included in the Alien Bill. If they were, he was to say that the Treaty of Commerce was in that case at an end. If the French were not included, he was to desire Lord Grenville to fix a day for M. Chauvelin being presented at Court as the Minister of the French Republic.'—W. A. M. See *Letter to the Prince of Wales*, London, 1808, p. 165.

[1] *Authentic Correspondence*, Appendix p. 89.

as to her conquests, as to the Scheldt, and as to general peace. Would not France explain herself if she sincerely desired to preserve peace? All chicanery grieves me—*toute va à travers*. I am distressed, and think of renouncing politics and burying myself in the country. Write, I pray you, a word of reply, and inform me if your Executive Council is willing to arrive at an accommodation.

Je vous souhaite le bon soir.

END OF THE FIRST VOLUME

www.ingramcontent.com/pod-product-compliance
Lightning Source LLC
Chambersburg PA
CBHW051850300426
44117CB00006B/340